Dublin in the 1950s and 1960s

Dublin in the 1950s and 1960s

CARS, SHOPS AND SUBURBS

Joseph Brady

FOUR COURTS PRESS

Typeset in 11pt on 14pt Garamond by
Carrigboy Typesetting Services, for
FOUR COURTS PRESS LTD
7 Malpas Street, Dublin 8, Ireland
www.fourcourtspress.ie
and in North America for
FOUR COURTS PRESS
c/o ISBS, 920 NE 58th Avenue, Suite 300, Portland, OR 97213.

ISBN 978–1–84682–661–0 hbk
ISBN 978–1–84682–620-7 pbk

A catalogue record for this title is available
from the British Library.

Printed in England
by TJ International, Padstow, Cornwall.

Contents

7

ACKNOWLEDGMENTS

9

SERIES EDITORS' INTRODUCTION

13

THE GROWING FOOTPRINT

20

PLANNING FOR FUTURE GROWTH

Getting a plan – The 1957 development plan – The road network –
Housing – Preservation and demolition – The first development plans –
Regional development – The Myles Wright report – New towns – Form
of the new towns – Comparisons with British new towns –
Implementation of Myles Wright report

65

THE URBAN LANDSCAPE

Changing dynamic – The 'bowl of light' – The Civic Offices – Mains
drainage – State projects – Memory and commemoration – The State's
response – The concert hall – The commercial landscape: skyscrapers
arrive – The commercial sector – The Georgian city – The urban landscape

162

THE CITY AND THE MOTOR CAR

Changing city structure – Congestion – Parking – Control of cars and
pedestrians – Public transport – Traffic problems – Road plans –
Schaechterle report – The Buchanan approach – Reaction to the
Schaechterle report – The Grand Canal route – Myles Wright – Dublin
Transportation Study and Travers Morgan – Future change?

220

THE SUBURBAN CITY

Challenges to the city centre – Retailing – What the census revealed –
The centre versus the suburbs – Self-service – Supermarkets –

CONTENTS

Shopping centres – Opening hours – Rationing – Car ownership – City centre redevelopment – Renewal in the city centre – The shopping experience – Grafton Street – Dealing with traffic – George's Street – Westmoreland and D'Olier streets – O'Connell Street – Henry street – Mary and Talbot streets – A polycentric city

330

DUBLIN FOR VISITORS

Dublin at the beginning of the 1950s – The culinary experience – Speedway – Dublin and tourism – Connectivity – Selling Dublin – 'With the authority of Dublin Corporation' – Bord Fáilte – *Seven Days in Dublin* – The end of an era of Ward Lock guides – The practicalities – Entertainment – Coffee table views

406

SOURCES AND BIBLIOGRAPHY

420

LIST OF ILLUSTRATIONS

427

INDEX

Acknowledgments

This is the seventh volume in the series *The Making of Dublin City* and we have now arrived at the period between 1950 and 1970. This is close to the time in which I grew up and it is interesting to revisit the period and see the extent to which my recollections are reflected in the sources. It has convinced me, if I needed convincing, that memory distorts and that memoir can only been used as seasoning on hard facts. Historians in Ireland used take this to an extreme and avoided studying the period in which they have lived or, indeed, in which their parents have lived. All that this ensured was that their connection with the time was even more tenuous than it might otherwise be and that their ability to understand the past was even more limited. Having lived in the period under consideration provides a context that is not otherwise possible, as long as the author remembers not to assume that his or her experience was somehow typical of others.

My sincere thanks must go to two mentors. Tony Parker introduced me to retail geography and from him I learned the mysteries of consumer behaviour. It was from Arnold Horner that I first heard about regional planning and the implications of the Myles Wright report which was being implemented as I began my undergraduate studies.

My editors, Ruth McManus and Anngret Simms, continue to do trojan work in bringing these volumes to completion. It is hard to believe that many years have passed since the first volumes in the series appeared but it is also wonderful that the appetite to continue is still keen.

My colleagues and friends in UCD have been invaluable. My thanks are due to Jim Byrne, Alun Carr, John Dunnion, Bryan Fanning, Tom Garvan, Frank Hayes, Andreas Hess, Alun Jones, Michael Laffan, Tim Mooney, Feargal Murphy, Gerald Mills, Niamh Moore, Wolfgang Marx and Ronnie Moore.

Illustrations are a hugely important element in this series and this volume is no exception. Many of them are the result of serendipitous finds on Ebay and their inclusion justifies the hours that I have spent trawling through the vast array of offerings there. Or at least that is what I tell myself! As a result I have a significant collection of books, pamphlets and ephemera on Dublin which have proved very important. I also want to express my deep gratitude to the late Frank Kelly for his generosity in giving me permission to reproduce material from *Dublin Opinion*. This is a wonderful source of material because it captures so well what was bothering the chattering classes. Likewise my thanks to the staff in Pearse Street Library who delved into their archive to produce some wonderful materials and also provided an oasis of calm in which to work. I wish also to acknowledge the value of the Crampton photo archive, now housed in UCD's digital library. Thanks also to Noelle Dowling, the archivist in the Dublin Diocesan Archives, for once again making me welcome and being of such great assistance.

Four Courts Press continue to be great supporters of this series; they produce books to the highest standards and they make a vital contribution to the academic world.

My deepest thanks, though, must go to Anne for her continuing and unfailing encouragement and support and without whom this book or any other would not have been written.

Series editors' introduction

I am delighted to welcome the latest volume in *The Making of Dublin City* series, which explores the everyday landscape of the 1950s and particularly the 1960s, at a time when the motor car came to dominate the city, not just affecting transportation, but also planning, shopping and commercial activities. In many ways, the increased need to accommodate the car symbolises the tension between the desire to create a modern city and the feared loss of its heritage which had become acute by the late 1960s. By the end of this period, Dublin had left behind the last hangovers of wartime rationing to embrace a modern booming economy with its various pleasures and pitfalls. As the commercial sector grew, it made a dramatic mark on the landscape, as modern glass and concrete office blocks began to proliferate, particularly to the south-east of the city centre. Dublin's first 'skyscraper', Liberty Hall, along with near-neighbours Hawkins House and O'Connell Bridge House, are now among the least loved buildings of the city. Nevertheless, they have become a fundamental part of its character and fabric. This volume presents the story of how and why such a transformation was wrought on the urban landscape, dovetailing with other publications on the modernisation of the capital in the 1960s, while emphasising the geographical approach.

This book shows how new pressures came to bear on the urban environment. In response, new planning mechanisms were necessary and, at last, Dublin Corporation produced its first formal, official plan. However, as this volume demonstrates, the process was far from uncomplicated. The work of Myles Wright in planning Dublin's future development in the late 1960s, ultimately leading to the designation of the western 'new towns' of Tallaght, Lucan-Clondalkin and Blanchardstown, will be familiar to many readers. Far less has been written about planning the city in the 1950s. In this volume, Joe Brady teases out the challenging experiences of that decade, and includes a detailed examination of the 1957 Draft Plan which reveals much of the official thinking about how the city should evolve. This helps to fill a void in our understanding of Dublin's planning history.

Dublin in the 1950s and 1960s provides a detailed exploration of the ongoing evolution of one city, but it is also clear that Dublin was not isolated from wider influences. Throughout the text, and particularly in discussing planning and development initiatives, Joe Brady takes a comparative approach. As in earlier decades, when the form of Dublin's new housing schemes owed much to the British 'garden suburb', planners in the 1950s and 1960s drew on overseas influences to inform their work. The consultants involved in devising what is commonly known as the 'Myles Wright' report would have been familiar with proposals for Stalingrad and more especially the developments in Britain which are outlined here. Indeed, understanding the nature of Britain's post-war new towns programme reveals much about how and why Dublin came to be shaped as it was during these years.

In his examination of the civic landscape, Joe Brady presents the differing perspectives of the city authorities, various representative bodies, journalists and the 'man and woman in the street'. Beginning with a seemingly insignificant monument, the 'bowl of light' which once graced the centre of O'Connell Bridge, the conflicting viewpoints of these diverse groups serve to show how spaces in the city were contested. The story is not just of this monument, but how the city centre was perceived by different interest groups. It is worth noting that, as early as the 1950s, the apparent 'decline' of the capital's main thoroughfare was being decried. Turning to the early debate around the proposed new civic offices for the city, Brady once again illuminates a previously under-examined area. This, in effect, is the pre-history of the Wood Quay controversy, from 1951 through to the end of the 1960s. It reveals considerable politicking and tension around the proposals, which augured ill for the ultimate project as it was developed, controversially, in the 1970s. Controversy was also a hallmark of the edifice most properly known as the 'Nelson Pillar', which met its demise in 1966. The discussion of this event and its aftermath leads into a broader consideration of commemoration in the city, at a time when other statues were also attacked, and the authorities grappled with the thorny issue of how to remember Ireland's various war dead.

The subtitle of this book highlights the role that the car had come to play in the city's geography. While earlier volumes in the series have considered the impact of car ownership in Dublin, it was during this period that their increasing popularity became a real problem. They did not just cause congestion as they clogged up the city streets, as we are reminded in some striking photographs. The very landscape of the city changed, as mass car ownership made it possible for the city's suburbs to grow at ever increasing distances from the core. The housing aspect is covered in *Dublin, 1950–1970: houses, flats and high-rise*, but here we see that other urban activities also became suburbanised, following the population in its outward movement –

with new office developments, factories and Ireland's first shopping centres catering for car owners. Shopping centres went hand in hand with a new type of shopping experience, as retailers began to grapple with the new and somewhat alien concept of self-service. Public transport was less and less able to cater for an increasingly dispersed population, and the belief that an expanded road network was necessary to accommodate the growth in car usage held sway. Fortunately, for Dublin, lack of finance hindered the development of the city centre motorways, which ultimately blighted the centres of many post-war British and European cities.

Although saved from some of the immediate physical impacts of new road construction, car-dominated suburbanisation had an insidious longer-term influence on the city proper. The impacts of this emptying out of the city centre were to be felt increasingly in the decades which followed. Dublin began to experience the 'doughnut' shape already characteristic of US cities at this time. As people, jobs and services moved to the suburbs, dereliction and decline were experienced in much of the centre. But there was a fight back, and plans to revitalise parts of the central area were devised from as early as the 1960s. Meanwhile, some quite central locations, particularly in the vicinity of the southern Georgian squares, acquired a new popularity for use as offices. Some of the developments proved highly controversial, with an emergent tension between those who favoured the retention of the centre's historic fabric (though not necessarily the central population) and others who promoted the development of a modern capital with its steel and glass structures.

This volume follows on from *Dublin, 1930–50* in its exploration of the shopping experience for Dubliners in the 1950s, including both the new shopping centres and also the long-established key shopping areas of the city centre. The detail and illustrations in this chapter help to give a real sense of the lived experience for residents, much as the subsequent chapter reveals what it was like to be a tourist in Dublin. Everyday life and common experience are melded with an understanding of the evolving geography of the city.

As with the previous volumes in the series, *Dublin in the 1950s and 1960s* uses a broad range of maps, photographs and illustrations to illuminate Dublin's story. While all serve a purpose, it is perhaps timely to highlight the value of the witty cartoons of *Dublin Opinion*, which are reproduced through the generosity of the late Frank Kelly. These are more than just amusing illustrations, as they reveal the debates considered worthy of comment at the time and give a unique insight into how contemporary society thought about such issues. Indeed, this volume as a whole helps us to get a sense of the lived city, as it was experienced by contemporaries, as well as an understanding of how the authorities intended it to evolve. As we learn more about the geography of Dublin's recent past, it is to be hoped that we will also endeavour to use that knowledge to plan wisely for the future.

RUTH MCMANUS

The growing footprint

As Dublin approached the 1950s, there was a sense of excitement (perhaps euphoria for a while) that the coming decade would offer more opportunities than the one coming to an end. With the exception of the North Strand bombing, Dublin had been spared the horrors of war but the decade had stopped the development of the city in its tracks and it had been a case of marking time. Now the opportunity was there to shake the dust off the projects that had been mothballed, to take the car down off its blocks and to see how the opportunities of the new Europe could be turned to the benefit of the city.

Housing is the most visible manifestation of the growth of any city. It is what visitors see if they approach the city by air and no other land use has quite the same impact. The development of the housing market in the 1950s and 1960s has been the subject of another volume in this series, Brady (2016), and this volume concentrates on other aspects of the city's development, which, though important, did not have the same spatial impact. Because of this, it will useful to be begin with a short summary of what happened with housing during this period.

The housing sector was in crisis from the very beginning of the twentieth century. The city was always trying to catch up with demand and to match the housing available with the needs of its population. It was a problem even in the private sector and it was not until the 1960s that home ownership in Dublin began to come into line with the experience elsewhere in the country. For those relying on social housing, the position was grim for the first two decades of the century as Dublin Corporation struggled to come to an understanding of its role in provision and the policies needed to underpin this. It was only when it was finally understood that suburban housing was a necessary (and perhaps even the dominant) element in any building programme and when projects began to be realized some hope for a solution began to grow. This was first crystallized in the north city survey, which the Corporation undertook in 1918 and in which it set out its stall with ambitious projects of urban renewal and suburban development. Marino and Cabra are shown with a geometric layout in both cases, together with a comprehensive redevelopment of the north inner city. Marino and Cabra were indeed developed, though with a longer lead-in time than would have been hoped and the 1930s saw further large suburban estates in Kimmage and Crumlin together with some inner city renewal.

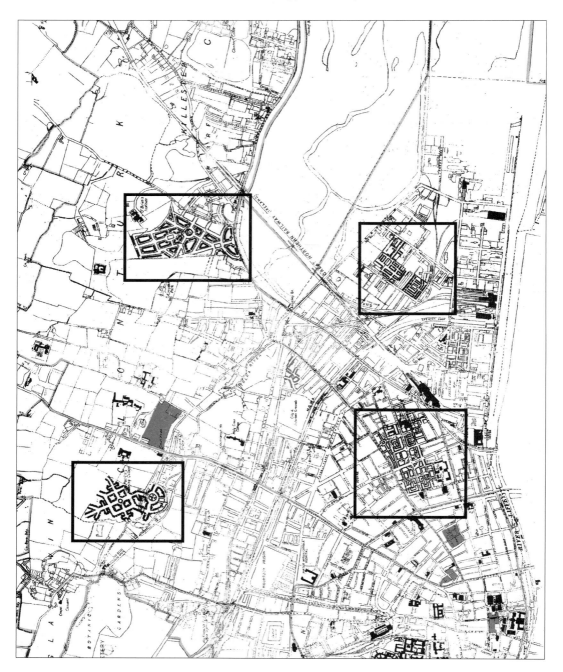

1. Extract from the north city housing survey of 1918 showing contemplated developments. (Report 13/1918.)

The population of the city had continued to grow during the 1940s and there was a pent-up demand for housing. In the social housing sector, Dublin Corporation had managed to keep building during the war and, when they reviewed their performance in 1944, they found that they had produced 8,257 dwellings over the previous five years. Their efforts had been hampered by a shortage both of materials and of skilled craftsmen as many of the latter found employment in the UK. Their plans for the next five years included an additional 7,500 dwellings. This was an ambitious target given the available resources but it was about half of what the Housing Inquiry, which reported in 1943, suggested would be necessary. It also turned out to be more than they could deliver and the slower than expected resumption meant that the Corporation managed to complete just under 4,000 dwellings by 1950. The next five years were more impressive and over 10,000 dwellings were completed by 1955. Thereafter, the programme was allowed to slow down in response to an increasing vacancy rate consequent on emigration only to have to pick up again in the early 1960s as demand once more increased.

Such were the demands placed on Dublin Corporation that, while continuing the policy of building cottages in the suburbs and flats only in the city centre, they were persuaded by the Minister for Local Government, Niall Blaney, to experiment with high-rise and system building. The Minister was anxious to end the problem of housing shortages for good and he became convinced that system building was the way to do this. The experiment was based in Ballymun and it was watched with interest by both public and private sectors as it took shape in the latter years of the 1960s. It had the potential to transform building and the future form of the city, though the developing evidence at that time from the European mainland suggested that it was not without problems. Even at the height of its enthusiasm, Dublin Corporation never found the approach *so* interesting that it re-oriented its major housing schemes towards high-rise and system building. Members of the Corporation continued to prefer houses with gardens in the suburbs and relatively low-rise flats in the city centre.

During the 1930s, the private sector building industry saw a shift towards bigger developments produced by larger limited companies. The days of the small-scale local builder who built a handful of houses at a time was coming to an end, though Dublin Corporation went out of its way to provide contracts that suited them for as long as was feasible. The southside was the favoured location and the semi-detached house with garden became the easiest way to differentiate private housing from social housing where the terrace was more common. McManus (2002) showed that there was never a clear distinction between public and private sector housing, with Dublin Corporation facilitating private building and private builders relying on people who were eligible for both State and local authority supports. This mutual dependence came into particular focus in the years immediately following the Second World War. Not surprisingly, private building was affected by wartime shortages to a greater extent than the public sector. Building materials became so scarce that one architect suggested that doors might be abandoned in favour of curtains. After the war, they also found that it took longer to get started again because of a government decision to focus building materials on the supply of smaller houses. Builders had to be pragmatic and hope for local authority tenders or else orient their output towards the lower end of the market, for which they might get a licence. This slowed down the recovery in the business but they had another bigger problem in that house prices and incomes had and were continuing to diverge. The early years of the 1950s were characterized by an over-priced market in which purchasers were squeezed by both high prices and an unwillingness among lenders to advance more than 75 per cent of the purchase price. Builders complained that they could not sell anything but 'subsidy houses'; houses that would get Small Dwelling Acquisition Acts (SDAA) loans and local authority supplementary grants. Price readjustment to bring builders and purchasers more in line had taken place by the middle 1950s but they then had the problem of emigration and a tight credit environment was sufficient to suppress demand. It was not until the 1960s with better incomes and better access to affordable financing that the private market began to take off.

When the market picked up again, the demand permitted the development of some large estates, especially to the north of the city. 'Estates' were suggestive of social housing so developers often sought to avoid the appearance of an estate by trying to give a distinctive character to what they built. They found useful marketing ideas in the United States and purchasers were wooed with images of graceful living in the 'colonial' or the 'vancouver' development. The term 'virginian' appeared in a few developments; resonating with the popular television series of the same name, though the connection was quite tenuous. Private houses moved towards a norm of four bedrooms though not necessarily with greater floor area than supposedly smaller houses. However, there was a demand for large and expensive houses in desirable areas such as Howth.

In the 1920s, the early Corporation schemes of Marino and Drumcondra were tenant purchase, whereby rents were actually mortgage payments. This policy was favoured because the various authorities liked the idea of developing a population of property-owning citizens. Such were likely to adopt middle-class values and to be conservative in outlook. At a time when Europe was engaged with the ideas of the emerging Communist USSR, it seemed less likely that property owners would overthrow the State in favour of a communist society. It was a short-lived focus because it was realized that these rentals were beyond the means of the majority of would-be tenants and Dublin Corporation moved quickly from tenant purchase to straight rental in the early 1930s. For a while, though, it looked as if owner occupancy could be more a feature of the social housing sector than in the private sector. The reality is that most people in Dublin rented: in 1946, the census of that year showed that 74.5 per cent of accommodation was rented. Dublin Corporation was a major player in this market but so also were the rental companies such as Associated Properties, which positioned itself to serve those with lower incomes, people who might be Corporation tenants or on the housing list if they had larger families. Then there were the house builders who retained a number of houses in their developments for renting. They seemed quite happy not to dispose of all their properties and to keep and manage some as rental properties.

Home ownership began to grow only in the 1960s as people found that they had more money in their pockets and the mortgage system became more affordable and accessible. Dublin Corporation returned in a small way to tenant purchase as early as the 1950s as they observed from the operation of the differential rents system that there was a substantial cohort of tenants or potential tenants who could afford to be purchasers. The biggest change came when the Corporation decided to sell off its property portfolio to its tenants. The Corporation, unlike many in the UK, never had an ideological objection to seeing its rental properties move into the private sector. Their concern was more pragmatic and focused on what might happen to the State support for repayments on loans that had been raised to build the houses. When these difficulties were sorted out in the late 1960s, they found considerable interest in their tenants becoming home owners. The upshot of all these policies was that Corporation rentals accounted for 41,819 dwellings in 1971. This was one third of the housing stock and while it was a clear statement of how important social housing had become in the city, it was now set to decline as tenants became owners. When other rentals were added to that total, about 51 per cent of accommodation in the city was some kind of rental.

Dún Laoghaire was always somewhat different to the city. In Dún Laoghaire in 1971 tenure was divided 45/55 in favour of ownership. Council housing accounted for around 23 per cent of the housing stock (3,108 units) and very little of this was in the process of being bought. Social housing was also relatively uncommon in the southern suburbs, which had grown strongly. Over 80 per cent of the 34,384 dwellings there were privately owned with only 6.4 per cent (2,189 units) rented from the local authority.

While apartment or flat living was commonplace in most European capital cities, this was not the case in Dublin. The middle classes abandoned the central areas of the city in the nineteenth century in favour of the rural idyll (or at least what passed for it) in the independent townships. There the idea of middle-class life being associated with individual houses was firmly cemented and there were very few attempts to tempt that social group into flats. The poorer sections of the population had long been used to living in multi-family dwellings and the only way in which to house a sizable proportion of this group in decent accommodation in the city centre, where their social networks were located, was by building flat blocks. The central areas of Dublin city became associated with the flat blocks of Dublin Corporation and philanthropic bodies such as the Iveagh Trust and it was almost a certainty that a flat dweller was in social housing. This began to change in the middle 1950s when developers began experimenting with middle-class flat developments in central suburbs. The locations chosen were in the desirable residential areas of the southern suburbs, generally central locations which would appeal to those who wanted a more urban lifestyle. They tended to be close to the inner city, but not in it, and almost entirely on the southside. With a small number of notable exceptions such as Ardoyne House on the edge of Herbert Park, the designs were pedestrian and unimaginative with rectangular blocks featuring strongly. What they offered was another form of urban life and it was generally believed that these would be life-cycle choices, appealing to professionals in the early stages of careers or to older people who wanted to downsize (though that term was still some years away). The latter would have needed to give the prospect careful thought as most of the first-generation blocks did not feature lifts. Flats were initially only for rent because of difficulties involved in getting mortgages and insurance in multi-occupancy units but this had been solved by the beginning of the 1970s and there was an increase in provision and interest as that decade went on. It was not until the 1990s that apartment living became a major feature of middle-class life as rocketing house prices turned flats from a lifestyle choice to a life necessity.

During the 1950s and 1960s, Dublin expanded its footprint mainly to the south and north. In the north, the construction of the new sewer opened up most of the remainder of the county borough to housing and Dublin Corporation capitalized on this by its developments in Finglas, Edenmore, Kilmore and Coolock. Private developers were also active here, especially in the eastern part and they and the Corporation ended the decade in competition for what little land remained. To the south, private development had expanded into the county area long before 1950 and this became the preferred location for private housing during the 1950s and 1960s, though there was also development on the western edge in Clondalkin and environs, before it was designated for large scale suburban development by Myles Wright. Dún Laoghaire too ran out of space and its suburbs spilled into the county. The result was that originally discrete suburban developments gradually merged to form a continuous belt of housing. With the exception of a few locations, Dublin had yet to expand greatly to the west. To this point it had been both unnecessary and also inconvenient because of the poorer communication routes. By 1970, this expansion was clearly a prospect. The city could not expand to the east, however desirable the locations might be. The coastal areas were fully developed and while there were occasional suggestions that building might be accommodated on Sandymount Strand, it was most unlikely that this would happen given the economic and social power of the local residents. To the north, the city was approaching the limits of development as it came closer to the airport corridor. Its only option here was to leapfrog the airport and develop in the suburban locations of Swords, Malahide, Portmarnock and even Skerries. Malahide and Portmarnock, with their excellent environment and fine beaches, were perfect locations for middle-class housing, once people came to terms with the nature of the commute. To the south lay the Dublin mountains. There were still some opportunities to build at lower levels but directing the city's growth there was never going to be an option. The Myles Wright report identified building to the west as the only reasonable option and it was no surprise that such was the direction of growth.

Planning for future growth

Despite the work of the 1938 Dublin Tribunal, there was no significant change to the governance structure of Dublin by 1950. The Tribunal had suggested that Dublin needed to be managed as an entity and not by a series of separate and disconnected councils. They had suggested a structure for this new council and a means of ensuring that the needs of urban and rural areas were properly addressed. They also made recommendations on the form of democratic structures and the functions that could be devolved to the officials and to the councils. The proposals were dramatic but hardly unexpected since similar proposals had been around for at least a decade and were discussed in the run up to the absorption of the Pembroke and Rathmines townships into the city area in 1930. In fact, the fractured governance of the city had been a matter of debate since the latter years of the nineteenth century.

The government of the day sat on the report and moved, at the last minute in July 1940, to incorporate the Howth borough into the city. This was done in haste and was accomplished with unusual speed. At the time, it was made clear that nothing else was in the mind of the government and it was safely and correctly assumed that nothing would happen for the duration of the war. Indeed, nothing happened after the war either, despite a number of changes of government. It seemed that nobody had the appetite to do what had been proposed. Rather, there was talk of boundary changes which would allow the various councils to absorb areas necessary for their development. Thus, at the beginning of the 1950s, the urban area comprised Dublin Corporation, Dún Laoghaire borough and part of the area controlled by Dublin County Council into which both boroughs were increasingly expanding. Any talk of the implementation of a single unified authority for the entire area simply faded away.

Getting a plan

This left planning in the hands of three authorities but with significant ministerial oversight. At the beginning of the 1950s, Dublin Corporation was involved in unfortunate litigation over its failure to publish a planning scheme for Dublin – what would now be called a development plan. They had taken significant powers to control development under the 1934 Planning Act but this also gave them the obligation to prepare the scheme with 'all convenient speed'. The made a good start by commissioning Patrick Abercrombie with Sydney Kelly and Manning Robertson to prepare a sketch development plan and this was duly delivered in 1939. This was taken as a framework for the statutory plan which was confidently expected by the early years of the 1940s. Thereafter, the process went off the rails for reasons that are not entirely clear, even after extensive airing in the courts. There was a change of mindset which caused the Corporation to come to see the making of the plan as an unnecessary and even dangerous undertaking. They felt that they did not have the resources to make the plan and they feared that they would be exposed to compensation claims from people who had proposals rejected or prevented because of the specifications of the plan. That was certainly provided for under Part XII of the 1934 Act, though there were also remedies for the Corporation. Rather, they preferred to continue under a concept of 'interim planning' where they had quite extensive, even draconian, powers to control development. This is not to suggest that they were suddenly against the concept of planning but rather that each submission was judged against a series of principles which were known only to the officials in the Corporation.

It was all quite surprising and against the grain. The Corporation and its officials had demonstrated a long engagement with the concept of town planning. Dubliners had been early enthusiasts for the ideas of Ebenezer Howard on garden cities and town planning and the decision to hold a competition for a town plan in 1914 was an indication of that enthusiasm. The subsequent engagement with Unwin and Geddes, two of the great names in planning (see Bannon, 1985; McManus, 2002), with Dublin Corporation was further evidence of this interest. Their decision to adopt the provisions of the 1934 Act was another indication that the concept of rational town planning was deeply ingrained.

Nonetheless, they were not disposed to make a statutory plan anytime in the near to medium term. While it seemed to suit the Corporation, it was open to an accusation of inefficiency and bias. It was a circumstance which could not last and it was inevitable that it would be challenged in court. The courts process began in May 1951 when Modern Homes (Ireland) Ltd, a developer with considerable experience in Dublin, obtained an order in the High Court on a conditional basis directing Dublin Corporation to make the planning scheme. To the surprise of many, Dublin Corporation challenged the ruling and it was in the courts over the next four years on technical matters and matters of principle. It has been dealt with extensively in a previous volume in this series (Brady, 2014) and it would not be appropriate to go into detail here. Suffice to say that Dublin Corporation took every opportunity possible to avoid their ultimate fate; a direction to prepare a plan. Eventually, and only when they had been told by a jury that 'all convenient speed' did not mean at the convenience of the Corporation, they were directed to produce a draft plan within two years, taken literally as 11 July 1955, some five years after the court proceedings were initiated and some nineteen years after they first undertook to produce the plan. Even then they did not make the date and were in the throes of mandamus proceedings in the High Court, having been accused of contempt of court, when the plan finally was published in October of 1955. Following an exhibition of the plan and an opportunity for interested parties to submit objections, it was approved in 1957.

The 1957 development plan
The draft plan that went on exhibition comprised a book of articles and three books of maps (R1/02/04). The maps were drawn on the 25-inch (1:2,500) Ordnance Survey series reduced to A3 size and bound in a folder. Each land use was coloured and the timing of the development was indicated by the colour. The plan had a forty-year time frame broken down into five phases of eight years. This was an incredibly long time frame over which to contemplate development and there was a real danger of encouraging decay. The justification was that the plan, once adopted, could not be modified without going through the entire process again. This proved to be the fatal flaw in the process because within the logic of this planning framework, it actually made sense to plan for a long period even though it demanded a degree of foresight and/or control to ensure that the plan would have any relevance a generation hence.

Each project was allocated to one of the five periods and the idea was that land acquisition would take place by the end of the eight year period which was indicated. Thus, the maps showed land whose acquisition was planned for some time within the next forty years. It is true that the plan allowed for affected property owners to develop their properties during the period of the plan but the fact that their ultimate fate was demolition in most cases would not have encouraged much useful development.

Book 'A' of maps showed the lands that were to be acquired by Dublin Corporation for road development, housing and a number of other uses. Book 'B' showed use and density zonation while miscellaneous provisions were set out in Book 'C'.

The *Book of Articles* was the statement of the draft plan itself and it comprised a large-format typescript which ran to 162 pages. It contained no

2. Dereliction in Liffey Street, late 1970s. (A.J. Parker.)

statement of vision for the city, though it must be admitted that there was no such requirement in the legislation. There was not even an introduction; it got down to business straight away with a table of definitions. The Corporation did not explain the kind of the city that they hoped would result from the provisions outlined and there was no sense of any philosophical basis. Were they, for example, going to accommodate the car? Did they have a policy in relation to social mix in residential developments? What was their view on the preservation of historic landscapes? None of this appeared in the *Book of Articles* and the reader must determine the priorities from the bald legalistic language of each of the parts within the book.

Neither was there any sense of the context for these plans. It would have been reasonable to expect some analysis of the likely population growth and distribution in the city to determine if the suggested roads would be adequate, whether the housing programme would meet needs. Compared to later plans, it was a very bald list of objectives.

The road network

Based on sheer volume alone, road plans were the single most important aspect of the text. These ran to 118 pages of the 162 pages of the text. These

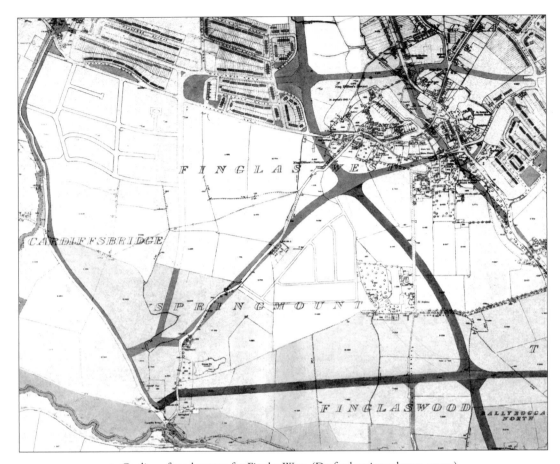

3. Outline of road system for Finglas West. (Draft planning scheme, 1957.)

set out in detail where roads were to be widened or created with an indication of the width of the road and the time frame for the road's development. For example, the Santry by-pass was provided for during the first time period and it was described as running approximately 1000ft (305m) east of the existing Swords Road with a width of 160ft (49m). The route outlined on the map was similar to what was eventually built. In the suburbs, a ring road was provided between Kylemore Road and the Long Mile Road. A substantial west–east routeway was also planned which would link Finglas with the coast and thus link up the new housing estates. It did not quite work out as planned here but Oscar Traynor Road and its linkages came to serve that purpose. What was proposed was complex, as figure 3 shows, and while a modified Finglas Road

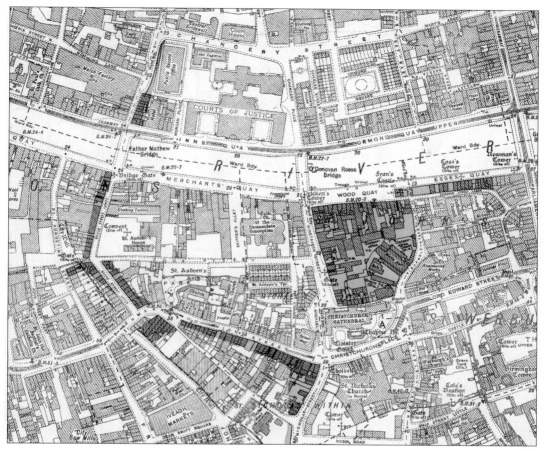

4. Portion of the new tangent route showing road widening in the High Street area. (Ordnance Survey plan, 1:2,500, Sheet 18(XI), 1938.) The demolition area for the Civic Offices in Wood Quay is also shown. Note that this is a simplified redrawing of the draft planning scheme using an older base map. The darker shade shows demolition.

can be seen, they had plans for another road of equal width to the west, which was never constructed.

One of the roads with the greatest spatial impact on the existing landscape was a new artery that would link the North Circular Road at Doyle's Corner with the South Circular Road at Leonard's Corner – in other words a tangent route. It would run from Phibsborough Road via Constitution Hill, Church Street (crossing the river by a widened Father Mathew Bridge) and then through Bridge Street, High Street, Nicholas Street, Patrick Street, New Street and Clanbrassil Street to the South Circular Road. The impact would be

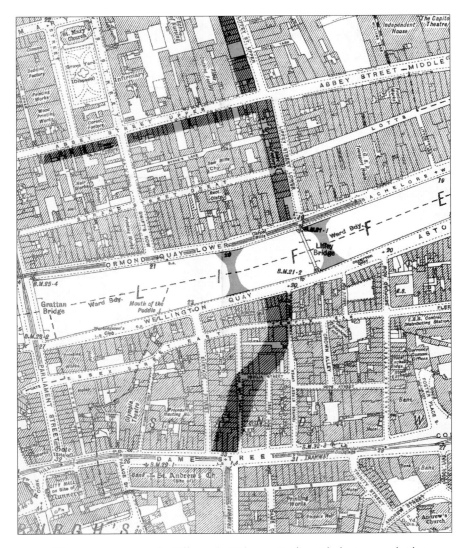

5. The new route across the Liffey at the Ha'penny Bridge with the two new bridges (Ordnance Survey plan, 1:2,500, Sheet 18(XI), 1938.) Note that this is a simplified redrawing of the draft planning scheme using an older base map.

particularly obvious in the medieval city where the historical road proportions would be lost in the widening of High Street. Overall, this was to be an 80ft (24m) thoroughfare and it will be noted that a similar proposal emerged from the various traffic plans produced a little later in the decade. This route would link with an important cross road, which would lead from Parnell Street, across Little Britain Street and, via Halston Street, into North King Street. Here too the demolition would have to be significant in order to meet the requirements of the 8oft (20m) routeway.

Abercrombie's legacy was evident in the proposal to extend South Great George's Street to the quay near the Ha'penny (Metal) Bridge. On the opposite side of the Liffey the new road would link Liffey Street, Parnell Street and Dominick Street to the tangent route at Broadstone. The map shows a curved route continuing from South Great George's Street across Dame Street to emerge at the quays at Eustace Street. Liffey Street and Denmark Street would be widened by the demolition of their western sides and the finished road on both sides of the river would also be 8oft (24m) wide. The Abbey Street junction would be simplified by widening Abbey Street on its southern side, west of Liffey Street, to the same width that it was on the eastern side. Traffic circulation would be managed by the building of two unidirectional bridges on either side of the Ha'penny Bridge, creating a large roundabout. It is unclear what was to happen to the Ha'penny Bridge. In previous generations it was unloved and proposals to remove it had been contained in Abercrombie's first plan for Dublin (1922) and it seemed taken as a given that this would happen by both Abercrombie and the Corporation. This time, there was no mention of demolition and it remained on the map. The reader will recall that Abercrombie (1941) had suggested this arrangement as a focus for the new cathedral that would be built on the north side of the river. There was no mention of the cathedral in the plan and no demolition to facilitate it; it seems that it had faded from the Corporation's consciousness as much as from that of the archdiocese.

These arteries would be supplemented by ring roads to the north and south. On the northside Griffith Avenue and Collins Avenue would be extended while, on the southside, there would be a route from Dundrum, through Rathfarnham and Greenhills, to Walkinstown. The saga of a bridge east of Butt Bridge, described in detail in Brady (2014), was not quite over. There was no bridge in the plan but the approaches were to be developed. Interestingly, some year later, Myles Wright (see below) felt it important enough to include a suggested system for a crossing over the Liffey at that point. As the diagram shows, it would have been a complicated entity.

There was little in this that was new and, while it did not follow the advice of Abercrombie directly as set down in his sketch development plan, it was without doubt a version of the road network that he proposed. Also, though there was no discussion, it seems reasonable to say that the underlying

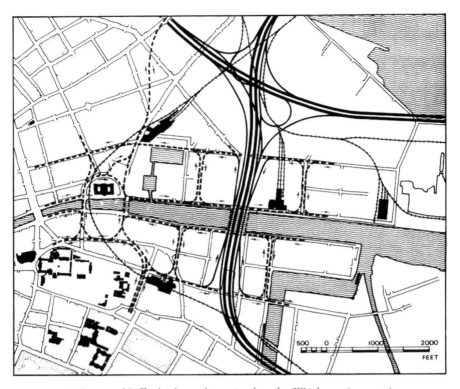

6. Suggested Liffey bridge and associated roads. (Wright, 1967, p. 34.)

principle was that of accommodation for the car. There was no particular concern expressed about changing the scale of the urban landscape by a dramatic alteration of the width of the roads in relation to the heights of the buildings lining the route.

The plan also presented a list of protected roads while a table outlined the approved distances from roadways for building lines. This was done in considerable detail. For example, a distance of 50–60ft (15–18m) was specified for Kimmage Road Lower on its east side from the northern gable of no. 274 in a north-easterly direction for 510ft (155m) approximately to the southern gable of no. 242.

In Part IV of this plan, the Corporation introduced the concept of land zonation and thus gave themselves an important tool in the management of the city. They divided uses into different categories:

- Residential
- Residential Services

- Residential and Offices
- Commercial
- General Business
- Industrial
- Special Industrial
- Public Open Space
- Agricultural
- Municipal Housing

These formed part of a zonation matrix where compatible (and by extension incompatible) land uses were shown. These were combined with what they called 'frontage zones', which could either be 'shopping frontage' or 'light industrial frontage'. They also developed a density table for housing. This was the only substantial statement made on housing in the entire plan, the remainder had to be inferred. It identified four zones in the city with an additional special zone for Howth Head designed to keep it at low density. There was a significant change between the draft plan and the final plan in that densities for flats were included in the final plan and back gardens were now specified in terms of both area and length. The figures below are from the plan as adopted.

Table 1. Dublin planning scheme 1957, maximum density expressed as average acreage required by dwelling. (Dublin Planning Scheme, Table K, 1957.)

Zone	2 storey	3 storey	4+ storeys	Terraced	Semi and detached
A	1/20	1/35	1/42	1/20	1/14
B	1/18	1/30	1/36	1/18	1/12
C	1/15	1/25	1/30	1/10	1/10
D	1/9	1/15	1/18	1/6	1/6

Table 2. Dublin planning scheme 1957, minimum back garden dimensions. (Dublin Planning Scheme, Table K, 1957.)

Zone	Length (ft)	Area	
		Terrace	Semi and detached
A	35	1/60	1/40
B	35	1/40	1/30
C	60	1/20	1/20
D	60	1/14	1/14

Heavy industry was to be located north and south of the docks with other industries located in such a way as to preserve the character of the city.

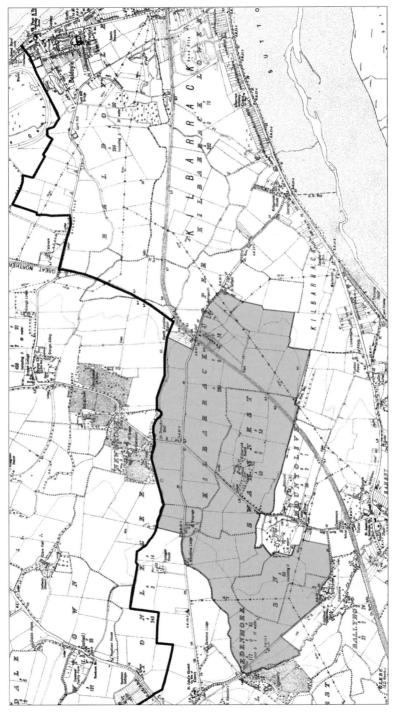

7. An example of the extensive land reservations for housing on the northern edge of the city. (Ordnance Survey plan, 1:10,560, Sheet 17, 1936–7.) Note that this is a simplified redrawing of the draft planning scheme using an older base map.

Housing

With the exception of the density standards there was very little written in the plan about housing in the city, even Corporation housing. The housing proposals were somewhat modest, even if they were confined to the first sixteen years. They planned to develop 62 sites which would total 180 acres (73 ha) within the canals for housing, and this would provide about 6,000–7,000 dwellings, most of which would be flats. Suburban activity would be focused on the Coolock-Raheny area, which was really the only area available to them, and they expected to take 1,000 acres (405 ha) which would provide a modest enough 6,000 dwellings. Twelve or thirteen thousand dwellings over a sixteen-year period was not a very ambitious target but the concentration in the city centre was of interest because it can be seen as an attempt to stem the loss of population from the area, consequent on the Corporation's own clearance programmes. There was quite a campaign underway at the time to keep people close to their original locations. There was certainly unease among some members of the Corporation about suburban dwellings and concern was often expressed by both councillors and tenants alike about the social and economic costs of suburban building. The plans would use up all of the development land in the city and either the Corporation had to seek a further extension to the area of the county borough or they had to begin to plan in conjunction with Dublin County Council. They had always eschewed a regional planning role, even though they had the legislative basis to adopt it, and it seems that extra-territorial planning was too much to contemplate in this plan.

The maps are much more eloquent. They make clear the impact of the various housing projects, though nothing was indicated about the nature of the provision in terms of layout or type of housing. Great swathes of land from Finglas in the west to Kilbarrack on the coast were marked out for development. There was nothing on this scale planned elsewhere in the city; the only opportunities depended on the new northern sewerage system. Within and throughout the inner city, blocks of buildings were marked for development, often in association with road widening.

Preservation and demolition

The demands of both road plans and housing plans necessitated a great deal of demolition and there was no discussion of this at all. It seemed to be understood that this was a necessary consequence. The creation of the tangent

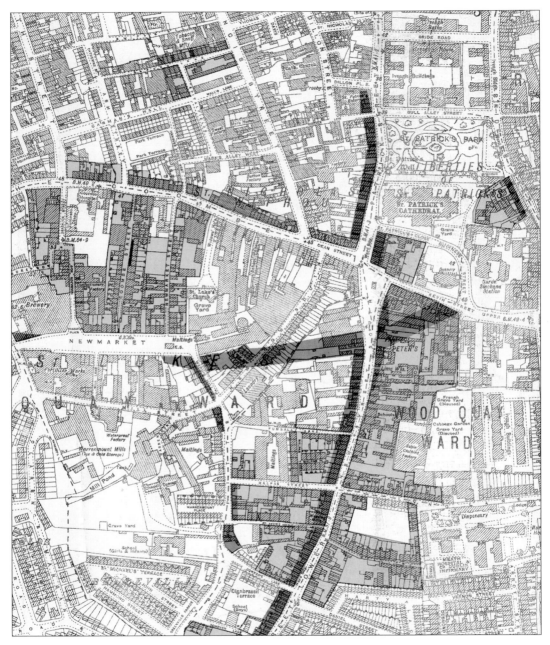

8. Demolition and renewal from Patrick Street and the Coombe into Clanbrassil Street. (Ordnance Survey plan, 1:2,500, Sheet 18(XV), 1938.) The lighter shading shows the area of housing renewal, the darker shading shows demolition for roadways. Note that this is a simplified redrawing of the draft planning scheme using an older base map.

9. Demolition and renewal along Clanbrassil Street. (Ordnance Survey plan, 1:2,500, Sheet 18(XV), 1938.) The lighter shading shows the area of housing renewal, the darker shading shows demolition for roadways. Note that this is a simplified redrawing of the draft planning scheme using an older base map.

route and the renewal of housing required the demolition of most of the east side of Phibsborough Road from its junction with the North Circular Road as well as the housing on Constitution Hill. Only the west side of Church Street would have survived. Together with the tangent route, the cross route along North King Street envisaged substantial demolition on both sides of the Church Street junction. This was particularly noteworthy because the acquisition of property had a deadline of the end of the third period, effectively sterilizing the area for a quarter century.

South of the river the tangent route would make its way up to High Street from Father Mathew Bridge, clearing property on the west side and especially on the south side of High Street where not only would property be demolished but the road layout would be changed. As it went southwards, the demolition of most of the west side of Patrick Street would be necessary and once the Coombe was reached, there was to be even more significant change. Here, a new route would be cut through from the west, leading from Dolphin's Barn, along Cork Street and into Newmarket where a large housing project was planned. From there it would join the tangent route via a new road cut through the existing built environment from the south-eastern edge of Newmarket to emerge on Kevin Street opposite the Garda station. The tangent road then proceeded southwards along Clanbrassil Street where widening and housing renewal would have seen not only the removal of the frontage along the street but also the housing in many of the blocks to the rear. It would become obvious to a reader of the plan that these demolitions, when combined with substantial planned renewal of the housing stock between Charlemont Street and Richmond Street, would have a dramatic impact on the streetscape of the early city.

Housing renewal would result in the loss of the Georgian houses on both sides of Dominick Street as well as nineteenth-century houses along Dorset Street and the area between North Strand Road and Ballybough, north of the Royal Canal. Gardiner Street and environs were relatively untouched, however, because the programme of renovation undertaken in the 1940s had extended their lease of life, though it was intended to widen Summerhill on its western side in the later periods of the plan. The focus of attention was on a small block on Gardiner Street between Waterford Street (now gone) and Deverell Place and on Grenville Street and Charles Street Great, both adjacent to Mountjoy Square.

It was not all demolition and renewal though and the Corporation saw value in the preservation of both natural and man-made features. A number

Ref. to Map Book C		Description
Sheet	Plan	
14	XIV	(a) King William's Rampart, Finglas, to north of Glebe House and lying approximately 120-ft. north-east of St. Patrick's Well.
do.	do.	(b) Old Finglas Church and Stone Cross, situated south of Church Street, Finglas
15	IX	Site of burials as shown on map to east side of Bonnybrook Townland.
15	XIII	Moat at Moatfield House situated approximately 300-ft. west of Coolock Bridge.
do.	do.	All Saints' Protestant Church, Howth Road, Raheny.
15	XIV	Ruins of St. Assin's Church, Howth Road, Raheny.

10. Example of protected structures in Dublin planning scheme, 1957.

of vistas and prospects were preserved and there was a section that specified particular trees, groups of trees and woodland areas. These are to be found in Tables M and N respectively and these locations are set out in some detail.

Protected vistas, for example, included the following:

- Land on the south side of the portion of the Custom House Quay from a point near the loop line bridge to 750ft due east shown on the map coloured blue and less than 30ft from the said Custom House Quay.
- Land on the north side of the portion of the George's Quay from the loop line bridge to 600ft due east shown on the map coloured blue and less than 30ft from the said George's Quay.

These protected vistas were not all in the city centre and included, for example, a portion of Anglesea Road or the summit at Howth Head and quite a number of coastal locations. Table P on page 160 outlined the buildings and structures which were given preserved status. Most were historical structures and included features such as King William's Rampart at Finglas or the ruins of St Assin's (Assam's) Church in Raheny.

The façade and steeple of St George's Church on Hardwicke Street as well as the nearby 'Black Church' were given protection. The city wall along John Dillon Street and St Audeon's into Cook Street were also for preservation, as was Powerscourt House on South William Street. It was a rather short and sparse list though. There was relatively little protection given to the streetscape of the city, though the concept was recognized. For example, the roofs and façades of buildings on all sides of Merrion Square and Fitzwilliam Square were protected. Similar protection was given to the north, south and west sides of Mountpleasant Square and the west side of Harcourt Terrace, a Regency

11. St George's Church in its heyday. (Bartlett in Wright, 1821.)

12. *(below)* Harcourt Terrace as it was in 2009.

terrace. However, these were the only protected streetscapes in the city. The Georgian northside was left to its own devices and streets such as Henrietta Street, the genesis of the Georgian city and site of some of the best houses in the city, was left to genteel decay.

Among the other projects was the completion of the municipal offices and more space for the car. The plan was to provide eighteen car parks with provision for 1,200 cars mainly on derelict or obsolescent sites, which were increasing in number.

It cannot be said to have been a dramatic plan or even an innovative one. Most of what was included was already part of a long-standing agenda and there was no vision provided for the future development of the city as an entity. There was no way that the social housing envisaged would meet the need and there was little attempt to control or manage private development, except in so far as it could not take place on land earmarked for social housing. The Corporation had the power under Part 2 of Schedule 2 of the 1934 Act to make regulations in terms of the size, character, height, spacing and frontage line of buildings and other structures but there was nothing said about these. It seems that the plan was designed to do what was necessary but no more.

Nonetheless, it was taken seriously by all of those who might be affected. The plan, including the articles and the maps, was displayed in the Rotunda of City Hall between 8 October 1955 and 8 January 1956. Approximately 6,500 people were believed to be directly affected by the proposals and the Corporation wrote to each person telling them of the potential effect. Objections had to be received by 8 December, two months following the display of the plan and by this deadline a total of 3,445 objections were received and a further 135 late objections were submitted. This was a meaningful deadline because once the plan was made, there was no further opportunity to object and the consequences could be long lasting.

The Corporation then began the process of considering the objections. There is no doubt that they set about the matter with dedication. As a first step, a 'board of officers' was established which comprised the assistant City Manager, Law Agent, City Engineer, City Architect, Dublin Planning Officer and the principal officers of the Housing and Engineering and Town Planning Departments with the Clerk of the Council as Secretary. All objections were considered by the Planning Officer and when he had undertaken the necessary consultations with other officers, he reported to this board. This completed the first step. A Special Committee of the Corporation was set up at its meeting on 4 October 1955 which comprised the Lord Mayor and the chairs of the Finance, Housing, Streets, Health, Cultural and General Purposes committees. The board of officers, having considered all objections, submitted their response and recommendation to this special committee for consideration and decision. Thus, it was the elected members of the Council who came to the final view on each of the objections and not the officials.

It was a hugely time consuming effort. The objections were looked at in two tranches with 1,800 dealt with in the first group. This required nine meetings of the board of officers and eight meetings of the councillors but they were in a position to report on these objections by March of 1956 with the remainder being dealt with by the autumn. These were reported in detail in Report 56/1956 and Report 75/1956. Most objections were denied since they would have nullified the proposals but it seems that the Corporation was open to alternatives when this proved possible. For example, it was decided to shift the widening of Malahide Road in Marino from the east side to the west side on part of the route because of the effect that it would have had on front gardens.

Not all amendments were the results of objections. The Corporation reconsidered aspects of the plan for four main reasons.

> In a number of cases widening proposals have been eliminated where it appeared that the improvement likely to be achieved in road conditions was not sufficient to justify the cost or inconvenience likely to result. A typical instance of such an improvement is where a widening of only 2 or 3 feet to an existing road was proposed and it was anticipated that the cost of acquiring the land and rebuilding the boundary wall would more than outweigh the value of the improvement. In a number of other cases the works shown on the Draft Planning Scheme have in fact been executed. A third class of change results from criticism of detailed design in road works put forward from time to time by officials of the Department of Local Government, and finally a number of changes in road design have been made at the instance of other departments of the Corporation.
>
> (Minutes, 14 January 1957, p. 24)

Some alterations were made to the housing schedule too but only in the detail of the individual proposals. There was no alteration in the scale or timing of the developments.

The plan was put to the Council in January 1957 and it was approved unanimously. In so doing, reference was made to the submission received by the Royal Institute of the Architects of Ireland. It was noted that this was received on 8 January 1957, some thirteen months after the statutory period for the receipt of objections. Given the dates in question, it is reasonable to assert that the RIAI did not have much, if any, influence on the nature of the plan but some of their comments are of interest.

As a general point, the Corporation felt that the RIAI did not understand the legislative framework in which the plan was made. The Corporation noted that it could not plan for State-owned property or property under the control of a range of agencies. While they found the RIAI's idea for a planning commission on the lines of the Wide Streets Commission worthy of mention, they questioned whether this would add anything to the efficiency of their operations. It all seems rather odd. The RIAI did themselves no favours by being so late and then to dilute their practical comments on the plan with airy-fairy ideas seems ill-judged. They also seem to have forgotten that much of the effectiveness of the Wide Streets Commissioners derived from their authoritarian and anti-democratic powers.

In more practical terms, they complained that the road schemes were less than ideal and did not meet the needs of traffic and convenience. However, the Corporation took the view that their proposals were pragmatic – decided by the needs of the city, how much money they had and the existing road network itself. The RIAI were more in favour of a bridge to the east of Butt Bridge than the Corporation was, as the latter's comments indicate. The Corporation took the view that there was now no pressing need for such a bridge and they felt that the eastward movement of the city was no longer the dominant force, given the development that had been sited to the west of the city, where it was noted that there was now a population of 70,000.

The RIAI was also worried that not enough attention was being given to preserving buildings and they asked that the number of buildings so scheduled be increased. Here, the Corporation's worry about money once again came to the surface. They expressed the view that it cost money to preserve buildings and there was a worry that the burden would fall onto the Corporation, forcing them to spend money that they did not have. Instead, its view was that:

> most of the buildings listed are controlled by responsible bodies that have either erected or preserved these buildings for many years. The listing of buildings in the Planning Scheme does not automatically provide the finance necessary to preserve them and though a considerable number of buildings listed by the Institute of Architects

are in fact listed in Table P of the Planning Scheme, the property in the hands of the State and Corporation have not been scheduled for the reasons, first of all, the State is exempt from planning control and, second, that the Corporation is unlikely to injure the important buildings under its control.

(p. 31)

The adoption of the plan by the Council was not the end of the matter. The Minister for Local Government had to give his assent and this was not a foregone conclusion. Because the process allowed objectors to restate their case to the Minister, this was effectively a rerun of the Corporation process. In the Corporation minutes for 7 December 1959, it was reported that over 1,200 objections had to be sent to the Minister for consideration. It was bound to take time but it should have been a disappointment to all that the plan had been neither approved nor rejected by the beginning of 1961. It was the only plan that had been approved by a council and sent for approval to the Minister. The legal process that enveloped Dublin Corporation must have had much to do with this and it provided justification, if any was needed, for other bodies to sit and wait to see the outcome. However, the Department faced the prospect of getting similar plans from the other boroughs, councils and urban districts, even if not in the immediate future. The Department, for its part, seemed overwhelmed by the enormity of what was involved in approving a plan and determined that it was not going to do it again. The 1963 Act was, in part, designed to ensure that. The Corporation had got close to its first development plan but did not quite get it over the line. But it had done the State some service in showing in a clear and practical manner that the provisions of the 1934 Act, even as amended by the 1939 Act, were unworkable and far from enhancing planning were likely to prevent it.

Of course, this did not really inconvenience the Corporation. It was now clear of its court actions and it had fulfilled its obligation under the 1934 Act. While the Minister was deliberating, it could use its interim powers, as it had done for twenty years, but this time safe in the knowledge that it was in conformity with the law. Thus, what had happened before continued to happen: the Corporation proceeded with elements of the plan as the opportunity presented itself. The Minister gave approval in 1958 to proceed to acquire land to widen Church Street. This included 73–93 Church Street and Lisburn Street (Minutes, 7 July 1958). The Housing Committee in 1960 proceeded to approve the inclusion of the Upper Rathmines Road–Highfield

Road junction in list of road proposals scheduled for execution in the first period of the planning scheme (Report 66/1960).

It has been noted above that there was no statement of philosophy in the document but some conclusions can be attempted. It seems that the Corporation was in favour of trying to accommodate the motor car and to solve the problems of city congestion by driving wide roads through the older and decayed part of the city. In this, they were little different to authorities in cities across Europe, as will be discussed later. The old city seemed to hold no historical interest for the Corporation and they were quite content to lose the streetscape despite it being one of the few remnants of the medieval city that had survived. The housing was also old, poor and generally in bad shape and it could go without it being too much of a loss. Even Henrietta Street, the genesis of the modern town house and the location of some of the finest examples of these houses, was not worthy of preservation because it was generally ruinous. Specific monuments were designated for preservation and the Corporation did recognize that the largely intact Georgian landscape around Merrion Square was a different proposition to that of other locations. It seems that money was the driving force, as it had always been. The Corporation was scared of taking on responsibilities for which it had no readily identifiable source of funding. Thus, it made sense to preserve Merrion Square but to leave well alone the decayed and more questionable landscapes to the west.

The first development plans

The 1963 legislation was a sea change in the approach to planning. The saga about the planning scheme in Dublin was an important catalyst in convincing the Minister that a new approach was needed. The experience that his Department had of trying to review the Dublin scheme was that it was too rigid and inflexible a mechanism for ensuring good planning.

The problem with the planning scheme concept was that once it was approved, it had the force of law. There were limited opportunities for people to object and once the window for that opportunity was passed, there was nothing further possible. It was a cumbersome process involving both the Corporation and the Minister and it was difficult to change. Any planning scheme stayed in force until it was replaced by another one or struck down by the Minister. Even minor revisions required that the entire process be gone through again. These were some of the arguments that the Minister for Local Government, Mr Blaney, made when he opened the second stage debate on the Local Government (Planning and Development) Bill, 1962 on 22 November 1962:

The 1934 Act had many defects. It laid down a procedure for the making of a planning scheme which was too lengthy and too cumbersome. The scheme itself once made would contain extensive powers to regulate development and control the use of land. The provisions of a scheme would, therefore, require the most detailed preparation, and elaborate investigations of the provisions would be an essential prerequisite to its being brought into force. It would require the Minister's approval and his approval could, in effect, be annulled by the Oireachtas or by the High Court. Once made, a planning scheme would have the force of law and could be amended only by a repetition of the procedure required for the making of the original scheme.

Since a scheme could not readily be adapted to changing circumstances, it should include all possible foreseeable developments. It would be impracticable to make a workable plan on this basis, especially in an era of rapid technological and social change such as the present. A planning scheme might entail a substantial aggregate of compensation liabilities as soon as it came into force. This would put a premium on timid and inadequate schemes. Even if the compensation liabilities could be met, there would be no guarantee that the provisions for development which occasioned them would ever mature. Compensation paid in respect of interim directions cannot be recovered. This means that a planning authority is more or less committed to including interim directions in the planning scheme.

(Dáil Debates, 197(10), col. 1768)

He went on to say that the planning scheme was about controlling development and not about promoting it. It set out what people could or could not do but it did nothing to advance projects. He wanted planning to make our towns better places to live and work in by improving their appearance, services and facilities. This meant that they had to be flexible and responsive and to be able to adjust to new and changing circumstances. It was a particular point of importance with him that the proposed legislation gave authorities the power to undertake urban renewal.

To that end, it would now be a requirement for all councils and authorities to make a plan that was solidly based on evidence. The plan would contain a written statement of policy. It would provide a mechanism so that people wishing to make developments could ensure that they were in conformity with the plan (planning permission) and 'the planning system must ensure that the public, including the land owner, the tenant, the house owner, the shopkeeper and the developer, will be enabled to know with as much assurance as possible how the development of their area is likely to proceed and how that development is likely to affect themselves'.

The aims of the legislation were fourfold:

- To set up a new and more flexible planning system to be operated by local authorities throughout the country.
- To enable local authorities to facilitate industrial and commercial developments and to secure the re-development of these parts of built-up areas which have become outmoded, uneconomic or congested.
- To secure that the amenities of town and countryside are preserved and improved.
- To relate compensation to property owners to the restrictions imposed on them by individual planning decisions rather than to provisions in planning schemes and to end their liability for betterment charges.

It was going to be quite an onerous process for a local authority and they had only three years from the passage of legislation to come up with a plan that would be comprehensive in its coverage. A plan was expected to deal with (a) zoning of land used for particular purposes; (b) securing the greater convenience and safety of road users and pedestrians by the provision of parking places or road improvements or otherwise; (c) development and renewal of obsolete areas and (d) preserving and improving amenities. Within that they could go into as much detail as they liked and they were free to include other areas of interest.

The biggest change was that the Corporation would now have control of their plan. While it was obliged to consult with the Minister and other designated bodies, it did not have to seek ministerial approval. The process was also designed to facilitate review and adjustment so that it could be agile in meeting the needs of the city.

The various authorities – Dublin Corporation, Dublin County and Dún Laoghaire – produced their draft development plans by the 1967 deadline, or close to it, but the process of final approval was drawn out. Dún Laoghaire published its development plan in 1970 but in the case of Dublin Corporation and Dublin County it took until 1971 before the plans were finally adopted, although this time the delays were approved by the Minister. To be fair, both councils needed time to digest the implications of the Myles Wright report, which will be looked at in detail below, and it would have been pointless to have proceeded to adopt a development plan without taking it into account.

Regional development

A most important influence on the planning of Dublin from the 1970s on was the strategy developed by the Myles Wright team of consultants. The Abercrombie plan for Dublin of 1922 and the Civic Survey of 1925 were earlier examples of an attempt to plan for the entire metropolitan region, even though at the time there was no legal framework within which this could be achieved; these plans have been discussed extensively in earlier volumes of this series. The attempted reforms of local government following the 1938 tribunal had come to nothing with the exception of the absorption of Howth into the county borough. There were still three local authorities in the metropolitan area: Dublin Corporation, Dublin County Council and Dún Laoghaire. The need for greater integration or, at the very least, greater co-operation was manifest especially as more and more of the new urban developments were going to involve the transfer of people from the city to the county, a transfer of legal authority as well as financial responsibility.

The possibility that such a legal framework might come into being was provided in the 1934 Town Planning and Regional Planning Act which, *inter alia*, gave Dublin Corporation the right to become the statutory regional planning authority for almost the entire east region as well as Dublin. This far-seeing piece of legislation was never acted on and Dublin Corporation restricted its own mandate to the county borough area. There were amendments to the city boundary in 1941, 1951 and 1953 but these did not keep pace with development with the result that the city gradually spread deeper and deeper into the south county and the physical gap between the city and Dún Laoghaire became less and less by the year.

Though the degree of co-operation between the councils increased, especially by the creation of a joint planning department for both city and county, planning for the city was far more complex than it needed to be. For example, Dún Laoghaire could block a road proposal by Dublin Corporation by simply refusing to continue it onto its territory.

The sketch development plan produced by Abercrombie and his associates in the late 1930s advised that the city area should not be allowed to grow unrestrained into the countryside but rather should be contained within a green belt. Growth beyond that greenbelt was to be accommodated in a series of satellite towns. The plan suggested that these might be located at Malahide, Portmarnock, St Margarets, Swords, Lucan, Blanchardstown, Castleknock, Clondalkin and Tallaght and might between them house 62,000 people, the largest of these being Malahide/Portmarnock with 20,000 and Swords with 10,400. Together with some growth permitted within the built-up areas, these initiatives would accommodate a final population of 765,300, which Abercrombie regarded as more than would ever be needed and he expressed the view that 'it is unlikely, in fact, that Dublin will arrive at such a size, but a margin to allow for a certain freedom of choice, should be permitted' (Abercrombie, 1941, p. 156).

The Corporation did not address the issue of satellite town development with any seriousness during the 1950s, largely because the locations were outside its functional area and they had not departed from the view that they would not become the regional planning authority.

Instead, they decided to continue with the safer system of fringe development, a policy that continued until the late 1960s, and if necessary to seek additional land through boundary revisions. They *did* adopt the idea of a green belt of between four and six miles (6.5–10km) wide which would enclose a city with a maximum population of 620,000, excluding Dún Laoghaire, with the exact location of the city limits determined by the potential carrying capacity of water and sewerage facilities. However useful as the concept of setting a limit to the population within the green belt might have been, the Corporation had no plans to guide it if the city population ever rose above this maximum, a problem that the satellite towns concept was designed to solve.

The Myles Wright report

The Myles Wright report grew out of the provisions of the 1963 Local Government (Planning and Development) Act and was commissioned, via An Foras Forbartha, by the then Minister for Local Government, Neil Blaney, in exercise of his function as the co-ordinator of development plans made by planning authorities under that Act. It showed the balance between central and local control which was now emerging. While councils were to have control of their own planning processes, the Minister was not letting go of all of the levers of power. The consultants were asked to plan for an area some 30 miles (48km) in radius from the city centre, effectively overriding the spheres of influence of the local councils. The report was therefore an implicit acceptance by the State of the inadequacies of the prevailing system of multiple authorities.

The terms of reference given to the Wright team of consultants in April 1964 were quite comprehensive. They were asked to prepare a plan which, among other things, would have regard to:

- The position of Dublin as capital city.
- The regional and national economy and the government's aim to expand the economy as a whole and to check emigration.
- The requirements of the 1963 Act with particular reference to:
  - the size and form of urban settlements;
  - major land uses;
  - green belt policy;
  - roads and communications;
  - public services and utilities.

The plan was presented to the Minister in December 1966 and published in 1967 and it set out the planning parameters for the region for the period to 1985.

New towns

The requirements of evidence-based planning necessitated the production of a series of population projections. There were three over-arching assumptions. The first was that the targets set in the *Second Programme for Economic Development* (1964) would be met and that it was reasonable to project growth out to 1985. This set the nation the target of increasing its GNP by 51 per cent in the period 1960–70, equivalent to a growth rate of 4.2 per cent per annum. The employment effect would be to increase the labour force by 7 per cent or 73,000 jobs, with the greatest increase coming in industry (32 per cent) while employment in services was to increase by 14 per cent. A second and more conservative assumption was that the metropolitan region would not exercise a centripetal effect on national economic growth and that there would be no change in the region's share of employment and investment. They also made assumptions in relation to reduced emigration.

It was assumed that population would grow strongly as a result of a slightly lower death rate and an increased birth rate resulting from increases in the numbers of families being formed. Within these parameters, two sets of calculations were employed to establish upper and lower bounds for the population estimates. The minimum was calculated on the assumption that natural increase would slow down in the period 1971–85 compared to 1961–71, mainly as a result of decreases in fertility, perhaps to the level experienced during 1956–61. Emigration would continue but at a reduced rate. The upper estimate assumed that migration would diminish as an influence and that the consequently younger population would experience greater natural increase as a result of more family formation, even if individual fertility levels were to reduce. The figures derived from these calculations are given in the table below.

Table 3. Population projections for the Dublin region, 1966–71. (Adapted from Wright (1967), Table 20.)

	Dublin City and County		Kildare, Meath, Wicklow		Total	
	%	,000	%	,000	%	,000
Natural increase	+16.9	121	+12.3	23	+15.9	144
Net migration	-4.8	-34	-8.2	-15	-5.5	-49
Total increase	+12.1	87	+4.1	8	+10.4	95
Population 1971		805		196		1,001

Table 4. Population projections for the Dublin region, 1971–85. (Adapted from Wright (1967), Table 1.)

	Dublin City and County		Kildare, Meath, Wicklow		Total	
	%	,000	%	,000	%	,000
Natural increase (max)	+27.0	216	+19.6	38	+25.4	254
Natural increase (min)	+21.0	169	+16.5	32	+20.0	201
Net migration (max)	0.0	0	-5.1	-10	-1.0	-10
Net migration (min)	-4.6	-37	-8.6	-17	-5.4	-54
Total increase (max)	+27.0	216	+14.5	28	+24.4	244
Total increase (min)	+16.4	132	+7.9	15	+14.6	147
Population 1985 (max)		1,021		224		1,245
Population 1985 (min)		937		211		1,148

The projections suggested a population of 805,000 in the city and county by 1971, an increase of 12 per cent over the 1961 figure of 718,000 and way over what Dublin Corporation had considered as the maximum population that could be accommodated within its green belt. The growth dynamic would then ensure further increase to between 937,000 and 1,021,000 by 1985. The report conceded that growth might be faster or slower than that predicted and on that basis presented an estimate of an extreme maximum population of 1,174,000 in 1985, based on the assumption that the projected growth would be reached by 1978; and an extreme minimum of 797,000 based on an assumption of very slow growth leading to the targets not being achieved until 1993.

Assuming an average family size of 3.3 persons, the estimates suggested that there would be between 227,000 and 313,000 additional families within the Dublin region requiring housing in addition to the backlog of housing need in Dublin. The consultants estimated that as many as 38,000 dwellings in the city (46,000 in city and county) were unfit, or would become unfit, for long term occupation during 1961–85. The study team extrapolated from Dublin Corporation's own experience and suggested that of the 38,000 houses that would become unsuitable for long term use, 10,000 or so would require urgent and immediate replacement during the period of the plan. Moreover, the current pace of development suggested that there would be a carry-over of housing need from the 1960s to the 1970s.

The assumption of the consultants was that every family requiring housing provision would be provided with a separate fit dwelling by 1985. This was in contrast to the view held by the Minister at the time that the future for the city lay, at least partially, in the high-rise concept being developed at Ballymun. This goal would require the construction of between 100,000 and 153,000 new houses in Dublin city and county in the period 1971 to 1885. This was a tall order, the rate of building necessary to achieve this being three times that achieved in the decade between 1955 and 1965, though it is admitted that the depression of the middle 1950s reduced the overall rate of building somewhat.

The major question then raised related to the location of these new houses. It was suggested that some of this growth could be accommodated in fringe developments added to the existing built-up city and it was indicated that the most likely locations for these would be (a) the northern suburbs, (b) the area along the line of the Dodder and (c) the area around Stillorgan, Foxrock and Killiney. Assuming a density of 19.1 persons to the acre (47.2 per ha), they estimated that the northern suburbs could accommodate a further 108,000, the Dodder Valley area an additional 53,000, while the Stillorgan area could cope with an increase of 100,000 people. However, some of this extra potential would be taken up by the expected redistribution of approximately 73,000 people from the city centre as a consequence of slum clearance. Therefore, the additional population that could be accommodated within the built-up city would be about 188,000 people or about 50,000 families.

The projected need would require the location of upwards of 100,000 families elsewhere and therefore the building of up to 100,000 new houses. The solution was the same as that suggested by Abercrombie back in 1939: new towns. They were not new towns in the British sense, though, because they were not designed from the beginning to be self-contained. The consultants felt that this might occur over time but that 'a new town is not likely to provide suitable employment for all its working population in its early years, although we recommend that special effort should be made to provide employment in step with growing population' (Paragraph 4:21). Though not self-contained, they felt it important that these towns should be far enough apart so as to spread the traffic load they generated as evenly over the city as possible. Moreover, they should be located so that journeys between them would not pass through central Dublin. This narrowed somewhat the choice of sites. The mountains to the south were not conducive to such a development and anyway needed to be preserved as a recreation area. The area to the north also offered limited possibilities since the presence of the airport made it undesirable to build within 3.5 miles (6km) of the control tower, and they even suggested that this control zone might extend all the way to the coast in the areas now occupied by Malahide and Portmarnock.

The consultants rejected coastal locations as being too difficult and placing great burdens on the transportation system. This left them with the area to the west of the city and this they chose, not only by elimination but also because they felt it had a number of distinct advantages. They felt that as most transport in the future within Ireland would be by road, these communities would be well located in terms of access to the major routeways and thus have advantages in terms of attracting investors and employment. In addition, there was abundant land here to permit the towns to be separate from each other and sufficiently apart from Dublin to prevent the development of a continuous built-up area. They proposed the creation of four new towns in the seven miles (11km) between Blanchardstown and Tallaght. Each town would grow westwards and would achieve a maximum population of between 60,000 and 100,000, giving a total for the system of 350,000 people.

Each town was to be provided with a shopping centre and 'other facilities which would meet all ordinary weekly needs' (Paragraph 4:31) but higher order functions would continue to be provided within Central Dublin. This concept seems to hark back to a much earlier idea from the beginnings of town planning in the modern era. When Ebenezer Howard published his hugely influential *Tomorrow: a peaceful path to real reform* in 1899, he saw his

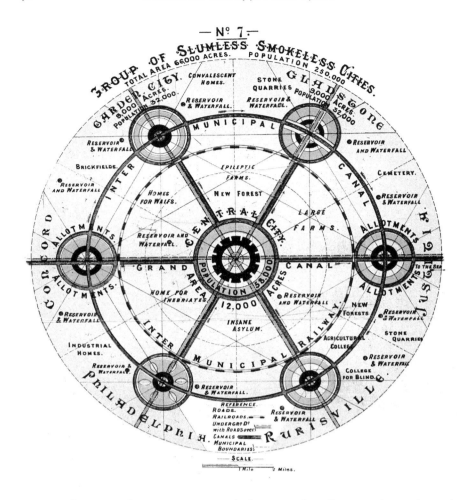

13. Howard's concept of a city system – a central urban area with satellite towns. (Howard, 1898.)

garden cities being part of a system of cities with the smaller satellites served by a larger town, though not of the scale of Dublin (see McManus, 2002).

The locations chosen for the towns were:

1. Westwards from Templeogue and Tallaght,
2. Westwards from Fox and Geese in Clondalkin,
3. Westwards from Palmerstown towards Lucan,
4. Westwards from Blanchardstown.

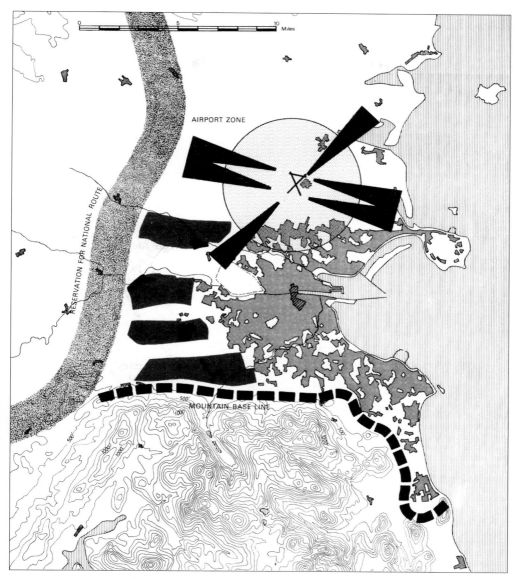

14. Wright's new towns in their regional context. (Wright, 1967, p. 21.)

The towns were designed to be long and narrow, in effect linear, and to be separated from each other and from the rest of the city by green belts. The separation of one from another was for the reasons described above but also so as not to cut off those living in the built-up city from access to the countryside. Blanchardstown was to be the first for development.

Form of the new towns

The report argued that the form of the new towns had to take account of transport needs. Therefore, they provided a linear layout which would both permit the use of private cars, *ad lib*, but also permit the economic operation of bus services. Linear designs are rare in urban form but they have been favoured because of the ease with which the design elements can be extended as the city grows. It is much easier to accommodate growth in a linear design than in other geometric shapes. The best examples of a truly linear design come from the Soviet Union and the work of Miliutin on Stalingrad and Magnitogorsk in the late 1920s. In Stalingrad the city was arranged as four major zones running in parallel with the River Volga. Nearest the river was the parkland onto which the residential zone faced. Its other face was onto the main transportation artery and across that was another green zone which ultimately led into the industrial or factory zone. A railway line served the

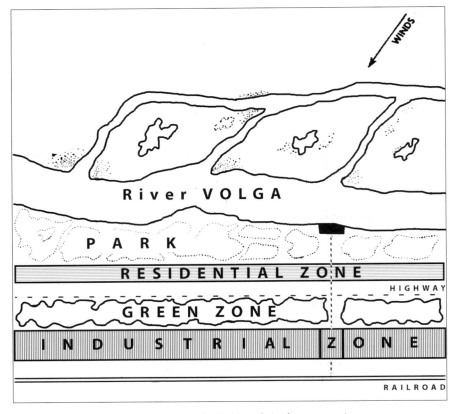

15. Miliutin's plan for Stalingrad. (Miliutin, 1974.)

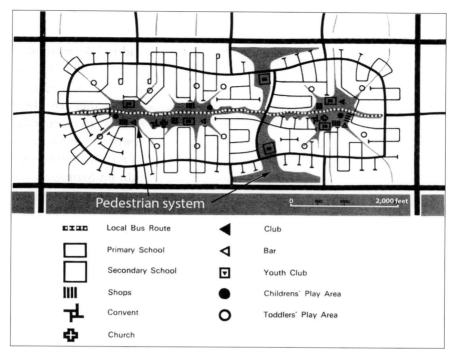

Pedestrian system

	Local Bus Route		Club
	Primary School		Bar
	Secondary School		Youth Club
	Shops		Childrens' Play Area
	Convent		Toddlers' Play Area
	Church		

16. Residential areas in the new towns. Though Wright believed that people would insist on using their cars, he provided for public transport systems. Here, a local bus route goes through the residential area, part of a loop system for local traffic. (Wright, 1967, p. 31.)

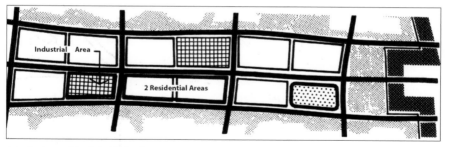

Industrial Area

2 Residential Areas

17. Industrial and residential areas in new towns. One of his options for local transportation was to have small buses operating up and down the central spine between these zones. (Wright, 1967, p. 30.)

industrial zone. Thus, most local journeys could be done on foot and while there was complete separation of work from residences, they were within walking distance. Similarly, the residential area gave access to both the main transportation route but also the recreational area. It was a highly planned, high-density solution.

Wright's solution was nothing as dramatic as had been attempted in Stalingrad but a high-density solution was favoured. The report did not envisage providing much open space within the urban area itself, since its linear form would provide easy access to the green belt around it. Instead, the consultants suggested that no more than 0.5 acre (0.2 ha) per 1,000 people be provided in the form of parks and the same amount for play areas within residential developments. Industrial areas would be provided within the urban area in the hope of developing a local employment base.

The residential areas would consist of a square or oblong area enclosed by, but separated from, the major traffic routes. There would be a system of access and distributor roads to bring people to and from the major roads. The diagram, reproduced here, shows culs-de-sac leading to a single internal loop road which has limited access to the main roads. Each residential area would be provided with a church, primary schools and six to ten shops. In order to ensure that these facilities would be no more than 0.5 mile (0.8km) from any house, it would be necessary to restrict the amount of open space to that provided for each individual house and the provisions mentioned above. Secondary schools would be located in some residential areas but would also serve neighbouring areas. Each residential area was assumed to contain two primary schools under the assumption that no infant should travel more than 0.25 mile (0.4km) but that older children could travel up to 0.5 mile (0.8km). However, the consultants did not prescribe the size of the school in each residential area and by extension they did not suggest population limits for each residential area. Instead, they suggested that different populations might be contained within the distance parameters stated above by varying the density from anything between 23.2 and 74.8 persons per acre (57–185 per ha). Finally, the report did not suggest that the residential areas have a completely separate pedestrian circulation system to that of cars: it was never going to be Radburn. Instead, they limited themselves to suggesting that underpasses be provided between the residential areas and the green belts. Thus, only the outer main roads were likely to have underpasses.

Comparisons with British new towns
The provision of additional housing in Britain became a priority after the end of the Second World War for a variety of reasons, including the need to replace war damage, the need to house returned servicemen, and the need to deal with the problems of overcrowding and congestion that had been the subject of analysis in such reports as that of the Marley Committee (1935).

The influence of the garden city movement had gradually grown so that the idea of building new towns had become more and more acceptable. The Marley Committee stated that they 'advocate the fullest adoption of the type of development usually associated with the idea of the Garden City' (p. 25). The Royal Commission of 1940 into the *Distribution of the Industrial Population* gave more guarded support for the idea of new towns but the Abercrombie plan for Greater London of 1944 was centred on the provision of a series of satellite new towns around the city. The argument in favour of building new towns was finally accepted in the terms of reference given to the Reith Committee, which were:

> ... to consider the general question of the establishment, organization and administration that will arise in the promotion of New Towns in furtherance of a policy of planned decentralization from congested urban areas; and in accordance therewith to suggest guiding principles on which such new towns should be established and developed as self-contained and balanced communities for work and living.
>
> (Ministry of Town and Country Planning, 1946)

Such was the speed with which the decisions were taken that the first Reith report was concluded within three months, a second a few weeks thereafter, and a third within another three months. Moreover, the last report was still in production when the New Towns Act (1946) was passed with the result that fifteen new towns were designated in the period to 1956. It must be said that the new towns programme was not the be all and end all of British town planning in the years that followed and that it made a small, though useful, contribution to housing provision. Nevertheless, Wright had the experience of almost twenty years of the new towns programme at his disposal when producing the report and therefore it is reasonable to make a number of comparative points.

The crucial difference to Dublin was that British new towns were designed to be independent of their 'parent' towns. Their progress was the responsibility of a development corporation appointed by central government. While the corporation could not compel any industry to locate in its new towns, its independence permitted it actively to seek industry and employment for itself and compete for jobs with other locations. No such independence was planned for the Dublin towns and therefore any relocation of industry to the new communities would depend entirely on the policy of the metropolitan councils who might have other concerns.

A key concept in the British new town approach was that they should be 'self-contained and balanced communities for working and living', although this proved very difficult to achieve in practice. This principle meant a number of things; the towns were to provide as much local employment as possible for those living in the towns; the structure of employment was to be varied to avoid dependence on a single industry; the facilities available in the town should meet the normal day-to-day needs of its inhabitants, including leisure and recreation; and the population should be balanced in terms of social class and age structure. The degree to which this formula was applied varied as did the success achieved (Thomas & Cresswell, 1975). One measure linked the provision of a house in the new town to having a job in the new town but achieving a balance in terms of social class was left much more to chance in that industrial projects were not filtered to see what impact their employment profile would have on the town. Some attention was devoted to the spatial aspects of class segregation with various proposals made over the years to try and prevent residential differentiation, such as mixing various social groups within each of the residential areas. This was the policy followed initially in Crawley though Peterlee favoured a policy of separate housing provision.

The achievement of a balanced age structure was also a concern, though not explicitly stated in the Reith report, in that it was recognized that most migrants would be young, given that the propensity to migrate declines with age. An unbalanced age structure would cause demand for facilities to wax and wane as the population bulge moved through the age cohorts with consequent problems for the efficient provision of facilities. This problem proved difficult to deal with in Britain with no comprehensive solutions proposed. Limited solutions were provided in the shape of giving houses to older people not tied economically to the town and providing housing for the parents of younger migrants. While it cannot be said that British new towns managed to become completely self-contained and balanced communities for working and living in terms of the criteria outlined above, Wright cannot have been unaware of the concept.

The Wright report contains no such aspirations about the desirability of creating balanced and self-contained communities. The concept of self-containment was not emphasized by Wright and would in any event have been difficult to achieve given the proximity of the new towns to Dublin. Even in Britain where the new towns were located at considerable distances from their 'parent' city, at least 18 miles (29km) in the case of London, the growth of car ownership made the possibility of self-containment difficult to achieve and it

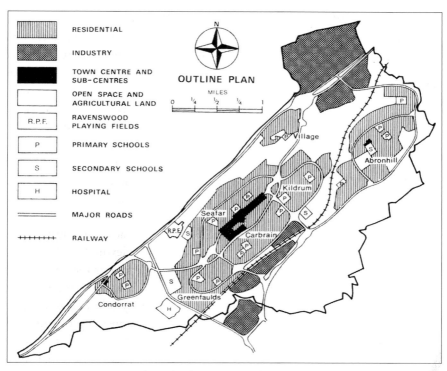

18. Outline plan for Cumbernauld. (Evans, 1972.)

19. Aerial view of town centre of Cumbernauld. (J.R. James Archive, University of Sheffield. Creative Commons Licence.)

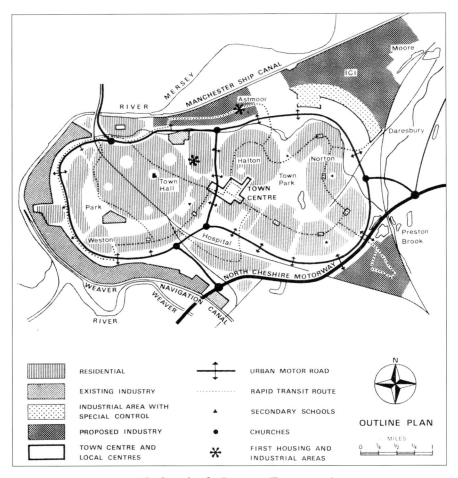

20. Outline plan for Runcorn. (Evans, 1972.)

may be that Wright, in planning for a car-owning population, decided not to try for what might be an almost impossible goal. Rather, Wright's view was that the communities would be part of Dublin and not separate urban entities. He advocated that employment should be sited in the new towns but this was in the context of his view that the entire metropolitan area needed to disperse its employment in order to make the city function better, especially in terms of its circulation pattern. There were no social desiderata set down and only the fact that the towns would house most of the urban growth of the city would indicate that they would have a balance of social class. The neighbourhood concept (Brady, 2016) was implicit in Wright's plans, a concept whose use varied considerably in the British new towns, though its presence or absence often depended more on definitions and labels than on the presence or absence of a structure whereby communities were structured into units of a given size and provided with day-to-day facilities. Thus, neighbourhoods were out of fashion in Reddich (1965) although the housing was still subdivided into distinct areas. Wright did not call his residential units 'neighbourhoods' but rather 'residential districts' but it is clear that he saw his towns structured into distinct residential areas, each with its own local services and facilities.

The layout of the new Dublin towns was an attempt to plan for a situation where car ownership would be high but where it would still be necessary to provide a comprehensive public transport system. In this regard, Wright's plans bear comparison with the plans for Cumbernauld (1955) or Runcorn (1964). Cumbernauld attempted to come to terms with the car age by building a town with a completely separate pedestrian and car circulation system (Gibberd, 1972). The town centre was a high-density, multi-level development on the lines endorsed by Buchanan. The feasibility of the pedestrian circulation system was ensured by building at high density, thus ensuring a very compact town where every facility was within walking distance. The road networks consisted of a hierarchy of roads designed to filter traffic out of the residential areas towards the main roads. This is also a feature of the Wright scheme where the main roads were on the outskirts of the residential areas but there was no provision for a separate circulation system for pedestrians.

Wright's approach to housing was for low-density development that was closer to Runcorn than to Cumbernauld. In Runcorn, public transport was seen as a key element of the design whereby it was planned to provide a rapid transit system in the form of a figure eight, with the town centre at its intersection, forming the spine of the residential development which was considerably more dispersed than in Cumbernauld. Wright believed that the proposed design would permit the development of an efficient public transport network. Express buses would run along the central spine to Dublin while small local buses would bring people to the express termini on a looped route through the residential areas. It was seen as a practical and necessary compromise between the demands of car owners and sensible planning and was in the spirit of the age. The designs do not have exact parallels in Britain, though perhaps there are echoes in the approach adopted for Milton Keynes some years later.

Implementation of Myles Wright report

In the event, the population projections of the Wright report proved too conservative and the city grew at a faster rate than had been anticipated. By 1971 the population of the city and county was 852,219 but by 1979 this had grown to 983,683 and to 1,003,164 by 1981. The maximum population growth estimate had been achieved by 1981, four years ahead of target. Nevertheless, the proposal that a considerable proportion of that growth be contained in a number of new towns on the western edge of the city became planning policy though the detail of the plans was significantly modified, particularly in that the two separate urban developments planned for the Lucan and Clondalkin areas were merged into one.

While there was no change in the governance structure of Dublin as a result of the 1963 Act, there had been some useful developments which had the potential to make the planning process more coherent. The creation of the post of City and County Manager and of a Planning Department which, though still structured on city and county lines, was under a single administrative authority was a positive move. It was not quite the reform needed since the individual councils still had the final say but it was an important step and one which was particularly important for the chances of a report like Wright's which transcended local authority boundaries.

The projected populations of the three satellites were somewhat modified in the first development plans with Blanchardstown and Clondalkin/Lucan both set to reach 100,000 by 1991 and in line with then current British New Town targets. Development had already begun in Tallaght by the time of the plan, despite Wright's choice of Blanchardstown as the place to begin development, and it was given a population target of 136,000, considerably greater than the other towns and well above the maximum suggested by Wright.

The plan accepted that the residential areas were to be built on the neighbourhood principle but the linear structure was not adopted. In fact, there was no attempt to provide anything innovative, instead the outline plan was for a number of distinct neighbourhoods clustered around the town centre. Within each neighbourhood there was to be provided a school, church and low-order shopping with the next level of services being provided at the town centre, which would be the focus of the settlement (see MacLaren, 1983).

In this respect the plans had much more in common with the early British new towns such as Stevenage (1946), the first of the programme, where each neighbourhood had a primary school at its heart and a subsidiary shopping centre. Harlow's (1947) structure was more complex where a number of

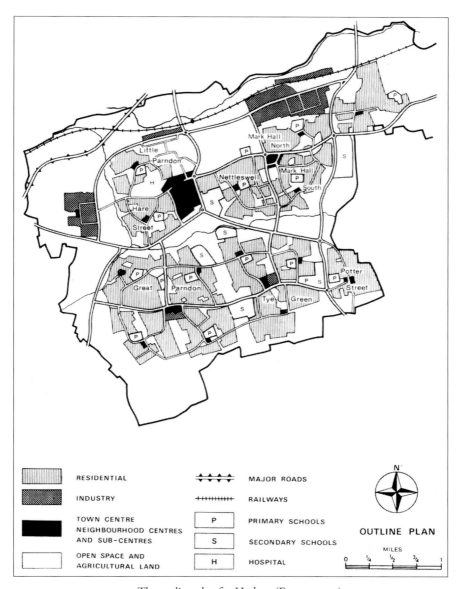

21. The outline plan for Harlow. (Evans, 1972.)

neighbourhoods share higher order shopping facilities to create a neighbourhood cluster, with four such clusters then being served by the town
centre. This intermediate layer was not adopted in the Dublin system which
moved directly from local provision to town-level provision.

22. Temporary local shopping provision in Tallaght as houses were completed in 1970s.
(A.J. Parker.)

There was some attempt to control traffic flow through neighbourhoods in the new Dublin towns, though this is better seen in the later developments. Earlier developments, such as the Old Bawn estate in Tallaght, tended to follow a rigid grid system with all roads connected to the main road. The later road systems were designed to bring into the neighbourhood only the traffic that had business there and gradually filter it into the culs-de-sac along which the houses are built. The building lines were varied in order to give some variety and there was considerable open space. This may be seen in the Corduff neighbourhood in Blanchardstown where there are only two entrances to the estate from the encircling main road with little development along the line of these entrance/exit routes. The plans contained aspirations for a comprehensive public transport system but progress on this aspect was slow with the result that the residents of the new towns became car users, as much from necessity as any other reason.

No mention was made in the development plan of trying to achieve an age balance in the new towns by perhaps varying the size and price of houses through the planning permission process. The result was that most developers, including the local authorities, decided to build for young families and so created residential areas with largely homogeneous age structures consisting of

23. The first 'town centre' in Tallaght in the middle 1970s. This was a long way from what the population might have reasonably expected. (A.J. Parker.)

24. The '3 Guys' shopping centre at Tymon, Firhouse, just prior to opening in 1977. The large parking provision is indicative of the importance of the motor car in the shopping process. (A.J. Parker.)

young couples, young children and little else. There was a greater concern with social differentiation and the plan attempted to achieve a mix of social classes by seeking a 60/40 ratio of private to public housing. However, although this was sometimes achieved within neighbourhoods, often it was achieved only in terms of the overall balance between neighbourhoods. The difficulty with such social engineering is that though the city planners might wish this kind of result to be achieved they can only facilitate development, they are in no position to initiate it. The residents of these new towns have also found to their cost that the limitations of the planners extended to areas other than social engineering. Services proved notoriously difficult to attract to the towns with developers recognizing that areas which comprised young families with children were unlikely to have much disposable income after the necessities have been taken care of. This led to Tallaght having to wait until 1990 for the opening of its town centre complex while the other new towns just had signs on green-field sites as the only indication of where their centres would be. Each of the new towns now has its regional level centre. The Blanchardstown centre was opened in 1996 and has since been extended. It currently claims to be Ireland's largest shopping centre with 140 stores, three retail parks and 7,000 parking spaces. The Liffey Valley centre was the last to be completed and is somewhat off centre to Clondalkin. Its location proved controversial and it serves as much as a regional centre for Dublin as for the 'new town'. It opened in October 1998 with a floorspace of about 250,000 sq. ft (23,000 sq. m) and seventy shops, somewhat small for a centre of its type. Consequently, it took some time and a more than doubling of capacity before it achieved a critical mass but it is now firmly integrated into the edge developments of the city.

In 1914 it was first suggested that Dublin should have a town plan and that future development should be managed using town planning principles. While the idea was quickly accepted, it took until the end of the 1960s for that plan to emerge. The 1957 plan had been a useful attempt but had not quite made it. Against that background, the progress of the 1960s was positively speedy. With the adoption of the development plan in 1971, Dublin embarked on a process whereby its planning would henceforth be governed by a series of principles set out in a plan and subject to regular review and amendment. That the outcome was not always what might have been expected is another story that has already been well told in McDonald (1985).

The urban landscape

Changing dynamic

Ever since city life began and especially since the Renaissance, urban authorities have sought to enhance the civic environment by building either landmark buildings or by the creation of urban quarters. Their ability to create magnificent urban environments spoke of their power and wealth and this was particularly important in a capital city, which aimed to set the tone for the country as a whole. There is an excellent treatment of this in both of Spiro Kostof's texts – *The city shaped* and *The city assembled*. It was easier to do this if control was in the hands of an autocrat or somebody with powers approaching autocracy and the classic examples of urban remodelling in the nineteenth century are Paris at the hands of Baron Haussmann or Vienna under the direction of the Emperor Franz Josef. Though not an autocrat, the degree of power given to Haussmann was such that he was able to sweep away most of medieval Paris. He was stopped before he could complete the clearance, which would have included Notre Dame. In his defence, it must be recognized that his is the city that is so loved today. Two twentieth-century autocrats, Hitler and Stalin, both embarked on ambitious projects to put their stamp on the landscape. Hitler's Germania, the new Berlin, would have outdone anything previously attempted in sheer scale and as statements of power. Stalin's remodelling of Moscow would not have been far behind; the Palace of the Soviets alone would have risen to 415m. Renaissance city planning concepts had a strong influence on these ideas, especially those of Haussmann, and this influence continues to the present day. When François Mitterrand decided that it was his turn to leave his mark on the landscape of Paris through his Grandes Operations d'Architecture et d'Urbanisme he was conscious of the symbolism of the urban heritage that he had inherited. Thus, the Grande Arche de la Défense (1989) was dovetailed into Haussmann's planning and lines up, for example, with the Arc de Triomphe, the obelisk in Place de la Concorde and the Pyramide in the Louvre. The City Beautiful movement that developed in the United States at the end of nineteenth century operated in a democratic political context but it too sought to create urban environments that owed much in design terms to the Renaissance. This was a middle-class agenda and its proponents wanted cities of beauty, harmony

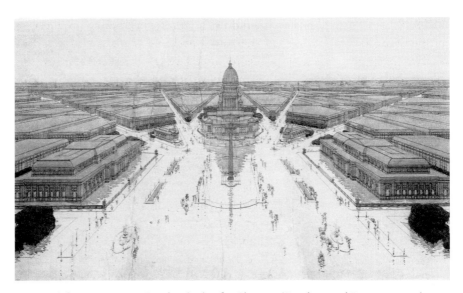

25. The city centre in Burnham's plan for Chicago. (Burnham and Bennett, 1909.)

and order not just for aesthetics but also because they believed that this would engender civic pride and benefit the urban economy because beautiful surroundings would encourage productivity. Perhaps the best known of the promoters of the concept was Daniel Burnham. Together with Frederick Olmsted he was the principal designer of the World's Columbian Exposition held in Chicago in 1893 to celebrate the 400th anniversary of Christopher Columbus' arrival in the New World. The buildings prepared for the exhibition owed much to the French Beaux Arts movement, which in turn was hugely influenced by Renaissance ideas. His plans for Chicago, which he prepared with his colleague Edward Bennett between 1906 and 1909, showed the development of these ideas in an urban setting.

In democratic societies it is common for many plans, no matter how worthy, to remain as drawings. Thus it was with most of the more ambitious parts of Abercrombie's first plan for Dublin, which would have seen the construction of grand civic buildings and the creation of impressive boulevards. It was usually a question of money and sometimes a question of politics. Certainly in Dublin there was never the money to build on a grand scale from the 1920s on and the 1950s and 1960s were certainly not the decades to be contemplating such projects. The times required focus on more practical and pragmatic projects. The push to address the scourge of TB saw the building of sanatoria in places such as Ballyowen in Lucan. There was a major programme of hospital building in train that would provide new hospitals: St Vincent's at Elm Park, a new maternity hospital at the Coombe, a fever hospital at Cherry Orchard and a new regional sanatorium at Blanchardstown. Significant investment was needed on the infrastructure for the planned national television station and towards the end of the 1950s the long-planned move of UCD to its suburban location began. The latter was the object of both amusement and relief. *Dublin Opinion* had provided a number of wry views of crowding in the Earlsfort Terrace buildings in the 1950s and it offered a view of what the campus might come to look like in its July 1960 edition that is not entirely far-fetched from the perspective of 2017.

The Royal Institute of British Architects visited the city for their Architect's Conference from 11–14 June 1947 and in their brochure for the event they recognized the reality as outlined above. They noted that no public buildings of note had been produced over the previous quarter century (they could have gone back further) because of the necessity of addressing the problem of the slums. They were hopeful that 'with growing appreciation of its architectural inheritance, Dublin looks forward with confidence to the time when great architecture, possessed of aesthetic qualities essentially Irish, will again be produced'. They ended their booklet with a quotation from Shakespeare's

26. View of Ballyowen Sanatorium. (Crampton photo archive.)

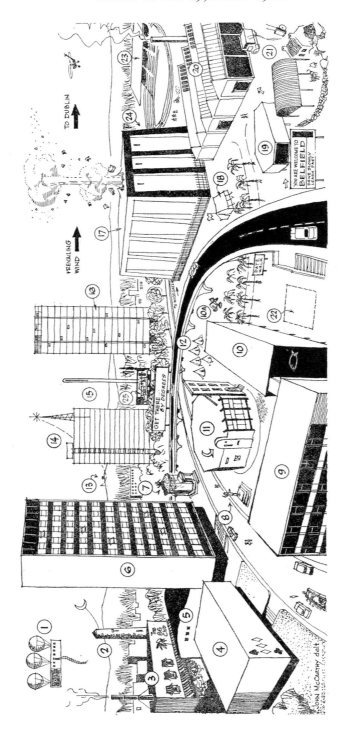

27. View of the Belfield campus. (*Dublin Opinion*, 1960, pp 144–5.)

Guide to UCD Campus	
1	School of Higher Mathematics and Suspended Animation.
2	Faculty of Celtic Studies, with Twilight attached.
3	The Espresso Building.
4	The Poker Institute.
5	Convocation Theatre.
6	School of External and Internal Politics.
7	The Classics Building.
8	The Myles na Gopaleen Monument (First Professor of the Codology Faculty).
9	History and Dates.
10	School of Secondhand Motoring.
11	School of Architecture (revolving) with Georgian façade.
12	The Earlsfort Exiles and Displaced Persons Camp.
13	The Hellfire Club.
14	The Television Faculty (Professor Andrews, Dean).
15	The Bodkin Tower.
16	Information Bureau for Posts Abroad.
17	Faculty of Nuclear Physics.
18	School of Nuclear Disarmament.
19	Pathology Block.
20	Summer School of Canning.
21	Faculty of Agriculture.
22	Site for Faculty of Forensic Medicine.
23	The Delany Stadium.
24	Helicopter Landing Ground for Students and others.

Henry V, 'for now sits Expectation in the air'. They were still expecting in 1951 when Charles Aliaga Kelly gave his inaugural address as President of the Architectural Association of Ireland. In a downbeat speech, he lamented the lack of engagement of architects with the planning of the city and suggested that perhaps they were too busily engaged with building semi-detached houses. He recognized, though, that there was little that might excite and that it was so disappointing that few public buildings, apart from hospitals, were being constructed. In other countries, the wealthy endowed swimming pools, libraries and so on but in Ireland they bought racehorses. The only buildings of major architectural interest that were regularly being constructed were churches but 'there is no doubt that the general standard of their design leaves much to be desired' (*Green Book, 1951–52*, p. 28). Towards the end of the decade there seems to have been a realization that the era of public and civic building was not coming back. The address by P.M. Delany in 1957 suggested that there was far too little interest by business and commerce in either good planning or good architecture. He was equally concerned about the impact of the motor car and he was in prophetic mode when he said 'the time is at hand in many of the world's great cities, and in not more than 10/15 years away even in Dublin, when either private motors must be excluded from the city centre, or the entire city must be rebuilt so as to provide separation of wheeled and pedestrian traffic, mammoth car parks, parking and waiting space within each building-site for all the vehicles attracted by the functions of the building' (*Green Book, 1958–59*, p. 29). He was wrong only in suggesting that the issue was ten years away; within five years this would be a live issue in the city. His successor, James Green, was hardly more confident about the demand for modern architecture. There was no public appreciation and therefore no demand for modern architecture and definitely no clamouring that Dublin or other Irish cities should be embellished in this manner. Indeed, the tenor of his paper was that architects and architecture had some considerable ground to make up. As he put it, 'ultimately the standing of the profession in the community depends on the value that the community sets on its services. If people don't think that architecture is sufficiently important to the community then there won't be any high esteem or prestige for architects' (p. 57).

There were some far-reaching changes to the civic landscape nonetheless as the world of commerce and public administration came to have a significant impact and transformative power moved from Dublin Corporation to the corporate sector. Whether they embellished the civic landscape is another matter. There was the addition of Dublin's first skyscraper as the Irish Transport and General Workers' Union built Liberty Hall on the site of the original building. The thorny issue of commemoration and memory also drove changes to the city's landscape. There was the loss of another tall building in that the Nelson Pillar was dramatically removed from O'Connell Street in 1966, much to the surprise of many who had been agitating for its removal for many years. Perhaps, though, the project that generated the most comment and stayed in the public consciousness for longer was on the face of it, a small and relatively insignificant modification of the island on O'Connell Bridge to accommodate the 'bowl of light'.

The 'bowl of light'

An Tóstal was the 1950s' version of 'The Gathering', though it was conceived of as a multi-annual event. It was entitled 'Ireland at home' and it was hoped

28. Landing in the pool. (*Dublin Opinion*, 1953, p. 45.)
Caption: Memorable moments, the first Saturday night motorist to land in the middle of the ornaments on O'Connell Bridge.

that a range of cultural and entertainment events would tempt tourists to visit Ireland around Easter each year, thus extending the holiday season. It was begun in 1953 and a set of commemorative stamps was issued to mark the event. Dublin Corporation wanted to make an impression on visitors to the city but money was tight and they decided to mark the event by the floodlighting of public buildings and the provision of flower beds in the principal streets. They provided a fund of £10,000 and hoped that this would be at least doubled by donations from businesses.

The highlight was to be a piece of public art, making use of the central median of O'Connell Bridge (*Irish Times*, 22 January 1953, p. 9). It was announced that a cut stone plinth with a central fountain with flower beds and two ponds of water would replace the walkway. It was to be illuminated by night and it was hoped to keep flowers growing all year. By April 1953, it was ready to be unveiled and, while it closely resembled the description above, what was unveiled was surprising. Its construction generated a great deal of public interest and large crowds gathered on the evening of 4 April 1953 on the rumour that the hoardings that had surrounded the construction were to be removed at midnight (Easter Sunday). When this did not happen, a mini riot ensued which resulted in windows being broken in O'Connell Street and some appearances in the courts the following week. The fountain (or whatever it was – it defied description) was formally unveiled on Easter Sunday evening, 5 April, when the Lord Mayor switched on the illuminations but there had been a constant stream of visitors all day to view it resulting in traffic jams more associated with a Friday than a Sunday evening (*Irish Times*, 6 April 1953, p. 1). In fact, the structure had to be protected by barrels for a number of weeks until it was felt that motorists had become accustomed to it and would be less likely to crash into it (*Irish Times*, 15 April 1953, p. 3). It comprised a large open concrete structure (not cut stone as expected), the length of the bridge, about 2m wide and about 1m high. The outer perimeter of the structure was given to a flower bed while the inner part comprised a water feature, a pool, with small fountains playing along it. It was the centrepiece, however, that really captured the attention. This was a basin of about 15ft by 18ft (4.5 x 5.5m) and it was this structure which held a 'bowl of light'. There was a copper bowl with a diameter of about 4ft (1.2m) which rested on a hemicycle of girders. In it was a series of multi-coloured plastic 'flames' which could rotate and which were designed to be illuminated at night. It was this element in particular that generated an almost immediate and hostile reaction from public and artistic circles alike. Hostile reaction was summed up very well in a letter from a John Hennig of Sutton:

> The permanent Tóstal 'memorial' is not 'beautiful', as the official programme says, but offends the elementary conceptions of taste.
>
> It is unfunctional to have a memorial, a flower-bed and a fountain in the middle of a bridge, to place on a granite bridge a concoction of concrete, steel tubes and twisted plastic, and to have between the fountains an unquenchable flame which, to top the horrors, can revolve at times. Plastics must not be used in a permanent memorial. The light green of the toy bridge, the medley in the flames and the pink of the flowers against a grey base form an objectionable colour-scheme. The concrete border is far too heavy for the flimsy structures of the bridge which has nothing to bridge and the torches which have nothing to hold them up.
>
> (*Irish Times*, 14 April 1953, p. 5)

However, the citizens did not get the opportunity to get used to the flames. In the early hours of 19 April 1953 Anthony Wilson, a TCD student, clambered on the monument, pulled the flames from the bowl and hurled

29. The Liffey returns the flames. (*Dublin Opinion*, 1953, p. 104.)

30. The bowl of light without the flames.

them into the Liffey. Drink, it was later suggested, had been taken! He was apprehended, having run down Aston Quay and was convicted in the District Court on 4 May and fined £48 7s. 6d. (*Irish Times*, 5 May 1953, p. 11). The monument had the effect of causing traffic jams for some time; first when people came to view it and then, when the flames were bemired in the slime of the Liffey, people came in the hope of getting a glimpse of the flames in the water. In April 1955, a diver from Belfast decided to attempt to retrieve the flames and some thousands came to view his efforts. Ernest Camlin made numerous dives between the central piers of the bridge but found nothing (*Irish Times*, 12 April 1955, p. 1). There seemed to be general relief at that outcome.

However, that was not the end of the saga. There was never any serious suggestion that the flames would be replaced but that left the remainder of the structure. People wondered what they should call it and a number of alternatives circulated. It was called a 'semi-submerged submarine', the 'long woman's grave' but the two names that found most favour were that of 'the tomb of the unknown gurrier', courtesy of Myles na gCopaleen, and 'the Thing'. It was 'the Thing' that resonated most with people because it summed up very neatly a feature that defied description. At the same time, it is hard to understand why it engendered such vitriol. The artistic and literary circles did not like it, certainly, but it is unclear why (or if) there were strong feelings among ordinary Dubliners about the item. It might be that it was felt to be cheap and to diminish the image of the city. The cartoon in *Dublin Opinion* for May 1953 may capture the prevailing mood: it has Daniel O'Connell and Nelson contemplating an ice cream from the bowl. Perhaps it was felt that this was the last straw for a street that lacked dignity as the main street of the city, given over as it was to ice cream parlours and cinemas.

Flinging the flames into the river might have been a hasty act but there was no haste in the deliberations of the Corporation. A motion before the Council in October 1953, in the name of Councillor Gallagher, that would have removed 'the Thing', was withdrawn. By November, the mood had shifted to thinking that something might be saved and that the water feature in the centre could be enhanced into a more dramatic fountain with the surround faced in dressed limestone. By the beginning of 1954, the idea of the fountain had been dropped and it was decided to fill it in and make it into a flower bed. It is not immediately clear why it was not simply taken away. Cost was probably a factor for though it cost approximately £90 to keep it in flowers per annum, it was estimated in 1956 that it would cost of the order of £1,200 to get rid of it (Minutes, 9 January 1956). It seemed much more harmless as

"*As for me, Nelson, I prefer a Chocolate Sundae or a Knickerbocker Glory.*"

31. O'Connell's ice cream soda fountain. (*Dublin Opinion*, 1953, p. 71.)

a flower bed and the photographs of the time do not suggest that it was particularly offensive. However, this did nothing to change the view of the object in the minds of opinion makers. In 1954, Erskine Childers, the Minister for Posts and Telegraphs, was stirred to wrath about it. The very fact that a minister of the State should have felt moved to speak about a flower bed in the centre of a bridge is indicative of how the object was viewed. The occasion was the annual meeting of the Friends of the National Collections of Ireland. It was not a meeting favourable to modern art and a purchase of a Henry Moore statue was the subject of an excoriating rebuke from Lady Dunailey in which she said the topic caused her to become not angry but frenzied. The Minister, whose role on the night was to propose the annual report, addressed his comments to the subject of the flower bed on O'Connell Bridge (*Irish Times*, 1 April 1954, p. 1).

> I would make one last desperate plea. If it has been decided that it is right that there should be banks of flowers on O'Connell Bridge for the 1955 Tóstal, I hope that instead of having that concrete casting of what looks like a semi-submerged submarine, the Corporation will contain the flowers in a structure which will be in conformity with the balconies of the bridge.

These are the opinions of a selection of fairly responsible men. They reflect the opinions of thousands of others, who are not specially articulate, or who have no platform from which to express their views. But here we are with the abominable Thing still defacing our main bridge two years after it was first wished on us and no sign of the people's wish being observed.

The matter faded somewhat from public attention after that and it was planted on a regular basis with flowers appropriate to the season. It provided a support for a Garda signalman's box for a time. But, as is often the case with these things, the matter continued to rumble.

It raised its head again at a meeting of the Council in 1956 when the City Manager was asked by Councillor Thomas Denahey for the cost of 'removing the obstruction and restoring the bridge to its former dignified beauty' (Minutes, 9 January 1956). The Manager repeated what would have been well known by then. It had been intended to face the fountain with polished marble or limestone but this could not be completed in time for the first Tóstal. This begged the question as to why it was not done subsequently because it was the appearance of the concrete finish that did much to annoy. Perhaps it was the fact that it was estimated to cost £3,000 to achieve the desired result and by then any enthusiasm for it had waned.

Mrs Una Mc C. Dix wrote to the Council in March of 1958 suggesting that a redesign of the flower beds would be a good idea. She felt that two beds of a graceful design separated by a small tower with an illuminated clock would be nice. She did not 'believe that there is any demand for the removal of the flower beds from the general public. The majority of us love flowers and do not see enough of them. Besides to remove them would seem to be giving way to a petty form of bullying' (Minutes, 10 March 1958).

The last comment might be the key to understanding why it took so long to remove it. Money was certainly a consideration, but it was not the only factor. This is evident from the fact that the Corporation was offered the money to remove the flower bed but declined to do so. The City Manager reported to the Streets Committee at the end of December 1958 that he had been in discussions with the Council of An Tóstal about the decoration of the city for the coming year. The Council had asked for £3,300, the same as had been voted in the previous year. *Inter alia*, they suggested that the time had come to replace the flower beds and restore the bridge to its previous shape. The Manager took the unusual step of appointing an advisory committee,

32. The monument as a flower bed, 1959.

33. Support for a Garda signalman.

"GENTLEMEN .... THE THING!"

34. The Councillors preserve 'the Thing'. (*Dublin Opinion*, 1959, cover.)

chaired by the architect Michael Scott, to look at this idea. It seems that he was aware of the sensitivities around any such proposal and he wanted to be sure of his ground. The advisory committee came to the view that the flower beds should go and the former features should be restored: three lamp standards and four sections of balustrade. In addition, Mr Scott indicated that they had word that an anonymous donor would meet the cost of removal and replacement.

The latter removed the financial impediment if such there was and the existence of the advisory committee allowed the Council to act on its advice rather than bow to external pressure. That seemed to be how the Streets Committee saw things, because on 8 January 1958 they recommended that approval in principle be given to the removal of the structure. They noted that the Port and Docks Board, who were the responsible authority for the bridge,

35. Adding to the weight of the structure. The author on the flower bed in 1959.

would have to be consulted but later consultations revealed the happy news that the original fittings had been preserved.

The matter was considered at a meeting of the Council on 10 March but the motion put by Councillors Lemass TD and Larkin TD was that they reject the removal proposal. It may well have been that most Dubliners were indifferent to the structure by then but there was certainly no great groundswell of opinion in favour of retaining it. It appears that a majority of the Council was rather annoyed at the pressure that was being put on them from bodies such as the Royal Hibernian Academy and the RIAI and they seem to have resented the suggestion of the Dublin Tóstal Committee. It seems to have been a rather petulant decision with the intention of showing the mettle of the Corporation in withstanding what they perceived to be unwarranted criticism. It merited the cover of *Dublin Opinion* with the Councillors shown toasting the retention of 'the Thing'.

In 1961, Alderman Frank Sherwin asked the City Manager, perhaps with a twinkle in his eye, if it was his intention to leave the flower bed there for an indefinite period and perhaps give it a face lift. The response introduced a new element into the discussion. First, the Manager made his own position clear and then noted that the flower bed might be seen as causing a problem for the bridge.

> When the City Council last considered what should be done about the structure on O'Connell Bridge a proposal for its removal was rejected. I do *not* consider that it should be left indefinitely. Apart from other considerations, it places additional weight on the bridge where gas mains cross, and this weight is increased on public occasions when numbers of people stand on the flower-bed.
>
> The matter is being re-considered in consultation with An Coisde Sráideanna. In the meantime the weight of the structure should not be further increased by materials for a 'face lift' or for any other reason.
>
> (Minutes, 6 February 1961)

Councillor Peadar Cowan took the bait and asked the following colourful question at the next Council meeting on 6 March:

> What is the weight of the structure on O'Connell Bridge. Who ascertained, and how and when, that the weight was a possible source of danger to mains under the Bridge; what advice on this point was given to the Corporation before the erection of the structure was authorized in the first instance or at any time since; if the original plan envisaged marble facing for the rough concrete and if, particularly for the benefit of those who can only see with the eyes, the marble facing will now be carried out especially as such facing will increase the dignity, beauty, charm and character of the Bridge and satisfy the aesthetic tastes of the ordinary citizens who appreciate the beauty of the flower displays and are untouched and untroubled by the presumptuous pomposity of those unfortunate individuals handicapped with crimped and wizened minds who, incapable of seeing beauty anywhere and least of all in nature, grouse their gerning way through life to the perpetual annoyance of everyone, including themselves?

It was now revealed that the engineering department had been long concerned about the additional weight that the structure put on the bridge and particularly on the gas main beneath. This concern had been evident from the beginning and the worry was increased when the structure was used as a viewing point by people watching parades. However, it had served the useful

36. The end of 'the Thing'. (*Dublin Opinion*, 1962, p. 81.)

purpose of cutting down jaywalking across the bridge and that seems to have been the reason for tolerating its 240 ton burden.

Despite the Councillor's concern, this was to be the pretext for getting rid of the structure but there was still a way to go. At the Council meeting on 5 February 1962, Councillor Richie Ryan TD asked the Manager if it was proposed to remove it and how much it would cost. He asked specifically for (a) the cost of erecting it; (b) altering it; (c) maintaining it and (d) removing it. The Manager responded succinctly that it had cost £3,500 to erect it, there was no proposal or estimate for altering it, it cost approximately £250 annually to maintain it and the cost of removal would be about £1,500. It fell to the Streets Committee to try again and it came to the Council in April 1962 with a proposal to remove the structure because of the potential impact on the bridge (Report 54/1962). This was put to the Council on 14 May but the Council voted to bounce it back to the Streets Committee for further consideration. Sensing the need for a new approach, they asked the City Engineer for a new design for flower decoration that would be lighter (Report 94/1963). The Engineer duly reported that flowers needed a certain minimum depth of soil in which to grow and even this would be too heavy. Clearly, he was not going to allow the opportunity to slip away. He recommended that the flower bed be removed, the Streets Committee agreed and this time there was no more to be said (Report 160/1963).

The City Engineer's estimates for 1963 contained a sum of £1,900 to remove it and restore the roadway. The earth was removed from the flower bed in October 1963 but it was not until 27 December 1963 that demolition actually began as a crew with jackhammers moved in to begin to restore the central median to its current state. The original lamps were restored.

The Civic Offices

While the bowl of light provided a distraction for the Corporation, it did not distract them entirely from the project dearest to their heart – the Civic Offices. A site near Christ Church Cathedral had been suggested by Abercrombie (1941) in his sketch development plan as being suitable and it had been one of the first suggestions endorsed by Dublin Corporation. It was going to be expensive and money did not exist for it during the 1940s. There was a small window of opportunity in the middle 1950s when it looked as if the project might begin, though it was recognized that completion might take as long as twenty years.

It is useful at this point to note that a semantic distinction began to be used in the debate. The Corporation began to draw a distinction between the 'civic centre' as suggested by Abercrombie (on their urgings) and the Civic Offices or municipal buildings that they were now proposing to build. This allowed them to say that they were not deviating from the suggestions of Abercrombie but were doing something different and more modest. In fact, as will be seen below, Abercrombie did not make any such distinction. He headed his section in the report as 'municipal buildings' and referred later to a 'civic centre'. It seems that he saw no distinction and it is equally unclear what the Corporation felt it was going to achieve by attempting to draw such a distinction.

The process began at the end of 1951 when the Finance and General Purposes Committee recommended that £60,000 be borrowed for the provision of new office accommodation at Winetavern Street. It was a modest proposal for a one- or two-storey building with between 20–30,000 sq. ft (1,850–2,800 sq. m) of space. They also recommended that it 'might be considered whether the site would be suitable for the provision of further additional accommodation at reasonable extra cost' (Report 109/1951, p. 282). There was also a concern to get the work done without the need for a public architectural competition, which would inevitably delay the process and probably add to the cost. When the report was debated, the Council decided to go further and appointed a committee of twelve members on 7 January

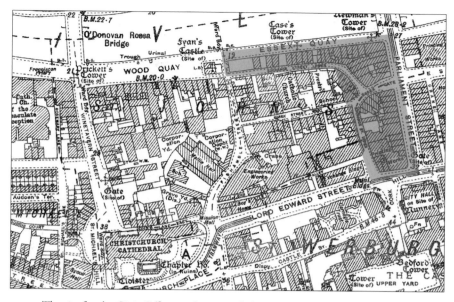

37. The site for the Civic Offices at the time of Abercrombie's sketch development plan. (Ordnance Survey plan, 1:2,500, Sheet 18(XI), 1939.) His suggested location (shaded) is on the eastern part of the extract at Parliament Street but the focus turned to the Wood Quay site between the cathedral and the river.

1952 (Civic Offices Committee) to examine how best to provide the necessary accommodation. While the borrowing of £60,000 was approved, this was not proceeded with pending the outcome of the committee's deliberations.

The Civic Offices Committee took the view that something more ambitious was needed than a single-storeyed block and the 'civic centre' came onto the agenda. With this in mind, they looked at location options and instead of sticking with a central site, they decided on St Anne's estate as the only possible site immediately available to the Corporation and asked the City Architect to report as to its suitability. This vacillation was to prove troublesome later and provided a pretext for stalling, even though the idea was a reasonable one at the time and in the context. The committee undoubtedly recognized that there would be difficulties in acquiring the necessary site in either Parliament Street (as originally suggested by Abercrombie) or in Winetavern Street because the Corporation did not own all of the properties that would be needed for a large-scale project and they knew from their housing experience just how long the process of compulsory acquisition could take. However, the view of the City Architect was not positive because of the distance of St Anne's from the city centre.

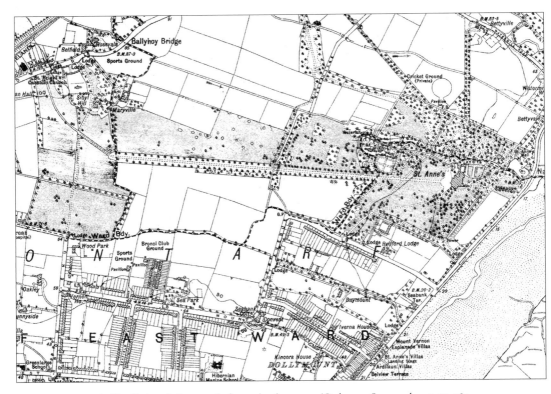

38. The St Anne's demesne before redevelopment. (Ordnance Survey plan, 1:10,560, Sheet 19, 1936.)

The Civic Offices Committee reconsidered and came up with a four point order (Report 132/1955).

1. To recommend Council to abandon the proposal to erect a Civic Centre on the site indicated in the Town Plan as the Committee considers it impracticable because of:
   (a) Cost of acquisition,
   (b) Uncertainty as to whether it could be acquired compulsorily failing agreement.
2. Request the City Architect to examine and report whether there is a site within a radius of ½ mile to 1 mile of O'Connell Bridge which can be made immediately available for the erection of a Civic Centre and to indicate for the information of the Committee where such site or sites are situate. City Architect to specifically examine the site at Constitution Hill indicated by the Right Honourable the Lord Mayor.

3. Request City Manager to indicate what Departments or portions of Departments he would recommend to be transferred to St Anne's if the Committee decide to recommend that site as the only one suitable and available.

4. Committee is definitely of opinion and will so recommend to Council that it is undesirable to hold a Competition and accordingly requests the City Manager to submit a panel of architects from whom an architect could be selected to design the new Civic Centre ...

In response the City Architect noted that the only site that he could recommend was the grounds of the Royal Hospital, Kilmainham, and that was not available. The uncertainty continued for some time but eventually the decision was taken to focus on the Winetavern Street site, which had been designated for a bus station in its lower reaches, while providing a clear view of the cathedral from the quays.

The committee approved the following order on 26 July 1954:

> [Civic Offices] Committee reiterates its previous decision to defer the immediate provision of a Civic Centre; it approves of the erection of blocks of offices at Winetavern Street and requests the City Manager to take immediate action to have preliminary details made regarding appointment of Architects, and preparation of draft plans, etc., to enable Committee report to Council; Report to indicate estimated cost and amount of accommodation to be provided in the next five years and asking Council if it does not approve of whole proposal to indicate what it will sanction for the first and second years for inclusion in the Rates. Necessary property at Winetavern Street to be acquired. Members of Council to be invited to inspect existing offices.

It should be noted that, in the committee's mind, this was not a decision to build the civic centre as proposed by Abercrombie, this was a decision to build some blocks of offices. Granted, this was on a grander scale than previously suggested and the costs were now estimated as being of the order of £500,000. The term 'civic centre' was now dropped (mostly) from discussions and the terms 'civic offices' or 'municipal offices' used instead. The committee returned to the matter later on in the year and sought to move things along by passing the following:

The [Civic Offices] Committee being of the opinion that in the interests of efficiency, proper administration, economical working and the health of the Corporation staff it is imperative that its decision of 26 July should be confirmed by the Finance Committee and submitted to the City Council for a definite and final decision. If the Committee's recommendation to provide the necessary sum annually from Rates does not find favour, the Committee feels obliged to point out that the urgently necessary office accommodation cannot be provided within a reasonable period.

(Report 132/1955)

The Finance and General Purposes Committee was a committee of the whole house and therefore was the voice of the Council. It had a concern about using the rates as the means of funding the offices, hence the reference in the paragraph above, because it would add 10d. to the pound to the rates at a time when the ratepayers were seen to be under considerable pressure.

Instead, they decided to ask the Minister for Local Government, via the Departmental Secretary, John Garvin, if the Minister would express approval in principle for raising a loan to cover the necessary £500,000. They wrote on 20 October 1954 and the response received was positive. The process was given greater impetus by the fact that problems were found with existing accommodation in Exchequer Buildings when work was due to begin on adding additional office space. It was found that the roof was dangerous and needed immediate work.

After some further consideration, the Finance and General Purposes Committee decided at its meeting on 13 December 1954 to proceed with building on Winetavern Street. Applications were to be invited immediately for the planning and supervision of a five- or six-storey building with net office accommodation of not more than 150,000 sq. ft (14,000 sq. m). With a degree of realism about funding, they asked that the building be designed as a whole but be capable of being delivered in stages, over at least four years. This decision would necessitate the acquisition of the remaining property in Winetavern Street and Wood Quay to the north of the Corporation depot and the Manager was asked to set this process in train.

At the next meeting of the Town Planning Committee in January, the shape of the building site was outlined. It was to be bounded by Winetavern Street, Wood Quay, Fishamble Street and John's Lane East. The Corporation had a cleansing depot on Wood Quay but the requisition for the site included

" He says he can't think of any suitable tune at the moment."

39. Rates and Dublin. (*Dublin Opinion*, 1956, p. 9.)

additional property on the quay – an open yard, licensed premises and some tenement houses with shops at the junction of Fishamble Street with Wood Quay. These were described as being in poor physical condition. There were houses at John's Lane which would have to be demolished together with a manufacturing chemist and two other small industries on Winetavern Street. In addition, the school attached to Christ Church Cathedral would have to go. The licenced premises in question was the Irish House, with a unique façade, and its potential loss did not seem to raise any concerns.

The City Architect produced a list of eight potential architects for the project and the City Manager chose the firm of Jones and Kelly of South Frederick Street and a meeting with them took place on 21 February 1955. It all moved very quickly after that and the Civic Offices Committee was able to report in May 1955 that it had a plan for the site. Following the municipal elections of later that month, the new Council terminated the work of the special Civic Offices Committee and the project was now taken over by the General Purposes Committee.

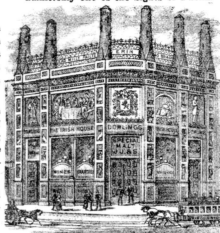

☞ WHERE TO GO?
To "THE IRISH HOUSE"

Visitors to Ireland's Capital should see this Architectural Gem, admittedly one of the Sights of Dublin.

There is to be seen Henry Grattan as he delivers his last Address in the Irish Parliament House, College Green.

Prominent, too, is the towering form of O'Connell unfolding the Act of the Country's Emancipation.

Erin is represented weeping on a Stringless Harp.

A lady is also represented gorgeously attired, with a wand in her hand, travelling through Ireland alone, to whom the Bard of Erin "Tommy Moore," dedicates his beautiful melody, commencing with the words—

" Rich and rare were the gems she wore ; And a bright gold ring on her wand she bore."

Various Emblems are to be seen both outside and inside of the Historic time of Ireland's Nationality and Ireland's Prosperity.

The interior is also beautifully and artistically decorated with Irish Emblems, including Arms of the Four Provinces, Round Towers, Ancient Irish Harps, &c.

40. Portion of late nineteenth-century handbill for the Irish House.

41. The Irish House and Wood Quay prior to clearance.

The *Irish Times* published a drawing of the building as it would look along Wood Quay (*Irish Times*, 18 August 1955, p. 7). The building fronted on to the River Liffey, and was to be approached by an open forecourt. The offices were designed on axial lines with a central block of six storeys facing the quays. The frontages on Winetavern Street and Fishamble Street were of five storeys and the two front blocks had four storeys. The plan was approved and orders were made for the employment of the various services needed to get the project, which would be built in a number of stages, underway. This was as good as it got for the Corporation. Their actions seem to have taken everyone by surprise, especially the unusual speed with which they had moved to implement their decision. Indeed, the time line from appointment of the consultant architects to publication of the plan was only a matter of months. Then the opposition caught its breath and two principal focuses of concern emerged.

The Royal Institute of the Architects of Ireland was displeased and a delegation was received by the City Manager on Saturday, 15 October 1955. They were particularly annoyed that there had been no public competition for the project. They characterized the plan as being 'wasteful of space, destructive of the amenities of the river bank and in basic conflict with the Abercrombie plans'. He had advocated a site to the west of Wood Quay for the offices, a park in the upper reaches of the Wood Quay site and a bus station set into the lower section. This would leave a clear view of the cathedral on the hill from the quays.

> Having examined various possibilities, we have come to the conclusion that the civic centre should include the existing City Hall. Parliament Street should be widened to 150-ft. and the new Civic Buildings should flank the widened Parliament Street on the West, extending from Lord Edward Street to the Quay. The block should be L-shaped with a wing extending along Essex Quay. This wing would give dignity, sadly lacking at present, to the quays on the South. It is proposed that East Essex Street be carried through the block of building with a flying bridge connecting the upper floors. This bridge could, if required, be duplicated, higher up Parliament Street over an entrance to an internal court, thus giving a symmetrical treatment to the facade facing that street. We are of opinion that, if properly treated, these bridges would enhance the possibility of attractive architectural treatment whether on classical or more free lines.
>
> (Abercrombie, 1941, p. 37)

With regard to the Wood Quay site, the plan stated that:

> It is, therefore, proposed that a site for a future omnibus station should
> be reserved on Wood Quay, extending from Winetavern Street
> approximately to Fishamble Street. The road parallel to the quay-Fleet
> Street-East Essex Street-Cook Street would bound the new omnibus
> station on the South. The area between the new station and Christ
> Church Cathedral would be left free of further building with the object
> of forming public gardens and giving a view of the Cathedral from
> Wood Quay on the South bank, and Upper Ormond Quay on the
> North bank of the river.
>
> (Abercrombie, 1941, p. 21)

The RIAI felt that what was being proposed was the Corporation's attempt at
a civic centre and they expressed the view that a project of such scale needed
to be developed in consideration of the wider spatial context, especially that
of the cathedral and the Four Courts. The City Manager attempted the
argument that this was only an office project. 'He said he would like to make
it clear to the Deputation that all the Corporation had in mind was the
erection of blocks of offices in stages to relieve overcrowding in present office
accommodation' (Report 132/1955, p. 254). He further argued that the
Corporation had decided not to proceed with the civic centre because of the
costs involved and the uncertainty of acquiring the property needed to
complete the project. It was also explained that in order to preserve a view of
Christ Church it would be necessary to 'sterilize' a significant portion of the
site. However, the Corporation officials indicated that if the RIAI could come
up with a plan that would preserve the view of the cathedral, then they would
be happy to consider it. The RIAI was disposed of, therefore, without too
much bother but the Church of Ireland proved to be a more difficult case.
Here, the Corporation was anxious to be more accommodating. The Church
of Ireland in the form of the Dean and Chapter of the cathedral objected on
the basis that the view of the cathedral from the river would be obstructed.
Meetings took place and some breaking of ranks was evident. The City
Architect expressed the view that he had never supported the Winetavern
Street site, while Dr Beausang, the Deputy City Engineer, made it clear that
his instructions from the City Manager and the Council were to be as
accommodating as possible. Accordingly, the architects were asked to modify
their plans, which they did reluctantly, muttering about their professional

reputation. The revision involved lowering the height of the main block and widening the wings so that the same amount of office space was produced. The Dean and Chapter of the cathedral were happy with the compromise plan.

It was at this point that the resolution of the City Manager began to falter. He had pushed the project forward at great speed but now he began to worry about the reaction to what had been announced. The reaction in the press had been negative and might be summed up by a letter to the *Irish Times* by Micheal O'Dea, Hon. Secretary of the Architectural Society in UCD who wished, on behalf of the students, to associate himself wholeheartedly with the RIAI and the Architectural Associations 'in their several condemnations of the scheme. Not only do we agree with these bodies regarding the unhappy choice of site, but further, we must question both the taste and integrity of the actual building' (*Irish Times*, 15 November 1955, p. 8). Indeed, the design had been likened to an early twentieth-century factory block on one of the best sites in the city. The debate soon widened as to whether alternative sites had been considered, given that the 'Abercrombie' site had been abandoned. The Corporation claimed that it had looked at other sites, including St Anne's Park, but returned to the basic premise that it needed to have its facilities centrally located. However, the news that the State had acquired the Royal Hospital further muddied the waters. This was a prestigious location, albeit not entirely central. It was never clear that the State was prepared to make it available to the Corporation but there were enough who believed that it was there for the asking.

Cover was needed. Despite the approval of the General Purposes Committee for the project, it had never been formally approved by the City Council, even though they were effectively the same body. This caused a motion to be put to the Council and this was discussed at a long meeting on the evening of 9 January 1956 where the full range of opinions was expressed. The Council agreed in principle to proceed with the plan on the Winetavern Street site but not to take action until the question of the availability of the Royal Hospital or Dublin Castle was decided. It was a classic fudge and a fatal blow but one that pleased many in the architectural community. Michael Scott was quoted as saying that he had been opposed to the Wood Quay scheme but he thought that the idea of building on the grounds of the Royal Hospital would be quite charming and he felt that the building itself could be restored for some civic purpose (*Irish Times*, 12 January 1956, p. 6).

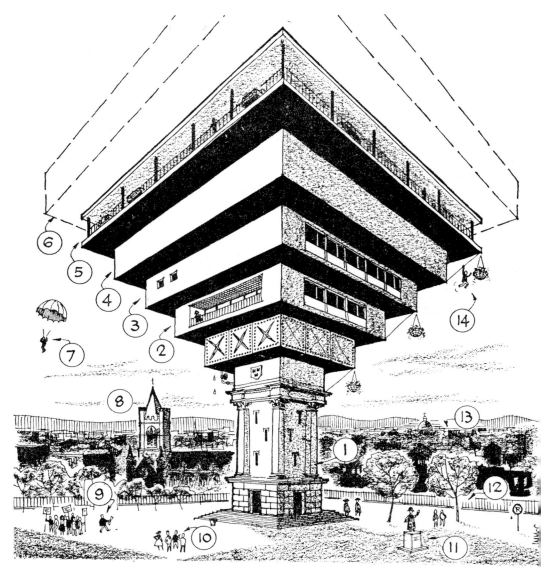

42. *Dublin Opinion*'s plan for the new offices. (*Dublin Opinion*, 1961, p. 361.)

There was a series of meetings of the Corporation and the consideration and reconsideration of the proposals until it was decided to shelve the project in 1957. The formal mechanism was the acceptance of a proposal from the Finance Committee that a loan of £18,500 be raised to cover the costs incurred in the

Design for New Dublin Corporation Offices				
By Our Staff Architect				
Our architect believes that his design is both functional and symbolic. It is his belief that this is the first top-heavy building designed for a top-heavy organization. The structural system is based on the optimum employment of distressed concrete.				
1	The Rates Department, on which the whole structure rests.		8	Unrestricted view of Christ Church Cathedral.
2	Afternoon Tea Verandah, placed, for convenience, immediately over the Waterworks Department.		9	Ratepayers delivering protest against building.
3	Department for Preservation of the Squares.		10	Group of Corporation employees enjoying coffee break.
4	Sealed chamber for Housing Consultants' Reports.		11	Statue to the Lord Mayor who will open the new building.
5	Car Park below roof level, for Corporation employees, reached by internal lift, with helicopter facilities on roof.		12	Two trees specially planted for the use of juvenile delinquents: they are kept under constant observation from the windows.
6	Provision for future expansion to keep up with the rates.		13	Distant view of unlucky ratepayers' dwellings.
7	Corporation official responsible for painting the dotted lines at 6.		14	Ex-Tóstal hanging baskets being watered by hanging gardener.

project. Given that the project was then estimated to cost up to £700,000, this was the effective end to it. There was no longer the prospect of raising the money as the State was in the middle of a credit squeeze and the focus was now on curtailing public expenditure (*Irish Times*, 10 January 1957, p. 7).

A question to the City Manager in January 1958 asked about the then current position with either the Winetavern Street site or the Royal Hospital in Kilmainham. The response was short: 'I can see no prospect in the foreseeable future of there being money available for the erection of municipal offices at Winetavern Street or any other site' (Minutes, 13 January 1958). That is not to say that the project was abandoned, rather that the momentum had been lost. While a lack of money was crucial, another factor that contributed was that a doubt developed as to the Corporation's powers to acquire property under compulsory purchase and to borrow money for a project involving municipal offices. This led to reluctance on the part of the

43. 'You must reduce'.
(*Dublin Opinion*, 1957, p. 76.)

" 'You must reduce,' says he.
'Not on your sweet life,' says I!"

city authorities to go down that route because of a fear of the litigation that might ensue. This issue was clarified and sorted out under the Local Government (No 2) Act of 1960. A collective sigh of relief was evident in the report of the General Purposes Committee (Report 128/1960), which asked the City Manager to proceed as soon as possible to acquire the site. In proceeding with the project, they noted that while the project might be completed in stages, it was necessary to present a full schedule to the Minister for Local Government before his approval could be obtained. The committee took the opportunity to note that the plans for municipal offices dated back to 1901 (at least). They finally dismissed the possibility of using the grounds of the Royal Hospital because, first, there was no chance that they were going to get it and, in any event, it was too remote from the city centre to be practical. Equally, there was no point in continuing to consider using the space in Dublin Castle. There was only one site that was suitable and that was the one that they had decided upon around Wood Quay and Winetavern Street. They must have known that this would continue to be a contentious matter because of the earlier comments on the suitability of the site. However, they would doubtless have argued that they had done everything possible to seek another location but none was available. They would also have argued as to the long and growing need to provide for an efficient administration and would have pointed to their willingness to do what they could to meet objections, within the context of building on the site. The seeds of the later intransigence of the Corporation can be seen in this report. The process had been going on for years and they had identified the only solution possible. It was this or nothing and nothing was not an option.

They also suggested that the project would be profitable in that while the principal savings to the Council would come in efficiencies and the elimination of duplication, there would be a saving of at least £18,000 per annum as a result of the release of property onto the market which was currently occupied by the Corporation. So, a decade after the first consideration, the Corporation had a site, in its view the only one that was suitable, and now had the legal powers to proceed. They might have hoped for some rapid progress, especially as the economic circumstances of the State looked more positive than they had for a long time.

It was still in progress in 1962 when it was reported that the compulsory purchase order had been made and the Minister had forwarded the list of objections to the Council in December 1961. However, they had not yet proceeded with the necessary public inquiry by the middle of 1962 because there remained the matter of deciding on the final shape of the project (Minutes, 2 July 1962). This involved a decision as to whether to try to house all of the Corporation's business within the new complex or to site some branches in alternative locations; it was considered by the General Purposes Committee at its meeting in December 1962. The recommendation to the Council was to proceed with a project that would house all of the departments of the Council at a capital cost of £1.84m (Report 163/1962). The report was approved by the Council at its meeting on 3 December 1962 and the necessary authority given to raise the loan required. The report also noted that the architects had redesigned the plans to improve the view of the cathedral: 'availing of this opportunity to open up a view of Christ Church Cathedral from the river, thus reflecting our tradition of placing public building along the river front' (Minutes, 3 December, p. 580). Work continued slowly as the site was gradually put together. In 1963, it was reported that a settlement with the various Church of Ireland bodies involved had resulted in an agreement to transfer to Dublin Corporation all of the church land that was required for the Civic Offices. In return, the church authorities were given options on other properties in the vicinity (Report 43/1963).

By 1967, the Corporation had demolished and cleared a considerable portion of the site. The main land use remaining was a depot for the waterworks department and moving that was entirely within the control of the authorities. They felt that they had reached a critical stage and that they had cleared (literally) the major physical issues with the project. They now needed to put funds in place and they needed to be creative about this because they knew none would be forthcoming from the Local Loans Fund, which had proved so useful in driving their housing project since they were first given access to it just a decade previously. The Corporation estimated the cost now to be in the order of £2m and it was agreed (Report 102/1967) to seek expressions of interest from development companies for a project that would provide not only Civic Offices but also shops, banking and a wide range of services. They also decided to reverse a previous decision and to incorporate a new council chamber into the offices. In other words, this was the civic centre project of old.

This phase of the process ended on 15 December 1967 when the opportunity to express an interest expired. It was deemed a success as forty-five developers expressed an interest and it was rumoured that there was considerable cross-channel interest (*Irish Times*, 19 December 1967, p. 12). Of these, eight were asked to prepare detailed proposals, which included a scheme for financing the project, by no later than 1 October and six submitted proposals (Minutes, 2 September 1968). There was a general welcome that the project had come so far because the area had seen accelerated decline and blight was a widespread characteristic. Not only would it bring redevelopment to the area, it was hoped that the presence of such a large block of office jobs would encourage other development in the location and dilute the dominance of the south-eastern part of the city in the commercial sector (*Irish Times*, 31 October 1968, p. 13).

The brief was for 340,000 sq. ft (32,000 sq. m) of office space and 700 car parking spaces with the requirement that the plans should enhance the heritage value of the cathedral, the chapter house, the Liffey, the quays, the Four Courts and that the visual relationships between the new buildings and the old, the vistas from various angles and routes as well as more distant vistas should all be given consideration. The project was to be worthy of the city's government. The nine plans (one developer submitted four variants) were put on display in City Hall and attracted a variety of comment. The RIAI were not at all pleased that the plans and models were put on display before the selection process had been completed. The plans, they argued, were only part of the submission but having them on display meant that advocacy could be brought to bear on the final selection process. They were very annoyed that architectural concerns were not to the fore and they feared that the decision could be made on other grounds, such as financial concerns (*Irish Times*, 16 November 1968, p. 13). Indeed, the plans did produce a reaction. One letter on 9 November 1968 in the *Irish Times* said that 'the best that can be said of any of them is that the cathedral is *still there*. A tiny parish church isolated in a wilderness of "leggo toy building bricks"' (p. 11). Others were more complimentary and debated the virtues of one plan versus another, although it can be said that the two-page spread which was published in the *Irish Times* on 21 November offered more to criticize than to like. The view expressed was that the choice lay between 'the proposals of Michael Scott and Partners and those of Stephenson Gibney for Green Properties. The remaining four, or rather seven (there being four versions of the one proposed by Desmond Fitzgerald), lack the directness of approach and regard for the site of the other two mentioned'. The paper was particularly critical of the approach by Fitzgerald, who was the architect for Gallagher and Co.

> Professor Fitzgerald for some extraordinary reason has produced four versions of the same thing. One can understand a designer being torn between a low-level development all over the site or a single large block, but not about whether or not the thing should be covered in thin or thick vertical stripes. The four versions are characterized by the sort of tiresome mediocrity that has got modern architecture the public image it has.
>
> (*Irish Times*, 21 November 1968, p. 11)

Hardwicke Ltd had employed the company of Tyndall, Hogan and Hurley. The *Irish Times* correspondent damned them with faint praise when it was noted that 'by comparison the work of Tyndall Hogan and Hurley, which is far less appropriate in principle on the site, is more satisfactorily handled, with a considerable degree of thought given to the site, the quays and the Cathedral. The resulting form of the building, however, bears little relation to the site'.

The two which found some favour, that of Stephenson, Gibney and Associations for the Green Property Company and Michael Scott and Partners for the G.&T. Crampton firm, did not escape unscathed. Of the former, it was stated that:

it is an open question whether or not the scale of the proposal relates to that of the Cathedral. Christ Church is not really massive enough to be very dominating and, robbed of its steep north side, it may very well seem weak in relation to buildings of roughly the same scale. The whole project lacks the monumentality that no doubt the city fathers seek; arguments such as those put forward by the architects in the brochure, that the cruciform shape of the office towers relates to the Cathedral plan, are just nonsense.

The Scott proposal was generally liked and 'there can be no doubt about the monumental quality of the project and much thought has been given to the visual relationship of the tower and its podium to the Cathedral'. Lest, however, the reader be lulled into thinking that all was good, the piece goes on to say that 'the fact that this project is totally different from the Cathedral, while carefully acknowledging its existence makes for an interesting and uncompromising design'.

In common with the RIAI, the writer laid it all at the feet of the Corporation for the paucity of their brief. It was finance that was the driving element and 'there can be no doubt from the original brief that the major consideration to the Corporation is cost'.

> Why must it then drag us through the fraces [sic] of all this competition business it is hard to say. The brief, which contains several pages of detailed instructions and questions regarding the financing of the project, has a few pages of the vaguest possible waffle about the architectural design. This boils down to saying: it's an important building, car parking is to be under cover, and it might be possible to have interesting views of the Cathedral.
>
> ...
>
> What the brief calls for, and what it must get, is another office block or blocks which will not contribute anything to the city.
>
> (*Irish Times*, 21 November 1968, p. 11)

The tendering process was not without issues either. It was suggested that at 'least two of these companies have managed to assemble the confidential financial details for the contracts submitted by their competitors' (*Irish Times*, 20 December 1968). The costs submitted varied greatly.

Ronald Lyon Estates	Seifert and Partners	£4.65m
Eblana (Cross Channel)	Building Design Associates	£3.23m
G.&T. Crampton	Michael Scott and Partners	£3.43m
Gallagher and Co.	Desmond Fitzgerald	£3.05m
Green Property	Stephenson, Gibney and Associates	£2.67m
Hardwicke	Tyndall, Hogan and Hurley	£2.57m

The space to be provided also varied from the 372,000 sq. ft (35,000 sq. m) proposed by Eblana to the 340,000 sq. ft in the Lyon design.

A committee comprising officials of the Corporation and the architectural community, with a majority from the Corporation, was appointed to judge the submissions. The plans were judged on the basis of architecture, environment and function and none of the plans were judged to score highly enough on all three criteria. Two of them were found worthy of further consideration (these also happened to be the ones that would produce the lowest rent cost) and a majority vote chose the plan submitted by the Green Property Company. This was for four square tower blocks of identical design but varying in height between five, seven and ten storeys. The second favoured scheme was that put forward by G.&T. Crampton and it comprised a twenty-storey tower, which would have been located to the east side of the site. It might have been the better choice.

In looking to finance the projects, the Corporation had at least three options under consideration. The first was to raise a loan for the entire cost of the scheme repayable over a long period, or a lease and lease back arrangement for 99 years with an option to the Corporation to purchase within a specific period, or a lease and lease back arrangement without an option to purchase (Minutes, 3 March 1969). In the view of the *Irish Times*, however, the prospect of obtaining a loan was not good and a rental agreement was more likely. This probably increased the significance of the rental costs associated with each proposal.

It should have been realized that trouble was brewing. The excavations in High Street during the previous few years had yielded a wealth of archaeological materials. Test bores on the Civic Offices site had revealed deep layers of detritus that would later be revealed to represent a thousand years of urban living. Since this had been the original location of the city, it was inevitable that the site would be rich in archaeology. Moreover, interest in 'medieval Dublin' was growing as more and more was revealed about the early history of the city (see, for example, *Irish Times*, 26 March 1969, p. 12). There

44. The Wood Quay site in 1977 showing portions of the city wall.

was also a growing and better organized conservation movement developing in response to the threats to Georgian Dublin. The *Irish Times* article is also interesting in that it was very positive about Dublin Corporation. It speaks of the commendable foresight of the Corporation in encouraging the excavation of their sites. However, what might be a key point is that the author noted:

> At High Street, and here again it differs from the usual Irish site, when the excavation is finished there is literally nothing left but a stretch of clean boulder clay. So far there has been no structure sufficiently substantial to merit preservation. If any permanent structures, such as a stone wall or house foundations did turn up it would be worth considering the possibility of leaving that portion of the site open …

The Corporation was able to approve a scheme to widen Nicholas Street and part of High Street in 1966 (Report 144/1966). They may have believed that Wood Quay would work out the same way and, indeed, they facilitated the early excavations. Certainly, there was no sense that they were expecting to find anything major as this reply from the City Manager in 1968 indicates – having been asked what measures were in place to safeguard items of historical interest and whether competent archaeological bodies would be allowed to excavate, he answered:

The Corporation will ensure that adequate steps will be taken to safeguard any objects of archaeological interest found on the site. The Commissioners for Public Works are aware of the proposals for the development of the site and any representations they may make on the matter will be considered.

(Minutes, 2 December 1968, p. 386)

The problem for them was that it was soon found that the site was rich in stone walls and house foundations and that the early city had been remarkably preserved. The stage was set for what was going to be an ugly period in the relationship between Dublin Corporation and its citizens.

The problem developed at a time when the Corporation had been dissolved by ministerial order and the city was being run by commissioners. It begs the question whether the outcome might have been different if the elected representatives of the city had been involved at an earlier point. Given the reaction of many of them when public protest over Wood Quay became a feature of the 1970s, it seems reasonable to suggest that the outcome would have been exactly the same.

* * *

As mentioned above, the idea of a civic-sponsored cathedral had faded from view by the early 1950s. So also had the notion of a Roman Catholic project. Merrion Square had been obtained by the diocese in the early 1930s for this purpose and the diocese had taken possession of the square in 1938. The Archbishop of Dublin, Dr McQuaid, had been careful to assert his prerogative during the 1940s in the face of the unwelcome Abercrombie suggestion for a quayside location and later from what seemed to be the intention of the De Valera-led government to build a government quarter in the vicinity. The photograph on p. 102 shows the square in the 1950s, without a hint of having been touched since the 1930s, except for the filling in of the air-raid shelters built during the Emergency. The tennis courts, one of the main sources of income, are visible.

This circumstance continued during the 1950s and for most of the 1960s. There was a capital fund for the construction project but there was no active fund-raising and it was only very occasionally augmented by donations. A donation of £1,000 was received in June 1964 as 'a contribution to the cost of the erection of a new cathedral in the city of Dublin' (LV/B/4/10). A more modest £40 was received in July 1967 for the Eucharist shrine in the new cathedral (LV/B/4/11/1). The stock market doldrums of the 1950s meant that

45. An aerial view of Merrion Square in the early 1950s.

the value of its investments remained below purchase price until the better times of the 1960s. A valuation for 9 February 1954 suggested a sale value of £79,652 for the various investments, in addition to which there were various deposits that amounted to £3,674, some £2,100 in savings certs and £1,852 in bank credit (LV/B/6/7/2(i)). Even if the investments had been valued at par, it meant that the total fund was a little less than £100,000, nowhere near what would be required. However, the square was not a great burden on the diocese. There was a small annual income from keyholders and the tennis courts and the main expenditure was the wage paid to the gardener. The annual cost to the diocese was around £200 during the 1950s and £300 during the 1960s. For example, expenditure exceeded income by £213 in 1957 and by £320 in 1965.

There were occasional inquiries as to progress and one such was received in March 1962. It received a more detailed reply than usual and it explained clearly how matters stood. The Archbishop wrote that: 'I have not found it practicable to start such an enterprise, for it has first been necessary to provide some thirty new churches. About ten further churches are needed, not to mention schools. When the basic needs of the Diocese are sufficiently met, it will be possible to take up the provision of a Cathedral worthy of the Capital City' (LV/E/4/2). Another response, this time from the Archbishop's secretary, made it clear that no preparatory work had been done and nobody had been authorized to take on such work, though it was noted that the architect, 'Vincent Kelly, 87 Merrion Square, Dublin 2, for his own amusement prepared some plans for a cathedral on the site' (LV/E/6/1).

The peaceful slumber of the site was about to be disturbed as the 1960s drew to a close. The lack of public access to the square became the focus of agitation from a number of quarters that included the Labour Party, Sinn Féin, Fine Gael, an Taisce as well as a number of individuals. Ruairi Quinn wrote on 23 January 1969 on behalf of the Labour Party in the South East constituency asking for a meeting at which he would ask 'on behalf of the people of South East to open Merrion Square to the public and hand over responsibility and maintenance to the Park's division of Dublin Corporation' (LV/C/10/10/5). Other correspondents, such as Peter Feeney on 12 May 1970, pointed to the large numbers of children living in the locality and the relative lack of places of recreation (LV/C/10/12/3), while An Taisce spoke of the environmental benefits of having the park more extensively used when they wrote on 30 June 1970 (LV/C/10/14/1). The standard response was that widening access to the park was not within the legal competence of the Archbishop and he made it clear to his Press Office in September 1969 that 'I do not intend to make, or authorize anyone to make a statement on Merrion Square' (LV/C/10/8/2). There was an attempt to put pressure on the Archbishop when a petition was circulated among residents in the locality under the heading 'Playground for Rich or a Park of the People'. More direct action from Sinn Féin on 11 July 1970 saw them obtain a key from a sympathetic resident and open the park. It was a gentle occupation, they played football, but it was made clear that they had lots of copies of the key and were prepared to make them generally available. The Prohibition of Forcible Entry and Occupation Act, 1971 provided some legal protection against such acts but it was recognized that the mood of the city had shifted. Arthur O'Hagan, the diocesan solicitors, wrote on 3 July 1970 that: 'notwithstanding the imminence of such legislation, I have a very strong feeling that the problem in relation to Merrion Square is more likely to increase with the passage of time' (LV/C/10/15). The 'occupation' produced some comment in the press. Máirín de Burca of Sinn Féin wrote in relation to the cost of annual subscription that:

> There are far too many children in the City of Dublin whose only playing ground is the street or a concrete yard in a block of flats. That, side by side with this situation, there should be a private park, whatever

the sum needed to 'buy' a key, is anti-social and a remnant of the
Imperialist tradition of keep the 'natives' in their places ... We have
already given the key of the park to people who asked for it and further
copies may be had on application to this office.

(*Irish Press*, 17 July 1970, p. 11)

This was high rhetoric, though not of such persistence or weight as would
normally bother the archdiocese, but in this case it does seem to have rattled
them. There was consideration given to a press release and legal opinion was
taken. This marked the beginning of a significant change in the approach to
the square's use. A statement was agreed and is dated 16 July 1970 but
publication was held off because it seemed that the heat had gone out of the
issue in the public mind just as quickly as it had boiled up. On the one hand,
the statement reiterated the position that it was not accurate to say that a
project of building a cathedral had been abandoned. However, there was a
subtle shift in relation to what use could be made of the square until such time
as it was needed for building. The final paragraph stated that: 'It has been and
it is the desire of the Archbishop and the Trustees that at an appropriate time
and when the legal aspects of the provisional and temporary use of the square
and other important ancillary matters can be satisfactorily arranged the
optimum use of the square should be made. To this end the Archbishop has
given and will consider to give the matter most careful consideration'
(LV/C/10/25/8). What they had in mind was doing what Ruairi Quinn had
asked. As a further indication that the cathedral was really off the agenda, the
diocese sought advice from its financial advisers in 1971 as to whether the
capital fund, then valued at about £220,000, could be used as a loan fund for
urgent parochial works (LV/B/6/17). They were warned off but the real
significance was that they were now happy to see the money set aside for the
cathedral used for purposes that would probably never see the money repaid.
The decision was made in their heads but their hearts were not yet ready to
announce it generally. So Quidnunc in the *Irish Times* was still of the view
some months later that: 'Dr McQuaid could make a gesture, either by
disposing of the site, or at the least, giving access to the countless people of his
diocese who remain deprived of its use' (*Irish Times*, 21 January 1971, p. 11).

The keyholders of Fitzwilliam Square came to an arrangement in 1971
which allowed them to maintain private access (*Irish Independent*, 21 October
1971, p. 9). The diocesan press office took the view in an internal note that
'we have been singularly fortunate in the absence of comment on Merrion
Square in recent times. Long may it stay so!' (LV/C/10/44).

Mains drainage

A mains drainage scheme, a euphemism for 'sewer', does not immediately come to mind when identifying important civic projects but it was vital, because it both permitted the expansion of the city and determined where that could take place. Ever since sewerage became essential to an urban environment, the provision of mains drainage is what has turned agricultural land into prime development land. The 1906 mains drainage system provided for a city with a population of 325,000 and involved a series of interceptor sewers that ended direct outfalls into the Liffey (a lot of the time anyway – see *Irish Independent* online, 14 February 2015) and routed it to the wastewater treatment plant in Ringsend. This was still only a primary treatment system and the sludge was taken by barge out to sea and dumped. The SS *Shamrock* served this purpose until 1958 and it must have been one of the more interesting employments offered by Dublin Corporation.

By the 1950s, the city had run out of developed land. The area within the county borough was largely built up, especially on the southside. Private housing dominated the south-eastern sector and new housing estates had spread beyond the borough boundary into the county. Social housing dominated the south-western sector and here too there was very little land left within the county borough boundary. There was more scope for development north of the river but even there the city felt constrained within its boundaries.

This led the city to seek an extension to its boundaries in 1948. It was an ambitious plan to take some 10,849 acres, 3 roods and 37 perches from the county area. It is reasonable to suggest that the county saw it as a land grab and the initial response was hostile. It was suggested by the Department of Local Government that consultation should take place between city and county to see if an acceptable agreement could be found and negotiations over a period of years led finally to an agreement that the city would expand by 6,891 acres (2,790ha) (Report 74/1951). The expansion was to take place mainly on the north side of the city but with some 340 acres (138ha) on the southside in Ballyfermot and Walkinstown. The land on the northside was undeveloped in that the drainage infrastructure was not sufficient to accommodate any significant increase in housing. So began an ambitious project to build a mains drainage system that would run across the top of the city with an outfall in Howth. The scheme, the North Dublin Drainage scheme, was begun in 1952 and completed some six years later with an initial estimate of £1m but a final cost that worked out at almost double that. It involved laying a drain across the city from Castleknock and Finglas, Cabra, Glasnevin, Donnycarney, Killester, St Anne's, Kilbarrack to Sutton and onwards to Howth. In all, the piping covered a distance of 14 miles (23km) and in itself involved 30 miles (48km) of piping. A tunnel had to be drilled under Howth Head to provide an outfall for the sewage. It was described as the biggest engineering project of its type since 1906, with pipes that varied in diameter from 48 inches to 60 inches (122–52cm) and would provide drainage for the entire north city, a population of about 265,000. It would be less enthusiastically received today because the sewerage was still largely untreated, except for screening, and simply pumped into the sea at a distance of about 200 metres from the nose of Howth. From there it was confidently believed that the tides and currents would ensure that the material was not returned to the shore but instead dispersed into the sea. A less extensive but also important drainage scheme was begun for Dún Laoghaire in 1954 and completed in 1958 at a cost of £300,000. The Kilbarrack area would be opened up for development by the completion of a sewer that would link to the North Dublin Drainage system but also provide a holding tank for discharge into that sewer at off-peak times. This would allow that mains system to service a greater population than would otherwise be the case. This was to prove particularly important in providing for the Ballymun area. In addition, a scheme was to be provided for Swords and Malahide and for the Tolka Valley, the latter would open up development lands in Finglas.

This was only part of the story though, because though it created the framework for the development of the north city, there was still work to be done in the city as a whole and in linking all of the elements. This took place during the 1960s and involved one of the more controversial projects of the time – which will be discussed later – the draining of the Grand Canal, one of the two major systems needed to service the south city. The Grand Canal scheme was designed to relieve existing overloaded sewers and to provide surface water drainage as well as permitting development in Clondalkin, Lucan and Blanchardstown. The Dodder Valley scheme was intended to serve the county area immediately to the south of the city boundary as far as Templeogue with extensions as far as Holylands, Tallaght and Baldonnel. In the south-east, a new system was being developed at Shanganagh.

These schemes were designed to service the needs for the city until 1972/73. It was estimated that a population of 672,300 could be maintained at a development cost of £9.2m. The most expensive elements in the plan were the Dodder Valley system at £1.377m, which would service 170,000 people, and the Grand Canal scheme, which was estimated at £2.35m (Report 24/1967). On the whole, it did the job reasonably well, if not always odour-free, until the present tertiary system was introduced.

State projects

If the Corporation had few opportunities to engage in grand designs, then the State was in an equally difficult position. There was little enough money around and a need for investment in more mundane capital projects that would accelerate economic development. However, whether they wanted to or not, one area that they could not avoid was that of commemoration and memorial. It is fair to say that every Irish government has been aware of the power of remembrance and particularly of the power of a physical presence on the landscape. The saga about the removal of Queen Victoria from her position outside Leinster House indicated just how difficult it was to keep a balance between competing interests and most Irish civic authorities learned to leave well enough alone in practical terms if not in rhetoric.

"I wish something big would happen. Whenever there's a lull in things someone starts the racket about removing me all over again."

46. Nelson concerned. (*Dublin Opinion*, 1954, p. 243.)

It is somewhat ironic that the most significant change in decades to the civic landscape – the removal of the Nelson Pillar – was not initiated by the civic authorities and precipitated a response that in its speed and impact was utterly at odds with normal practice. The saga about the Pillar has been written about in other volumes in this series and dealt with comprehensively in Whelan (2003). The essence of the story is that once Dublin Corporation took on a nationalist character in the wake of the changes to representation that occurred after 1841, there were regular calls for the removal of the monument and the normal pretext was that it was a hindrance to traffic. The nearest any group got to its removal was in 1891 when a private bill introduced into the Westminster parliament got to a second reading. Post-independence, there were regular calls and occasional motions placed before Dublin Corporation calling for its removal. The Council was asked by way of motion to remove either the Pillar or the statue on 8 January 1931, 9 August 1948, 7 December 1953, 14 November 1955 and 5 March 1956. These were no more than ritual opportunities for appropriate speeches to be made and reported in the newspapers. Everyone knew that the Corporation had no power over the Pillar. It was private property, managed by trustees, who used the income generated by the visits to the top to maintain it. While the traffic argument for the removal of the Pillar was advanced from time to time, Dublin Corporation seemed content in 1955 to settle for the removal of the admiral. They wrote to the trustees asking them to permit the Council to remove the statue and to place it in the National Museum or some location of the trustees' choice. The trustees responded on 5 December 1955 that they had no powers to deviate from the original arrangements of the Trust. That satisfied the Corporation and the only action was to have the response noted in the minutes (Minutes, 6 February 1956). Indeed, the Corporation, perhaps inadvertently, deflated the argument about traffic improvements in 1960, which left them with a problem. The City Council at its meeting on 4 January 1960 asked the Streets Committee to report on the desirability of improving traffic conditions in O'Connell Street by removing Nelson. In turn, the Streets and Traffic committees had asked the Traffic Study Group, which had representatives of the Garda and Corporation officials as members, for their recommendations in relation to traffic flows on O'Connell Street, including the question of the Pillar. They took the question seriously and they came back to the Corporation committee with the following conclusions, which caused such surprise that the entire Council asked to be furnished with the materials that the committees had been given (Report 80/1960).

- That the presence of the Pillar in O'Connell Street was not the main cause of traffic congestion in the street;
- that the removal of the Pillar would not effect any major improvement in availability of traffic space unless all other monuments, etc., obstructing the full length of the centre of the street were removed also;
- and that the removal of these monuments, etc., would not have the desired effect on traffic flow. Traffic travelling northwards of the Pillar mainly proceeds in that direction via the 'bottleneck' at Cavendish Row. The benefits to traffic resulting from the additional space that would be made available in O'Connell Street by the removal of the monuments would be lost when traffic would reach Cavendish Row. The carriageway here would not be of comparable width to balance the capacity of this section with O'Connell Street as widened.
- In the event of the monuments being removed, amenities such as car parks, cycle parks, taxi ranks, etc., would be lost.
- The Group felt that from a traffic point of view there did not appear to be a case for the removal of the Pillar.

The findings were unsurprising; the surprising element was that the committee decided to report them. It might have been expected that they would turn a 'Nelson eye' to them. At one move, they removed the main non-political argument for the removal of the monument and the recommendation to the Council was that 'no action be taken'; a position approved in April 1960. Thereafter, with that fig leaf removed, any attempt to remove the rights of the trustees would have been seen in overtly political terms. Though primary legislation involving the Oireachtas would have been necessary, it would not have been complicated to draft, as was demonstrated after 1966. All in all, the best course of action seemed to be to let the matter settle once again, perhaps indefinitely.

Though the city authorities had a good record in avoiding iconoclasm, the 1950s saw a renewal of attacks on monuments by suspected republicans. The equestrian statue to Lord Gough was regarded by many as one of the finest examples in Europe but that did not save it from destruction at 12.40 a.m. on the morning of 23 July 1957. It had been attacked the previous November when the rear right leg was blown off and the horse was subsequently supported on a wooden peg. The statue survived the second blast reasonably well and lay on its side beside the plinth, the latter being largely unscathed. While restoration might have been possible, the decision was quickly taken to

47. The monument to Lord Gough in the Phoenix Park. (*Ireland in pictures*, 1898.)

remove both horse and plinth. The horse now lives on in Ballymun, though in facsimile and not yet in a public space. John Byrne, the Belfast-born sculptor, decided to fashion a replica of the Gough horse for his sculpture 'Misneach', which depicts a young, tracksuited teenage girl on horseback (see fig. 49). The sculpture was unveiled to a mixed reception, more to do with the subject matter than the quality of the execution, on 17 September 2010. It remains the only significant equestrian statue in the city.

The Carlisle monument had stood serenely in the middle of a flower bed in the Peoples' Gardens in the Phoenix Park since its unveiling. It was efficiently detached from its pedestal about 2 a.m. on the morning of 28 July 1958. The force of the explosion was such that the statue was propelled upwards and landed almost intact in the flower bed but embedded to a depth of two feet. It is debatable as to whether it could have been restored but no serious consideration seems to have been given to that, though the plinth

48. Statue of Lord George Carlisle in the Phoenix Park, unveiled on 2 May 1870.

remains unoccupied to the present day. Less well known but dispatched equally efficiently on the morning of 26 August 1958 was the statue to the thirteenth earl of Eglinton and Winton, located on the north side of St Stephen's Green. There were also ineffectual attacks on the war memorial in Islandbridge, to be discussed below.

The attack on the Pillar could not therefore have been wholly unexpected. It was certainly unwelcome because it forced action to be taken where inaction was the desired position. The explosion, timed at 1.30 a.m. on 8 March 1966, resulted in substantial damage. The visiting platform disappeared and a significant portion of the column was destroyed. However, the basic structure seemed intact and solid as the image here shows (fig. 50). What is interesting is the speed with which the authorities moved to decide that the monument was to be demolished. With a focus that had never been evident in the previous hundred or so years, nor was evident in many other cases, it was decided within days not to rebuild but rather to demolish.

49. 'Misneach' in the grounds of Ballymun Comprehensive School. There remains a long-term intention to move the statue to a more prominent public location once the regeneration project and the proposed rapid transport links are completed.

The speed was remarkable. The explosion took place on 8 March but by 11 March, the Government Information Bureau had announced that it was to be demolished by the army on the following Sunday. No reasons were given and it appears from newspaper reports that the Lord Mayor found out at the same time as the newspapers (*Irish Times*, 12 March 1966, p. 1). He was aware that there had been pressure from the Department of Local Government for the removal of the obstruction to traffic in O'Connell Street. Presumably this meant the debris from the original explosion. Indeed, the report made to Dublin Corporation some time later clearly differentiates between the practical actions taken by the Corporation to clear the street and make safe the structure and the Government decision to demolish it. 'The Government decided that the remaining part of the column should be demolished at the Government's expense by the Army Corps of Engineers by use of explosives' (Minutes, 4 April 1966).

A last-minute attempt by the RIAI to delay the demolition until interested citizens had had the opportunity to consider the matter and put forward proposals came to nothing. The O'Connell Street Traders Association had asked for such a pause on 11 March to allow this consultation. They argued that the Pillar added dignity and character to the street. The RIAI sought an injunction on the night/early morning of 13–14 March in a special meeting

50. The Nelson Pillar post-explosion on 8 March 1966.

of the High Court before Mr Justice Teevan in his private home. They lost on the basis that they did not have *locus standi* but on that basis it seems that the government did not have the power either; Dublin Corporation was the

51. O'Connell Street after Nelson. Note that the traffic arrangement remained unchanged.

appropriate body (*Irish Times*, 14 March 1966, p. 1). With commendable speed, the army engineers demolished the stump at 3.30 a.m. the same morning in an explosion that did not quite go to plan. It was intended to topple the stump northwards like a chimney fall but instead the lower part burst outwards and the column collapsed into its own space. The army, while expressing satisfaction with the outcome, suggested that the reason lay in structural faults in the column which would not have been obvious before demolition.

There was little debate about this and little debate afterwards, despite the attempts by Fine Gael to raise the matter in the Dáil. Mr Richie Ryan, TD, asked on 22 March 1966 by what authority the government had demolished the Pillar but got little or no answer (Dáil Debates, 221(12), col. 1896). The effort required in demolition is the most powerful proof that the monument was not fatally damaged in the explosion and that restoration would have been possible. It took the army engineers a significant quantity of explosives to blow up the shaft and then a crane with a wrecking ball had to be employed on the base.

There can be a number of reasons for the unusual haste. It might be taken at face value that there was at last an opportunity to clear a hindrance to traffic. The fact that no realignment of traffic flows took place in the aftermath would seem to put paid to that. It could be that it was too good an opportunity to miss to be rid of a hated monument and it was desirable to have it all done before the commemorations of the 1916 Rising, which were due at Easter. However, it is not at all clear that ordinary Dubliners really hated 'the Pillar'. It was the focus of the city, a popular meeting spot and many huffed and puffed their way to the top for a good view of the city centre. The fact that the statue could not be seen from the viewing platform must have added to a sense of detachment of the Pillar from Nelson. It seems much more likely that nobody wanted to ignite the inevitable debate as to who would replace the admiral on the plinth. To this might have been added a lack of appreciation of the aesthetic value of the Pillar. The *Irish Times* suggested as much in a leader on 11 March:

> It is unlikely that many Ministers will, aesthetically, regret the loss of a Doric column any more than they would a pillarbox. They have proved themselves immune to appeals on the destruction of beautiful Georgian houses. The professional, apparently, prefers modern office blocks, shops and luxury hotels to buildings of grace. It is a valid point of view for officialdom. We hope they and we will not have our fill of demolition before all of us are very much older.

Little was learned during the debate on the Nelson Pillar Bill on 15 April 1969. This Bill provided for compensation to be paid to the trustees of the Pillar allowing for loss of income and in recognition of their transfer of the property to Dublin Corporation. The total amount of money involved was only £22,000. In addition, it was noted that the total cost of malicious damages claims that had been paid (including those on foot of the army's detonation) to date was £39,082 of which all but £1,622 had been paid by the State. There was no debate on the pros and cons of the decision to demolish and there was no argument about replacement.

When the time eventually came, some thirty years later, to replace the monument, the chosen design was a postmodern, non-figurative stainless steel needle (*Irish Times*, 26 November 1998, p. 3). There were 205 entries to the international competition that produced the Dublin Spire but none of the three shortlisted entries were for a personalized memorial. There was only one with an overtly nationalist theme and very few with a religious orientation, though a gigantic Celtic cross was on offer (*Irish Times*, 12 January 1999, p. 7).

Memory and commemoration

As the action with the Nelson Pillar demonstrated, Dublin was not the sole preserve of Dublin Corporation. Its status as a capital city meant that the government of the day also felt that it could change its landscape as required. This was not particularly difficult to do, given the centralized system of governance that was in place. The question of an appropriate commemoration for Ireland's war dead reached a decisive, though not conclusive, point in the 1960s. This particular issue had rumbled on since the late 1930s when an impressive memorial to those who died during the First World War was completed in Islandbridge with State funding. Though it was the focus of an annual march and commemoration, the State, in the form of its government, tended to ignore this memorial and it was allowed to fall into decay. Even as the Islandbridge memorial was nearing completion, the government of the day was developing its plans for an alternative. It was this alternative that was eventually completed in 1966.

The war memorial was located at Islandbridge on a sloping site on the south bank of the river, following the decision that Merrion Square was

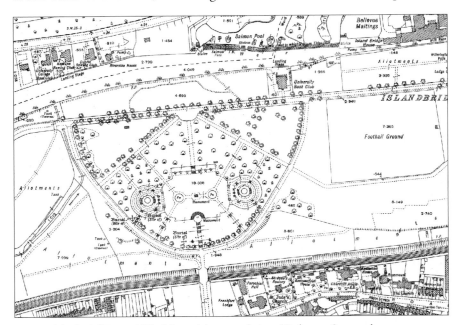

52. The Irish National War Memorial at completion. (Ordnance Survey plan, 1:2,500, Sheet 18(X), 1948.)

neither available nor appropriate. It has been argued in a previous volume, *Dublin, 1930–1950*, that it was the interest in the square as a site for the memorial that helped revive interest in finding a site suitable for a Catholic cathedral. The decision to proceed with the war memorial at Islandbridge was endorsed by the Cumann na nGaedheal government and the services of the noted architect, Sir Edwin Lutyens, were secured to design it. Work continued during the 1930s and by the end of the decade the British Legion was looking forward to the day when there would be an official inauguration of the memorial by the government of the day. In the event, they had to wait for over five decades by which time the gardens had fallen on hard times and were in decay. A restoration project was undertaken by the Board of Works during the 1980s and on 10 September 1988 they were opened to the public following a ceremony of dedication by representatives of the four main churches in Ireland. However, it may be argued that they were not formally endorsed by the State until the commemoration to mark the ninetieth anniversary of the Battle of the Somme on 1 July 2006 which was attended by the President and Taoiseach.

Though the gardens were not officially recognized from their completion in the 1930s, they were used for an annual commemoration of the war dead on Remembrance Day. The *Irish Times* is a very useful source of description of these events, which were segregated on a religious basis. They normally took the form of a religious service involving a parade of veterans with the largest event held under the auspices of the British Legion and the Church of Ireland. The Roman Catholic version involved a mustering of former soldiers at Bachelor's Walk and a march to the Pro-Cathedral for Mass followed by a return march to Bachelor's Walk. There was no interaction with the activities of the Church of Ireland, which tended to involve a service in St Patrick's Cathedral in the morning followed by a march to the memorial gardens in the afternoon where a commemoration ceremony was held. The afternoon parade, which in the 1950s attracted a large attendance, followed an assembly in some central location, Smithfield perhaps or the Phoenix Park. At Islandbridge, wreaths were laid and prayers were said. These were attended by representatives of the British Legion, representatives of the various regiments in which the fallen had served and a significant representation from diplomatic missions, especially Commonwealth countries. No representation from the Irish national government nor from the Corporation attended the event and there were no wreaths laid on their behalf.

In the years immediately following the accession to the British throne of Queen Elizabeth II, the Church of Ireland and British Legion events took on a particular character. Thus, in 1953, the *Irish Times* reported that several thousand marched from Smithfield to Islandbridge. Wreaths were laid by various contingents of the British Legion, the regiments, various diplomatic missions and a variety of organizations such as the Kildare Street Club, the Irish Rugby Football Union, British Ministry of Pensions and the Bank of Ireland. It was noted that as the last wreath was being laid, some members of the congregation began singing 'God Save the Queen' and that this was taken up by the majority present. A similar outpouring took place at a service in St Patrick's Cathedral and the report said that virtually everyone in the congregation joined in the singing (*Irish Times*, 9 November 1953, p. 7). The singing of the British national anthem was repeated in 1954, 1955 and 1956 but it seems to have faded thereafter. It seems that the sense of 'otherness' was felt by the participants also.

The pattern of commemoration continued into the 1960s and, for example, in 1964, there were the usual separate services in St Patrick's Cathedral and the Pro-Cathedral in the morning and then the commemoration at the war memorial in the afternoon. In the morning, the parade assembled in St Stephen's Green and marched to St Patrick's Cathedral. In the afternoon, the parade formed in the Phoenix Park and made its way to Islandbridge where eighty wreaths were laid. The other parade assembled at Bachelor's Walk and made its way to the Pro-Cathedral for Mass.

These events generally did not attract much incident. The annual parade was banned from 1939 for the duration of the war but there was surprise that it was also banned in 1945. Such was the level of outcry that, whatever the intention, the parade resumed thereafter. What is interesting is the language used to describe the commemoration. It was seen by the government as nothing to do with them. The reference below, for example, is to '*these people* honouring *their dead*' (author's italics), and not 'our dead'. It was an explanation of tolerance rather than recognition of a shared history. This was Mr Boland's (the Minister for Justice) response to an impassioned denunciation by Mr Dillon, during an adjournment debate in the Dáil on 15 November 1945, of the decision to ban the 1945 parade because of a perceived fear of a breach of the peace:

> I have very little to add to what I said yesterday, but at the outset I should like, lest there should be any misapprehension, to correct what Deputy Dillon said about me—that I myself banned the parade. I did not. I was informed beforehand that the police proposed to ban it for

the reasons that I have stated. Deputy Dillon would certainly gather that we were out against those men honouring their dead. As I pointed out yesterday, they got greater facilities this year than in past years in the matter of processions. They were allowed to hold church parades on two Sundays this year as against one day in previous years, and they were allowed to sell poppies on the Dublin streets on two days this year as against one day in other years, and there was no restriction whatever on house-to-house sales. If the police feel that there is likely to be a breach of the peace, they have the right to ban a procession, and that is what they did on this occasion.

I have no more to say. I am not capable of following the line that Deputy Dillon adopted, and there is no necessity to do so. There is no necessity for him or anybody else to tell me that people have the right to honour their dead. I need not be told that. Every decent man or woman everywhere will agree on that, and Deputy Dillon should not try to put me in the position that I was trying to prevent these people honouring their dead. Everybody in this country and, I hope, men everywhere, would be only too glad to see people coming together to honour their dead comrades; and to say that I have tried to prevent people doing that is altogether wrong.

(Dáil Debates, 98(10), col. 1248)

As part of the general pattern of attacks on monuments in the 1950s, there were two small explosions at the cross in the memorial gardens. The first was on the morning of Christmas Day in 1956 at about 1 a.m. Though it was estimated that a large quantity of explosives was used, there was relatively little damage to the cross. The second took place in October 1958, but again no substantial damage was done (*Irish Times*, 8 October 1958, p. 1). In November, on the eve of Remembrance Day, the memorial was daubed with paint (*Irish Times*, 10 November 1958, p. 1) but the paint was removed by the Garda before the event took place. Tensions seem to have been higher in the run up to the fiftieth anniversary celebrations of the 1916 Rising. In 1963, it was reported that a group of men broke into the offices of the British Legion on the eve of the annual commemoration. They beat up the Garda who was on duty and damaged some wreaths (*Irish Times*, 11 November 1963, p. 5). This resulted in increased security for the following day but no incidents occurred.

The State's response

The government moved onto a parallel track in 1939. In 1935, Oscar Traynor and other members of the Dublin Brigade of the Old IRA proposed that the government take over the Rotunda Gardens and turn it into a park dedicated to the memory of those who died in the cause of Irish freedom. It turned out that the hospital authorities had intended to build a nurses' home on the site but that would still leave a portion of the site (about 1.5 acres/0.6ha) available. The hospital committee of management decided to offer this portion of land to the State and the offer was accepted. This led to a token estimate of £10 being moved in the Dáil on 15 June 1939 (Dáil Debates, 76(8), col. 999) to secure the transaction. The State did not commit itself to a garden of remembrance (it was under consideration) but it was generally assumed that this would be the purpose to which the site was put. Indeed, from the beginning there was a suggestion that the site was too small and too confined for the purpose. The total sum involved in the transfer was £2,070 but most of the money was found in the current budget of the Office of Public Works (OPW). The image here shows just how confined the site was. There had been considerable space in the gardens but the recent construction had left only a small residual site available.

It is not surprising that the project moved slowly over the next few years because of the war, and the change of government in 1948 probably did nothing to advance the project. A competition in 1946 produced a winning design by Dáithí Hanly. The outline design reproduced in the *Irish Times* is not unlike what was eventually opened in 1966. It shows a sunken cruciform pool with seating on either side leading towards a raised area with another pool in which is placed a monument. What was suggested was 'bronze sculptured figures of Ireland guarded by four warriors with provincial shields' (*Irish Times*, 7 September 1946, p. 5). A semi-circular wall with patriots shown in bas-relief terminated the design.

On the face of it, it was an unprepossessing site. It was a rather small and confined space and it severely limited the scale of the memorial that could be accommodated. Despite being very close to O'Connell Street, it was still rather remote from the day-to-day life of the city. This prompted some to believe that the commitment of the government to the site, even after a winning design had been announced, was not strong and that ultimately a more suitable location, perhaps in the Phoenix Park, would be found (*Irish Times*, 12 September 1946, p. 4). The inter-party government of Fine Gael–Labour Party–Clann na Poblachta–Clann na Talmhan and National Labour had no difficulty delaying the project. The Minister for Health, Dr Noel Browne,

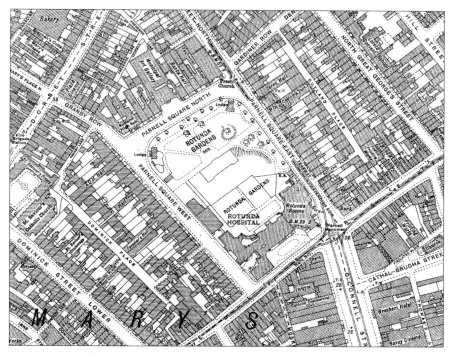

53. The Rotunda Gardens. (Ordnance Survey plan, 1:2,500, Sheet 18(VII), 1939.)

54. An aerial view of the Rotunda Gardens, looking south in 1949.

announced in April 1949 that the land was to be returned to the hospital for a number of years to permit it to be used for clinical purposes. There was concern about the level of neo-natal deaths in the city and the hospital authorities needed to make additional provisions for which there was no room in their current facilities. The need was felt to justify the delay to the project. However, it was the vagueness of 'a few years' that caused alarm bells to ring. This resulted in a cranky exchange in the Dáil in 1950 between Mr MacEnree of Fianna Fáil and the parliamentary secretary to the Minister for Finance, Mr Donnellan. The government was accused of abandoning the project but it responded that the delay was temporary and that the site could be retrieved at any time (Dáil Debates, 120(10), col. 1439). It got even nastier on 20 June, when, in response to a similar probing by Mr MacEnree, the Minister for External Affairs, Seán McBride, answering for the Minister for Health, gave details of the 10,000 sq. ft (929 sq. m) that were to be occupied by the hospital out of a total site area of 80,000 sq. ft (7,400 sq. m). This prompted Mr MacEntee to wonder why the hospital needed the entire site and that it was now clear that other locations in the city could have been used. The underlying suggestion was that this was an easy way for the government to get out of commemorating the 'Dublin Brigade of the IRA'. This produced a waspish response that 'the Deputy would be rendering a good service to national remembrance in this country if he ceased to try to exploit attempts made to provide for the children of this city, who are dying because of want of accommodation by his administration' (Dáil Debates, 121(14), col. 1392).

The goading worked, though, because in January 1951 (and before Fianna Fáil were returned to power later in the year) it was announced that the project would go ahead at a projected cost of £23,000. The hospital buildings, which were of wooden construction, would be transferred to another location. The return of Fianna Fáil to power between 1951–4 did not produce a speeding up of the project. It was 1958, with Fianna Fáil back in power again, before the hospital authorities advertised for tenders to replace the temporary buildings. Tenders were then sought by the OPW for the gardens and it was reported in October 1959 that these tenders were being considered (*Irish Times*, 7 October 1959, p. 3). Work finally began in 1961 and it was completed in time for the 1916 commemorations in 1966. In fact, it was almost complete. The question of the sculpture in the upper pond was still unresolved by the opening. Oisín Kelly had submitted a design for a piece depicting the metamorphosis of the children of Lir into swans in January 1962 but the government did not like the concept.

55. Garden of Remembrance as opened without the signature sculpture.

56. The 'Children of Lir' installed in the Garden of Remembrance.

57. William III in context in Dame Street. (*Ireland in pictures*, 1898.)

58. Thomas Davis statue in Dame Street. Note that the fountain is working in this image.

Discussions between Mr Kelly, the Arts Council and the OPW dragged on for years and it was not until February 1966, too late for the opening, that it was agreed to proceed with the original design. Mr Kelly professed himself unsure as to the reason for the delay. Asked why there had been such a delay, he was quoted as saying 'I've no real idea. I may be doing someone an injustice because I don't really know, but I have a vague impression that there was a feeling somewhere that the work might be thought generally incomprehensible' (*Irish Times*, 28 February 1966, p. 1). He may well have been correct in that impression. In the event, the gardens had to put up with a rather disappointing fountain until the 'Children of Lir' was installed in 1971.

Having taken so long to create the gardens, it then seemed that the State did not know what to do with them. The earlier suggestions that the site was unsuitable would seem to be borne out by the fact that the gardens did not come to play a central role in commemoration. Indeed, it was noted as quickly as 1967 that it had failed to replace the GPO as the central point for national commemoration. It seems reasonable to wonder if the State was really ever totally committed to the project. It was allowed to drag on for decades, despite some reasonable interruptions, and the scale on which it was constructed contrasts with the grander vision of the war memorial in Islandbridge, which occupies 8 hectares. Better sites were available and could have been used but there seems to have been no attempt to contemplate this.

Another project of commemoration that was delayed was the statue to Thomas Davis in College Green, replacing the equestrian statue of William III. August 1945 was the centenary of Thomas Davis' death and the work of the Young Irelanders was celebrated with enthusiasm, with a week devoted to events commemorating the patriot. A tablet was placed in College Green marking the site of a future statue. A committee was duly established but it does not appear to have got very far and it seems that the initial enthusiasm faded quickly. A model of a monument that comprised a central figure of Davis with two minor figures and a fountain was submitted by the Irish sculptor, John Kavanagh, soon thereafter but nothing was done. Interest seems to have revived later in 1952 when the Arts Council got involved but that petered out too (*Irish Times*, 5 March 1959, p. 4). It was only in 1961 that the project received an injection of energy.

In that year, the Arts Council asked Edward Delaney to submit a design. This comprised a paved platform measuring about 55 feet by 18 feet by 9 inches (17m x 5.5m x 23cm) high with bronze figure of Davis on a pedestal, approximately 10 feet (3m) high, and a pool embellished with bronze reliefs depicting Young Ireland. The design was further elaborated but the basic elements of the first design were those finally constructed. Davis stands on a plinth at one end of a platform. The main feature on the remainder of the platform is a circular pool into which four bronze angels blow a spray of water through trumpets. The statue was finally unveiled on 16 April 1966, more than twenty years after the laying of the tablet marking the site. There appears to be no particular reason for the delay. The statue was estimated to cost about £15,000 in 1963 and this might be the simple reason why it slipped off the agenda, only to be revived as the anniversary of 1916 loomed.

In any event, it has not proved to be a particularly successful piece. The fountain is prey to those who add washing up liquid to it and it has probably spent more time in the off position. However, it has provided one of the better of the irreverent names for statues, a feature of Dublin life – 'you're a nation once again'. Say it quickly and think of the angels!

The concert hall

This is a project that did not see the light of day during the 1950s or '60s and it is one of those 'could have been impressive' additions to the city. Looking at the city from the perspective of the twenty-first century, it seemed that Dublin in the 1950s was pretty well served with entertainment venues. There were several fine music halls cum theatres cum cinemas such as the Capitol, Gaiety, Olympia, Queen's and, of course, the Theatre Royal. These hosted a great range of musical events from opera at its highest level to revue and farce. A young Pavarotti impressed audiences at the Gaiety in 1963 with his performance as the Duke in *Rigoletto* for the Dublin Grand Opera Society. Nonetheless, it was felt by many that Dublin needed a concert hall if only for reasons of urban prestige – few cities of Dublin's scale lacked one. The idea was given impetus by the establishment in 1953 by the Music Association of Ireland of a company called the Concert and Assembly Hall Ltd, with the aim of building not only a concert hall but also a venue that could be used for meetings and conferences. One of the early suggestions was that it might contain a hall for 2,000 people, a smaller hall for 500 people with rehearsal rooms and restaurant. The company set about planning but it was 1958 before it was stated by the *Irish Times* that 'Dublin likely to have concert hall soon' (*Irish Times*, 23 June 1958, p. 4).

The company recognized that a public appeal for at least a portion of the estimated cost of £500,000 would be necessary in the straitened economic times. They felt that Dublin Corporation had an excellent site at the junction

59. Opera in the Gaiety in May 1941.

Gaiety Theatre

WEDNESDAY at 7.45 and SATURDAY MATINEE at 2.30

"LA BOHEME"

By GIACOMO PUCCINI

(By arrangement with G. Ricordi & Co.)

Dramatis Personae:

Mimi (a Seamstress)......................................MAY DEVITT
Rudolph (a Poet)..JOHN TORNEY
Marcel (a Painter).......................................JOHN LYNSKEY
Colline (a Philosopher)......................................N. I. LEWIS
Schaunard (a Musician)....................................SAM MOONEY
Benoit (a Landlord).....................................STEPHEN BLACK
Musetta (a Coquette)..................................EILY MURNAGHAN
Alcindoro (a Councillor of State).......................STEPHEN BLACK
Parpignol (a Pedlar)......................................H. SHERIDAN
Custom House Sergeant....................................J. SHERIDAN

Conductor...Capt. J. M. DOYLE

Boys:—Masters P. Kerwin, P. Holmes, J. Sparks, B. Coughlan, M. Kern;
T. Ryan, C. Douglas, J. Farrell

Students, Workgirls, Citizens, Shopkeepers, Street Vendors,
Restaurant Waiters, Boys, Girls, etc.

First Produced: Teatro Regis, Turin, February 1st, 1896

Libretto by Guiseppe Giacosa and Luigi Illica

Opera produced by...................................JOHN LYNSKEY

This Theatre is Disinfected throughout with Jeyes' Fluid

of High Street and Nicholas Street and were confident of getting it. Once again they made the point that 'a concert hall would fill a void in the cultural and civic life of Dublin, and that not only Dubliners, but all Irish citizens share a feeling of inferiority because Dublin is perhaps the only European capital which has not got such a hall'. They set to raising funds but it was a slow process and complicated by the fact that the Royal Dublin Society (RDS) announced that they would examine the possibility of taking responsibility for the building and administration of the hall (*Irish Times*, 3 November 1961, p. 6). By 1963, the RDS had come to the view that they would spend £150,000 on more provision for concerts, assemblies and exhibitions at Ballsbridge. This allowed Dublin Corporation to defer consideration (in fact, it had been given very little consideration) of the application from the Concert and Assembly Hall Ltd (*Irish Times*, 29 January 1963) until the form and scope of the RDS development became clearer. However, the project was about to receive a great boost of support from a most unlikely source.

The assassination of President Kennedy on 22 November 1963 created shock waves in Ireland. His hugely successful visit to Ireland was still

60. The concert hall.
(*Dublin Opinion*,
1952, p. 242.)

" Somebody told him the Concert Hall for the City of Dublin was actually being built."

resonating when the news of his death was received. There was a great sense of personal and national loss and a widely held belief that his memory had to be commemorated. This was felt in the Oireachtas just as much as among the general public and matters moved so quickly that the government announced in the Dáil on 3 December 1963 that it had decided that a State memorial would be erected to the late president and that it would seek the advice of the Arts Council on the matter. It was to be State funded with no need for public subscription: money would not be a problem. The consultation was dealt with expeditiously, quite the exception when compared to almost any other similar proposal, and an announcement was made on 17 January 1964 that the memorial would take the form of a concert and assembly hall in Dublin. It was also announced that a nine-person committee drawn from the three main parties in the Dáil would be set up to examine the legislative and other arrangements that would be necessary. In keeping with the rapid progress of the project, it was announced in May (*Irish Times*, 5 May 1964, p. 9) that the

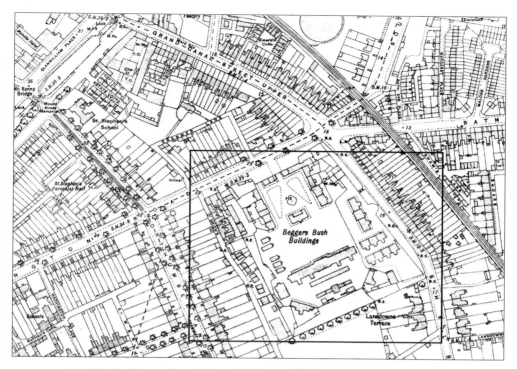

61. The Haddington Road / Beggar's Bush site. (Ordnance Survey plan, 1:2,500, Sheet 18(XII), 1938.)

architect would be Raymond McGrath, the chief architect of the OPW, thus obviating a national or international competition which would have delayed matters. The all-party committee for the John F. Kennedy Memorial Hall went on a fieldtrip to look at some contemporary halls in Europe with a view to using the best design for Dublin. Among others, they visited the Beethovenhalle in Bonn, the Liederhalle in Stuttgart and the Philharmonie in Berlin. This ultimately led to a design concept for the Dublin hall of a main auditorium which would seat about 1,840 people, a chamber music hall which would accommodate about 460 people with associated rehearsal spaces, library, bars and restaurants, all in a spacious design. The main hall would accommodate a full orchestra of up to 120 players with a choir space for 200. The stage was to have a proscenium arch and a cyclorama, together with a hydraulically operated orchestra pit for 90 players (see *Irish Times*, 13 November 1968). This would create a space with the maximum amount of flexibility and permit opera, theatre and ballet to be staged as well as music concerts. There was also talk that a convention centre would be incorporated into the design.

But it was all too good to be true; the question of the most suitable site was not as easily solved as the other questions. This has been a perennial problem in Dublin when any project has been discussed. There were many possible locations. The barracks site at Haddington Road / Beggar's Bush was proposed and generally favoured, just as it had been for the signature offices of the Departments of Health and Social Welfare (see below). Into the mix, though, was added the Royal Hospital, the Christian Brothers site in Marino, various locations along the quays, Morehampton Road and the Phoenix Park. The Phoenix Park site received much detailed consideration because space clearly would not be a problem. It was not greatly liked though among the architectural or artistic communities because it was seen to be peripheral to the city and a more central location was favoured. There was a belief that while Dubliners might go to an afternoon race meeting they would not venture to the park at night for a concert. Typical of the response was a meeting sponsored by the Architectural Association of Ireland in the Mansion House (*Irish Times*, 12 October 1967, p. 6) where it proved nigh on impossible to get anyone to speak favourably about the Phoenix Park. That this took place late in 1967 shows just how much steam had gone out of the project after the early enthusiasm. At that juncture, the State was no nearer proceeding with the project than it had been three years before. The Haddington Road site moved in and out of favour as other locations were suggested such as the Model School site in Marlborough Street or the site of the ruined house in St Anne's Park (scarcely better located than the Phoenix Park though it was pointed out that it was nearer the airport). This deceleration also allowed mature reflection to take place as to whether the cost of about £2m, per the initial estimate, could be borne. At the time of the decision, it would have seemed churlish to raise such concerns, if anyone had them, in the raw emotion of the times. Voices were now raised about competing interests such as houses, hospitals and schools, always an impossible choice, or why Dublin should be so endowed at the expense of the rest of the country. The government was forced to deny as early as January 1966 that the project had been abandoned because of escalating costs (*Irish Times*, 17 January 1966, p. 1) but even then the all-party committee was meeting less frequently. Indeed, one Cian O hÉigeartaigh of Edinburgh was moved to note that 'it seems strange that a site for concert hall is so hard to find: office blocks can be put virtually anywhere with no bother, yea even in St Stephen's Green' (*Irish Times*, 18 October 1968, p. 11). It also seems that Dublin Corporation was not particularly enthusiastic about any of the sites and does not appear to have actively engaged in the project. The Corporation did facilitate a proposal to change the name of Westmoreland Street to President Kennedy Street but it did not propose it. It agreed to hold the usual plebiscite on 6 February 1967 and the result was agreed on 6 April 1967 (Report 122/1967). The usual rule requiring four sevenths of property owners to agree was applied but what was different in this case was that most of those voting were businesses and not individuals. A total of 80 were entitled to vote, 61 ballots were received but the proposal fell short of that required with only 33 voting in favour.

It is not surprising that once the initial heat was removed, the project stalled. It was agreed very quickly, perhaps hastily, and enthusiastically taken up because the project addressed a long-felt need. But there was no assessment as to whether Dubliners would actually use it and whether it represented good value for money. As these realities dawned, the project receded into another of those good ideas that would be undertaken at some time in the future.

The commercial landscape – skyscrapers arrive

In the 1960s, Dublin saw something of a boom in office jobs and a surge in demand for office space. While some possibilities were offered by existing buildings, the demands of modern commerce required that modern office blocks be constructed and this not only led to the creation of a new sector in Dublin, it also offered the possibility for statement or signature buildings, taking over that role from the Corporation or State. This has become the established norm these days with commercial buildings outdoing each other in terms of the statement that they make and being given distinctive names, such as the 'Gherkin' or the 'Shard' in London. This need not be done on a grand scale as the 'Fred and Ginger' building (the Dancing House) in Prague demonstrates.

The single most dramatic change to the urban landscape was the construction of Ireland's first skyscraper for the Irish Transport and General Workers' Union (ITGWU) but the overall scale of office development was impressive too. There was nothing particularly novel about a high-rise building. They had been in use for millennia. The insulae of Rome rose to ten storeys, though they had a tendency to collapse. Equally, the mud brick homes of Shibam, a town in Yemen, have reached the same kind of height since the sixteenth century, at least. However, in the modern era, high-rise became a common feature of large cities, especially in the United States, towards the end of the nineteenth century. One famous example is the Guaranty Building in

62. The Dancing House in Prague.

Buffalo, New York, which was completed in 1896 by Louis H. Sullivan and Dankmar Adler and rose to a height of 46m. More spectacular because of the nature of the site on which it was fitted, the Flatiron (Fuller) building in New York city was designed by Daniel Burnham and completed in 1902. At 87m, it was one of the tallest buildings in the city at the time. Both were made possible by innovation in building methods which allowed for lighter but stronger structures but, more importantly, their functioning was made possible by the development of modern lift systems. The Otis company was to the fore in this area and this permitted the rapid movement of people to the various storeys of the building. People did not have to use the stairs.

63. The Flatiron building in New York.

The attraction of high-rise rests on two principles, intimately related. The first is prestige. It has long been a feature of cities that building high was one way of demonstrating prestige and position. The towers of medieval Italian cities rose to phenomenal heights as families sought to outdo each other. The tallest in Bologna still rise to over 97m. Even a medium-sized town, such as San Gimignano, could boast over seventy such towers with heights of over 50m. The modern skyscraper fulfilled that same role in the corporate world.

64. An aerial view of the Liberty Hall site in the early 1950s at the junction of Burgh Quay and Beresford Place. The substantial premises of Brooks Thomas can be seen in the middle right.

65. The Liberty Hall site cleared.

66. Liberty Hall under construction.

67. Liberty Hall completed.

However, it also made economic sense. Urban land was expensive and the use of high-rise allowed prestigious and expensive sites to be used to the maximum degree.

These two principles applied equally well to the project for the ITGWU. The site was a prestigious one. Liberty Hall had been the headquarters of the Irish Citizen Army and was one of the iconic locations of the 1916 Rising. The union also needed accommodation for its workers, whom it had to disperse to other locations in the city partly because the original Liberty Hall was no longer suitable for use. Building a high-rise on the site would maintain the association with the sacred site, it would demonstrate the strength and vigour of the union and it would permit the centralization of activities once again.

What drove the project was that Liberty Hall had been condemned by Dublin Corporation as unfit for use. An investigation into the building suggested that in its first use it had been jerry built, having been built in a hurry and to a poor standard. The activities of the *Helga* in 1916 had not helped matters either and by the 1950s the walls were out of plumb and the timbers had rotted. The ITGWU was forced to abandon the building and this was the immediate impetus for the reconstruction. It was achieved with remarkably little fuss. There was some discussion with the Corporation about the design but there seemed little concern in official circles about the impact of Dublin's first skyscraper. Not all of the architectural community welcomed it. For some, there was concern that it would dwarf the Custom House, for others there was concern about its mass in a low-rise area. There was a feeling that it would be better on a site that was not so heavily built up. However, the relative slimness of the tower diminished these concerns somewhat, while the element that stands along Burgh Quay blended quite well into the existing buildings. The person who caused the most fuss was a tenant of the union who had a lease on a public house that would have to be demolished as part of the process.

The building stands approximately 197 feet (60m) above ground level and has sixteen storeys. Much of the space is given over to offices but there is a large meeting hall at first-floor level. This is Liberty Hall itself and its 5,000 sq. ft (465 sq. m) has space for 800 people. Car parking provision is modest with only forty spaces being provided (see *Irish Times*, 1 May 1965, for a detailed description).

It might have had competition from a government project to provide a joint office complex for the Departments of Social Welfare and Health on its Beggars Bush site, also proposed as the concert hall site. This would not have

" Taking a bit of a liberty with the skyline, if you ask me ! "

68. Liberty Hall as an addition to the urban landscape. (*Dublin Opinion*, 1960, p. 361.)

69. The site for Busáras being cleared in the late 1940s. The indirect nature of the existing road network can be seen.

70. A design for the new Port and Docks HQ. (*Dublin Opinion*, 1954, p. 9.)

had the same urban impact because of its suburban location but it would have robbed Liberty Hall of its status as the city's tallest building. In 1962, plans were unveiled for a great block that would be 200 feet long and 50 feet deep (61m x 15m) and rise to height of 260 feet (79m). The twenty floors above ground would house 1,400 staff and present great walls of glass to the streets around. The design called for a wide plaza with an impressive water feature. However, the plans for the complex were shelved almost as soon as they were announced and, while the next few years saw the construction of some tall buildings, some central and some suburban, they did not eclipse Liberty Hall's dominance of the Dublin skyline. In fact, it held the title of Dublin's tallest building until the Millennium Tower (207 ft, 63m) in George's Dock was completed in 1998, though County Hall in Cork took the title of Ireland's tallest building in 1968 when it reached 220 feet (67m).

The Port and Docks Board had had long-standing ambitions of its own. It had outgrown its Ballast Office and in 1951 it was looking for a signature headquarters if it could get a satisfactory price for the Ballast Office. Their chosen site was on the newly constructed 'quadrant road' that was being completed as part of the Busáras project. This road would provide a direct link from Amiens Street to the quays and complete Beresford Place. To that end, they commissioned an architectural competition in May 1953 and the advertisement appeared in the *Irish Times* on 11 May (p. 10). It invited designs for a building on the 'old dock site' and it offered four prizes to suitable designs of £700, £500, £200 and £100. There was a three-person panel of adjudicators – John Fairweather, Vincent Kelly and Alfred E. Jones. Unfortunately, the competition did not work out as well as the Board would have hoped. Twenty-eight designs were exhibited in the National Museum in February 1954 but none was deemed worthy of the first prize. The second prize was given to Alan Hope of 50 Merrion Square and the board began a long period of discussion with him. They were still discussing the project in 1956 when Mr Hegarty, General Manager of the Port and Docks Board, declared of the move that 'it is definitely on the map' (*Irish Times*, 21 January 1956). On the map it might have been but it was to be a long time before it took shape on the ground and not in the location originally chosen.

The commercial sector

Liberty Hall was not the first significant office block in the city centre. It achieved iconic status because of its height but the replacement of the Carlisle Building with O'Connell Bridge House probably had a more dramatic effect on the urban landscape. With the completion of D'Olier Street and Westmoreland Street by the Wide Street Commissioners, the city had an impressive vista across the Liffey looking southwards. This was captured very well in the Brocas engraving *View from Carlisle Bridge*, which was published in 1820 and shows two fine streets with a unified architecture. D'Olier Street was terminated by a view of Trinity College while Westmoreland Street provided views of the Bank of Ireland and Trinity College. The quayside was completed by buildings of similar style and standard on either side of the focal point of the two streets. This vista was still largely intact in the late 1950s, though the central block had been much modified and given a mock gothic look.

The Carlisle Building, the eastern element of the ensemble, was put up for sale in June 1957 and demolition work began some four years later. The plans, approved by Dublin Corporation in 1959 with little comment, provided for a ten-storey building (eleven storeys if the penthouse is included) and a total floor area of about 43,500 sq. ft (4,000 sq. m). It was to be built in steel and

71. View from Carlisle Bridge, renamed O'Connell Bridge in August 1880. (Brocas, 1820.)

72. View from O'Connell Bridge in the 1930s.

concrete. The tolerance for signage on significant buildings is interesting. The *Irish Times* noted that 'as the building occupies a prominent site in an area in which illuminated signs are an important feature, it has been designed in such a way as to permit these signs to be erected as a part of the building' (*Irish Times*, 4 September 1959, p. 6). People were well aware of the significance of the site and it was noted that it could be seen from a wider range of locations than the Nelson Pillar, yet there was little concern about the impact of a tall,

73. O'Connell Bridge House in place.

white building on the surrounding environment. The delay in completion of the building had nothing to do with any objections. There was a dispute with the owner of the adjacent building but it was the delay in vacating the Carlisle Building that caused the timescale to be longer than anticipated.

As this project moved on, there was another dramatic development taking place in the blocks behind the Carlisle Building. The Theatre Royal on Hawkins Street had been demolished and in its place was rising a large office complex. The plans for the Theatre Royal site were unveiled in June 1962. It was a development of the Rank Organization, which owned the Theatre Royal and which decided that the theatre had no future in the changed world of cinema. Instead, they proposed a twelve-storey office block, which would help meet the needs of a developing city. Sir Thomas Beckett, the architect, was quoted as saying that Dublin needed economic and efficient buildings and that workers expected to be housed in offices with proper amenities. 'The average man should be housed in a first-class manner and that could not be done with hashed-up buildings' (*Irish Times*, 22 June 1962, p. 4). The office space was substantial at 128,000 sq. ft (11,900 sq. m) over twelve storeys and rising to 135ft (41m) and built of reinforced concrete and glass. It was anticipated that it would house up to 1,200 workers but only 128 car parking

74. Hawkins House, the replacement for the Theatre Royal, from Liberty Hall.

75. Office building and showrooms for Heiton McFerran Ltd, Tara Street, 1967.

76. Hume House, Ballsbridge, 1967.

77. Lansdowne House, Ballsbridge, 1967.

78. Fitzwilton House, Grand Canal, 1969.

spaces were provided. This is interesting in light of the discussion elsewhere in this volume about transport systems. It was also interesting that the architects noted that there was ample toilet provision for staff but a special toilet would be provided for directors and senior staff. With buildings such as these it was anticipated that more commercial development would be attracted to the location and that the existing quay front might be replaced with similar office developments, producing a distinctive modern commercial zone in the city. This was not to happen but other substantial office blocks began to appear in a variety of locations in the city such as the four-storey Irish Life Building on Mespil Road or the eight-storey Sugar Company Building on Leeson Street/Earlsfort Terrace, which would dwarf the Georgian and Victorian buildings around it. This was the beginnings of a concentration of commercial activity into the south-eastern sector of the south inner city and across the canal into Ballsbridge (Bannon, 1973). Many of the office buildings in the 1960s were quite unremarkable and few have become iconic in a good way in the period since. There were those whose scale made an impressive economic statement as well as changing the architectural landscape, especially in Ballsbridge, as the images above, all constructed by the G.&T. Crampton Company, demonstrate.

Table 5. Office development in Dublin, 1960–70. (Adapted from Malone, 1990).

Year	Developments	Area in sq. feet	Area in sq. metres
1960	5	76,225	7,080
1961	2	34,975	3,250
1962	1	39,000	3,620
1963	3	82,090	7,625
1964	3	225,865	21,000
1965	4	129,265	12,000
1966	5	189,305	17,590
1967	2	75,750	7,040
1968	5	159,600	14,830
1969	11	335,110	31,130
1970	9	223,300	20,750
Total	50	1,570,485	145,900

The data offered by Malone (1990) above suggest that fifty new office developments were added to the city during the 1960s. Before the middle of the decade, developments were small in scale but both the number of developments and the scale of individual developments increased as the decade progressed. In fact, Dublin was in its first office boom by the beginning of the 1970s and it was estimated that there were about 70,000 office workers. Most of that office space was added to the south-eastern sector. Up to 1970, no new office space was added to the city north of the Liffey and only 44,000 sq. ft (4,100 sq. m) in the northern suburbs. In contrast Ballsbridge had 349,000 sq. ft (32,400 sq. m) of development between 1965–9. This had important consequences for all parts of the city. It put pressure on the built environment of the south-eastern sector and resulted in significant change in what were the best preserved Georgian and Victorian districts. It also contributed to the decline and decay in the remaining parts of the city because commercial development generally avoided these locations. This was particularly the case to the north of the city centre. There were a number of reasons that drove this process. The most important was that much development was speculative and developers chose locations that had been successful in the past. They were not prepared, in the absence of incentives, to invest in locations that were not tried and tested. For their part, tenants wanted to occupy good, if not prestigious, locations. This would reflect well on their businesses and they could acquire status by being associated spatially with organizations with high recognition value. It was very difficult to persuade businesses to locate near tenements, for example, even when the quality of office accommodation was good and connectivity excellent. The south-eastern sector met these conditions. This had been the most prestigious part of the city since the middle of the nineteenth century following the slow decline of the Gardiner estate. It had maintained this status into the twentieth century and high-class suburban growth had occurred in the same sector. It had good connectivity, though the concentration of so much business there was now causing pressure on parking. Finally, it was always argued that business relied on a great deal of face-to-face contact and that this was best achieved by locating in commercial centres. It was somewhat ironic that the State was the biggest consumer of this space because of its need for offices for government departments. It took about half of the new space provided in the second half of the 1960s, the period when the boom in office development really took off. It is a pity that they did not use their purchasing power to achieve a more balanced commercial distribution. It might have saved some of the effort required in the urban renewal projects of the period from 1980 onwards.

It had been recognized in the developing plans that high-rise blocks would be a feature of the city. However, there was little sense of how their development might be controlled or whether they should be allowed in all areas of the city. There was a bye-law that limited the height of buildings to the width of the adjoining street but this was not always enforced. There was recognition that higher buildings offered possibilities that were important but also a growing realization that there needed to be greater consideration of their impact on the areas in which they were being inserted (see *Irish Times*, 5 September 1959, p. 5).

There was now yet another contrast between the southern and northern parts of the city centre. It is not unusual for development in a city to be uneven and for some areas to be favoured over others; sentiment can be very important in business. The north city centre had seen much of its business sector either decline or move to suburban locations and much of its housing stock was in a poor state. New commercial development could have been accommodated there much more easily. The issue was that no commercial developer was interested in taking the risk of investing in a location which was seen as less than desirable. Murphy and Vance (1954 a,b), as part of their work on the concept and definition of the Central Business District (CBD), identified these different locations as zones of assimilation and zones of discard. The zone of assimilation is an active area into which business uses expand, displacing older uses. Growth and change here is dynamic and there is the potential for conflict between the old and the new. The zone of discard is in a downward spiral and though it offers possibilities for redevelopment,

79. ESB offices on Fitzwilliam Street, perhaps the best example of the conflict between the old and the new.

80. The cause célèbre of Stein, the opticians, who stood against the demolition of their shop in 1983.

81. Advertising hoarding from the 1980s inviting development projects in the north city centre.

there is often a significant delay before these opportunities are taken up. Such was the low level of demand in the northern city centre that many sites remained unwanted for years, even a number of decades, playing a useful part as 'bomb site' car parks in the 1970s and 1980s. It was to take active State involvement to change this.

The Georgian city

While a boom in commercial activity was good for the city's economy and was a manifestation of a modern western society, it was inevitable that it would have a dramatic impact on the Georgian streetscapes of the city. An active zone of assimilation puts considerable pressure on the landscape and the tendency is to replace rather than try to retain and reconfigure. It was also inevitable that it was the best preserved part of the city that would face the greatest challenge. There were many parts of the Georgian city that were in decay or even derelict during the 1960s and where the commercial sector would have found it easy to locate. However, the best preserved streetscapes were in the best areas, the ones with the highest prestige and it was that quality that was also attractive to commercial developers. A contributory factor was that streetscapes or vistas were not seen to be of as much interest as individual buildings. In a later chapter in this book, there is an examination of how the city was presented in guide books and this suggests that Dublin's population in the 1950s and 1960s were not much different to previous generations in failing to recognize the value of urban vistas. Dublin Corporation, as has been shown above, were also leery about protecting too much of the urban environment. It is not that they were hostile but they had a deeply ingrained fear of being made liable for the costs of preservation. They happily left that to the owners, secure in the belief that much was in the hands of State agencies who could be trusted. In fact, it turned out that the State agencies could not be trusted and were far more moved by notions of the bottom line than by notions of heritage. The modern concept of planning permission came with the enactment of the 1963 planning legislation but the power that this gave to Dublin Corporation to control development was somewhat diluted by the existence of a direct appeal to the Minister for Local Government. All in all, it is easy to see how vulnerable the urban landscape was.

The process whereby Dublin lost so much of the best elements of its Georgian landscape has been dealt with comprehensively by McDonald (1985), while Hanna (2013) has detailed a number of episodes in the developing preservation movement from the late 1960s. What follows here will therefore only be a brief discussion and the reader is encouraged to look at both texts. Getting the general public concerned about what was happening was a slow process but the issue with the ESB's treatment of its property on Fitzwilliam Street was an important milestone. The line of buildings from the National Maternity Hospital along Merrion Square south and on into Fitzwilliam Street offered one of the finest Georgian vistas in Europe.

The ESB had acquired a run of houses on Fitzwilliam Street over the previous thirty years and had converted them to office use. By the end of the 1950s, it was felt that the buildings were unsuited to modern needs and that they needed to be demolished and replaced. The Board noted that the buildings were in bad condition and that Dublin Corporation's dangerous buildings section was concerned about them. The view of the ESB was that there was no way in which the buildings could be saved and that they had devoted large sums already to their preservation to no lasting effect.

They could have moved and left the houses for someone else to deal with. Dublin Corporation would not have welcomed that particular chalice and this is where cost came into the equation. At the same time, there was recognition that demolition was a major step. Indeed, it was reported in the *Irish Times* that Erskine Childers, then Minister for Transport and Power, was taking an active interest in the matter (*Irish Times*, 24 October 1961). It will be recalled from the discussion about the bowl of light that Mr Childers was quite capable of getting involved outside his ministerial remit. The ESB were advised to contact Sir John Summerson which they duly did. Even at this stage, though, the discourse was not about retention but whether replacement could be done in such a way as to preserve the streetscape. Sir John Summerson was one of the leading architectural historians of his time and his views did not do much to help preservation. He did not like the houses much and noted that their only value lay in their contribution to the vista. He did not like that much either and was of the view that it was merely accidental and did not have great aesthetic qualities. He was against retaining the existing façade or creating a pastiche version and instead argued for a bold architectural statement. So that was that! The Board decided to proceed with a competition for a design but felt it prudent to take a large advertisement in the *Irish Times* setting out their logic and quoting extensively from Summerson (*Irish Times*, 7 December 1961, p. 3). Nor, indeed, was Summerson out of line with the architectural community. A piece in the *Irish Times* when the final design was announced liked the manner in which the façade blended well but wondered why this was a necessary consideration at all. In the writer's view the 'corridor street' was dead and new buildings would offer only their flanks to the street (*Irish Times*, 10 November 1962, p. 10).

> In my opinion the winners have succeeded brilliantly in doing this. The bays of the structure are sharply defined at regular intervals which are at very nearly the same spacing as the party walls of the existing separate houses, and the windows, while large enough to provide modern standards of day lighting in the offices, themselves have a vertical emphasis similar to their older neighbours. The total effect when viewed obliquely – and this is the aspect that matters from the townscape point of view – will echo closely the accent of the street vista as a whole.

In the meantime, Dublin Corporation granted permission to demolish in 1962 but reserved its position on replacement until it saw the designs. It did not like the plans and refused permission to build on 23 May 1964. This resulted in an appeal to the Minister for Local Government, Mr Blaney, and, not for the first time, the Minister took a view on what was good for the city. He gave permission to proceed, subject to some modifications that were designed, he said, to improve the integration of the building into the vista.

82. The houses on Upper Mount Street following demolition in February 1989.

83. The restoration process almost complete in 1990.

The ESB grasped the Minister's approval and by 20 November were in a position to report that they had incorporated the Minister's 'suggestions' into the plans. That was that and demolition began in March 1965. Though Dublin Corporation theoretically had the power to plan for its city under the new planning legislation, the appeals mechanism demonstrated the reality that the only ones with power that mattered were the Minister and his civil servants. At the same time, it is important to note that the forces ranged against preservation were very strong and represented the respected establishment.

Later events may have shown that the ESB was reasonable in its assessment that the buildings were beyond salvation. In 1989, in what was seen by many as an act of atonement, the ESB decided to restore and renovate a terrace of eight Georgian houses on Upper Mount Street and two on Fitzwilliam Street. Unfortunately, during the restoration process in late February 1989, two of the houses suffered a major collapse and had to be demolished. While this was an embarrassment to the ESB and, indeed, to the architects, it did give credence to the earlier argument that the houses in the block had been weakened over the years by alterations and lack of maintenance. So, in an ironic twist, the ESB ended up creating a modern reconstruction of two houses, though it did an excellent job on the others.

The next test for the city was not long in coming and it focused on a run of Georgian houses on St Stephen's Green at the junction with Hume Street. While there had been an ESB Fitzwilliam Street Protest Group who were able to attract significant crowds to public meetings (see *Irish Press*, 15 January 1962, p. 4), they were easy enough to brush aside in the process.

The Hume Street campaign was notable for a number of reasons. First, the use of direct action by a small group of students who occupied the buildings was pivotal in directing public attention to the issue. It forced politicians and public bodies to engage to a degree that would not have otherwise happened. It also demonstrated how poor the ability or interest of public bodies was in preserving the resources in their care. The OPW facilitated the acquisition of key buildings that the developers needed to maximize the utility of the site. The shortcomings of Dublin Corporation's interim planning process were made manifest. The conflict also showed that there was no agreed definition among the body politic as to what constituted 'heritage' and therefore what should be a priority in preservation or, indeed, the degree to which preservation should be a priority.

Like many development companies, the Green Property Company was looking for opportunities in the south-eastern sector of Dublin in the 1960s.

St Stephen's Green was a good location and there had been other developments there. In 1965, Green Properties enquired of Dublin Corporation if nos 44–5 St Stephen's Green or 15–19 Hume Street were on their land reservation schedule. This was an important part of any development process because in the absence of a development plan, a developer had to second guess the Corporation as to their plans for any particular site. Land reservations had been included as a major part of the 1957 development scheme but that had never been ratified by the Minister. When they were assured that the houses were not on the list, they went ahead and purchased them. Similarly, when the three adjacent houses (47–9), known as 'The Dominican Hall', came on the market, they were purchased. This is where the narrative becomes complex and contested. According to the developers, the Office of Public Works intimated that they were prepared to dispose of their interest in 1 Hume Street and 45 St Stephen's Green – the key corner properties. They then sought outline planning permission to demolish and rebuild on the site of 46–9 St Stephen's Green and 1 Hume Street. Green Properties were given outline planning permission on 2 May 1966 for a five-storey office block. On receipt of this, they obtained the freehold of 46 St Stephen's Green and bought 2 Hume Street. Now the developers were the OPW's ground landlords but they still could not realize any overall project without the OPW's surrendering of a thirteen-year lease.

In the row that developed, it was said of the various interest groups that they had their chance to object to the original planning application and they chose not to do so. They were accused of being unfair in raising objections later when the intentions of the property company were plain for all to see. Indeed, there could have been an appeal to the Minister for Local Government against the award of outline permission but none was lodged. Equally, when Dublin Corporation changed its mind, they were accused of crumbling before the pressure of vested interests. Whatever about the first criticism, which it seems was true as a matter of fact, the particular criticism of Dublin Corporation was wide of the mark. They did not have a development plan, one was in preparation and they had only their interim powers to work with. These buildings were not in the schedule of buildings that Dublin Corporation had included as part of its 1957 plan. That was a sparse list, for reasons set out above. Permission would only have been refused if Dublin Corporation was prepared to risk a compensation claim from the developers and, as has been argued above, that was the last thing that the Corporation wanted or needed.

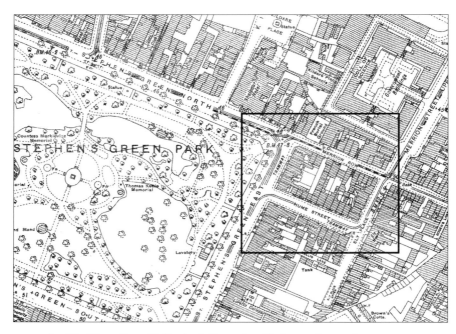

84. The Hume Street/St Stephen's Green site. (Ordnance Survey plan, 1:2,500, Sheet 18(XI), 1939.)

85. Oblique aerial image of the east side of St Stephen's Green in the early 1950s.

For their part, the developers lost no time in demolishing 47–9 St Stephen's Green. That knocked a hole in the façade that made it much more difficult to argue about the integrity of the vista. Emboldened by this level of success, they made an application on 30 April 1967 for detailed permission to erect two office buildings on 44–5 St Stephen's Green and 18–19 Hume Street as well as on 46–9 St Stephen's Green and 1–2 Hume Street. They must have been stunned when Dublin Corporation not only refused permission on 16 June 1967 but listed 46 St Stephen's Green and Nos 1 and 19 Hume Street for preservation. In all honesty, this made a nonsense of the permission previously given and left the developers with property that they could not develop. Why Dublin Corporation did a volte-face is not easy to determine. What was different was that they now had a draft development plan and it was within their remit to zone and designate buildings. But, it was only a draft development plan; it would be some years before it was finally adopted. They had to have understood that they might be found liable for compensation if the developers were ultimately refused. Whatever their motivation, the grounds for refusal were fourfold and comprehensive:

- that the development would involve the demolition of a number of buildings, the preservation of which was an objective of the draft development plan;
- that the plot ratio was excessive;
- that off-street car parking was inadequate and
- that the elevation and treatment would be inconsistent with the general character of the area.

However, it was not going to rest with them. The Minister for Local Government was brought into the frame and the developers appealed to him on 4 July 1967. This produced an oral hearing in December 1967 and the evidence given broke along expected lines. The position of the developers was that they had made an investment in good faith that was now worth less than 50 per cent of what they had paid. The city would lose an excellent opportunity for new commercial uses and, in any event, the buildings were in bad shape and could not be economically repaired. The latter was contested and it was argued that the buildings formed an architecturally coherent group, which in itself was contested (*Irish Independent*, 12 December 1967, p. 6). The Minister deliberated and eighteen months later, in July 1969, he decided that permission should be given.

This is when the matter became interesting. Just as demolition was about begin a group of students occupied 45 St Stephen's Green and the 'Battle of Hume Street' began. In and of itself, this should not have made such an impact. It was a small group of students but what they were doing seemed to resonate with a wider section of the population who saw it as a David and Goliath struggle, Goliath in this case being a foreign-controlled development company. The development company must have seen that too because they offered the buildings for what they had cost to An Taisce or any other bodies interested in their preservation (*Irish Times*, 15 January 1970, p. 5). This was done very quickly, a month after the occupation began. It seemed that the public was beginning to awaken to the question of planning permission, who planned and for whom planning was done.

The occupation also moved the matter into the political arena and the debates that took place offer useful insights into the varying political opinions of the day. On the one hand there was the contribution by Justin Keating of the Labour Party:

> We have witnessed the matter of conservation in Dublin become an issue that is now much more deeply cared about than it was previously. It is due partly to the bully-boy tactics of a firm of private investigators, which are beginning to look like an enforcement agency, and partly due to the extraordinary sense of public relations that was involved in breaking into a building at 4 o'clock in the morning and bashing up the people inside.
>
> This has become a big issue. It highlights the point that there is no way, under present legislation including the Planning Act, for an organization such as the Office of Public Works to discharge with justice and dignity their duty towards the properties they hold in the centre of the city and of which they wish to dispose. There is the impossible dilemma, if we accept the present system of developing our city, that if you sell for the highest possible price property you no longer wish to retain, that is desirable from one point of view but, if you get the highest possible price, you guarantee the desecration of the city in the process because the people able to pay the highest possible price are people who want to put up office accommodation.
>
> (Dáil Debates, 247 (8), col. 1122)

Then there was the contribution of the Minister for Local Government, Mr Kevin Boland. In the course of a lengthy riposte on 11 March 1970, he delivered what must be one of the must vituperative attacks on the conservation movement every produced. He claimed that he was not against the conservation of Georgian Dublin but he did not see it as the State's business to fund it. His view was that money for capital projects was scarce and that it had to be put to the best use possible and he was not going to divert a penny from housing, water and sewerage provision:

> I make no apology whatever for saying that the physical needs of the people must get priority over the aesthetic needs of Lord and Lady Guinness and Deputies Dr FitzGerald, Drs Browne, Desmond and all the other Deputy Doctors that we have. I make no apology for saying that, desirable as is the preservation of old buildings of architectural merit, while I am Minister for Local Government and while the needs of the people for housing, water and sewerage services remain unfulfilled, not one penny of the capital allocation that it is possible to make available to my Department will be spent on such preservation, desirable as it is. That is not to say that every possible effort should not be made to conserve as much as is feasible of this part of our national heritage for as long as possible.
>
> (Dáil Debates, 245 (1), col. 168)

The truth of it was that he did not really understand why people were bothered about Georgian Dublin, any more than Deputy Jim Tunney, who summed it up neatly later on in the year when he said on 16 June 1970 that:

> In honesty, I must admit to not having the same interest in or the same architectural knowledge of Georgian buildings as have Deputy Keating and other speakers who may see all that is best in Irish heritage and culture in the preservation and the conservation of such buildings. In passing, I might say on that particular point that at times I am at a loss to reconcile this expressed regard for our heritage that seems to manifest itself only in regard to physical heritage and which has no regard at all for the spiritual and linguistic traditions of the Irish people. When I look at the demonstrators who have been credited with such maturity by Deputy Keating I wonder whether they are genuinely interested in all that is best in Irish culture or whether their interest is purely architectural.
>
> (Dáil Debates, 247 (8), col. 1128)

It is tempting to see this kind of exchange as the manifestation of a post-colonial bitterness and the dismissal of the colonial power's heritage. There may well have been some of that in the responses but it is too simplistic to draw a straight-line between 'Georgian destruction' and 'a hatred/dismissal of the works of the conqueror'. There are too many steps in between for such a neat linear relationship. It is true that neither Tunney nor Boland had much appreciation for the earlier architecture of the city. For them, their ideal of material heritage was to be found in the natural landscape. This is hardly surprising given that most people at this juncture in Irish society were either immediate immigrants from the countryside or the children of such. Moreover, though they might not have appreciated it, they were the inheritors of a nineteenth-century romantic tradition that elevated rural life and diminished that of the city. What complicated that equation was that Irish cities, especially Dublin, were colonial constructions. Dublin was never an Irish town. It was built and developed by various groups of colonizers and was only recently getting used to being the capital of an Irish country. Thus, in elevating the rural above the urban, they were reflecting both a long-standing view of cities as places of exile and a rejection of something that was non-Irish. The telling phrase above comes from Tunney when he asks 'whether they are genuinely interested in all that is best in Irish culture or whether their interest is purely architectural'. Irish culture, it seems, did not encompass architecture – not just colonial architecture but any kind of architecture. He, and others like him, suffered from a visual illiteracy – the result of an education system that omitted this aspect. Tunney was as 'modern' as anyone else and saw the straightforward commercial benefits of wealth creation. This is exactly the problem that Manning Robertson had identified in his *Cautionary Guide to Dublin*, published in 1933, when he wrote:

> Some acquaintance with the elementary principles of design should take its place as an essential part in the education of the coming generation. Only in this way can a sound public opinion be built up. Without a sound public opinion our position will be without hope, since no legislation can instil a cultural attitude of mind, neither can we expect our Local Authorities to exert adequately any powers of control that may be conferred upon them if they know that the electorate is indifferent or hostile to any restraint exercised for the public good.

(p. 5)

Boland was no different. He did not understand why people were prepared to go to such lengths to preserve buildings that were needed for a better commercial purpose. They were, after all, only buildings. He saw the protestors as middle-class dilettantes with the time and money to indulge a minority interest in some obscure form of art while he had to deal with the realities of life for the betterment of the lives of the people. It was bafflement as much as annoyance; the same kind of bafflement that sometimes attends the announcement of the latest Turner award recipient. This lack of appreciation and understanding of the built environment prompted the outburst that always comes to mind whenever Boland is mentioned in the context of Hume Street:

> Of course, I can understand that the consortium of belted earls and their ladies and left wing intellectuals who can afford the time to stand and contemplate in ecstasy the unparalleled manmade beauty of the two corners of Hume Street and Stephen's Green may very well feel that the unskilled amateurish efforts of Mother Nature in the Wicklow Mountains are unworthy of their attention. Indeed, it may be that the Guinness nobility who pull the strings to which the Georgians dance may consider that as long as the private mountain amenities of Lough Tay and Lough Dan are preserved free from the intrusion of the local peasantry and uncultured mob, it is all right to permit an architect closely associated with a prominent An Taisce personality to intrude a manmade building in an unspoiled area like Glenmalure.
>
> (Dáil Debates, 245 (2), col. 267)

The question was how to bring this matter to an end. The students had ensured that it had been thrust firmly into the public arena and their occupation lasted a lot longer than anyone had anticipated. Eventually, the developers lost patience and decided to act in the manner of the Wide Streets Commissioners; they sent people into the house in the middle of the night to evict the students and to make the house uninhabitable by removing the roof. This was seen as 'bully boy' tactics and it backfired both publicly and politically; the company was forced into an agreement that any development would reflect the Georgian character of the area. On that basis, the occupation ended and planning permission was duly obtained.

This was only a victory of sorts for the conservation movement. The buildings were demolished and they were replaced with office blocks with a

Georgian pastiche finish. Whether that was better than a modern office block is a matter of debate and personal taste. The developers got more or less what they wanted, though they had to settle for a less intensive use of the site. What was more important about this saga was what it revealed about the strength of the planning process, the value of militant action and the gap in public appreciation of what constituted heritage. The big challenge was to educate the public as to the meaning of heritage and why it needed their attention so that it would not be necessary to engage in fire brigade action in the future.

The urban landscape

With the development of a distinctive commercial sector in the south-east of the city, one of the final elements of the modern city was now in place. It was inevitable that this part of the city would be the favoured location for the developing office sector because, in the absence of incentives to do otherwise, speculative builders were going to invest in areas that were already seen as attractive. There had been a smaller commercial sector there since the nineteenth century and this was the zone of better residences and fewer slums. It seems counter-intuitive that better residential zones should become the focus of commercial development but it makes perfect sense. These were addresses that carried a cachet in the 1960s and that quality translated to the commercial development quite easily. Thus, it was far more attractive for a company to say that it had its headquarters in Ballsbridge rather than in Gardiner Street. The latter would have provided a far cheaper location but it would not have 'said' the required things about the company.

Thus, the south-eastern sector of the city was set to become the commercial hub of the city close to the city centre and the prime residential zone further out. The residential element had been begun in the nineteenth century and its social position had been confirmed in the residential development decisions of the twentieth century.

In the 1960s, therefore, the most comprehensive transformation of the urban landscape was the result of the growth of the commercial sector. Their modern office blocks, taller than their neighbours and made of glass and concrete, were a very visible manifestation of the changing world. The other changes were important but, with the exception of the loss of the Nelson Pillar, were relatively limited in their spatial impact. There were some new statues on the landscape and O'Connell Bridge had had a brief transformation before being returned to its former glory. There was now a Garden of

Remembrance to those who died in the cause of Irish freedom but even at this early stage in its history it seemed as if it was going to be little used. After thirty years it also seemed as if the Civic Offices project was finally going to be realized. This had been a long-held ambition of the Corporation, it had figured strongly in the Abercrombie plans for the city and was reinforced in the city's own planning scheme, itself something that had been long awaited. At last they had a modern design and the means to finance it. They must have felt that they had been careful enough to avoid the pitfalls that caused their 1950s' attempt to come to nothing. The design was sympathetic to Christ Church Cathedral and the other buildings of note in the locality. They were going to facilitate archaeological investigation before building; this had worked out very well on High Street. However, while the Civic Offices plan offered the hope of a counter pole to the south-eastern sector, it may well have been that its optimum time had been lost. The growing interest in the city's medieval past could not have come at a worse time for the city authorities. Their preferred site was right on top of the core of the medieval city. At the time though, very little of the physical structure of the city had survived above ground and the medieval character of the city was not a strong element in anyone's consciousness, at least until the excavations of the High Street area in the 1960s. These revealed an affluent and sophisticated urban area and there was a growing realization that there was more to the old city than two cathedrals, a castle and fragments of a city wall. Who could have known what was going to emerge once the layers of rubbish accumulated over a millennium were removed from the Wood Quay site and what that would mean for the Corporation's plans?

The city and the motor car

Changing city structure

Dublin has always had a problem with managing its traffic flows. The problem is almost as old as the city itself but came to a head in the middle of the eighteenth century when the issue of street vendors and the narrowness of some streets prevented the expeditious access of the Viceroy to the Castle and ultimately led to the establishment of the Wide Streets Commission. While it achieved much in the redesign of the city – the city centre of today is largely its creation – it did not achieve a city with free-flowing traffic. By the middle of the nineteenth century, whatever benefit the new streets had offered had been overwhelmed by increases in flows and complaints about congestion were once again commonplace. When Butt Bridge was opened towards the end of the nineteenth century it was hoped that, in conjunction with the new Tara Street and Lord Edward Street, it would make a significant improvement to flows. It proved not to be. The bridge was too narrow from the beginning and there were attempts from the 1920s to 1940s to find a solution in the widening of Butt Bridge and the building of a new bridge further east. This would have been further augmented by the traffic management plans that were set out in Abercrombie's sketch development plan (1941). These envisaged a new bridge to replace the Ha'penny Bridge and improved flows in the centre as a result of new and realigned roads. Butt Bridge was widened in 1932 but neither the plans for a replacement to the Ha'penny Bridge nor the plans for a new bridge to the east had come to anything by the beginning of the 1950s. In fact, the latter was firmly pushed into the future when, in 1954, a report commissioned by the Port and Docks Board recommended that the issue of an eastern bridge be considered in terms of an holistic assessment of the traffic needs of the city.

Congestion

Despite poor economic times, the number of vehicles of all kinds continued to rise and in 1956 there were 65,556 registrations in the city and county compared to 55,568 in 1953 and 24,480 in 1939. More control measures were introduced, tweaked and changed again in an effort to bring some order. There were bans on right-hand turns at busy junctions and alterations to

" *How do you account for your part in the accident?* "
" *My vision was obstructed by the Parking Warning sticker some Guard stuck on my windscreen.* "

86. Court appearance. (*Dublin Opinion*, 1952, p. 252.)

" *When will you fellows learn to respect the traffic laws?* "

87. Regulations. (*Dublin Opinion*, 1954, p. 378.)

traffic flows on congested streets. It was believed that parking was part of the problem, in fact it was argued in some quarters that it was *the* problem. There were already stringent parking regulations over much of the city centre in the

1950s but there was still a great deal of on-street car parking. There also seemed to be a great deal of disobedience of the regulations, despite regular reports of errant motorists receiving substantial fines in the courts. The regulation that prohibited waiting for more than twenty minutes between the hours of 8.30 a.m. and 6.30 p.m. was extended to more streets in the city centre in 1950. This meant that motorists had to park in authorized places only across most of the city centre (*Irish Times*, 19 August 1950, p. 1). After 6.30 p.m. on-street parking was permitted but not everywhere. Many streets were designated as prohibited streets and this even prevented people from parking outside their own houses. This was seen by many as overly restrictive and the reasons advanced for them, such as the need to facilitate street cleaning, were viewed with some skepticism.

It was noted in 1953 that 'an all-out effort is being made by the Civic Guard authorities to alleviate and, if possible, solve the present chaotic condition of traffic … From the circular it is obvious that from now on neither the pedestrian, the motorist, nor the cyclist who transgresses will "get away with it"' (*Irish Times*, 6 June 1953, p. 9). It would appear that enforcement of this kind did not solve the issue and a more nuanced message was adopted that blended enforcement with good civic practice. One such appeared in the *Irish Times* in 1956 when the Commissioner of the Garda, Mr Daniel Costigan, warned of greater enforcement while pleading for better behaviour. What he outlined suggested that behaviour was pretty bad and he noted that:

> Motorists should follow these rules for the relief of congestion:– Don't leave vehicles standing (1) at or near a 'No Waiting' sign; (2) at or near a street junction; (3) alongside another standing vehicle; (4) opposite or nearly opposite a vehicle standing on the other side of a narrow street; (5) at or near road repairs; (6) at or near a bus stop; (7) at traffic lights between the road pad and the lights; (8) on a pedestrian crossing or opposite a pedestrian refuge.
>
> (*Irish Times*, 7 July 1956, p. 9)

It was also argued that there was plenty of parking space if motorists would make the effort to go to the designated off-street car parks. It was noted from time to time that these were rarely used to capacity while motorists sought to park on every inch/centimetre of the street. In 1956, there were such parks at Bride Street, Redmond's Hill, Mercer Street, Cuffe Street, York Street, Cornmarket, Essex Quay, Cole's Lane, Townsend Street and Waterford Street, St Stephen's Green South and Parnell Square. The Waterford Street park was only minutes from O'Connell Street but though it had space for 300 cars, it seems that there were rarely more than a few dozen there (*Irish Times*, 17 August 1956, p. 4). A lack of knowledge of the existence of the car parks was suggested for their lack of use but it was probably as much to do with the fact that people wanted to park as close to their destination as possible – a practice and an intent that remains just as strong today. The same kind of plea was made in 1959, though the number of vehicles in the city and county was now close to 80,000. Superintendent Charles Ryan set out much the same list of bad behaviours in the District Court and once again the plea was for better observance rather than a reliance on enforcement (*Irish Times*, 15 April 1959, p. 9).

There were other examples of bad behaviour, which were highlighted from time to time. In 1950, the sequence of lights was changed to what is in use today by removing the amber light from the sequence of red to green (*Irish Times*, 11 January 1950, p. 11). This caused a little annoyance to drivers who had become used to starting off on amber. However, they discovered that by moving forward a little over the stop line, they could see the changing sequence on the other set of lights and jump their light. At some lights, it was decided to create a period where lights were red in both directions to permit traffic to clear the junction. However, this facilitated the jumpers once they worked out how long the gap was. Though traffic lights were a common part of the urban landscape by the 1950s, it seems that numbers of motorists considered them as optional facilities. Councillor J.H. Douglas of Dublin Corporation felt it useful to recommend to the Garda that they institute regular checks at traffic lights to catch motorists and cyclists who ignored them (*Irish Times*, 4 March 1952, p. 1). In 1956, it was still found necessary by a district justice to remark while convicting a motorist of crashing a light that they were 'not put up as ornaments. They were erected for the protection of all traffic – of all users of the road. They must not be ignored' (*Irish Times*, 29 November 1956, p. 10).

By the middle of the 1950s, the Council came to the view that it was time to plan in a formal way for improved traffic flow in Dublin. They were not yet convinced that the city had a major problem but it was understood that a coherent and 'joined-up' approach was needed. Specifically, the Council wanted steps to achieve the following:

Car Parking	Measures to relieve traffic congestion due to parking, provision of alternative parking facilities and supervision thereof.
One-way Traffic	Extension of this system.

Mechanical Control   With special reference to O'Connell Street and
                           O'Connell Bridge areas.

Suburban Rail Services   Possible contribution to better city services and relief
                           of road congestion. Committee also to report on
                           steps which may be taken to implement Council's
                           previous resolutions in favour of Speed Limit, safer
                           Pedestrian Crossings and Major Road Halt System.

This necessitated a survey, which involved routes being driven in a test car, an
Austin A40, 1952 model. From their consideration of the results, their overall
conclusion was that there were no serious problems in relation to traffic
circulation in the city and that the average speed, even in the congested city
centre, was no worse than in other cities, though there were specific issues to
be addressed (Report 42/1957).

Parking
As the consultants' reports would later confirm, the Corporation's study
identified an issue with commuter parking. There was a considerable volume
of all-day parkers and a census taken by the Garda on 28 May 1954 found
8,329 cars parked in the central city area but there was 'appointed street
parking' for only 1,805. While the main routes were reasonably clear, the side
streets were jammed with this volume of cars. The Council was concerned
about the cost involved in providing off-street car parking on the scale required
and the area that would have to be devoted to it. They estimated that ground-
level parking would need about 30 acres (12ha) and this was not available.
This got them thinking about multi-storey car parks but, in 1957, it came
down to the fact that it would cost about £800 per space to provide and this
would be a significant burden on the rates.

The report was not hugely enthusiastic about one-way streets. There were
twenty-eight of them in the city in 1957 but, while the powers existed to
increase their numbers, it was felt that they were merely palliative and could
lead to an increase in journey time as well as encouraging more parking.
Likewise, while there were forty-eight intersections controlled by traffic lights,
it was planned to add no more than four in the near future. The problem was
that the technology did not exist to control junctions as complex as O'Connell
Bridge and manual control was the better option. There was greater scope at
the Parnell Street end where the junction was simpler. Neither was there any
great enthusiasm for the railway. The coastal route worked well but they could

88. Multi-storey car park in Marlborough Street. It was to be the 1970s before these made any significant impact on Dublin traffic.

not see any potential to link growing suburbs such as Finglas or Ballyfermot to the centre by rail. In the case of Finglas, where no rail line existed, the cost would be prohibitive and while it would be possible to build a station in Ballyfermot the fact that it would have to lead to either Kingsbridge or Amiens Street meant that it would be little used.

So it was just as well that they felt that Dublin could manage its current level of traffic because there was little or nothing in this report that would suggest innovation or dynamism in finding a solution. The Streets Committee considered the report at its meeting on 2 April 1957 and concluded that no dramatic action was needed for the city centre in the immediate future. In turn the report was considered by the City Council and it accepted that there was a shortage of car parking spaces and recommended that all suitable sites be made available for temporary car parking. They also agreed that suitable sites should be advertised for letting for the erection of multi-storeyed car parking. Further, it was recommended that the proposal for the widening of Church

Street be expedited so as to facilitate north–south bound traffic. As part of a strategy to manage better the interaction between pedestrians and traffic, it was accepted that further consideration be given to the introduction of underground pedestrian crossings in the central city area and to the reduction, as far as possible, of cross traffic at O'Connell Street and Westmoreland Street (Report 42/1957, p. 202). This had long been a source of complaint from pedestrians who felt it was necessary to take their lives in their hands while attempting the crossing.

That report was much more sanguine than might have been expected. The dominant perception among Dubliners was that there was a problem of traffic congestion and more typical would have been the complaint made at a meeting of the Dublin Council of Irish Unions on 10 January 1956. Here, it was pointed out that even on main streets, buses could not get into the kerb to pick up passengers. In Parnell Street at busy times, there were two lines of parked cars right to the edge of the monument (see the images here).

More fun was the opinion piece in the *Irish Times* for 18 February 1956. This was a little bit of 'out of the box' thinking by A.F.J. It was suggested that O'Connell Street could be widened by removing some of the smaller monuments and car parks in the centre and by narrowing the footpaths an extra lane could be obtained. There was a lot of unused space in Parnell Square and Mountjoy Square and some of this could be used for car parking for 'as regards the public playground in Mountjoy Square, surely there is less need for it than for a solution to the traffic chaos'.

Not a fan of railways, A.F.J.'s suggestion was to move the rail termini at Westland Row and Amiens Street to other locations, out of the centre such as Fairview, where a new cattle market could be established in the city, thus removing the need to drive cattle along the North Circular Road. Neither was A.F.J. a fan of cyclists (it seems that they had few fans) and the suggestion was to ban them from the centre at peak times. Finally, to improve the capacity of traffic to climb such hills as Gardiner Street or Winetavern Street, the suggestion was to lower the gradient. 'All these changes would cost a lot of money, I admit. But would be a long-term policy, and we will have to spend money on a city face-lift anyway. Why not do it well?'

Daft as these suggestions might have been (and one cannot help but wonder if the writer's tongue was firmly in his cheek), one of the features of planning in Dublin is how the same ideas recur in different generations. One such, which resurfaced at the end of the 1950s, was that of covering over part of the Liffey for use as parking. This had previously been proposed in 1931

89. Parking on O'Connell Street near Parnell monument.

90. Parking on O'Connell Street Lower.

(see *Dublin, 1930–1950*) but the idea had quietly dissipated into the ether. The City Engineer and the Planning Officer were asked by the Streets and Traffic Committee to look at the project in 1960. The City Engineer was dismissive. He argued that any structure within the walls of the river would obstruct its flow and increase the risk of flooding. He suggested multi-storey car parks. The Planning Officer gave a more developed answer. He suggested that there might be two possible ways to do it. The first would be to cover over the Liffey with a sort of very wide bridge. This would pose considerable engineering difficulties and it would be difficult to provide headroom underneath. The second would be to build out from the quays on a cantilever basis. To make this worthwhile, the projection would need to be at least 35 feet (11m) in depth. However, the Planning Officer invited the committee to consider the river from an aesthetic point of view as well. He argued that 'the Liffey, as it runs through Dublin, forms probably the most important single characteristic of the city and that which establishes its character most of all. Most cities of the world have rivers, squares, parks and building, some of them extremely fine. The proportions between the width of the river, the width of the quays and the heights of the buildings flanking it are important' (Report 58/1960). He went on to argue that the cantilever proposal would reduce the river to a canal while the overhang of the platform would form dark gloomy recesses. Figures were produced which showed, in any event, that it would not be worth it for the number of parking places created:

Section of river	Parking spaces created from	
	total coverage	30-feet projection from quays
Butt Bridge to O'Connell Bridge	300	125
O'Connell Bridge to Metal Bridge	300	125
Metal Bridge to Grattan Bridge	400	150

The committee accepted the arguments and the idea disappeared once more.

Control of cars and pedestrians

Of course, nature abhors a vacuum and the difficulties in finding and getting into parking spaces saw the emergence of the parking attendant. These self-employed parking consultants appeared by magic in parking locations and by dint of uttering the magic phrase 'lock hard', they ensured that the driver could get the car into any space. A gratuity was then expected for the service. There was a well-developed system of pitches by the 1950s, which were passed down the family, and woe betide any interloper or, indeed, any motorist who

91. Prospects. (*Dublin Opinion*, 1950, p. 285.)

92. The ever-present attendant. (*Dublin Opinion*, 1954, p. 305.)

felt it might be possible to dispense with the parking service and/or the 'minding' service that attended it.

Indeed, so well developed was the concept that one such was moved to sue for libel as meters were introduced. There had been a cartoon in *Dublin Opinion* in the early 1950s on the topic of the earning power of these attendants and it seems to have been correct. A John Wright of 68 Mercer House, Mercer Street, sought damages against the publishers of the *People* newspaper claiming that he was libelled in an article which they published on 2 May 1965 under the heading 'No Wonder the "Parking Pirates" are worried! The Meters will filch their sweet Pickings'. In the article it was suggested that there were 300 such people in the city and John Wright was quoted as saying that he could earn £20 per week in the summer and that it was a bad week when he could not earn £14 per week. Mr Wright, who was 56 years of age and had eight children, had been a parking attendant for eighteen years. He argued that he looked after about thirty-six cars on the St Stephen's Green side of the Dawson Street–Grafton Street segment and worked from about 8.30 a.m. to 6 p.m. but that he could hope to make no more than about £10 per week. He lost his case with costs going against him (*Irish Times*, 12 May 1966, p. 11).

The pedestrian needed protection from the traffic flows too, though they were also notorious for ignoring all regulations. The big initiative was the intention to build more central street traffic islands. These were felt to have the effect of slowing down traffic and forcing vehicles to keep to the centre of their lanes. The fact that vehicles had a tendency to crash into these islands was put down to bad driving rather than an inherent fault in the concept. However, the phrasing of the comments of one quoted official must raise a smile. He noted that 'the islands give the pedestrian a fair chance to cross the road in comparative safety and he has only to deal with one stream of traffic at a time' (*Irish Times*, 10 December 1955, p. 4). Later regulations required traffic to stop at the actual stop line and not encroach onto the pedestrian crossing. It was also determined that the vehicle should stop on amber unless it was so close to the junction as to be unable to stop in safety (*Irish Times*, 1 February 1957, p. 4). Zebra crossings also began to appear in the city about this time and by late 1957, there were fifty-seven of them in the city. It seems that pedestrians took to them easily and were quite happy to assert their right of way. The feeling that pedestrians were seen as prey by motorists was widely held. At a meeting of the Dublin Council of Irish Unions on 10 January 1956, it was said that one took one's life in one's hands trying to get across the road

"*Nine minutes forty seconds manoeuvring your vehicle IN leaves you forty seconds rest before commencing to manoeuvre the aforesaid vehicle OUT again. . . .*"

93. Twenty minutes only. (*Dublin Opinion*, 1955, p. 400.)

in Fairview and that a bridge over the North Strand was the only way to accomplish that traverse in safety.

Other measures were going to be necessary, given that enforcement and appeals to the good nature of motorists were less than effective. The parking regulations were already draconian by today's standards but it also seemed that they were regularly ignored. Nonetheless, there was shock when it was decided to eliminate parking entirely from some streets. This was introduced in time for Christmas 1960 and it involved the banning of parking from major streets with rigorous enforcement of the regulations by the Garda. Such was the effect of the threat of enforcement that retailers on Grafton Street complained that people were afraid to come and do their shopping there, even though there were plenty of legal parking spaces in nearby streets, though the limit was still twenty minutes. There was some good news though because it was finally accepted that twenty minutes was not enough for even the best-planned shopping trip. The authorities decided not to enforce the twenty-minute limit and to give upwards of an hour in the designated areas.

As part of this new approach a total of twenty-four new one-way streets was introduced. It cannot be said that this was dramatic in effect because they were pretty narrow streets to begin with but the demonstration effect was useful in that it showed that the authorities were prepared to take action. The new one-way streets were:

- Chatham Street, east to west.
- Chatham Lane, south to north.
- Clarendon Street, south to north.
- Balfe Street, north to south.
- Harry Street, east to west.
- Mary Street, east to west.
- Upper Abbey Street, west to east.
- Great Strand Street, east to west.
- Upper Liffey Street, south to north.
- Lower Liffey Street, south to north.
- Denmark Street Little, south to north.
- Jervis Street, north to south.
- Swift's Row, north to south.
- Wolfe Tone Street, south to north.
- Moore Street, north to south.
- Little Strand Street, east to west.
- Little Mary Street, east to west.
- East Arran Street, north to south.
- St Mary's Abbey, west to east.
- Little Green Street, north to south.
- St Michan's Street, south to north.
- Halston Street, south to north.
- Townsend Street (between Tara Street and College Street), west to east.
- Fleet Street (between D'Olier Street and Westmoreland Street), east to west.

As with many temporary measures, the parking changes became permanent and were incorporated in new parking regulations which were approved in 1962 and came into force in March 1963 and which applied in the city of

Dublin, Dún Laoghaire and Balbriggan. Statutory instrument 11/1963 set out the rules and regulations for parking and five schedules provided detail for the streets to which they applied. The fact that five schedules were necessary tells the reader that there was nothing simple about this arrangement. One novelty was the concept of a 'cycle track' which was described as 'a part of a road designed for use only by pedal cycles and in respect of which there is a traffic sign indicating that it is a cycle track'. That idea seemed to get lost somewhere along the way.

One schedule set out 104 parking locations where parking was limited to one hour between 8.30 a.m. and 6.30 p.m. The second schedule comprised fifty-four streets, mainly close to the central city area, where parking was either for two hours or generally between 8.30 a.m. and 6.30 p.m. Signs on the street would indicate which. One positive thing was the end of the hated and impractical twenty minutes parking regulation. Then there were two lists of streets where parking was prohibited between the same hours, the difference between the lists being whether it was permitted to stop to set down passengers or to load or unload goods. Parking was specifically prohibited on Grafton Street's west side at all times. The final group was locations where cars had to park nose-in rather than parallel but with no time limit.

Together with these came the concept of fixed penalty or 'on the spot fines'. This was a big change because the previous system required a court appearance and it was as troublesome for the authorities as for the malefactor to have large numbers of summons. However, from now on, penalties would apply to those 'parking a mechanically propelled vehicle in a prohibited place, at a prohibited time, for a prohibited time, or in a manner prohibited. If a civic guard has reasonable grounds for believing that any of these offences is being or has been committed, he may (a) serve a notice on the driver on the spot, or (b) fix a notice to the vehicle, alleging the offence and indicating that, if payment of 10s. is made within 21 days at a named civic guard station, a prosecution will not follow'. Within a year the fixed penalty was increased to £1 because it was found that motorists were not being sufficiently deterred. This was greeted with 'horror and anger', with the AA suggesting that it was outrageous to do this when there were so few legitimate parking spaces available. The spokesman went on to suggest that nobody would park irregularly if there were legal parking spaces available. That touching but misplaced belief in human nature aside, the reality was more likely to have been that the relationship between the size of the penalty and the probability of being caught was not well aligned (*Irish Times*, 30 July 1964, p. 1).

94. Parking meters and nose-to-kerb parking on Eden Quay.

This was never going to be enough though. Charging for parking was inevitable. This was doubly attractive because it allowed a scarce resource (parking) to be monetized, producing an income for a cash-strapped Council and it could be done in the name of good city management. It took a long time to introduce though (nothing unusual there!) and for a long time it seemed as if it would never happen. In 1957, the Streets Committee of Dublin Corporation discussed the possibility of introducing parking meters on the streets. No decision was made on costs but it was noted that it cost motorists 2*s*. 6*d*. for each eight hours they were parked in a private car park in London. At the time, they were informed that the necessary legal powers did not exist but that was remedied by 1962. In a piece by their Motoring Correspondent in 1959, the *Irish Times* took a wry look at the prospect.

> … there is something to be said in favour of the devices. For one thing, they would be a vast improvement on the allegedly living money-collectors who operate at present. Parking meters cannot wave you on airily, when a slight push on their part would provide enough space for your car. They cannot be rude, uncivil and un-co-operative, as some of the present incumbents are (though of course, they cannot keep a space for you against all comers, and doff their cap at you for a suitable fee,

either). But they have one thing in common with attendants – they expect money while giving no service whatsoever.

(*Irish Times*, 14 April 1959, p. 8)

By 1963, the Corporation was ready to act and it proposed to seek an amendment to the parking bye-laws (section 5) to allow for the installation of meters. In July 1963, the Streets Committee, having consulted with the Garda, reported to the Council that the following streets had been recommended for meters (Report 114/1963). This was most of the core area of the city centre.

- O'Connell Street, Upper and Lower.
- Eden Quay.
- Abbey Street Upper – south side.
- Abbey Street Middle – south side.
- Abbey Street Lower – between Presbyterian Church and south side of Beresford Place.
- Abbey Street Lower – between Marlborough Street and north side of Beresford Place.
- Beresford Place between Eden Quay and Abbey Street Lower – west side.
- Cathedral Street between O'Connell Street and Thomas's Lane – north side.
- Cathal Brugha Street between O'Connell Street and Marlborough Street – both sides.
- Cole's Lane between Henry Street and Sampson's Lane – east side.
- Denmark Street Little – east side.
- Findlater Place – south side.
- Henry Street – north side.
- Liffey Street Upper – east side.
- Liffey Street Lower – east side.
- Mary Street – north side.
- Marlborough Street between Parnell Street and point opposite No. 87 – east side.
- Marlborough Place between Marlborough Street and Talbot Lane – both sides.
- Northumberland Square – North of Lr Abbey Street – both sides.
- Parnell Street between O'Connell Street and Wolfe Tone Street – south side.
- Sackville Place – north side.
- Talbot Street between Amiens Street and No. 5 – north side.

The Council noted these recommendations at its meeting of 12 August 1963 and invited the Garda to develop the necessary draft changes to the bye-laws. These were received by November (Report 178/1963). It was a rather convoluted method of doing things but though neither fees nor penalties had been agreed, it was felt by some that charging could be in place by August 1964 (*Irish Times*, 29 November 1963, p. 1). It was January 1964 before the City Council adopted the recommendation, though not unanimously. It was argued that it was prudent to move slowly on the matter as the experience in the UK had not been favourable to that point (*Irish Times*, 14 January 1964, p. 1). Organizations such as the AA argued that other solutions remained to be tried before charging was introduced, including a greater use of one-way streets. An attempt by Councillor Walsh, P.C., and Councillor Kelly to prevent the introduction by the following motion was defeated (Minutes, 13 January 1964). Their motion suggested that: 'In the light of experience gained in large cities in other countries and because of the reported financial loss sustained and the inconvenience caused to the public, this Council is of opinion that the question of installing parking meters should be referred back to the Streets Committee'.

The *Irish Times* report had been optimistic about the timescale because it was reported in 1968 that it was possible that Dublin might have parking meters by the following year. A proposal was made to the General Purposes Committee that would have seen the installation of 2,500 meters from March 1969. The scheme would be administered by traffic wardens and existing off-street car parks run by the Corporation would cease to be free when the charges were introduced. The area initially envisaged was bounded by Capel Street, Parnell Street, Gardiner Street, Butt Bridge, Lombard Street, Merrion Street, St Stephen's Green, Aungier Street, South Great George's Street and Parliament Street (*Irish Times*, 20 May, 1968, p. 11). The charges would not operate on Sundays or public holidays. This time the proposal was approved after a period of public consultation and the meters were in the course of installation by the end of 1969. Dublin Corporation announced its intention to double the number of meters as soon as they had gained the necessary experience from the first tranche of 2,500. A start date of mid-January 1970 was envisaged and the Corporation denied in the most vehement terms that the initial locations had been chosen so as to exclude government departments, local authorities and semi-state bodies. They made the point that once the extensions were in place, officials working in the Custom House, Merrion Square, St Stephen's Green, City Hall and Dublin Castle areas would certainly be affected (*Irish Times*, 13 December 1969, p. 1). By March 1970, they had

1,500 meters in place and were reporting occupancy of 50 to 55 per cent. This was below the expected usage of 80 to 85 per cent but motorists were being pushed into a smaller and smaller zone of free parking, so the usage was inevitably going to increase.

Public transport

Dublin continued to have an extensive bus service during the 1950s and 1960s, despite the emphasis on providing accommodation for an increasing car-owning population, for whom the ownership of a car was an important status symbol. Up to the end of the 1960s, it was still possible to get home at 'lunch time' from the city centre to as far away as Raheny and still have time to read the newspaper before returning to work. In many households, 'dinner' was still eaten in the early afternoon, between 1 and 2 p.m.

Even in the early days of public transport, the network of trams had reached out into the distant suburbs of Rathfarnham and Howth. It had been established early on that the system needed to begin in or around 7 a.m. and to continue until about 11.30 p.m. Sunday services were curtailed, starting later and ending earlier, and this too changed little over the years and seemed to meet the need. The new CIE entity continued to expand its routes as the suburbs developed but largely along existing radial routes. They did not experiment with grid-based or other network ideas but they were active in increasing capacity. In 1952, they announced that they were replacing many of the 58-seater buses with 66-seaters on busy routes such as the 46A or the 48 and increasing the frequency at peak times. They extended routes and introduced new ones. For example, the number 14 from Dartry was extended across the city to Annamoe Drive on the North Circular Road. Luncheon hour services on the 44A to Mount Prospect Avenue were increased (*Irish Times*, 10 December 1952, p. 4). A new route, the 78B, was introduced in June 1957 to serve Upper Ballyfermot while the 40 route was extended to serve Cardiffsbridge Road and the 16 was extended to Shanard Road. It is very difficult to get an objective view of how good or bad the service was. It was certainly not difficult to find criticism of the service as being unreliable and expensive. One example would be the letter from 'P.B. Dublinman' of Ballsbridge to the *Irish Times* on 29 April 1958. In it he complained that Dublin commuters were being used to subsidize uneconomic rural routes and that the company's 'bouquets to its best regular customers are an increase in fares and a reduction in service'.

Myles na gCopaleen was not a fan in 1955 when he wrote that:

> A business call brought me to Clare Street, just beyond Merrion Square. Afterwards, I wanted to rush to the office of this newspaper in Westmoreland Street. At a stop in Nassau Street, just beyond the Kildare Street Club, I stood with several other people from 5 minutes past 12 noon until 12.31, and *no bus of any denomination whatsoever passed in that time*. I do not mean that packed buses passed without stopping. No bus whatever passed. The street is used by not fewer than five separate bus lines but on it, at the busiest hour of the day, there was no public transport last Friday for nearly half an hour. If that is not a good one, write and tell me a better. (I feel like withdrawing that last challenge). On second thoughts I am sure there is many a better!
>
> (*Irish Times*, 13 July 1955, p. 6)

Now it might be objected that the walk would have done him good and he would have been there in a fraction of the time that he waited but that would be to miss the point. Dubliners were out of love with their bus company. Objectively, the company had 548 double-decker buses and 110 single-decker buses in service at the end of 1955. They built their own in Inchicore and in that year they were turning out 66-passenger double-decker buses at the rate of about three a week. While they aimed not only to replace older buses but to increase the fleet by 220, they did not see the capacity for further increases because of the problem of congestion. In their view, the roads were too congested (in contradiction of Dublin Corporation's report) and made worse by the parking issue and adding new buses would only add to the problem of delays. The General Manager of CIE, Mr Frank Lemass, was reported as describing the parking regulations as 'a joke' (*Irish Times*, 25 October 1955, p. 7). They had to add extra buses to routes just to keep the timetable working. The timetable itself was probably another source of annoyance because it was of little practical use. There was no indication at individual bus stops as to when a bus was due, never mind as to when it was likely to arrive. Until very recently, the best that was given to commuters was the departure time from the terminus and the frequency of the service, allowing them to work out the probability of an arrival within a particular time frame. Factor into that an estimated delay of a given bus during busy times of anything up to thirty minutes and the capacity for frustration is easy to understand.

There were also accusations that the service was expensive. This was a perennial complaint among those who had relocated to better housing in the new suburbs. They now faced a significant additional cost in getting to work. The company was often criticized for being unresponsive to this problem but they pleaded that their governing legislation required that they break even. Fares seemed to rise on a regular basis. There was an increase of 7½ per cent in 1951, another 5½ per cent in 1953, a further increase in late 1955 and so on. However, it was claimed that by restructuring the stages of the fares, only a minority of people actually paid the increase. On the other hand, increases were regular and there was another round of them in January 1960. Once again, the company attempted to explain that matters were not as bad they seemed. They argued that the minimum fare of 3*d*., which was paid by about 32 per cent of customers, was not going to rise. The 4*d*. fare, paid by about 30 per cent of passengers, would rise to 5*d*. and the 5*d*. fare would also rise by a penny.

There were incentive fares such as a 2*d*. shoppers' fare for off-peak travel which was defined as 10 a.m. to noon and 2.30 p.m. to 4.30 p.m., time bands that would be in place for many years. This allowed people to travel from the Parnell monument to the St Stephen's Green corner of Grafton Street, to South Great George's Street, Westland Row and similar distances around the city. More stealthy increases were achieved by narrowing the stages to which each fare applied, thus making it more expensive to do a particular journey though leaving the fare structure untouched. This was done in 1962 and the company promised that fares would not increase by more than a penny (*Irish Times*, 6 January 1962, p. 1).

Despite the company's defence that increases were never as bad as they seemed, the data show that between 1965 and 1970 fares increased by 110 per cent – double the increase in salaries and four times the increase in the cost of living. An analysis was offered in the *Irish Times* by Garrett Fitzgerald (5 November 1970, p. 15), which argued that CIE was in an unsustainable pattern of trying to make up for decreases in passenger numbers by increasing fares. Fares, especially for short journeys, were not particularly good value and car ownership was increasing. The bus company was literally driving people to use cars, a drift that needed no encouragement. People did not calculate the relative values of car versus bus on a per journey basis, taking all costs into account. If they did, the bus would win without difficulty. If they made any price comparison, it was the cost of bus fares versus petrol and that was a much narrower gap. The problem with the bus service would only have been solved by a policy shift to focus on public transport as a solution to congestion and away from the unthinking policy of reducing the attractiveness of public transport by making it more expensive while making it less efficient.

The suggestion that common sense was missing from analysis of the problem is supported by what went on at a meeting of a Danish/Irish symposium on Environment Planning at the Kilkenny Design Workshops in April 1968. Mr J.F. Higgins, manager of Dublin city bus services, spoke and told the participants that, at that point, the company was in profit but it was not going to stay that way because of the factors that Garrett Fitzgerald later identified. Bus speeds reduced from 11 miles per hour (18km/hour) to four miles per hour (6.5km/hour) at peak times, the car was replacing the bus for weekend activity while the gap between income and costs was widening. What was of greater interest was the fact that the speaker reported that he did not detect a clear view among policy makers as to the future role of public transport. CIE had been consulted as part of the Corporation's draft development plan but were not central to it, a fact that surprised some of the delegates present. Higgins was clear that it was 'not possible to adapt our cities for the uninhibited use of the motorcar, and it will not be possible to accommodate fully the expected growth of motorcar usage in inner Dublin. Public transport will, therefore, be encouraged and public transport vehicles given priority in traffic'. Yet, as one delegate put it, 'it appear[ed] that CIE [were] fighting one isolated corner'. It was not an auspicious start to the era of formal city planning.

If there were issues about the bus service, the railway was even more of a Cinderella. Abercrombie had not been enthusiastic about the future role of railways in solving the commuting problem in his sketch development plan (1941). He reckoned that commuters would decide that nothing could beat the convenience offered by the car. Because people were prepared to walk only short distances to or from a station, the railway's attractiveness was limited only to a narrow hinterland around each station. It was further limited by the coastal location of the main north-south route and the location of the terminus for the main western link in Kingsbridge, quite a distance from the city centre.

The level of service in the mid-1950s was reasonable, if complicated. The 1955 *Red Guide* for September showed that the first train from Killiney into Westland Row was at 6.35 a.m. and it reached its destination at 7.19 a.m.; an elapsed time of less than 45 minutes. It then crossed the Liffey and got to Amiens Street some six minutes later. The next train was not until 7.22 a.m. but there were trains at 7.54 a.m., 8.06 a.m. and 8.25 a.m. People living in

GREYSTONES, BRAY, WESTLAND ROW and AMIENS STREET

Weekdays

UP			A.M.	A.M.	A.M.	A.M.	A.M.	A.M.	A.M.	A.M.	A.M.	A.M.	A.M.	A.M.
Greystones	dep.		7 40			8 10				8 35			9 25	
Bray 46	arr.		7 52			8 22				8 47			9 37	
Bray 46	dep.	6 35	7 22	7 54	8 6	8 25				8 53	9 20	9 40		
Killiney		6 44	7 31	8 3	8 15	8 34				9 2	9 29	9 49		
Dalkey		6 50	7 37	8 9	8 21	8 40		8 50	8 9	9 20	9 36	9 55		
Glenageary		6 53	7 40	8 12	8 24	8 43		8 53	9 11	9 23	9 38	9 58		
Sandycove		6 56	7 42	8 14	8 26	8 46		8 55	9 13	9 25	9 40	10 0		
Dun Laoghaire		6 58	7 45	8 17	8 20	8 29	8 48	8 52	8 58	9 16	9 28	9 43	10 3	
Salthill		7 1	7 48		8 23	8 32		8 55	9 1		9 31			
Seapoint		7 3	7 50		8 25	8 34		8 57	9 3		9 33			
Blackrock		7 6	7 53	8 22	8 28	8 37	8 53	9 0	9 6		9 36	9 48		
Booterstown		7 8	7 55		8 30	8 40		9 2	9 8		9 38			
Sidney Parade		7 11	7 58		8 33	8 43		9 5	9 11		9 41			
Sandymount Halt		7 14	8 1		8 36	8 45		9 8	9 14		9 44			
Lansdowne Road		7 16	8 3		8 38	8 47		9 10	9 16		9 46			
Westland Row	arr.	7 19	8 6	8 30	8 41	8 50	9 0	9 13	9 19	9 27	9 49	9 56	1015	
Tara Street		7 22	8 9	8 33	8 44	8 53	9 3	9 16	9 22	9 30	9 59	10 18		
Amiens Street		7 25	8 12	8 36	8 47	8 56	9 6	9 19	9 25	9 33	9 55	10 2	1021	

Weekdays—continued.

UP		A.M.	A.M.	A.M.	P.M.	P.M.	P.M.	P.M.	P.M. E	P.M. S
Greystones	dep.	9 49		11 5	1215			1 35		
Bray 46	arr.	10 1		1117	1227			1 47		
Bray 46	dep.	10 3	1015	1120	1230	1 20		1 50	2 0	
Killiney			1024	1129	1239	1 29		1 59	2 9	
Dalkey			1029	1135	1245	1 35	1 51	2 5	2 15	
Glenageary			1032	1138	1248	1 38	1 54	2 8	2 18	
Sandycove			1034	1140	1250 E	1 40	1 56	2 10	2 20	
Dun Laoghaire		1019	1037	1143	1253	1 23	1 43	1 59	2 13	2 23
Salthill			1040	1146	1256	1 26	1 46	2 2	2 16	2 26
Seapoint			1043	1148	1258	1 28	1 48	2 4	2 18	2 28
Blackrock			1046	1151	1 1	1 31	1 51	2 7	2 21	2 31
Booterstown			1049	1153	1 3	1 33	1 53	2 9	2 23	2 33
Sidney Parade			1052	1156	1 6	1 36	1 56	2 12	2 26	2 36
Sandymount Halt			1055	1159	1 9	1 39	1 59	2 15	2 29	2 39
Lansdowne Road			1058	12 1	1 11	1 41	2 1	2 17	2 31	2 41
Westland Row	arr.	1032	11 0	12 4	1 14	1 44	2 4	2 20	2 34	2 44
Tara Street			11 5	12 7	1 17	1 47	2 7	2 23	2 37	2 47
Amiens Street 65	arr.		11 8	1210	1 20	1 50	2 10	2 26	2 40	2 50

95. An example of the up-line service between Greystones and Dublin in 1955.

Dalkey had an even better service and it seemed that there was a demand for trains between 8.50 a.m. and 9.55 a.m. because there were five services, including three with only limited stops between Dún Laoghaire and Westland Row. Commuters from Greystones had to wait until 7.40 a.m. for their first connection and the service from here or Bray was less frequent than for stations further up the line but there was the alternative Harcourt Street line for those heading into the city. Service throughout the remainder of the day was variable with two to four trains per hour and a copy of the timetable was an absolute necessity not only because of the variability in schedule but also the variability in stations serviced. The final train of the day arrived in Amiens Street at 11.44 p.m. The service from town to Greystones was similar; most trains took travellers as far as Killiney but Bray and Greystones were not as well served. There was better service to the stations between Westland Row and Dún Laoghaire on the down timetable and not as many express trains.

Anyone socializing in the city centre had until 11.10 p.m. to get the last train to Greystones which reached there at a respectable 12.16 a.m. Sunday retained its character as a day of rest with a reduced service.

The service on the coastal railway on the northside was not as useful as it had only a limited number of stops. It stopped at Clontarf (soon to be closed), Killester, Raheny and Howth Junction. Thereafter, it split into services for Portmarnock, Malahide and onwards to Drogheda. In 1955, there would not have been many commuters from Portmarnock and onwards. The other branch went onto Sutton and thence to Howth with travellers to either station being able to avail of the summit tram. Travellers from Howth to the city were not particularly well served. The first train was at 8.08 a.m. and while there were four trains up to and including 9 a.m., thereafter the service was patchy with trains at approximately hourly intervals only. As compensation, those socializing in Howth could wait until almost midnight to get the last service into town and they would have been standing on the platform at Amiens Street by 12.20 a.m. Those on the town side of Howth Junction could also use the service from Drogheda and that meant that they had five services before 9 a.m., the first being at 7.13 a.m. and a further three up to 10 a.m. As with the southern line, a timetable was vital, giving the variability in timing and in the stations served. Train travel was not a spur-of-the-moment thing. It was a similar story getting out of Dublin. There was a train that stopped at most places at 5.15 p.m. and another at 5.45 p.m., 6.05 p.m. and 6.35 p.m. and the last train of the day was at 11.30 p.m.

Of particular interest was the Harcourt Street line. This deposited travellers right in the city centre, five minutes from St Stephen's Green and it ran through the middle-class heartland of the city. The areas serviced included Ranelagh, Milltown, Dundrum, Stillorgan, Foxrock, Carrickmines, Shankill, Bray and Greystones. If there was a route with commuter potential in the city, it was the Harcourt Street line. In 1955, the service was as good as any other. The first train of the morning was from Bray at 6.57 a.m. and pulled into Harcourt Street at 7.30 a.m. and there were ten services between then and noon. In the other direction, the first departure was at 7.50 a.m. and it arrived in Bray at 8.25 a.m. There were six evening departures between 5 p.m. and 7 p.m. and the final train out of Harcourt Street was 11.20 p.m., which arrived in Greystones at 12.15 a.m. The service was at its best in the morning, evening and at typical work times; the timetable became more complicated between noon and 5 p.m. with some services in operation only on Saturdays or not on Saturdays.

It was the city's only true commuter line, all the other services ran on inter-county lines, and it was a measure of how the railway was not seen as a mass transit mechanism that this line was chosen for closure in the re-organization and rationalization of CIE in the late 1950s. The decision to close was taken in October 1958 and implemented on 1 January 1959. The justification was that the line was making unsustainable losses and that CIE could not sustain these losses under its governing legislation. They hoped to save £71,000 annually by the closure and they offered the usual sop to the displaced commuters by promising an enhanced bus service. There was remarkably little protest. At a public meeting in Bray in November 1958, chaired by the chairman of Bray Urban Council, the most radical proposal they could come up with was to stay the closure for a year, reduce services and alter the schedule and see if the people of Bray actually wanted it (*Irish Times*, 22 November, p. 5). With that level of protest and that level of alternative suggestion, there was never any question of a reversal. In fact, the greatest energy was generated by the suggestions for what to do with the rail bed when the railway closed. It had an obvious use as a roadway and various proposals were made. One such was for a limited access highway to Bray and was advocated in a piece by Hugo Munro (*Irish Times*, 29 December 1958). Unfortunately for commuters, the railways had got themselves into a terminal loop of declining numbers and increasing fares to compensate for declining numbers; a fate that was being predicted for the buses.

Train fares bore favourable comparison to bus fares but people complained about them too. The first-class fare to Killiney in 1955 was 1s. 5d. but it rose to 2s. 10d. for Greystones. Third class, though less salubrious, was 11d. to Dún Laoghaire or Shankill and 1s. 11d. to Greystones. Taking Shankill as an example, return fares were even cheaper and could be had for 1s. 6d. while weekly tickets were available at 8s. 2d. and monthly tickets at 32s. 8d. Further savings were possible on quarterly and annual tickets.

Table 6. Third-class fares from Harcourt Street Station in 1955.

Station	Single	Excursion	Weekly	Monthly
Ranelagh	2d.		2s. 6d.	10s. 2d.
Milltown	3d.		3s. 5d.	13s. 6d.
Dundrum	5d.		4s. 3d.	16s. 11d.
Stillorgan	8d.	11d.	5s. 1d.	20s. 3d.
Foxrock	8d.	11d.	5s. 1d.	20s. 3d.
Carrickmines	9d.	1s.	5s. 8d.	22s. 6d.
Shankill	11d.	1s. 6d.	8s. 2d.	32s. 8d.

Bus fares were increased in October 1955 to howls of protest and declarations that they were unaffordable. The fares on the 46A bus route offer a useful point of comparison to the trains and show that the bus fares were more or less the same. The maximum fare to Dún Laoghaire was 1s. while it was possible to get to Newtownpark Avenue for 7d. and Foxrock for 8d. Rail fares also continued to increase – the fare to Greystones was 2s. 2d. in 1958 – and this did nothing to help the travellers' perception of the railway as inconvenient, uncomfortable and expensive. Even so, the decision to close a line running into the heart of a growing commuter belt has to rank as one of the more bizarre planning decisions taken. It seems that this was not the railway age and it looks as if Abercrombie had accurately captured the views and wishes of commuters some twenty years previously.

Traffic problems

This was all the more depressing because as the city continued to expand its footprint and car ownership and usage continued to rise, Dubliners began to experience traffic jams on a more regular basis, even in the 1950s. The phenomenon of the Monday morning and Friday evening traffic slowdowns became well established and it was understood that the space around O'Connell Bridge to College Green was best avoided. Gradually, the capacity of the system to cope with any excess or special demand reduced and Christmas began to be troublesome. Thus, at Christmas 1961, there was a headline in the *Irish Times* that noted 'fears of traffic chaos in Dublin'. By this time, there were 54,880 motor cars licenced in Dublin city and county. To this needed to be added the 18,514 motor cycles of various kinds, the 13,111 goods vehicles and a further 1,901 buses, taxis and other public service vehicles. This gave a grand total of 93,542 vehicles and it appeared that all of them wanted to park in the city centre in the run-up to Christmas.

It seemed that there was little spare road capacity by 1963 when what was also described as 'traffic chaos' (*Irish Times*, 24 October 1963, p. 4) resulted from a number of major road repair projects that were undertaken simultaneously. There were twelve different locations with roadworks but the focus of the problem seemed to have been work on Pearse Street, which necessitated a temporary one-way system be put in place. Delays of up to thirty minutes on bus services were reported and traffic was described as moving at a crawl in all parts of the city. As had been the case for nearly a century and remains so today, the major bottleneck was College Green. The same kind of problem was repeated in 1965 when resurfacing work at Butt

96. Bumper to bumper traffic on Grafton Street in the 1960s.

Bridge caused a major traffic jam that persisted until late into the evening. Motorists wondered how the closure of one crossing could cause so much trouble and one was quoted as saying that 'it just shows what a wonderful easing of traffic there would be if the authorities would make up their minds at last to provide another bridge east of Butt Bridge' (*Irish Times*, 26 June 1965, p. 1).

It can be argued that these were exceptional events that resulted from non-standard traffic flows and that the city, as a whole, was still coping well with the traffic demands. Jams were sufficiently rare to merit discussion in the newspapers. This is probably a reasonable view but it can be seen that less and less dramatic events precipitated a crisis as time went on. On a Friday evening in October 1969, the breakdown of an articulated truck on Newcomen Bridge combined with a two-car crash in Lincoln Place conspired to produce a memorable traffic jam – one that was destined to be remembered for many years (*Irish Times*, 31 October 1969, p. 9). The city came to a standstill for hours from late afternoon and into the evening. Delays of two and a half hours in cross-city journeys were reported as were tailbacks that were two miles long in places. It also resulted in the suspension entirely of some bus services as journey times doubled. The causes were two entirely separate and individually trivial events, separated by a considerable distance but they brought the city to a standstill. The problem was exacerbated by the bad behaviour of motorists who entered junctions without a clear exit. It became obvious to all sensible observers that normal business in the city was on a knife edge and that decades of failure to engage with the traffic problem had produced its inevitable consequences. It would be overstating matters to consider this traffic jam as a defining moment in the story of the car in Dublin but it did help shape a change in attitude. Just to reinforce the point, in the run up to Christmas of that year, it was reported that Dublin had experienced its 'second worst' traffic jam – 'worse than any Friday except the famous very bad one in October'. From 11 a.m. to late evening, traffic was almost at a standstill in the city centre. The problem was a simple one. The flows of pedestrians at the O'Connell Street crossing at Henry Street were such that they disrupted the normal flow of traffic, itself augmented by large numbers of potential shoppers. The *Irish Times* described it thus.

> Henry Street was a mass of parcel-carrying humanity at this stage. When traffic slowed down on O'Connell Street the pedestrians took full advantage of the opportunity to try to establish a right-of-way between North Earl Street and Henry Street. A spokesman for the gardai commented: 'we have every man out on the street to control pedestrians because they insist on crossing the road and this caused chaos'.
>
> (*Irish Times*, 23 December 1969, p. 1)

Road plans

During the 1950s and 1960s much attention was devoted to road planning, though perhaps fortunately not as much to road building. The employment of international consultants became an essential feature of these plans. The plans that emerged were no more than a variation of the same themes and it is difficult to understand why so many were commissioned. There was a pressing need to remove traffic from the city centre and this required new routes to the west and to the east. It also made sense to join these to the north and the south. Each plan varied, of course, in the detail of the route and in the impact on the landscape but the intention of them all was that Dublin would be criss-crossed by high capacity roads, just as many European cities were being transformed. The plans also bore out the uncertainty expressed above about the role of public transport. It was seen as 'important' but it was unclear what the balance between public and private transport should be.

These were big money, high stakes projects but, certainly in the 1950s, this level of investment was not going to happen soon. Therefore, what actually happened in road terms was relatively minor but, to reiterate a point made previously, the plans had the effect of sterilizing land in areas likely to be affected.

A small but important project was the link between Beresford Place and Amiens Street, to improve the main route to and from the city centre for places such as Clontarf and Fairview. Work was underway in early June 1952 but it had been a matter of very protracted negotiations between Dublin Corporation and the Port and Docks Board. It also took a long time to build: at the official opening on 25 September 1952, only the smaller part of the route, that linking Amiens Street with Beresford Place, was complete. The remainder was expected to take some additional months. It was a point of note that the necessary ducting had been put in to permit the installation of traffic lights and that sufficient width had been left in the footpaths at the Beresford Place end to permit the installation of a subway if traffic flows proved it to be a necessity. A small start was also made on the three arterial routes that Dublin Corporation had planned, of which the eastern bridge route was one and the reconstructed Ha'penny Bridge was the focus of a second. The third route would have had a more dramatic effect on the landscape and this has been examined in some detail in a previous chapter. Even before it was approved as part of the Corporation's draft planning scheme, it was the focus of a public inquiry relating to a compulsory purchase order on 14 October 1954.

The arterial route in question was to join the north and south circular roads to the west of the city centre and thus relieve some of the pressure on O'Connell Street. The order was only in respect of a 750 yard (0.7km) segment of the road at Church Street where a new width of about 80 feet (24m) (50 feet for the roadway and 15 feet each for two footpaths) was in contemplation. The inquiry was into the compulsory acquisition of eighty houses which included some business premises, tenements and part of the Four Courts Hotel. It was contested on the grounds that it would not produce the necessary alleviation of city centre traffic and, on the face of it, that argument seemed well grounded. In fact, Mr Miley, who represented the Four Courts Hotel, was quite far-seeing in his comments. He objected to the plan being progressed in this way when only a small portion was going to be realized at that time. He argued that it was unfair on those south of the river who were going to be affected by the plan but who had no opportunity to object. They would not be able to contemplate any development of their property and it would inevitably decline in value allowing the Corporation to

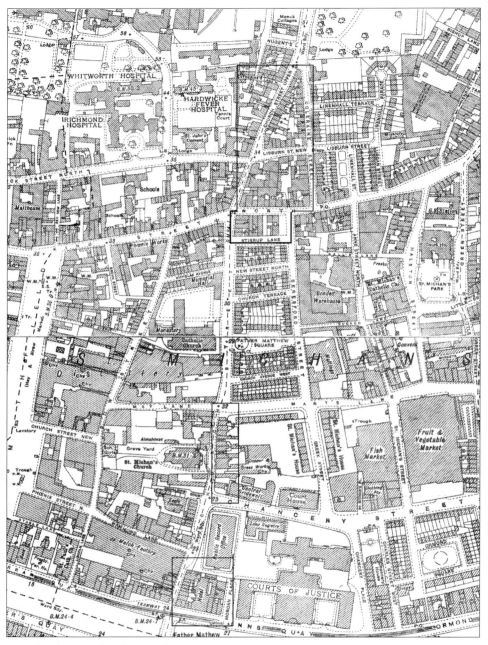

97. Church Street demolitions. This particular CPO was for the buildings next to the quays but later clearances resulted in almost all of the properties north of Stirrup Lane being demolished. The plan shows the approximate extent of the major demolitions directly affecting Church Street. King Street North was also significantly affected. (Ordnance Survey plan, 1:2,500, Sheet 18(VII) and (XI), 1938.)

get it for a much reduced price when the time came (*Irish Times*, 21 October 1954, p. 10). Despite the objections, this routeway was later adopted as part of the ill-fated planning scheme but the southern part of the route was still a matter of live debate and public protest before it was completed in 1987 and not before much of the route had succumbed to the inevitable dereliction.

Schaechterle report

The Schaechterle report was an important milestone in the relationship between the city and the car. On the one hand it supported the belief that it made sense to accommodate growth in car usage by building bigger and better roads. However, it recognized also that there was a balance to be struck and that it was neither possible nor desirable to accommodate all demands. In 1959, Professor Feuchtinger, an expert from Ulm in Germany, was asked by Dublin Corporation to advise on the traffic issues of Dublin and he prepared a preliminary report in December that year. This led to a decision to undertake a comprehensive, evidence-based analysis of the future road network based on the projected demands for 1985. It fell to his colleague Professor Schaechterle to complete the study as Professor Feuchtinger died in 1960.

Schaechterle's analysis was based on a comprehensive traffic census, involving both counts and questionnaires, undertaken in Dublin in April 1961. The data it yielded were analyzed over the next number of years with the first report being presented to Dublin Corporation in April 1965. One obvious limitation, however, was that the analysis was based on the county borough of Dublin while it would have made more sense to take an overview of the entire urban area. In many respects the results were unsurprising but they gave numerical weightings to views that had been long held. His basic finding was that the southern inner city and the southern inner suburbs were the main destination for the city's traffic flows and that action was needed to manage these flows.

His census, taken over a twelve hour period, found that 64,612 motor vehicles crossed the outer cordon (the borough boundary). The numbers crossing into the inner city were considerably greater at 114,374. There was a 'rush hour' but the peaks were somewhat later than today and more limited in time. The morning peak was between 9 a.m. and 9.30 a.m. and between 5.30 p.m. and 6.30 p.m. in the evening. When they combined inward with outward flows they concluded that central city traffic was dominated by passenger cars (71 per cent) with the remainder made up of motor cycles (11 per cent), commercial vehicles (12 per cent) and buses (6 per cent). In addition, they logged a total of 84,747 bicycles, showing that the bicycle was still an important mode of transport within the city. Buses added significantly to the load on the streets because of the radial pattern of routes with a focus on the Nelson Pillar.

Traffic came into the borough mainly from the south and the south-west with routes such as Rock Road, Stillorgan Road and Clonskeagh Road carrying considerable volumes while Drimnagh Road, Naas Road and Lucan Road also had heavy traffic. In contrast, while the Swords Road in the northern city was heavily loaded, there was much less traffic from Ballymun, Finglas or the Navan Road. This was a straightforward reflection of the social geography of the city and the location of the main out-of-county roads. They estimated that over 70 per cent of the traffic crossing the borough boundary was heading for the city centre and it was joined along the way by the considerable volumes generated in the city itself.

The traffic within the borough had its own complex flows but they found that the bulk of the traffic on the south side of the city was heading into the south-eastern inner city. Some 42 per cent of south city traffic crossed the inner city boundary compared to only 13 per cent of that from the west. About one third of traffic originating in the north of the city crossed the north inner-city boundary. Most of this was for destinations in the north city but there were considerable flows across the river too. The main destinations will not come as surprise to the reader; the cars were heading into the business and shopping districts of north and south cities, wards such as Mansion House, Royal Exchange and North City.

The question of a bridge over the Liffey to the east of Butt Bridge was once again raised. The study showed that O'Connell Bridge and Butt Bridge took the heaviest loads of cross-city traffic. Just as Abercrombie had noted in the 1940s, this was traffic that was heading to the docklands or the east inner city and it was forced into the centre because there was no bridge to the east of Butt Bridge. It had been agreed, almost since the moment that Butt Bridge was built, that a new bridge to the east was needed. Indeed, significant effort had been put into the planning process for such a bridge, only for it to run into the sand in the 1950s.

Interestingly, they found that through traffic – traffic travelling from and to destinations outside the outer cordon – was relatively insignificant. They estimated that it made up about 8 per cent of the volume and that removing it would not solve the city's congestion problem. Rather, the solutions were to be found in a system of new and upgraded roads that would manage the flows

98. 'Save our strand'. A growing awareness of the dangers facing Sandymount Strand characterized the late 1960s.

better and get traffic that did not need to be in the city centre out of those central flows. The road along the Grand Canal was seen as an important distributor of this traffic on the southside but it was noted that no similar route existed on the north side of the city. Such new roads were to be developed in tandem with what they called large interceptor parking places or multi-storey car parks. They would be located on the southern fringes of the south inner city and around Phibsborough on the northside and would prevent commuter traffic travelling all the way into the city centre.

The report recognized that there was a very high density of bus traffic in the city and that the main entrances to the city were South Great George's Street and Grafton Street on the southside and Amiens Street and Parnell Square East on the northside. If public transport was to work efficiently in the city centre, then it was necessary to deflect from the city centre the traffic that did not have a destination there, while in heavily loaded traffic streets, the use of bus lanes was suggested.

They offered four scenarios as potential solutions. The first three were variations that they further examined to produce a fourth scenario, which they felt was both feasible and which would meet the needs of the city. Because the possibilities for widening existing routes were limited in the south-east of the city, they proposed a new coastal route from Dún Laoghaire using Strand Road. Though they did not say this (and there was a lot that they did not say), this would inevitably have required building on Sandymount Strand since they suggested that this road would have four lanes of traffic.

The other main route would be from Enniskerry and would run tangentially along the border of UCD. Modifications to existing routes would result in the Naas Road feeding into Davitt Road and traffic would then travel along the canal route. Bypasses would be provided for Finglas, Santry and Coolock. Griffith Avenue would be extended to the Navan Road in the west and to the Howth Road in the east. Terenure Road would be extended to Palmerstown Road to Milltown Road and from Walkinstown Avenue to Kylemore Road. The latter two initiatives were designed to facilitate the distribution of traffic along a west–east axis by connecting up all of the main radial roads. This would get them to their destinations without bringing them closer to the city centre.

For their ring road, they produced their most noteworthy proposal and one that they believed to be central to the success of the entire scheme. This was the creation of an 'express traffic road' (p. 44). In scenario four this would run along the route of the Grand Canal and the North Circular Road/Royal Canal with the new Liffey Bridge connecting the two rings at Guild Street – Macken Street. This was to be the location of the Transporter Bridge, later the Lift Bridge of fond memory. What was now proposed was much more significant in that the bridge would accommodate eight lanes with a median separation.

The report proposed a one-way system between Finglas Road and this new Liffey Bridge. This would make use of Richmond Place, North Circular Road for one direction and the bed of the Royal Canal for the other. Further west the road would make use of Cabra Road and follow the line of the railway towards Phoenix Park. It would either use the rail bed or be built on either side of the rail line. All of this, they argued, could be accomplished with 'comparatively small interference with existing buildings' (p. 48). The scheme can be said to involve comparatively small interference only if the overall impact on the landscape is ignored. Individual buildings might have been unscathed but the fabric would have been transformed. The full impact may be understood only when the detail of the main routes (p. 86) is examined. It was a requirement that the ring road between Davitt Road–Leeson Street–Liffey Bridge and Drumcondra Road be constructed as a six-lane highway with separated carriageways and flyover junctions; though they believed it might be possible to retain single level junctions at some points. While the intention in the north was to use the railway line, it is clear (but never mentioned) that the only way that this could be achieved south of the river was by building over the Grand Canal.

In the inner city, they proposed what they called a 'tangent square' (p. 48). These were four roads which were designed to funnel traffic away from the very centre of the city. The northern segment would be along Parnell Street and North King Street. This would link in the west with a southwards route along Kingsbridge, Steeven's Lane which would break through to Cork Street. The southern link would join with Cork Street and run eastwards through the Coombe and break through to St Stephen's Green South. The final element in this square was a complicated linkage from St Stephen's Green East to Merrion Street into Westland Row and then across Butt Bridge to Gardiner Street where it would link with Parnell Street. Pearse Street would become one way, complemented by Townsend Street. The impact of these roads would be very significant and, for example, they indicated that Merrion Row would have to accommodate six lanes, as would Butt Bridge, while the Coombe would have four lanes. Further analysis convinced the consultants that the western side of the square was too far to the west and they proposed moving it closer to the city to run along Queen Street, Bridgefoot Street, Pimlico and Ardee Street.

However, this was not enough. In order to manage traffic within the central areas, it was necessary to have what they called a 'street square' (p. 49). This lay within the tangent square described above. It shared Parnell Street as its northern edge and linked with Church Street – Bridge Street on the west and then High Street – Dame Street on the south before flowing into the Tara Street and over Butt Bridge. These routeways were to be developed in conjunction with an extensive system of one-way streets. The dominant principle behind these various traffic cells was to sift and sort the traffic so that it reached its various destinations in a more efficient way. In association would be the provision of parking spaces along the various tangent routes to encourage drivers to stop their journeys without proceeding further into the centre.

The plans were designed to cope with the demands of a city in 1985 and were an interesting mix of accommodation and control. It was assumed that the city would be able to cope with a large volume of commuters bringing their cars into the city. Not only would it cope but these arrangements would permit 'new town planning perspectives in the formation of the city centre' (p. 67). They suggested that it would be possible to consider better public transport in the city and more pedestrian areas and that the plans were required for a 'sensible urban renewal' scheme in the inner city. This would be the means whereby it would be possible to achieve a 'desired restoration and renewal of individual portions of the inner city by means of which a business centre can arise suited to the future traffic requirements of city inhabitants. This relief was also a pre-requisite for the creation of pedestrian shopping precincts' (p. 94). This was not unlike the compromise that underlay Buchanan's ideas of suiting the planning of city areas to their purpose and which will be discussed a little later.

Central to their proposals was the provision of sufficient parking in key locations to get people to leave their cars before heading right into the centre. They published a report on parking provision in 1968, based on data gathered in 1966, which focused on the inner city, largely the area between the canals. This drew a distinction between that part of the city and the central business district (CBD), the shopping and commercial districts on both the north and south sides of the Liffey. A total of 35,948 parking spaces were identified, of which 93 per cent were on the street, leaving only 2,609 spaces in public car parks. There was an additional 7,733 private parking spaces, largely in the southern part of the CBD. Outside the CBD, most of the parking was on-street. The larger off-street car parks at the time were as follows:

High Street	110
Winetavern Street	90
Wood Quay	130
Hogan Place	90
Dominick Street Lower	285
Dorset Street – Frederick Lane	200

Most were temporary by nature, the result of demolitions and clearances and the land awaiting development. These were manifestations of the bomb- site approach to development and car parking which was to plague the city for many years. There were 9,802 spaces available in the CBD, of which 17 per cent were in off-street parking lots. There were time restrictions on 1,349 spaces that generally limited parking to two hours or less. The main off-street parking lots are listed below:

Charlemont Street	200
York Street – Mercer Street	220
Golden Lane	105
Townsend Street PMPA	80
Denmark Street – Cole's Lane	140
Waterford Street	550

Overall, there was a good supply of parking spaces in the inner city and capacity was generally available during the day but not where it was most in demand. There was overcrowding in the CBD and a great deal of illegal parking. The results indicated that the number of parked cars exceeded capacity by 43 per cent at peak times and that the off-street car parks were generally full at peak time. About half of all vehicles were parked for an hour or less with approximately one third staying for more than two hours. When this was translated into an occupancy rate for each spot, they came to the view that over 54 per cent of the available parking hours was taken by those staying more than four hours. That rose to 78 per cent when those staying longer than two hours were factored in. This pointed out the difference between the numbers of parkers and the occupancy of the spaces. Even in 1966, most of those parking in the city centre were short-term parkers but the space was being occupied by long-term parking.

Their conclusion was that there had to be more restrictions placed on parking in the very centre of the city to ensure the more rapid turnover of the spaces there and to make them available to business users and shoppers. This pointed to the introduction of parking meters, a solution that was soon adopted. Long-term parkers could be accommodated by the provision of new facilities on the edge of the city centre and some of them might be deflected to public transport though no indication was given as to how this might be done. In addition, larger businesses should be 'encouraged to provide their own private parking facilities for their employees' (p. 18).

To cope with future demand, the report suggested there would be a need for a parking provision within the inner city of between 57,000 and 59,000 parking spaces. This was based on a projected increase in car usage from 167 per 1,000 people in 1966 to 341 vehicles per 1,000 people in 1985. They wanted more parking taken off the streets in the city centre to allow for better traffic flows and so the focus moved to the provision of off-street parking in multi-storey car parks, or 'parking houses' as they referred to them (p. 33). A large unspecified proportion of these were to be located close to the city centre to ensure that the walking distance was no more than 300–400 yards (275–365m) at a maximum. They reckoned that the provision of the full 59,000 spaces might be a challenge and that perhaps 45,000 places was more realistic, of which about 18,500 spaces should be in multi-storey car parks. This led them to contemplate the doomsday scenario of having to rely on public transport if neither space nor money could be found for these car parks.

> Should the policy of limiting parking time not succeed in closing the gap between parking demand and the parking facilities and should the provision of additional spaces prove impossible either because of planning or financial reasons, then the consequences must be faced and the role of public transport will be all the more significant in the future.
>
> (Schaechterle, 1968, p. 39)

Nowadays, these suggestions would be regarded as too accommodating of the car. Current policy is to deter people from bringing cars into the centre of the city by reducing the number of on-street parking spaces and charging significant fees for those spaces that remain. There are fewer than 10,000 paid parking spaces in the inner city and a declining number of free spaces, which the City Council aims to eliminate. Parking provision in new buildings is greatly reduced while there is nothing like the number of off-street parking spaces that were envisaged, though multi-storey blocks have been built. However, the Schaechterle report was written at a time when it was believed that car usage could be managed. The days of laissez-faire usage were gone and the significant parking restrictions in place have been discussed above, but it was still felt that the city could deal with an increasing use of cars and that included using these cars to come to the city centre. Reports such as this promoted a rational use of space so that cars would be directed to where they needed to be in the most efficient manner possible. Congestion was to be avoided by a layered system of roadways so that the car only entered local space when it was necessary to do so. Commuters, though, could not be accommodated to any greater extent because it was necessary to have turnover in parking spaces to accommodate those who had business to do. However, commuters were still to be provided with long-term parking spaces on the edge of the city centre and no more than a modest stroll imposed on them to reach their ultimate destination.

The report generated less debate than might have been expected and was not extensively reported except by the *Irish Times*. It is not an easy read and it is more of a research paper than a report for public consumption. The consultants developed their argument throughout the report and refined and revised their recommendations based on each incremental set of analyses. The recommendations were not particularly clearly set out and there was no impact analysis on the city. There were no visuals, diminishing the impact on the reader, and the precise details of the road network were left to more detailed analysis to come later.

The text focused on roads and only on roads. This is not a criticism of it or the consultants since that is what they were asked to do but it is a criticism of the specification for the report. It should have been clear to all that road planning of this kind could not be done without a significant impact on the urban fabric and that should have been a consideration in the outcomes recommended. Instead, this is very much a road engineer's view of the city. If what is wanted is a city that can accommodate the car, then this report outlines how it should be done. In such a context, it is not relevant that to achieve this it will be necessary to clear much of the existing fabric. Schaechterle recognized this and the final paragraphs of his report note that:

> By means of the present traffic investigation it will be possible to take necessary decisions concerning traffic development in the city of Dublin. The development of the main street network is an absolute necessity if the capital city of Ireland, with its significant economic strength, is to maintain itself in the age of motorisation. Closely connected with the decisions about traffic development are, at the same time, the measures for a renewal of the inner city.
>
> It is an urgent necessity that all city constructional considerations and projects be included within the scope of co-ordinated city and traffic planning. Traffic and city building cannot be separately treated any more.
>
> (Schaechterle, 1965, p. 101)

The Buchanan approach

The approach to traffic planning by Schaechterle was in line with that suggested in the influential 1963 Buchanan report but the Buchanan report looked at solutions in a more holistic manner. The impact of Buchanan's report was enormous, perhaps because it was written in simple, straightforward terms and also because it offered a number of practical case studies which showed how the solutions might be implemented in actual towns. Its importance was underlined by the fact that Penguin Books were commissioned to produce a special edition of the report that would be more accessible in cost terms to the general public. The HMSO version of the report was available at 50s. but the Penguin edition was sold at 10s. 6d. It was described as a condensation of the original report but in fact it contained all of the essential elements and most of the text. Buchanan's analysis was that the car was here to stay as a method of transportation. It was simply too flexible and offered too many advantages for it to be discarded. He dismissed arguments that the growth of car usage would be self-limiting in terms of congestion. This view suggested that there was a limit to the congestion that people were prepared to tolerate and that car usage would not grow beyond that. Equally, he did not accept the suggestion that the problem was insoluble and that money spent on trying to deal with it was wasted. His solution was offered as a sensible accommodation of the car and its integration into the urban environment. It was important to see it as a component of urban life and not some alien threat.

The essence of the problem, as he saw it, was that the inherited system of roads was unsuited to the car. The car worked best when it has an uninterrupted run but in the city it was slowed by junctions, parking, right-hand turns and so on. He saw the challenge as to 'contrive the efficient distribution, or accessibility, of large numbers of vehicles to large numbers of buildings, and to do so in such a way that a satisfactory standard of environment is achieved' (Buchanan, 1963a, p. 40). This is where his approach differed from Schaechterle. In his principle, a town or city would identify its environments and decide what levels of traffic were acceptable in each. They would then develop the road network to ensure that only the traffic that needed to be in the environment would actually get there: 'the one thing that is never allowed to happen is for an environmental area to be opened to through traffic' (p. 41).

In his city, there would be good environmental areas, places where people could 'live, work, shop, look about, and move on foot in reasonable freedom from the hazards of motor traffic, and there must be a complementary network of roads – urban corridors – effecting the primary distribution of traffic to the environmental areas' (p. 42). He was not suggesting that the environmental areas would be free of traffic. They needed traffic to function but he was suggesting that the level of traffic would be appropriate to the function of each area. The road network would have a hierarchy of distributor roads with the traffic being gradually filtered down the hierarchy as it came closer to its destination. In this system, he saw only two categories of roads – distributors, which were designed for movement, and access roads to serve the buildings.

He also suggested that there was a need to consider new forms of urban environments – environments in which the car was a fully integrated component. There was nothing new in this. Le Corbusier had suggested the integration of all forms of traffic with business and living in his design for the 'city of tomorrow' in the early 1920s. Buchanan also saw the virtue in redesigning urban environments to make use of different layers for different purposes.

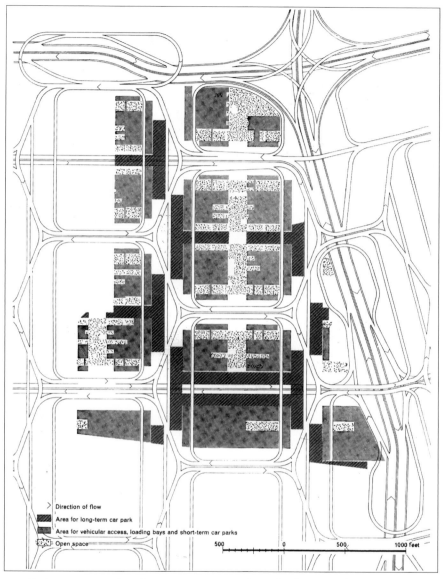

99. Buchanan system of roadways servicing a complete redevelopment of an existing centre. This provides a high level of managed access while ensuring the minimum traffic within each zone. (Buchanan, 1963a, p. 137.)

Thus, there could be a transportation link underground, the ground-level streets used for traffic while the city functions were developed on a deck above at whatever number of levels was desired. Of course he recognized that this

100. A schematic for a multi-level centre. (Buchanan, 1963a, p. 143.)

kind of development was suited only to particular areas and there were many parts of the city where there would be no sense in trying to change its character.

For the road systems, Buchanan was quite happy to see highways within the central area involving flyovers and separated junctions, where this was possible within the particular environment. It was all a case of the roadways being in the appropriate locations. Equally, parking needed to be provided in appropriate locations and there was no difficulty having multi-storey car parks. He recognized that full redevelopment was not possible in all cases but there was value in even a partial redevelopment of a city centre. One example given of a partial development was Newbury, where the historic core was preserved, pedestrianization improved, new multi-level environments created and traffic managed by a distributor system around the centre (p. 75). An impression of a multi-level development was offered in the analysis of an inner city area of London between Euston Road and Tottenham Court Road (p. 137 or p. 143, depending on edition).

There was urgency about dealing with the issue. He argued that it was not possible to make these changes over small spatial areas and 'that unless the public accepts that there has to be comprehensive redevelopment over large areas, then the opportunity for dealing imaginatively with traffic will all be lost and, in the end, this will severely restrict the use that can be made of motor vehicles in built-up areas' (p. 47).

Reaction to the Schaechterle report
The *Irish Times* gave the Schaechterle report considerable coverage on 17 and 18 November 1965 and provided a diagram of the new road network in the latter edition. It was a good summary of the proposals but there was no hint of the potential impact. In fact, the headline item was that the plan showed 'that a new Liffey bridge is urgently required east of the inner city to relieve the traffic load. With this new bridge, an efficient main traffic route should be developed running at a tangent to the inner city in the north-east, east and south-east' (17 November, p. 1). The focus on the bridge was not really surprising because that seemed to be in peoples' minds but this was hardly the most dramatic of the proposals. This bridge was also the concern of an article anticipating the report that appeared in the *Irish Times* on 13 August 1964 (p. 11). It began 'that report is expected to deal, among other things, with long-standing demands from many quarters for additional crossings over the Liffey, particularly on the seaward side of Butt Bridge'. The comments reported were concerned with this aspect of the anticipated plan, although one comment from the Lord Mayor, John McCann, was interesting in what it revealed about attitudes to the urban fabric. He noted that demolition or falling down of buildings in the past year made it easier to facilitate the plans.

> The number of clearances in vital areas of the city in one year – information on which has been made available to the German expert – could eventually be turned to ease many problems in the city, he said. In fact, one problem the Corporation had was that of trying to convince people not to demolish buildings that structurally were sound.
> (*Irish Times*, 13 August 1964, p. 11)

Even so, a cursory reading of the plan must have revealed that it could not be realized without significant demolitions, some quite near to the city centre. The Grand Canal route was central to the plan and building over the canal was inevitable if the road was to have six or eight lanes with freeflow junctions. After all, the present roadway is only four lanes along most of its length. The lack of concern at this planning stage seemed to stem from a belief in official circles that canals were now more of a nuisance than a resource. They had ceased to serve a useful economic purpose and were derelict along considerable stretches, especially in the case of the Royal Canal. CIE, which had responsibility for their upkeep, saw them as no more than a financial burden and they were anxious to be rid of them. They succeeded in getting rid of the Royal Canal in 1961. The Transport Act of 1960 allowed CIE to close the canal by giving suitable notice and this was done with effect from the beginning April 1961. Its decayed state was recorded in pictures and text by the *Irish Times* in 1963 (16 November) and it was commented that 'the decay evident everywhere is abundant proof that if a canal is to be maintained at all, it has to be well maintained' (p. 6). This canal had few friends in Dublin, probably because of its northside route. The Grand Canal was to prove more problematic.

The Grand Canal route

Dublin, especially south Dublin, needed more sewers in the early 1960s. In particular, a sewer from Blackhorse Bridge to the Ringsend outfall would provide for development to the south-west of Inchicore and Ballyfermot. The City Engineer advised in 1960 that the most economical route would be along the bed of the Grand Canal. Discussions were held with CIE and there was seen to be a coincidence of interests. The Streets Committee accepted such a proposal in November 1963 and it went to the full Corporation for decision. While it would be later argued that the intention always was to restore the canal to a waterway once the work was complete, the proposal from the City Engineer suggested that the waterway would cease to be a stepped high level waterway, managed by locks, and would become a graded underground culvert with a grade sewer alongside. The proposal was agreed by Dublin Corporation the following week on 11 November. Cost was the primary concern. It would cost about £1m to complete the work contemplated and about £2.5m to follow any other route. Interestingly, Mr Rory O'Brolchain, the Deputy City Manager, was reported as saying that the small use made of the canal as a waterway must suggest consideration of its use as an arterial road (*Irish Times*, 12 November 1963, p. 6). So it seems that the sewer project was the battle line. If it was successful, then the arterial road became a possibility. There was a vote in Dublin Corporation and the proposal to build the sewer was passed by 15 votes to 12 out of a total membership of 45. The voting does not seem to have been along party lines and did not appear to have spurred the interest of the Council since many members were absent. It did show that support, among those who were interested, was finely divided and, thus, the proposal was destined to rumble on for some time. It was because of this that no great attention was paid to Schaechterle's ring road proposal despite it being central to his plan.

By 1967, it seemed that Dublin Corporation had won the day when it was announced that a section of the Grand Canal would receive government approval for an 'indefinite' closure (*Irish Times*, 21 October 1967, p. 1). However, it fell to the Minister for Finance, Charles Haughey, to clarify what was meant when he answered questions on the matter on 8 November 1967. As time passed, a considerable public lobby in favour of saving the canal grew in fervour and politicians took note. The government and Mr Haughey answered very carefully that they were prepared to support the Corporation's proposal if they were satisfied with it and that the canal would be restored as a waterway. Mr Haughey emphasized that latter point: 'I think we need have no worries about that. All the Government have decided at the moment is that the Corporation may take it that provided a satisfactory scheme is put forward, permission to close the canal temporarily will be given, but the Government's firm intention is that the closing will be nothing other than temporary' (Dáil Debates, 230(13), col. 2053). This was really the end of the matter, since it was never the intention to reopen the canal, and consideration moved to other solutions and it took until 1972 before the matter was finally decided. In that year, control of the Grand Canal passed to the OPW and it was announced in October of that year that a three-mile tunnel costing £3.5m would run alongside the Grand Canal from Dolphin Road to Grand Canal Street. The contract was award to C.V. Buchan and Co. from the UK and it was estimated that the project would take five years to complete (*Irish Times*, 26 October 1972, p. 13).

This was also the end of the ring road but there was a decision to proceed with the 'tangent square' part of the proposal. It was a decision taken only in principle (see *Irish Times*, 26 1968, p. 13 for an outline of the discussion at the General Purposes Committee of Dublin Corporation) and it was not intended to begin work before 1972. What was decided was close to the suggestions of the consultants and involved a road system that was to be about 5 miles (8km) in length and which was to cost £22m. The route envisaged was from Gardiner Street in the east, along Parnell Street, North King Street and then south along Blackhall Place to cross the river via a new bridge. From there it was to head south into Pimlico before beginning its generally easterly journey along the Coombe, Kevin Street, St Stephen's Green South to turn north again via Merrion Row, Merrion Square and Pearse Street. The route would cross the river via a one-way system involving Butt Bridge and a new

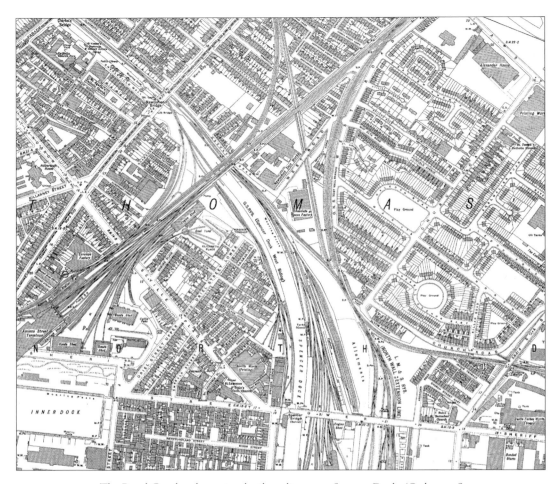

101. The Royal Canal and associated railway lines near Spencer Dock. (Ordnance Survey plan, 1:2,500, Sheet 18(VIII), 1938.)

bridge to the east of the Custom House and thence into Gardiner Street. It was set to involve several flyovers and underpasses and a number of new streets were required. The Corporation emphasized that no buildings of value would be damaged and, as an example of their sensitivity to the urban landscape, they pointed to the fact that they had rejected proposals for a flyover near St Patrick's Cathedral.

This was seen as a start and a start had to be made somewhere. It was felt that this element of the plan would relieve congestion on O'Connell Street, O'Connell Bridge and D'Olier Street (*plus ça change*) as well as permitting Dublin Bus to develop circular bus routes.

One of the other proposals was for an enhanced routeway that would run along the coast from Merrion to Sandymount and thence into the city. This inevitably would have encroached on the strand and provided a barrier between the residents of the district and the seashore, no matter how creatively the roadway was made. The confrontation here was set for the 1970s but the proposers of the roadway were always going to lose. The residents' associations in the area were the most experienced and well organized in the city, having honed their skills in the middle 1960s in relation to the Port and Docks Board plan to build a number of industries on reclaimed land near the port.

Myles Wright
In tandem with Schaechterle, Myles Wright produced his analysis of the ideal transport arrangement for Dublin in the light of the creation of four new towns to the west. It is much more conceptual in design and the level of detail is nowhere near as great but the essence of it was to transform the radial system into a grid system. The four new towns recommended by the plan – Blanchardstown, Lucan, Clondalkin and Tallaght – were designed to be spatially separate and to grow westwards as linear settlements along the major arteries that ran through them. The consultants were not unaware of the effect of increasing car ownership on the city. They thought it desirable to encourage the dispersal of employment throughout the existing city so as to prevent congestion in the city centre by reducing traffic flows. Similarly, they argued that the future road system for Dublin should be on the basis of a grid system instead of a radial system, thus permitting travel between any part of the city without the need to go towards the centre. This grid was to be developed over time but the framework was to be anchored to a basic system of high-quality major routes capable of taking large quantities of traffic. In this they adopted and adapted a number of the proposals of the Schaechterle study of Dublin city.

The report accepted that most employment would continue to be located within the canal ring and called for the improvement of central routes and the provision of more parking spaces. However, these changes would be expensive to achieve and, arguing the case for dispersal of employment, the report noted that 'they [the traffic improvements in the centre] will be costly and slow in construction and cannot be provided in step with rising volumes of motor traffic [while] rail access to the centre for daily workers has a precarious future' (Wright, 1967, paragraph 4:37).

The report therefore proposed a series of new roads which would permit easy cross-city movements without the need to travel through the centre, making a distinction between what was described as a traffic route and an access road. The report made the point that existing cross-routes comprised lengths of access roads that differed widely in character and convenience, and were on the whole discouraging to the motorist (Wright, 1967, paragraph 4:38).

The recommendations were for five major routeways:

- A Northern Cross-Route from Blanchardstown to the coast, which it was hoped would link the new employment centres in Blanchardstown with Ballymun (still the vision of the future at the time), Baldoyle and on to Howth.
- A route that would largely follow the line of the Royal Canal across the north of the city, which would facilitate the development of the port of Dublin, providing easy access to the west.
- A Southern Cross-Route that would link Dún Laoghaire with the new town of Tallaght and thence to the Naas Road, the main route to the south and south-west.
- A north-south route that would run west of the Phoenix Park linking Blanchardstown with Tallaght, which would form the spine from which the new towns would radiate outwards. This was the essential linking route between the new towns as well as completing the ring around the city.
- A route that had already been proposed by the Schaechterle group, who suggested a coastal link between the Belfast Road and the main road south to Wexford. This would run east of the Custom House across a new bridge to be built for the purpose.

These routes would form the framework of a new grid of traffic routes, incorporating some new roads. Wright did not see much future for commuter rail traffic without major subsidy and detected reluctance among workers to travel by rail, involving as it did the necessity to travel first to a station and then take the train, something Abercrombie had noted previously. The report is generally portrayed as being unenthusiastic about public transport but this view is unfair. Certainly the view of the report was essentially that as people get more money they will buy more cars and they will want to use these cars. The provision of the new framework of roads would give the people of the suburbs such mobility that public transport would be unable to compete, though it would have to be provided for those without a car. At the same time

Wright recognized the futility of trying to plan for complete freedom for the car in the city centre. In the second part of the report, which provides more detail about the proposals, it states that:

> even if it were thought desirable to maintain a high level of radial movement towards the centre, it is highly improbable that roads could be built at a rate which would match the growing demands of traffic, with the result that as the new roads were completed they would be immediately filled to congestion. The result of attempting to meet the demand would be the destruction of much of the best of Dublin, both by the enlargement of the radial roads and by the creation of vast parking areas in the City centre, where cars would stand idle all day on some of the most valuable land in the country.
>
> (Wright, 1967, paragraph 17.36)

The report recognized that the majority of journeys to work in the city centre would have to be made by bus and that parking restrictions would have to be imposed in the centre and at a cost that would make commuters consider whether it was worth the effort to bring a car. However, commuters would demand a fast and frequent public transport service and suggestions were made for the provision of limited access bus routes to speed the movement of buses from the suburbs into the city centre.

On reading, it seems quite a balanced report which depends for its success on the building of the new road system and the removal of as much employment from the central area as possible. In the absence of the latter, the need or the usefulness of the cross-routes would be seriously undermined. The problem with the Wright Report is that, like many others, only bits and pieces were put in place and the report's authors were then criticized when the result was not what was expected.

Dublin Transportation Study and Travers Morgan

The reader will be aware that elements of these plans were implemented over time but that the overall concepts never happened. That was partly due to an increasing level of activism in the population so that road plans now attracted considerable public debate and often downright opposition. It was also due to a major change, once again, in the approach to road planning that saw the emphasis shift to motorways and new roads. This was the outcome of the Dublin Transportation Study, which was undertaken by An Foras Forbartha in 1971. This study took the view that more was needed than just

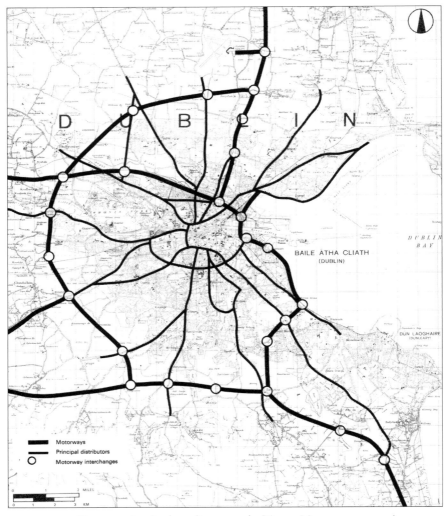

102. Transportation Study outline network. (Travers Morgan, 1973, p. 4.)

improvements to existing roads, though they did seek to discourage the use of the car for commuting. They proposed an orbital motorway system, elements of which are recognizable today – the M1, the M50 and the M11. However, this system was intended to have a motorway along the line of the Royal Canal as well as one along the coast, then south-westwards along Foster's Avenue towards Sandyford where it would join with the outer ring. Closer to the city centre, a key element of Schaechterle's plan was an inner tangent ring road or 'tangent square'. The Corporation had accepted the need for such a road in

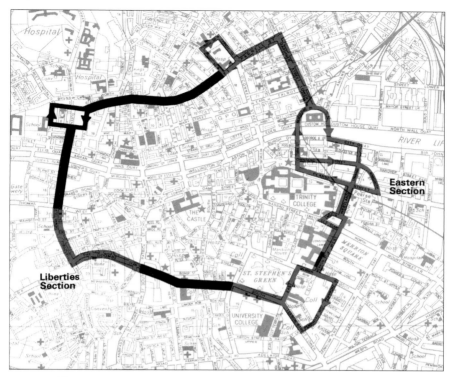

103. Dublin Corporation's plan for an inner tangent square. (Travers Morgan, 1973, p. 2.) The lighter shading shows the 'sensitive areas'.

principle and consultants R. Travers Morgan were given the task in 1971 of developing the plans and integrating them into the orbital motorway system described above. The brief took much of the route of the inner tangent as given but the consultants were asked to examine the impact of the tangent square in what were described as two sensitive areas – the Liberties in the south-west and the Georgian area of the south-east. In the event, they agreed with the Dublin Transportation Study and deleted much of the eastern segment of the tangent.

Travers Morgan's overall concept for the city centre can be seen in their schematic which is reproduced here. It was for a distributor system where traffic is filtered into smaller and smaller cells at it approaches its destination and it involved a road system of different scale from motorways to local access roads. There was little specific provision for public transport though two bus-only routes were suggested for Camden/George's Street and along Nassau Street. The northern section of the tangent followed closely on what had been

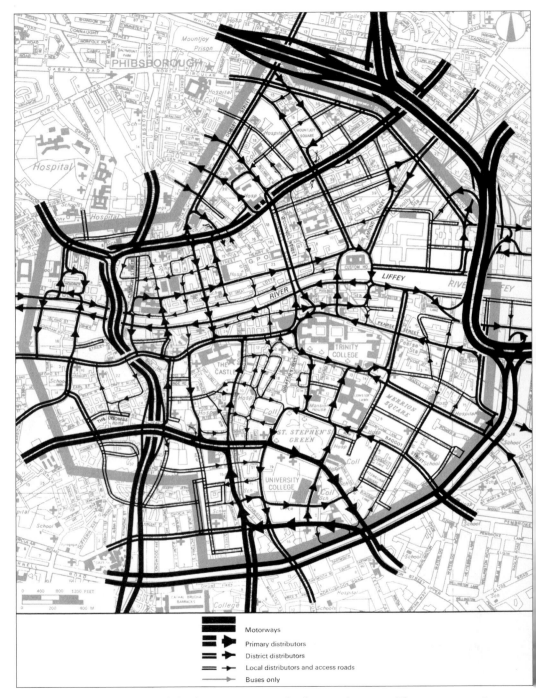

104. The recommended plan by Travers Morgan for the central city area. The tangent route is part of their system of primary disbributors. (Travers Morgan, 1973, p. 76.)

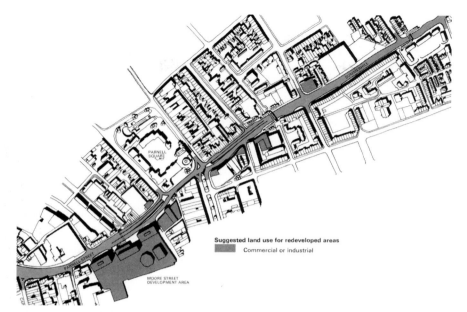

Suggested land use for redeveloped areas
Commercial or industrial

105. Recommended route for the northern part of the tangent. (Travers Morgan, 1973, p. 78.)

suggested previously. It was suggested that it link to the new Airport Motorway and the Royal Canal Motorway via an interchange near Ballybough Road. It would then follow a route westwards along Summerhill and Parnell Street and then cut across North King Street to join up with the western route near Smithfield. It was envisaged that there would be an underpass at the junction of Parnell Street and O'Connell Street and that the Parnell monument would have to be moved. This was to be a dual two-lane carriageway but with dual three lanes at difficult junctions. Most junctions, though, were to be at the same level, 'at-grade'.

The western route snaked southwards between Smithfield and Church Street. It crossed the Liffey to the east of St Paul's Church in Arran Quay and then continued between Patrick Street and Francis Street. From Kevin Street to Clanbrassil Street, it followed the line of Blackpitts. This was to be a very imposing road. They anticipated that it would need to have two three-lane carriageways with grade-separated interchanges. This was inevitably going to be controversial.

The southern element would have spared the Coombe by running on a more southerly route between Cork Street and Patrick Street. From there it proceeded across Kevin Street and cut through Cuffe Street, which would need to be widened on its southern edge. From there it would feed into the one-way

106. Recommended route for the western part of the tangent. (Travers Morgan, 1973, p. 79.)

107. The Kevin Street/Patrick Street interchange as imagined by the *Architectural Review*, 1974, p. 289. The view is towards the north with St Patrick's Cathedral on the right of the image.

system that had been introduced around St Stephen's Green. This element of the tangent would be like the northern element and comprise two two-lane carriageways.

The consultants were concerned about the impact of their plans and noted that 'recent opposition to road proposals in Dublin has shown clearly that without general public acceptance of proposals there is little hope of their implementation' (p. 5). To that end, they included measures for noise abatement and the minimizing of visual disturbance.

The scale of the western route was such that its impact on the urban environment was going to be severe. At Kevin Street, they required a grade-separated junction with an underpass for north–south heading traffic. They recognized that the scale of the junction was going to be large because of the volumes of traffic but they did not make any particular issue about this. Northwards towards High Street, they intended to make use of the geography so that the west side of the road would run between 1m and 3m below ground, though the east side would be an equivalent height over ground. At Thomas Street it would about 3.5m below ground level and it would run beneath the existing road at Cornmarket. However, it would not return to ground level to cross the Liffey. Rather, an overpass would be constructed at 8m above the river. This one would be for through traffic while there would be two other bridges, at quay level, on either side of the main bridge. They recognized that this would be visually intrusive but they argued that this route was the best route of all the ones that they had studied.

However well they argued the case, there is no doubt that the road would have cut a swathe through the urban fabric and made Dublin Corporation's earlier proposals for the area seem no more than a scratch on the landscape.

108. The Liffey bridge as suggested by Travers Morgan. (Travers Morgan, 1973, p. 80.)

109. The Liffey bridge as imagined by the *Architectural Review*, 1974, p. 289.

With only limited crossing points, it would have been a dramatic barrier in the landscape, as dramatic as a river or a canal. This point was returned to in an analysis of Dublin undertaken by the *Architectural Review* in a special issue published in 1974 and entitled 'A future for Dublin'. They described these proposals as 'traffic solution or blitzkrieg' (p. 288). They produced their own set of drawings to illustrate in their view what the impact of these solutions would be. They argued that their illustrations gave an indication of:

> the environmental havoc which the traffic proposals would create (this havoc is played down in the report by a sketch on p. 80 of the 'Traffic Plan' which makes the operation appear quite innocuous). The consultants proposed a grade-separated crossing of the Liffey with a

high level bridge for through traffic about 80ft wide and raised some 26ft about quay level. Flanking this bridge would be two lane slip roads jointed by quay-level bridges. The result would be a gap over 200ft wide blasted through the terraces in 7 [the illustration]. 9 shows the present tight built urban setting of St Patrick's Cathedral and 10 the dreadful effect of carrying out the underpass proposals shown on the plan.

(p. 288)

The consultants did not expend much effort in providing a realistic view of the impact of this routeway; their bridge over the Liffey is seen from a distance. The images shown in the *Architectural Review* show an entirely different kind of reality. Fortunately, whatever the reaction to the plan, its price tag of at least £14m ensured that it would not become a reality anytime soon. Thus ended the grand plan for the tangent square. It did not prevent, however, a return to earlier concepts of tangent routes and their ultimate construction.

Future change?

At the end of the 1960s, there was a dawning realization that a key moment had been reached in the relationship between the city and the car. It was still believed that there was scope and necessity to expand the road network to accommodate more cars at greater speeds. There seemed to be no fundamental objection to the concept of urban motorways where great swathes of concrete would segment the city into different quarters. It was understood that car ownership was set to grow, the city was set to be more suburbanized and traffic was inevitably going to increase. It was an absence of money rather than of desire that prevented these projects from becoming a reality and this is undoubtedly something for which Dubliners should be grateful and not for the first time.

It was also understood that planning for traffic could not be done in isolation from planning for the city. Both Buchanan and Schaechterle had recognized this but traffic planning in Dublin was far more advanced than city planning. The *Irish Times* published a three-part series on traffic in Dublin in November 1969. These pieces, written by the local government correspondent, Henry Kelly, looked at the nature of the problem and the actors involved in developing solutions. He did not offer any great hope for the immediate future. He felt that there was still complacency about the problem and it seemed not to make much sense to be thinking about implementing a plan

110. A view of the M8, Glasgow's inner ring road. Begun in 1965 and intended to encircle the city, the project was stopped in 1972 and formally abandoned in 1980 with just over half of the ring completed.

with a fifteen- to twenty-year window when decisions about the future growth of the city had yet to be taken. The worry was that:

> In discussing the general traffic problem of our cities, one finds a growing concern for what those cities are going to look like. Wholesale destruction of property that is both historical and beautiful would not be acceptable to the citizens of Dublin, one presumes: yet this could happen, piece meal, without their knowing.
>
> (*Irish Times*, 20 November 1969, p. 14)

He made a crucial point towards the end of the piece that traffic was growing faster than we appeared to have the power to control. Controls were necessary in themselves and not merely as a stop gap measure while the plans were put into practice. A sense of this growing awareness is obtained from an answer to a parliamentary question in the Dáil. The Minister for Local Government, Kevin Boland, answered on the transport problems of Dublin on 30 October.

His emphasis was still on road solutions but there was recognition that the car needed to be controlled too.

> With the natural increase in the city's population, the growth in economic activity and the increase in prosperity and consequently in the ownership of motor vehicles, the demands on the street system are bound to increase. It is necessary therefore to envisage activity on different fronts—traffic management measures to get better value from the existing streets, a construction programme, for the immediate future, of such priority schemes as can be undertaken with the resources likely to be available in that period, longer term measures involving more ambitious road schemes and possibly other transport arrangements and of course the overall physical planning of the city and its environs. Regional planning also has a part to play.
>
> (Dáil Debates, 241(13), col. 2266)

It was still believed that the city could accommodate more traffic. However, the changing wind was signalled at the end of his answer when he indicated that there was a limit to what could be done:

> It must be recognized that Dublin's traffic problem cannot be solved simply by providing road and parking space for everyone wishing to use his own private car.
>
> To do so would pre-empt practically the whole of the financial resources likely to be available in the foreseeable future. Policy overall must therefore aim at reducing commuter car traffic and encouraging greater use of public transport ...
>
> I trust that what I have said will bring some reality into discussion of Dublin's traffic problem and convince people that there is no ready or magic answer and that for the near future at least congestion can be reduced only by checking the flow of commuter traffic.
>
> (Dáil Debates, 241(13), col. 2268)

The suburban city

Challenges to the city centre

The dominance of the city centre for business and shopping was a characteristic of traditional cities. Most transportation routes focused on the city centre and this gave it a comparative advantage in terms of accessibility. The relative ease with which people could reach the centre compared to other locations meant that businesses which were located there could attract from a far wider hinterland. This greater access provided superior business opportunities, which in turn required them to pay more for the location that they were occupying.

This was the classic structure of urban land-use models. The best known, the Alonso bid-rent model, set out how much particular business types were prepared to pay for particular locations. Those who could derive the greatest return from highly accessible locations would outbid other uses. There would be a changeover point at a certain distance from the city centre where the balance would shift in favour of another land use and so on. In this model, the most accessible and therefore most expensive locations were occupied by retailing. At a short distance from the city centre, the locations were not quite as accessible and footfall would be lower. Therefore, retailing could derive less of a return, would be prepared to bid less and would be displaced by commercial land uses, which were better suited to these good but not absolutely central locations. So it would go with apartments eventually giving way to private family houses.

In this simple model, the city centre was home to high-end retailing and to the commercial sector. Whatever residential component was in the city centre would be high density and expensive. The basic and simplified structure for a city structured according to the Alonso model was that of a series of concentric circles around the city centre, each circle dominated by a particular land use. This structure would be complicated by any interference in the operation of the capitalist land market, such as that resulting from the provision of social housing or, indeed, by the physical geography of the city.

The model was a reasonable description of Dublin up to the 1950s. Most people were reliant on public transport, bicycles or walking and the centre dominated the retailing and commercial life of the city. There was a hierarchy

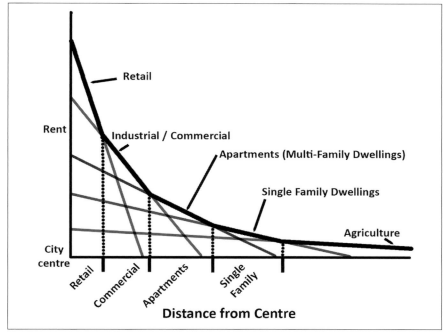

111. The basic Alonso bid-rent model.

in shopping provision with frequently purchased items being provided locally, some 'village' concentrations such as Rathmines or Drumcondra, but the city centre dominated the market for less frequent purchases – the high-order goods.

The model was useful as a simplification of reality as long as there was only one core area. This began to change as relative accessibility changed and the main cause of this was the increasing availability of the motor car. Now many parts of the city enjoyed superior accessibility and land uses that previously could only have survived in the centre began to explore the possibilities that this offered. So began the development of the suburbs as alternative locations for commerce and business. While this process began in Dublin in the 1950s, it only began to accelerate in the later years of the 1960s.

Retailing

What the census revealed
The first census of distribution, covering wholesaling and retailing, was undertaken in 1933 but the exercise was not repeated until 1951. There was

a census in 1956, 1966 and 1971. This census differed from the census of population in that there was not complete coverage; the 1971 census, for example, achieved a response rate of 76 per cent. Estimates were made for non-respondents but for this and reasons of classification changes, it is important not to make much of small changes over time.

The number of retail shops declined over the period in question but there were two phases. Between 1951 and 1956 there was an increase in the number of shops both in Dublin (defined as Dublin and suburbs) and in the State as a whole. In Dublin, numbers declined thereafter so that between 1956 and 1966, there was a reduction of 11.2 per cent and an even greater decline of 15.6 per cent in the period 1966–71. This was almost five times the decline for the State as a whole and indicates that some dramatic changes were afoot.

Table 7. Shop numbers in Dublin, 1951–71.

Year	1951	1956	1966	1971
Grocery	1,540	1,736	1,376	1,024
Grocery & public house	86	26	22	5
Public house	570	624	646	618
Fresh meat	363	427	460	376
Bread & flour confectionery	74	82	154	130
Dairy produce	193	92	14	8
Fish & poultry	55	63	76	41
Fruit & vegetables	248	214	178	138
Newsagents	790	937	586	448
Boots & shoes	112	106	111	118
Menswear	77	86		159
Womenswear	132	125		186
Drapery	300	357	555	117
Motor vehicles	81	146	395	106
Garages	179	126		208
Drugs	259	325	297	252
Hardware	181	148	154	164
Radio & electrical	109	99	117	151
Jewellery	80	109	79	90
Leather fancy goods	43	79	80	77
Books & stationery	83	102	66	66
Furniture & carpets	105	99	80	97
Other non-food	144	222	220	18
Total	**5,852**	**6,412**	**5,696**	**4,810**

Source: census of distribution 1951, 1956, 1966, 1971.
Note that the columns do not sum to the totals because not all shops were classified.

The data for Dublin city shows that grocery-type stores were the single largest category in 1951 with 26.3 per cent. Newsagents came next with 13.5 per cent and then, unsurprisingly, there were 570 public houses and these accounted for 9.8 per cent of the total. Local provision (food stores, newsagents and pubs) together accounted for over two-thirds of retail provision, though this was lower than in the State as a whole. Clothing stores were the most important non-food outlets (10.6 per cent) and the traditional drapery store was most important within the category. The remainder was distributed across electrical, hardware, books, furniture and the growing motor trade.

The increase between 1951–6 resulted in 6,412 shops in Dublin in 1956, compared to 5,852 in 1951. Most categories, including grocery and other food shops, increased in number but there were some declines in outlets for higher-order goods such as in hardware and furniture. The increase in Dublin was due to suburban development and the provision of local stores in these areas. Dublin Corporation, for example, had a policy of locating small runs of shops in its developments. The decreases were a first manifestation of the changing nature of retailing and of the economy. The mixed grocery and public house and the dairies were going; they reflected an earlier era.

Ten years passed before the next census but this time the picture revealed was one of decline. The total number of shops was down to 5,696, which was lower than the total for 1951. The big decline was in the number of food shops, especially grocery and other local provision outlets. This undoubtedly reflected the spread of the supermarket idea and the concentration of retailing into a smaller number of larger stores, something that will be discussed in more detail below. The final year for which information was available was 1971 when an even greater decline in numbers was recorded. There were now only 4,810 stores in Dublin, one thousand fewer than twenty years previously. The decline was marked across all kinds of food provision outlets and there were now 500 fewer grocery stores than in 1951 with a similar decline in the number of newsagents (see also Parker, 1973; 1974).

This did not necessarily mean a decline in the floor space devoted to retailing, however, as the trend in store size was towards larger and larger units. In 1956, almost 1,800 stores employed only one or two people but by 1971, this had declined to 1,450. In contrast, the census of 1951 did not record any stores with more than 100 employees but there were 55 stores employing between 50 and 99 people. Some of these stores grew in size but there were also new entrants so that by 1971 there were eighteen stores with between 100 and 200 employees and twelve stores which employed more than 200 people in the Dublin and Dún Laoghaire areas.

Table 8. Shops classified according to employment numbers, 1956–71.

Number employed	1956 Dublin	1956 Per cent	1966 Dublin	1966 Per cent	1971 Dublin	1971 Per cent
1	815	14.9	621	14.2	551	14.0
2	1,157	21.2	926	21.2	898	22.8
3	981	18	746	17.1	722	18.3
4	726	13.3	571	13.1	468	11.9
5–9	1,251	22.9	963	22	795	20.1
10–14	231	4.2	244	5.6	213	5.4
15–19	108	2	98	2.2	99	2.5
20–29	56	1	89	2	70	1.8
30–49	54	1	54	1.2	67	1.7
50–99	55	1	37	0.8	34	0.9
100–199			13	0.3	18	0.5
200+			11	0.3	12	0.3
Total	**5,434**		**4,373**		**3,947**	

Source: census of distribution 1956, 1966, 1971.
Note that Dún Laoghaire is included in the figures for Dublin. Its total in 1956 was 467 stores. The data relate to respondents only.

The centre versus the suburbs

High-order comparison goods are those items that are bought infrequently and where it is important for the shopper to be able to compare and contrast what is on offer. This includes clothing and shoes as well as white goods. The census of distribution for 1956 found that 78 per cent of business in the north city centre was for higher order comparison goods compared to 86 per cent in the south city centre but only 16 per cent in the suburbs. This was all about to change and the geography of the city would be changed fundamentally because of the coincidence of a number of factors. The city centre was increasingly congested and hard to travel to. Land there was expensive and retailing and services were limited in the amount of street-facing space retailers could afford. For those with a car, difficulty with finding parking added to the problem. Cheaper suburban locations offered the possibility of much more extensive operations where economies of scale could be derived. But how would customers get to these locations? Public transport reflected an older reality and was focused on the city centre. It was not easy to reach locations that were not on main routes and nodal points. This is where the growing availability of the motor car became important. The car offered flexibility and it changed the accessibility of suburban locations. Locations previously difficult to reach were now just as convenient by car as locations in the city centre. This was further emphasized by the growing suburbanization of population. The city centre was becoming more and more distant for an increasing proportion of the population and thus journeys to the city centre became more and more troublesome. Suburban locations were now closer to home in many cases. The city was about to become multi-nodal.

Self-service

Another process that would help drive change was the arrival of self-service because this allowed much larger units to be managed with relatively small staffs. Self-service was not entirely a new phenomenon in the Dublin of the 1950s. Woolworth had introduced the concept of self-service in the 1930s whereby shoppers could browse from goods set out on counter displays rather than having to commission the goods from a sales person. However, the transaction was still completed at the counter from which the goods were chosen. H. Williams experimented with the idea briefly in 1949 in their Talbot Street store but soon returned to conventional retailing. Self-service was set, however, to change how retailing was done and its adoption was a necessary step in the changing scale of retailing that occurred in the 1960s. It was first experienced in the grocery sector in Dublin but the idea soon spread into other areas. Grocery shopping was largely local in the 1950s. People would often shop several times a day and stores were typically quite small. Even in 1971, when the concept of the supermarket was well established, the census of distribution showed that, of the 1,717 food shops in the county borough and suburbs, almost half employed only one or two people. Similarly, over 1,200 of these occupied less than 500 sq. ft (46 sq. m) or about the ground floor area of a standard house. Despite their relatively small size, many such shops offered a sophisticated level of service. They might have delivered and they probably offered credit. Many households would have a 'shop book' in which orders would be written, processed by the shop owner and an account rendered. Accounts might be settled weekly or monthly or in a variety of arrangements. Self-service shopping changed this relationship. Deliveries and credit were not compatible with this new model but there was an advantage in that prices could be lower.

A sense of the difference may be seen in a letter to the *Irish Times* from the Irish Housewives' Association. It was at a time when there was a debate about retail resale price maintenance as a tactic to prevent price cutting.

> We are satisfied that the cash price stores fill an important need, particularly for the lower-income groups. If housewives are prepared to pay cash and carry home their purchases they are entitled to buy their goods at a keen price. It is fully realized that the credit grocers who deliver must pay messenger's wages and have capital to offset long-paying and non-paying customers. The cash grocer has none of this expense, and in consequence can sell at a lower price.
>
> (*Irish Times*, 14 February 1955, p. 5)

Surprisingly, perhaps, there was a hostile reaction to the idea of using self-service in some segments of society. Not everyone wanted to be seen to be shopping somewhere because of 'price'.

The genesis of the self-service idea dates back to the 1920s in the United States and, though it was a well-developed phenomenon there before the Second World War, it was well into the 1950s before it really took hold in Dublin. Retailers were somewhat wary of the idea but the grocers' lobby group, RGDATA, were generally positive about the value of the idea by the middle 1950s. They felt that it would improve turnover on the basis that 'if it can't be seen, it won't be bought' (*Irish Times*, 14 December 1956, p. 3). At the same time, it was recognized that a new phenomenon, 'pilfering', would have to be accommodated. By that year, shoppers in Dublin could enjoy the self-service experience in Cummiskey's self-service at 45 Grafton Street. Such was its novelty that they felt it necessary to explain how it worked in a newspaper advertisement (see, for example, *Irish Times*, 26 July 1956, p. 8). They emphasized the advantages of comparison shopping and the speed at which the task could be completed. This was combined with lower prices and the fact that 'when you get you get home, you will find something in your basket that you did not ask for. An itemised Receipt for all your purchases, with the correct mechanically-added Total at the bottom'.

The process was explained as follows:

> Thus when you enter our Store, you need not wait until a clerk is free to wait on you. Just take one of the baskets provided for your use, put the merchandise you select into the basket, and take it to the Check-out counter near the exit of the Store.

Successful implementation required the availability of pre-packaged goods, replacing the loose goods of the grocery counter. H. Williams argued that it

112. Self-service comes to Grafton Street. (*Irish Independent*, 31 July 1956, p. 1.)

The World's Most Modern Business Now Open

— CUMMISKEYS —

| IT'S QUICK | SELF – SERVICE | IT'S CLEAN |
| IT'S CHEAPER | GROCERY STORE | IT'S ACCURATE |

45 GRAFTON ST.

"Where the best costs less"

It gives us great pleasure to offer you—our public and customers—this modern and up-to-date Shopping Method which has proved

Our Recommendation

Thousands of satisfied customers testify to the enormous success of this Self-Service Store, which opened just a week ago in Dublin's Smartest Street.

COME, SEE FOR YOURSELF!

SUCH A GREAT SUCCESS THROUGHOUT THE WORLD

We have been advised, helped and assisted by the leading Grocers and Economists, including Self-Service Experts, on our undertaking and now can offer it to YOU AS YOUR FUTURE METHOD OF SHOPPING

"You Will Like It"

CUMMISKEY'S

SELF-SERVICE

45 GRAFTON STREET

(BESIDE ROBT. ROBERTS)

was the unavailability of sufficient pre-packaged products that stymied their use of self-service until the end of the 1950s. The trade catalogues of the time also offered a great variety of display units and food producers often provided display units either free of charge or at a greatly reduced price in order to secure good selling positions. In advocating the concept of self-service, smaller retailers sometimes argued that it had no real impact on employment, just a redeployment of people into other roles. However, this was to miss the point. It was probably true that a small grocery shop took the same number of staff to run either in a traditional format or as a self-service. However, the self-service model allowed for a far larger unit to be managed by the same staff numbers and there were significant economies of scale available. This was an impact that the small grocery shop was about to experience.

By 1971, the data suggested that most grocery establishments were still non-self-service but change was well under way and the balance of power had shifted. In Dublin, there were 194 units who described themselves as 'self-service' but 724 who said that they were not. The self-service units were the larger stores and the 26 stores who each employed more than 50 persons had a combined turnover of £20.7m, compared to the combined total of £13.7m for all non-self-service grocery stores.

Supermarkets

The potential for scale increases saw the development of the supermarket. These days, the 'supermarket' is a generic term for grocery and day-to-day shopping but in the early days the concept of scale was very important. The CSO focused on size and on the method of selling and a supermarket was defined as having at least three checkouts and a selling space of at least 2,000 sq. ft (186 sq. m). On this basis, it was at least four times larger than most traditional grocery stores. The emergence of supermarkets onto the city's landscape can hardly be described as rapid. Census data are not complete but the data for respondents for 1971 suggest that there was of the order of 109 supermarkets in the State, of which almost half were in Dublin or Dún Laoghaire, though it should also be remembered that there were other supermarket-type stores which did not meet the definition above. These employed about 1,600 staff. Thereafter, diffusion was rapid. From almost the beginning they began to have an international dimension as local businesses came into competition with what would now be called multinationals. Early locations were often in the city centre. H. Williams, for example, had their first store in Henry Street and later, in 1963, opened a supermarket in part of the Pims department store in South Great George's Street. This was directly in competition with a Power supermarket across the road at the junction with Exchequer Street and a Dunnes Stores opposite. However, they realized very quickly that there was no real future in city centre locations. The cost of land was too high for the scale of operation required. Moreover, the range of goods on offer tempted consumers to undertake larger and larger 'shops' and this in turn was facilitated by those who had a car. Suburban locations where land was cheaper suited all concerned. It meant that the stores were closer to their customers. It allowed larger, more spacious stores to be opened, with wider and wider ranges of goods and it permitted generous parking availability. So, by the early 1960s, H. Williams had stores in Killester and Churchtown, and by 1968 had eleven stores that included a 7,000 sq. ft (650 sq. m) store in Sandymount and one in Dún Laoghaire on Upper George's Street. They were planning another Dún Laoghaire store, also on George's Street and were acquiring the old Pye factory in Dundrum where they had 40,000 sq. ft (3,700 sq. m) available to them, though they did not intend to use all of this space for their supermarket. This supermarket opened on 10 January 1968 and

113. H. William's 'hypermarket' in Dundrum in the early 1970s. (A.J. Parker.)

114. Five Star supermarket in Rathmines in 1968. (Crampton photo archive.)

almost immediately was in competition with the new Dundrum shopping centre.

The international element came in the form of Associated British Foods, Garfield Weston's company. They were already a major presence in the British market under the Fine Fare brand. In Dublin, they chose a location across the road from H. Williams on South Great George's Street and it opened on

1 August 1963 under the Power supermarket brand. They began an aggressive process of expansion and soon had supermarkets on Henry Street and Talbot Street. In fact, the degree of supermarket provision became somewhat over-heated on Henry Street/Mary Street very quickly. By the final quarter of 1965, there was a H. Williams, a Power supermarket, a Home and Colonial (Liptons) store at the western end as well as a 5,000 sq. ft (465 sq. m) food hall in Roches Stores and one in Todco (run by Power Supermarkets). The suburban expansion followed a dual track of independent development and the acquisition of existing operations. Thus, in March 1965, they acquired Finn's Food Market Ltd which had stores in Raheny, Killester, Rathmines and Ranelagh and these were added to the shops in Dolphin's Barn, Kilmainham and Ballyfermot.

Into this market came the Five Star brand. This was owned by the Williams family of Tullamore who replaced their network of general merchant's stores with supermarkets. Although most of their activities were outside Dublin, they had stores in Cabra and Dalkey and they expanded quickly by opening a new supermarket at 21 Upper Baggot Street on 3 December 1965 as part of a major expansion programme that included a store in Rathmines (see the image above). To this was added a very large store of 30,000 sq. ft (2,800 sq. m) in Dundrum in 1968. In that same year, they announced the transformation of the Drumcondra Grand Cinema into a 10,000 sq. ft (930 sq. m) supermarket (*Irish Times*, 18 October 1968, p. 14), though it turned out to be much smaller than that.

A further entrant into the Dublin market was Quinn's Supermarket Ltd, which had its original base in Dundalk. They targeted the out-of-town market from the very beginning with Feargal Quinn, its managing director, quoted as saying 'the majority of people who were opening up supermarkets in Dublin and other cities, opened in the city centre, and expected shoppers to travel in from the suburbs. There were many who could not do this, who could not leave children at home, or who found it expensive and tiring' (*Irish Times*, 12 February 1964, p. 7). They analyzed the American market and noted that Saturday had become a day out when people drove to the supermarket. Their analysis was that there was a gap in the market in the developing suburb of Finglas, a gap that was later noted by Power Supermarkets. The Quinn operation in Finglas was in the heart of the village, where they bought the Casino Cinema and proceeded to develop a 9,000 sq. ft (835 sq. m) shopping area with a further 5,000 sq. ft (465 sq. m) devoted to parking. They expanded the concept of the supermarket to include a restaurant, newsagents, pharmacy and electrical goods. This store was operational by 1964 and it was joined in late 1967 by one in Sutton. Here

115. Superquinn in Finglas. (A.J. Parker.)

116. Finglas shopping centre in the 1970s.

they acquired the Sutton Cinema and this allowed them to develop an 11,000 sq. ft (1,022 sq. m) store with parking for 100 cars.

These were not the only players in the market. There were individual operators as well as other chains and competition was intense. Power Supermarkets decided to expand their operation in Finglas from 4,000 sq. ft (372 sq. m) to 14,000 sq. ft (1,300 sq. m) with parking space for 400 cars. They probably felt that there was room for both operations in the rapidly developing suburb but there were also casualties. Stewart's Cash Prices Ltd went into liquidation in January 1967 with debts of over £300,000. One of the stores was taken over by Elephant Markets Ltd. This was a 10,000 sq. ft (930 sq. m) outlet in Ballyfermot and it was ahead of its time in its approach to merchandizing. With a slogan of 'pile it high and sell it cheap', goods were displayed on pallets rather than on normal display shelves and there was no storeroom. By far the best known casualty, however, was the Findlater group. Established in 1823, these had been high-class grocers and a household name with branches throughout the city and very much a middle-class appeal. They could not withstand the changing retail environment. They had tried converting ten of their stores to self-service but they also hoped to retain their market by the introduction of a telephone shopping service in late 1967. This involved the establishment of a home delivery service with a call centre at Carysfort Avenue, Blackrock, which would handle the phone orders for most of their branches, with the exception of Howth and Malahide. The orders would then be passed to staff 'shoppers' who would pick the goods in the stores and they would then be dispatched by delivery vans. Orders were available either on credit or cash on delivery and customers were assured that they would get supermarket prices (*Irish Times*, 28 November 1967, p. 12). They were ahead of their time in that this is now the model for online grocery shopping. However, it was not enough and on 30 December 1968, it was announced that the Power Supermarket group would take over the company (*Irish Times*, 31 December 1968, p. 1). Power Supermarkets were interested only in a handful of the stores, such as Dún Laoghaire, Rathmines, Baggot Street and Dalkey, and they indicated that they would dispose of the premises in Howth, Malahide, Dorset Street, Blackrock and Foxrock. Figures produced at the time indicated the stark reality. Findlater were generating £1 per sq. ft per week on cash sales whereas Power were generating £2 per week on the same basis. Findlater neither had the capacity to advertise nor the scale in their shops to match the selling power of their competitors.

Dunnes Stores had been selling food and fresh fruit as well as drapery using the supermarket model since 1960 when they opened on South Great George's Street but they dramatically changed the scale of operations and firmly placed the suburbs in competition with the city centre when, in October 1966, they opened their Cornelscourt store. It was described at the time as a shopping

117. The Findlater store in O'Connell Street, Dublin.

118. Findlater site post-redevelopment.

centre, which, if accurate, would make it the first such in Ireland. However, it does not fit quite the definition of a multi-unit operation since it was a wholly owned business. The store had 25,000 sq. ft (2,325 sq. m) for its drapery operations and a large supermarket. It was opened by the Taoiseach on 28 October 1966 and when fully developed it offered 700 car parking spaces and it was planned to offer additional services on a concession basis. As Mr Ben Dunne put it, 'people on their shopping expeditions from that area, accessible to the inhabitants of Foxrock, Blackrock, Stillorgan, Sallynoggin, Dún Laoghaire need no longer trek to the traffic ridden city for their needs' (*Irish Times*, 8 October 1966, p. 10). Cleverly, he introduced shoppers to the store from far-flung places such as Bray and Dún Laoghaire by operating special buses in November 1966, just as bargain train fares had been used to lure shoppers from the country to Dublin stores. He charged 1s. for a return fare and used the ordinary bus stops as pick-up points.

Dunnes was not to be the last entrant into the market. By the end of the decade Quinnsworth had emerged as a flamboyant force. Though still small in numbers, their stores were large in scale. The Ballymun store had 56,000 sq. ft (5,200 sq. m) of floor space and over twenty check-outs. Together with the Ballyfermot and Rathfarnham stores, they controlled over 100,000 sq. ft (9,290 sq. m) of shopping space. As scale grew, a new term – the hypermarket – began to be mentioned in retail circles. These were units large enough to service an entire region and, indeed, replace the normal shopping units within a town (see Parker, 1975).

So by the end of the 1960s, there was a well-developed, large-scale supermarket retailing sector that had both a major presence in the city centre and in the suburbs. It was a serious problem to the small, traditional grocers who had no ability to compete on the same basis. If Findlater, for all its status and longevity, could not survive, it is hardly surprising that there was a major clearance of smaller local stores.

The potential to take the supermarket idea even further was recognized even if the technology was not quite as developed as it needed to be. An experiment in Wallasey, near Liverpool, sought to exploit the growing availability of electronics. The idea was that instead of going around a supermarket and gathering up the goods to bring to the checkout, the shopper instead gathered up punched cards. Where the item was displayed, a punched card was available. The shopping cart, therefore, comprised a series of these punched cards which, when presented to the checkout assistant resulted in an itemised bill and an instruction to the store to assemble the order. All the shopper had to do was pay for the shop and then collect the assembled order. This was seen to offer the advantage to the retailer of allowing many more lines of goods to be on display in the store and it was reported that pilfering was dramatically reduced. There were also reduced costs in merchandising and shelf-stacking and the owner had an efficient stock control system. Though there were a number of examples of this and similar schemes, the idea quickly faded; it was a step too far for the times. The cards were fiddly and the systems were not always as efficient as they were supposed to be. But the main problem was that the customers liked to choose their own products, even when they were pre-packaged and non-perishable.

Shopping centres

Up to this point competition between the centre and the suburbs was largely confined to food retailing but a final stage would widen the competitive base to all aspects of retailing. This was the shopping centre. While the concept goes back to the nineteenth century and perhaps before that, the modern shopping centre dates from the early years of the twentieth century. They emerged in the United States with the decentralization of general merchandise stores into sites at the junction of major routeways. Soon these were developed by enterprising businessmen into strips of shops that fronted onto the streets but provided parking for customers at the rear or the side of the strip. These strip centres were very common in the United States by the end of the 1920s. From there it was a logical step to add comparison good shopping and to extend the range of what was on offer. Some early developments were the Country Club Plaza in Kansas city in 1922–3 and the River Oaks Centre in Houston in 1937. These were developed to service a high-status residential area but, in both cases, the main roads ran through the centre. Another example was the Highland Park Centre in Dallas but, in this case, the shop frontages were turned away from the street and from this developed the basic model for a shopping centre. This was suggested by Dawson as having 'the site all in one piece, not bisected by public streets, with individual stores built and managed as a unit with a unified image, under single ownership control and with the amount of on-site parking determined by parking demand' (Dawson, 1983, p. 6). With the need for significant redevelopment in Britain in the post-war period and the new towns programme, there was ample opportunity to introduce the shopping centre concept there. Shopping centre development was not confined to green field sites in the suburbs, it also formed part of extensive redevelopments in the city centre. The opening of the Bull Ring

119. Kansas City Country Club Plaza in the 1940s.

120. The Highland Park shopping centre in Dallas.

centre in Birmingham in 1964 or the Elephant and Castle scheme in London in 1965 demonstrated the potential for change within existing urban environments. While land here was not as cheap as in the suburbs, it was felt that planned shopping centres could better leverage city centre locations and,

121. The Bull Ring shopping centre in Birmingham.

122. Elephant and Castle in London. (*Illustrated London News*, 3 April 1965, p. 9.)

with parking provision and the concept of 'one-stop shopping', compete with suburban centres. While developers were enthusiastic about these possibilities, the transformation of urban landscapes, especially in smaller towns where the potential for growth was limited, often led to the abandonment of the old centre and its replacement with a shopping centre.

A clear hierarchy quickly emerged. At the bottom were the neighbourhood centres. These were designed to service the day-to-day needs of shoppers. They were not fundamentally different in scale to the strip developments of an earlier generation. For example, it was noted in the previous volume how one of the selling points of the Mount Merrion Estate had been the provision of a local shopping centre – an arcade of shops. The main difference now was the separate location and the provision of car parking spaces. It was the next level at which services similar to those available in the town centre appeared. These were often referred to as 'community centres' and offered greater depth and breadth in shop types. These would typically range in size from about 10,000 sq. m to 30,000 sq. m. An important concept in a shopping centre of this type was the 'anchor tenant'. This was the shop that was the main draw for people to the centre, it generated the footfall that sustained the other shops. The anchor would either be a supermarket or a department store or sometimes both. Competition would be managed so that the mix of shops was such as to provide a wide range of comparison shopping but not such as to dilute business. Thus, it would not be usual to have two supermarkets in a centre of this size, though larger centres could sustain them. However, there was no fundamental problem in having larger and larger centres and very soon the regional shopping centre began to appear. This, as the name implied, aimed to service an entire region and one centre could have more than the entire floorspace of a city centre. These might have several department stores and/or several supermarkets. They proved to be a very controversial entity as they had the potential to wipe out business in many adjacent city and town centres. In the UK, an example of a modern day regional shopping centre is the Trafford Centre, which is near Manchester and within minutes of the M60. The centre offers 185,000 sq. m of shopping space, over 200 shops and parking for 11,500 cars. It has numerous department stores, supermarkets, food halls and is located so that 10 per cent of the UK's population is no more than a 45-minute drive away. It is estimated that it gets in the order of 35 million visitors per year. However, this pales into insignificance when compared to what is being built currently in China.

It was to be a long time before regional-scale shopping centres became a feature of Irish cities or even of Dublin. The majority were neighbourhood or

123. An aerial view of the Trafford Centre. Note the extent of the parking provision.
(Google Earth.)

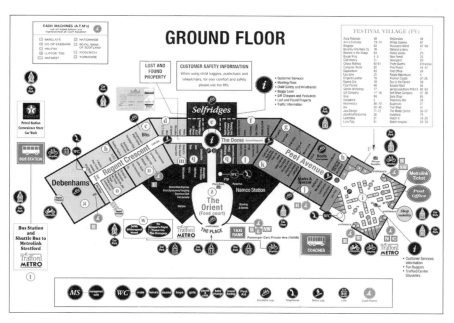

124. Ground floor of the Trafford Centre.

community centres but the community level centres were of sufficient scale to cause competition for the city centre. The first shopping centre in Dublin was opened in Stillorgan. Its formal opening date was 2 December 1966 but because it was not fully operational until 1967, it is the latter date that is generally used. It offered parking and a range of shops arranged in a series of malls. As was common for the time, the entire centre was not climate controlled and people were exposed to the elements as they wandered to and fro, despite the provision of a covered walkway. Most of the major facilities were at ground-floor level, though there were upper floors with some smaller shops within some units. However, the design in Stillorgan was of a much higher standard than some of the anonymous blocks that were built later in other locations.

Comparisons were made with the Lijnbahn in Rotterdam, then regarded as one of the innovative approaches to shopping within city centres. It comprised a long-straight pedestrianized street with shops on either side and marketing displays along the walkway. Completed in 1953, it replaced the main shopping street, which was destroyed during the war. Mr Hardie, chairman of MEPC who developed the centre, commented at the opening of the Stillorgan centre that he thought that the centre would add something architecturally to Dublin (*Irish Times*, 2 December 1966, p. 12). That might be arguable but what was not was that it marked a signal shift in the geography of the city. When it was first announced in May 1965, the plan was for 56 shops and parking for 600 cars on a 280,000 sq. ft (26,000 sq. m) site with a built area of approximately 110,000 sq. ft (10,200 sq. m). There were to be three anchors, two supermarkets and a department store, and among the facilities was to be a nursery and a playground for children (*Irish Times*, 11 May 1965, p. 6). As was common, the circulation flows were managed to ensure that shoppers were drawn past several stores. This was done by dispersing the anchors throughout the centre to create a circular flow.

The mix of tenants was managed. In addition to the anchors, there were butchers, chemists, dry cleaners, clothing stores, newsagents, electrical goods stores, delicatessens, a wine merchant, jewellers, carpet sales, a travel agent, an optician and a barber. Competition was permitted in that more than one outlet of a particular kind was allowed, especially in those areas where comparison shopping was the norm. The catchment area was estimated to have about 150,000 people within a three-mile radius (5km) of the centre and this was expected to rise to about 220,000 by 1971. The maximum drive time that would be tolerated was estimated at being twenty-five minutes but it was

125. An example of uninspired shopping centre design. The Boyne shopping centre in 1979.

126. The Lijnbaan in Rotterdam in the 1950s.

reckoned that the hinterland would comprise those within a fifteen-minute drive. This suggested that shoppers would come from as far away as Donnybrook, Dean's Grange, Cabinteely or Foxrock, with those with access to the main arteries coming from further afield. This was solidly middle-class Dublin with average incomes of about £2,000 per year but disposable income

127. Stillorgan shopping centre and environs upon opening.

would have been relatively limited in the early years because the residents were mainly younger families with children.

At the time of opening, it was claimed that 85 per cent of the units had been reserved. The selling point of the letting agent, Osborne King & Megran, had been the concept of 'one stop shopping' (*Irish Times*, 28 July 1966, p. 12). This was the introduction of a Continental concept whereby shoppers were offered the opportunity to do a range of shopping in one location within easy access of their car. There was more car parking than could be fitted along both sides of Grafton, Henry and George's streets (if it was allowed), there were no limits to the time that could be spent and there was nobody to require the car to move or impose a fine. In short, the argument was that there was no need to proceed beyond the Stillorgan centre and make one's way into the city centre. However, the centre was not an overnight success despite its very positive reception in the press. The press believed that there was a need for additional shopping provision in the suburbs. It was seen as the 'answer to the suburban dweller's shopping problems'. A puff piece in the *Irish Times* on

128. The Stillorgan shopping centre upon opening. (Crampton photo archive.)

11 December 1967 described how everyone shopping was smartly dressed and young. A piece by Terry Keane the previous summer had also noted how up to the minute was the place. She described a new 'fashion supermarket' for the young. The clothes were described as being 'way out and the prices are way down' (*Irish Times*, 4 July 1967, p. 6).

The original supermarket anchor was going to be Findlater but following the demise of the brand, the anchor role passed to Quinnsworth. There had been a Quinnsworth store in the centre from the beginning but it sold variety goods rather than food. It was decided very early on that the future of Quinnsworth lay in food retailing and they took the 4,000 sq. ft (372 sq. m) store that had been destined for Findlater. By the early 1970s, this had been transformed into 15,000 sq. ft (1,390 sq. m) of selling space. However, in an interview in 1971, Mr Quinn noted that the early days had been bleak.

At that time the Stillorgan centre was known by the representatives as 'the morgue'. They used to say that Ben Dunne used to start laughing out at Donnybrook and usen't to stop till he got to Cornelscourt – used to drive by it (the Centre) just for a bit of fun.

(*Irish Times*, 20 October 1971, p. 13)

There was turnover in the units, even in the very beginning, but the arrival of Bewley's in 1969, their first outlet outside of the city centre, was an important vote of confidence. If this was an unsteady start, it was only temporary because the shopping centre concept was well established by the end of the decade. It was seen as part of a developing affluent society where time costs involved in such activities as shopping detracted from other possible activities. A piece in the *Irish Times* in 1970s made the point explicitly that the established city centre had to look to its laurels. For the first time, there was recognition that large out-of-town centres could be real competition. The author suggested that 'the only way to compete is by putting the like of Henry Street and Mary Street under one roof, knock the whole lot down and rebuild a shopping arcade that will bring back all the excitement of town shopping. Allied to all the advantages of ease of shopping, ease of parking, low price, great variety' (*Irish Times*, 31 October 1970, p. A3).

It was not long before a second shopping centre was developed south of the river, this time in Dundrum, and it was almost complete at the end of the decade. It was on a rather small site, not more than 18,000 sq. m, but it had the advantage of being very close to the existing village centre. It was a relatively small centre, about 60,000 sq. ft (5,600 sq. m) and architecturally it was rather disappointing. However, its anchor was a 30,000 sq. ft (2,800 sq. m) supermarket with the Five Star brand, directly competing with the H. Williams development in the old Pye factory. The centre was set to offer chemists, restaurants, fish and poultry shops, newsagents, shoe shops, a garden centre and a car showroom with a total of about twenty plus shops and with parking space for 500 cars. Unlike the Stillorgan centre, which aimed for a very large hinterland, this was smaller in scale and aimed to serve the 5,500 new households in Dundrum.

The Phibsborough development, which was opened on 24 October 1969, was different in many respects. It was located in the north inner suburbs – unlike both the Stillorgan and Dundrum centres, which were suburban and were drawing on new housing developments. Phibsborough was a well-established local village with its own shopping provision. The housing areas

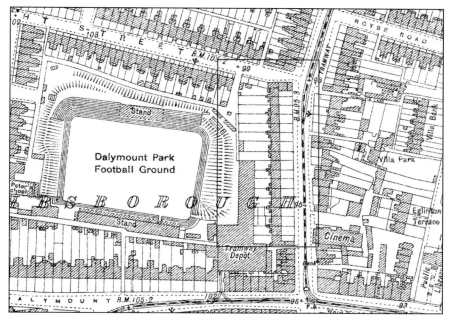

129. The site for the Phibsborough centre. (Ordnance Survey plan, 1:2,500, Sheet 18(III), 1939.)

130. The Phibsborough centre with a Power supermarket in 1969.

in the locality were mature, the local authority developments to the west in Cabra dated to the 1930s and 1940s. It was not welcomed by the local traders and the building was delayed by at least three years because of this. The local traders appealed in May 1966 against the planning permission for the centre on the grounds that local shopping provision was already adequate and the area was already congested (*Irish Times*, 17 May 1966, p. 5). The centre involved the demolition of a row of twenty-one cottages, with substantial gardens front and rear. This was held up by the *Irish Times* in 1969 as a good example of urban renewal. It quoted Thomas Murphy, of MBK auctioneers and valuers, as saying:

> I knocked at the doors of 21 cottages at Phibsboro. They were single storeyed and sad and depressing and had been dying for about 50 years. A few had fought back but the most modern amenity of many was a toilet at the bottom of the garden. Most of them were occupied by old people, and many had lived there for over 60 years. It was not, accordingly, just a matter of money but of individual human problems.
>
> (*Irish Times*, 1 November 1969, A10)

It had been reported some six years previously that tenants had been offered £500 to move (*Irish Times*, 6 July 1963, p. 13). The tenancies had been taken over, it appears, by the developers or their associates and there was underlying threat that those who did not leave would be evicted, in line with the law. It is an interesting window into the time. The development was seen positively by the *Irish Times* writer and the replacement of housing with shops and office blocks and the displacement of elderly long-term residents did not produce negative comment. Today developers might be less likely to explain how they went about getting vacant possession from elderly and vulnerable people who had spent perhaps the greater part of their lives in the houses.

The centre was also different in that it was a mixed office and shopping development. The main and distinguishing feature was the office tower that, at eight storeys, dominated the local skyline. It contained approximately 34,000 sq. ft (3,160 sq. m) of office space and it was apparent early on that is was going to be dependent on a State letting to fill it. The shopping provision was relatively unimaginative. It comprised a strip development with about fifteen shops and about 30,000 sq. ft (2,800 sq. m) of shopping space with a Power supermarket as the anchor. Parking provision was both awkward and limited with 270 spaces (they claimed) on different levels.

The Ballymun shopping centre development promised to be the most interesting of all. This was a green field site and an opportunity to showcase the potential of suburban developments as part of the innovative Ballymun housing scheme. It was still being referred to as a 'new town' during this period and had the advantage of an over-arching plan and a single developer. In August 1966 the Minister for Local Government, Mr Blaney, invited developers to make submissions indicating their capacity to undertake the brief for the centre which was intended not only to provide shopping but also to serve as the town centre with a variety of community services, including a swimming pool. The provision of swimming pools as a community service was a developing policy at the time and part of a wider agenda of providing both leisure activities and exercise opportunities (Talja, 2014).

Unfortunately, the centre proved to be a disappointment. Its design was uninspired and bleak, even when new, though it did enjoy some early success, particularly with the Quinnsworth anchor. A footprint of 350,000 sq. ft (32,400 sq. m) was provided for the entire centre and the various walkways into the residential area focused on it. The shopping centre itself comprised a simple cross design, giving four shopping 'streets' with the main anchors at the junction of the arms. The shops faced inwards along 'streets' and there was protection from the elements. The original plan envisaged 111,800 sq. ft (10,400 sq. m) of retail space over two levels with two department stores, two supermarkets, some fifty shops and two pubs plus filling stations, an entertainment area and a swimming pool. The completed centre, not as originally planned, was named the 'Seven Towers Shopping Centre' in recognition of the most distinctive element of the local housing design and had its own advertising jingle, heard on radio: 'seven towers shopping centre … a better place to shop'. The intention was that it would serve not only Ballymun but become an important draw for the entire northside. To that end, the developers were prepared to contemplate the building of multi-storey car parks if necessary.

Unfortunately, the building of the town centre was not phased in time with the housing development. This was a mistake, a fact recognized by Mr Kerr of Holland & Hannen & Cubitts (Property Management) Ltd, one of the agents involved in the development, but he absolved the planners.

> With hindsight part of the town centre should have been built a lot earlier in the schemes. But I think the problem was that to launch this housing scheme was a fairly vast enterprise and perhaps the largest one

of its size in Europe at the time. The planners could, I think, be forgiven if [they] did not appreciate the urgency of getting the town centre off the ground.

(*Irish Times*, 29 May 1968, A6)

This was a housing development on the edge of the city with little public transport and no other facilities within walking distance. It would have beggared belief that any planner could fail to understand the need to provide for the population who were being located to this new world. The reality was that the planners were well aware of the problem and, as has been discussed in the previous volume, *Dublin, 1950–1970*, Dublin Corporation made sterling efforts to have the services in Ballymun provided at the same time as the houses.

As a result, over 2,000 residents had nowhere to shop for a considerable period of time and this necessitated the provision of temporary shopping facilities (*Irish Independent*, 31 August 1968, p. 12). Kerr also said that he was disappointed that the centre was not bigger but this too was entirely within the control of the project team.

These were undoubtedly elements in a rapid disillusionment with the Ballymun project and it was already beginning its downward spiral just as the centre was nearing completion. The town centre project was a wasted opportunity to show what could be created in a context of a brand new residential development where there was next to no competition and where there were no constraints on getting the design right.

Opening hours

Restrictions on opening hours had been part of the retailing environment for decades. The motivation seems to have been a desire to bring order to capitalism and to improve the lot of employees. This seemed particularly to be an issue in smaller shops where owners and employees felt it necessary to open all hours in order to maximize their business. The fear was that anyone who closed earlier than anyone else would lose out, yet all recognized that there was only the same quantity of business to be done. Larger stores, in contrast, did not see the virtue in round the clock opening and were generally quite content with the restrictions that were placed on them. The legislative basis for control was the Shops (Hours of Trading) Act which came into force in 1938. Wartime imposed further controls but these were replaced in 1947 by comprehensive regulations.

The amendments (S.I. No. 362/1947) instituted a general prohibition on shops opening before 7 a.m. and maintained the distinction between certain types of shops (early closing) and ordinary shops in the Dublin County Borough. There was a long list of what constituted an ordinary shop in Dublin but the principle was that it was an early closing shop unless it was included in the list of exemptions. There was no mention of Sunday trading and no regulation of the weekly half-holiday.

Closing hours for a Dublin City (early closing hours) shop were 6 p.m. from Monday through Friday and 10 p.m. on Saturday. Otherwise, and for all shops in the remainder of the city (including Dún Laoghaire), the hours were different with the seasons. From October through March, shops were required to close by 8 p.m. on Monday through Thursday, at 9 p.m. on Friday and 10 p.m. on Saturday. During April and September they could stay open for an additional 30 minutes between Monday and Thursday while during May through August, they could open as late as 9 p.m. on Monday through Friday.

Without a great deal of debate, the government moved to suspend this order in all areas outside Dublin, Dún Laoghaire and Cork in October 1952 and then to revoke it completely for all areas from 27 December (S.I. 355/1952). It cannot be said to have been greeted with universal approval by organizations such as RGDATA who feared a return to an 'open all hours' system. For its part, the government saw this as an attempt to drive competition and hopefully keep prices down at time of fiscal crisis. They did not revoke any special orders made in respects of specific employments and one such that remained in place in Dublin to the end of the 1960s applied to butchers. This was under pressure though in the latter years of the decade as supermarkets increasingly incorporated butchers within their store and they wished them to be open for the same hours as the remainder of the store.

Rationing

It took some time for food retailing to return to normal after the Second World War. In addition to rationing, there were price controls on a wide range of goods which included food, wearing apparel, fuel, light and power, household goods, industrial raw materials, building materials, fertilizers, maize and maize meal, agricultural implements, and many miscellaneous goods. A look at the *Irish Independent* for 4 January 1951, p. 4, will show just how comprehensive the control was. Rationing ended in the first week of July 1952 but a maximum prices order was retained on sugar, butter, bread and wheaten meal. There was a further bizarre control on the sale of butter for a while.

Under an order of 4 July 1952, Irish Butter was permitted to be sold throughout Ireland but not in Dublin (S.I. No. 205/1952). Dubliners (including those living in Bray) had to buy imported butter, mainly from New Zealand. This apparently was designed to ensure that butter supplies, which were under pressure, would not be deflected from their production areas. However, as these controls disappeared or were diminished over time, so the changes to retailing outlined above began to have an effect. One immediate effect of the removal of rationing was that shoppers could once again shop around and the reports from the time suggest that they started to do so quite quickly. Another effect was that prices began to rise as goods began to find their market price in the absence of a controlled and subsidized rationing market. Thus, for example, tea under rationing was controlled at 2s. 8d. per lb but by September 1952, it was selling at between 4s. 8d. to 6s. 2d. Some local grocers reported a drop in sales as shoppers took to larger stores in the city centre in search of value. The opportunity for supermarkets, cash and carry shops and other approaches could now be fully exploited.

Car ownership

Increasing car ownership was a key element in the shift in people's shopping habits. While the registration of new cars dipped significantly in the early 1950s – to the extent that there were layoffs in the assembly companies – the trend was upwards by the third quarter of the decade and continued that way. In 1958, there were 40,934 private cars registered in the city area, compared to 37,750 in 1955. There were 11,265 commercial vehicles in 1958, slightly down on the 1955 figure of 11,290. There were also lots of motor cycles, some 12,733 in 1958 but unfortunately no estimate of the number of bicycles, though Schaechterle's research indicated that they were numerous. The choice of car was limited by the import regulations and what the assemblers were prepared to put together but there was still a good range. In the 1950s, Ford dominated the market followed by Morris and Austin with a smattering of Volkswagens and Hillmans. It is said that a house followed by a car are the two largest purchases that a person is likely to make in his or her lifetime. As has been discussed in a previous volume, the price of houses rose steadily during the 1950s and 1960s. A standard three-bedroomed house could be had for somewhere in the region of £2,300 in 1952 but people could expect to pay in the region of £4,000 in 1960 and more than £5,000 in 1964.

In 1955, the cheapest Ford was the Popular, available at £350. The Anglia was available for £454 and the Ford Prefect would have cost £488. Moving up market, a consumer would have paid £564 for the Consul and £564 for the

131. Advertisement for Ford Prefect in 1952.

The Prefect

saves you money from the start;
this lively car is roomy enough
to take four people in comfort.

ONLY
£460
Ex Works

THE PRICE IS RIGHT

YOU SAVE All the time on Running Costs:
The Prefect costs amazingly little to run and maintain. It's easy on petrol, oil and tyres. After many thousands of miles of trouble-free motoring your Prefect can be restored to brand-new performance through the famous Ford Engine Exchange and Parts Exchange Schemes.

YOU SAVE All the time on Service:
Spares, repairs and other servicing jobs are smaller items in the Prefect owner's budget. They are all carried out at low charges, and the Ford Dealer Service operates *everywhere*.

YOU SAVE Through Constant Reliability:
A reliable car is an *economical* car, and the Ford Prefect is super-reliable. It will give you efficient service for a long, long time, and even the toughest of country-road driving comes easy to a Prefect.

When in Cork visit the Ford Factory · Monday to Friday · 10 a.m. to 3.30 p.m.

Ford Motoring—the best at lowest cost

HENRY FORD & SON LIMITED · CORK

Centre of Attraction

Zephyr Six

In Town and country alike

people turn to admire the Zephyr Six. Here indeed is 6-cylinder luxury coupled with the world famous 'Five-Star' features. Long sweeping lines . . . brilliant performance. . . a revolutionary O.H.V. 'over-square' engine . . . and a score of mechanical refinements. It's a car to be proud of, proud — not only of its superb appearance but of its remarkable economy. Find out more about the Zephyr Six — without delay—at your local Ford Dealer's.

★ *Revolutionary O.H.V. Engine 6 cyl. 2,262 c.c. ("Over-Square" engine design for exceptional power and long life.)*
★ *Entirely new type Independent Front-Wheel Suspension with built-in double-acting hydraulic shock absorbers.*
★ *Hydraulically-operated brakes and clutch.*
★ *Centre-Slung seating.*
★ *All-Steel Welded Integral Body Construction.*

ZEPHYR SIX—23.4 h.p. Fordor Saloon, plastic leathercloth; tyres 6.40 x 13 £666 . 0 . 0 ex works. Extra for Genuine Leather £19 . 0 . 0 Extra for Heater £15 . 0 . 0 Extra for Radio £28 . 0 . 0 Extra for White Sidewall Tyres £6 . 15 . 0

See your Ford dealer NOW!

Ford MOTORING-THE BEST AT LOWEST COST

HENRY FORD & SON LIMITED · CORK

132. Advertisement for Ford Zephyr in 1952.

133. Advertisement for Vauxhall cars in 1955.

Zephyr. At the top of the range was the Zephyr Zodiac at £728 and the Customline V8 at £1,150. These were ex-works prices and the final price would have depended on what deal could be done. Renault offered their four-door 750 for £499 and there was a full range of Vauxhall cars. At the same time, an Austin Cambridge five-seater cost £599 for the A40 (1,200 cc) or £625 for the A50 (1,500 cc). Both offered the luxury of a heater and demister. A Volkswagen came with these features but cost a more modest £499. The Wolsley four forty-four was more in the luxury class and cost £797 while the MG Magnette was a pricy £865. Its 1.5 litre engine boasted a top speed of over 80mph (130kph), but where could it get to that speed? Newspapers offered regular motoring columns and double-page spreads were not unusual. There was a large second-hand market. All in all, despite the economic circumstances, there was a market and a wide interest in motoring.

Prices rose steadily but not dramatically – there was even an occasional drop in prices – but, even so, a car was a major item of expenditure given the level of salaries. The Anglia cost £515 in 1960 before reducing to £493 in 1964. The Austin A60 cost £788 in 1965 with the automatic version at £878 and a diesel version at £898. The customer was a hardy animal because a heater was yet an optional extra at £15. The Ford Zephyr 4 was now £855 but it had a heater while a Cortina would have cost between £800 and £900 in 1968. It must have been only Austin users who relied on rugs to keep warm because the Morris 100 included a heater (as well as lots of space) for its price of £705. A more exotic Renault 8 with disk brakes on all four wheels plus a host of built-in extras would have cost £719 in 1966. House ownership increased significantly during the 1960s, so it is not surprising that car ownership also increased, facilitating the processes described above.

City centre redevelopment

It was evident by the end of the 1960s that the dynamic in the city had changed and that it was becoming polycentric in common with most other cities of its size and scale. Though this posed a new and serious challenge to the city centre, there had been recognition for some time previously that redevelopment was desirable. Decay and dereliction was an increasing problem in the central area, especially as the tenements were being closed and people rehoused. The arrival of the age of the shopping centre made this redevelopment an imperative.

In 1966, for the first time, the Census of Distribution offered a picture of the city centre. It confirmed what had long been understood to be the case, that it dominated the higher-order shopping of the city. They defined the central area or central business district (CBD) as shown in the map on p. 255. It was bounded by Parnell Street in the north and stretched to York Street in the south. In the west, the boundary was South Great George's Street and Capel Street but with a small salient into the markets area around St Mary's Abbey. To the east it was Kildare Street, Tara Street and Amiens Street but without the housing areas around Gardiner Street. While it would not be an uncontested view of the main business area of the city, it encompassed the main shopping areas, though it included quite a number of non-core streets as well.

Shop numbers decreased in the central area but the rate of decline was lower than in the metropolitan area as a whole; many of the losses were suburban. That said, convenience shops such as grocery, fresh meat and general food shops experienced a considerable drop in numbers. Butchers and other meat sellers fared worst of all. Their decline resulted in some measure from the rise of the supermarket but was due, to a far greater extent, to the process of slum clearance which removed their clientele to suburban locations. Looking at the 1971 figures, although grocery shops, food shops, butchers and pubs accounted for over 23 per cent of the shops by number, they contributed less than 14 per cent to the total turnover of the central area.

Table 9. Central area shopping profile, 1966–71.

Type	1966 Stores	1966 Per cent	1971 Stores	1971 Per cent	1971 Turnover £000	1971 Per cent
Grocery	55	5.3	44	4.6	3,679	4.3
Public house	125	12	108	11.4	6,607	7.6
Fresh meat	50	4.8	29	3.1		0
Other food	57	5.5	38	4	1,574	1.8
Newsagent	95	9.2	60	6.3	2,576	3
Clothing	236	22.7	167	17.6	26,190	30.3
Chemist	40	3.9	30	3.2	1,887	2.2
Vehicles	16	1.5	16	1.7		0
Durable goods	94	9.1	119	12.5	7,510	8.7
Other non-food	262	25.2	239	25.2	36,474	42.2
Total	**1,038**		**950**		**86,497**	

These figures confirmed what was apparent on the landscape; city centre retailing was about clothing. After all, they occupied the best locations and the data now showed that they had over 30 per cent of the turnover, despite a decrease in the number of stores between 1966 and 1971. As would be expected, the three categories, durable household goods, other non-food and clothing, occupied over 85 per cent of the retail floor space. It was this business sector that was under threat from the shopping centres and there was a need for a central area response.

Renewal in the city centre

The impact of Charles Abrams' United Nations memorandum on dealing with Dublin's population growth, produced in 1961, was far reaching in that it influenced much of what was to become the Local Government (Planning and Development) Act, 1963. It also looked at the growing need for renewal in the centre of Dublin as a consequence of population loss. In particular, the study team seemed quite shocked by the apparent dereliction of the Moore Street area where they described the push-carts as giving the impression of

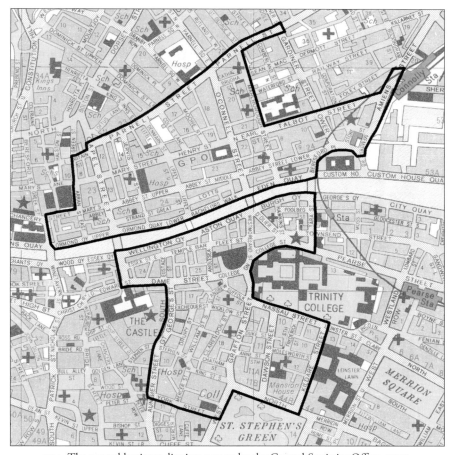

134. The central business districts as seen by the Central Statistics Office, 1971.

activity amid squalor. The *Irish Times* report was pleased with this recognition but the greatest concern of the writer was that any redevelopment would include a provision for parking for the streets around, as every nook and cranny was jammed (*Irish Times*, 14 November 1962, p. 11).

Armed with stronger legal powers to acquire land, courtesy of the 1963 Act, the Corporation moved to redevelop the Moore Street area. In 1966, Nathaniel Lichfield and Associates were given a brief to produce a preliminary appraisal of shopping redevelopment in the centre of Dublin. Lichfield had already prepared an outline plan for development of the north city centre in 1964. This was for an area bounded by O'Connell Street, Parnell Street, Capel Street and the quays and it involved about three million sq. ft (280,000 sq. m).

It was to be a multi-faceted plan that would involve residential development, a new bus station, an entertainment complex and factories as well as improving the shopping experience. Such a plan was, of necessity, a longer term proposal and Lichfield's own view was that it would take at least ten to fifteen years or even twenty-five years to realize. In fact, it was still no more than an idea when an opportunity arose to redevelop and expand the shopping provision in the Moore Street/Chapel Lane areas. This was not quite ideal because of its location on the edge of the area and there was concern that it might produce an alternative pole which would could upset the overall integrative focus of the wider development plan. Yet, the opportunity could not be ignored.

As part of Lichfield's study, a survey of shoppers was undertaken and it showed that the vast majority of shoppers came directly to the city from home. This was 77 per cent in the case of the north city centre and 65 per cent in the case of the south city centre. Those shopping before, during or after work accounted for the bulk of the remainder. Retail spending had been buoyant during the 1960s and it was anticipated that it would continue to grow, as a result of both population growth and economic development. Because much of this growth would be suburban, it was to be expected that there would be faster growth in suburban trade. However, Lichfield was sanguine about the position of the centre. He said that 'this, of course is not to imply that the centre will not grow or that a new centre may emerge to rival it. Both events are highly unlikely. It implies that there will be some shift in the distribution of spending, with the rate of growth in the city centre being somewhat slower than that in total throughout the suburbs' (Lichfield, 1966, section 3.4).

At this time, Lichfield anticipated only the opening of the Stillorgan shopping centre and the proposed centre for Ballymun. He felt that it was doubtful whether further similar developments would be operative by 1971. He did not foresee the much more rapid spread of shopping centres and he anticipated that the balance of trade between the centre and the suburbs would only have shifted from 56 per cent in favour of the centre in 1966 to 57 per cent in favour of the suburbs by 1986. This had to be understood against an anticipated increase in total business and it was a decline in the relative share of business taken by the city centre and not the absolute amount. This meant, he argued, that there was certainly scope for further shopping development in the centre. He suggested that the increase could be 12 per cent in the period to 1971 but that the total space could increase by 25 per cent on the 1966 figure by 1986.

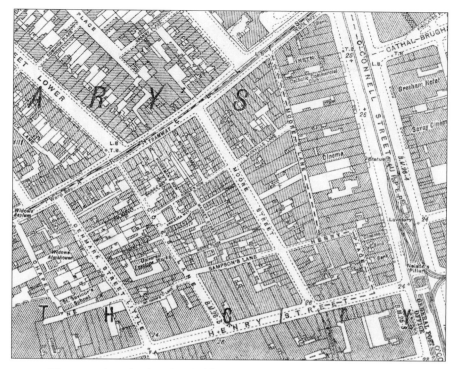

135. The area to be redeveloped in Dublin city centre. (Ordnance Survey plan, 1:2,500, Sheet 18(VII), 1943.) The map shows the warren of small streets and lanes which had slipped into dereliction by the time of the proposed project.

The proposed development was of a site which was bounded by Moore Street, Parnell Street, the rear of Henry Street and Chapel Lane. It covered an area of about 305,000 sq. ft (28,300 sq. m). It was going to be a multi-level development with over seventy retail units, two department stores and a supermarket. It would encompass the existing street market and replace it with a managed open market within the scheme. Lichfield estimated that the scheme would use up about half of the estimated growth potential in the city centre up to 1971. He worried, however, about the concentration of so much new space in the north city centre but felt that this could be accommodated because Dublin was a twin-centre. Lichfield would have preferred a better sequencing with earlier redevelopment taking place closer to the quays and ensuring the development of more integrated shopping north and south of the river. This development was going to be spatially distinct for quite some time. The Planning and Development Committee of Dublin Corporation asked the City Manager at its meeting on 9 November 1965 to engage with local

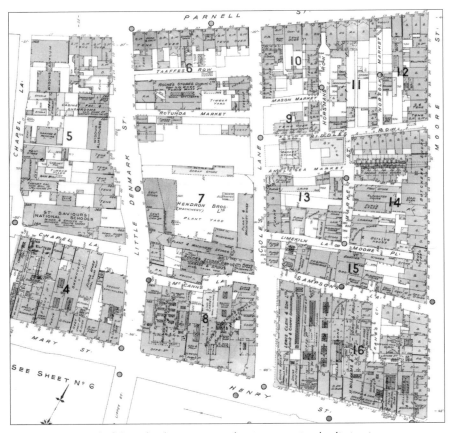

136. Detail of the redevelopment area, showing extensive dereliction in 1957.
(Goad Fire Insurance plans, sheet 3.)

interests and to gauge reaction. This produced a report to the City Council in April 1967 (Report 46/1967). It was generally positive. The view was that a phased development would be best and it was important not to have a razed landscape while development was taking place.

The business owners were keenly aware of the likely impact on their business from the developing suburban centres. It was their view that they could only succeed if the area was developed as a modern, in-town shopping centre on the model of European cities with traffic segregation and lots of parking. They were quite advanced in their thinking for the times and very much in line with what was regarded as best practice elsewhere. The Corporation was keen to reassure traders that they would be treated fairly and there was a general acceptance of this by the traders. That said, the welcome was not universal. A significant group, particularly the street traders, opposed the plans and their position became more entrenched as time went on. Their opposition resulted in a public inquiry into the compulsory purchase orders.

The approach was going to be via what would now be called a public-private partnership. The largest land owner in the area at the time was the Irish Property Corporation Limited. This company was the main driver of the project and the intention was that the area would be developed together with Dublin Corporation, which was the second largest owner of property. It was proposed that the Irish Property Corporation Limited would buy up as much property as they could. The Corporation would use its powers of compulsory purchase to facilitate this when necessary. This was a powerful tool in the hands of any developer and it is not clear that the Corporation spent any length of time considering whether this was ethical. It significantly diminished the rights of property owners in the area and made them much more vulnerable. The Corporation seems to have been of the view that the area needed redevelopment and that this was a good way to do it. Under the deal the freehold in the property so obtained would pass to the Corporation entirely free of charge but the lease on the development would be for 125 years.

The plan was to have the following elements with a capital cost estimated at £4 million:

- A retail selling area of 150,000 sq. ft (14,000 sq. m).
- Storage attached to retail selling area restricted on initial plans to 64,000 sq. ft (6,000 sq. m), but subject to possible extension by agreement with Dublin Corporation.
- A non-retail area of 40,000 sq. ft (3,700 sq. m), which would include 10,000 sq. ft (930 sq. m) of ancillary uses such as showrooms, restaurants, cafeterias, ticket agencies, hairdressers.
- Hotel with ancillary accommodation.
- Entertainment facilities including cinema and bowling centre.
- Minor residential units.
- Car park up to 1,000 cars with petrol filling station and showroom.
- Offices providing a nett usable area of 92,000 sq. ft (85,500 sq. m).

This was a fairly standard mix and it was designed to ensure that one-stop shopping could be a feature of the centre and that there would be a ready-made, on-site clientele. This led to a compulsory purchase order for an area bounded by Moore Street, Parnell Street, Denmark Street Little, Mary Street (nos 33–8), Chapel Lane and Sampson's Lane (Report 101/1967). The order was contested, particularly by the Moore Street traders and the required public inquiry was held in September 1968. It was explained that development was both necessary and timely. Moore Street's hinterland was described as a 'shambles of makeshift, dilapidated structures' by James Culleton, a member of the City Architect's office (*Irish Times*, 26 September 1968, p. 8). The new development would involve the creation of a new streetscape in which there would be no traffic other than pedestrians. Service traffic would be facilitated by using ramps to bring the traffic to first-floor levels. In total, the order affected 164 houses, shops, factories, public houses, restaurants and other buildings. However, others noted that there were no structural defects in the buildings on the west side of Moore Street and therefore no need for urban renewal there. It was again confirmed that the open-air trading element of the district would be retained but it was clear that it would be done in a different way. It was going to be brought up to modern standards!

The approach to the project (and that for the Ballymun and Northside shopping centres) was approved by the Corporation following a fieldtrip between 24 October and 2 November 1968 when a delegation visited central area developments in Coventry, Birmingham, Solihull, London, Stevenage, Cambridge, Amstelveen, Amsterdam, Rotterdam, Cologne, Essen and Dusseldorf. The detailed report of the trip (Report 22/1968) made the point that they were aware that 'that there is much more at stake for Dublin than the cost of the bricks and mortar. So far as the central area of Dublin is concerned the problem is one of revitalizing an integral part of the capital city and safeguarding that undoubted tremendous retail potential of this area. It is a truism worth repeating that a city that is not living is dying'. The places visited were an eclectic mix of developments – first-generation new towns, centres that needed post-war redevelopment, centres in major cities but not the city centre, the city centre of smaller towns. They saw the degree to which it was possible to integrate a multi-level development into an urban fabric, how vehicular and consumer traffic was managed, how access in more or less congested cities was controlled and they also examined how the development process was managed.

Stevenage was the first designated new town in the post-war programme of new town building in the UK. As with many, it was grafted onto a pre-existing settlement that had its own shopping facilities. Whereas in other new towns, shopping developed as traditional on-street provision, because Stevenage was delayed – there was fierce local opposition – its shopping

137. The town centre of Stevenage.

138. The town centre of Amstelveen.

provision was developed as an in-town pedestrianized shopping centre – the first in Britain. Looking at it from today's perspective it is rather unprepossessing and resembles the Lijnbaan, mentioned above. It comprises a series of low-rise linear blocks with shops on the ground floor and offices and housing on the upper floors. While there were projecting roofs from the shops, the shopping experience was an outdoor one. The most distinguishing feature was its clock tower but there was the advantage of seats for weary shoppers and the convenience of the nearby central library. It is now seen as dated and there are well-developed plans for a comprehensive redevelopment, currently on hold due to a lack of funds. However, at the time, it would have provided the Corporation with a lot of food for thought. Here was the integration of shopping, commerce and housing with the provision of social services such as a library. The customer was separated from the traffic but at the same time there was both good transport links and access for cars.

Amstelveen is now a suburb of Amsterdam on the way to Schiphol airport. The town centre of the 1960s, now redeveloped, would have appeared to the visitors as having a lot in common with Stevenage. It comprised low-rise blocks with projecting roofs with shops on the ground floor, surrounding a paved central area which was restricted to pedestrians. The centre was also open to the elements.

The Elephant and Castle redevelopment (see above) was on a somewhat greater scale than the two examples above. Here the project involved the renewal of an area that had been destroyed by bombing during the Second World War. The scheme involved high-rise commercial development, rising to 55m, and comprised three free-standing blocks, two of seven storeys and one of eighteen, grouped around a central piazza. The main occupant at the time was the Department of Health. The shopping centre, completed in 1965 at a cost of £2.5m, was distinctive in that it was the first covered shopping centre in Europe. The glass roof was designed to be retracted in good weather so that the shopping could be in the open air but this rarely occurred. It was multi-level with shops on three levels and two levels of underground car parking (*Illustrated London News*, 3 April 1965, p. 9). When the delegation visited it was still struggling to establish itself commercially and had less than one third of the anticipated 115 shops in place. It still exists today but there are plans to replace it as part of a wider redevelopment plan.

Another stop was Cologne where they looked at the pedestrianization of existing streets. Hohlstraße and Schildergasse are at right angles and were important shopping streets in the pre-war era. In fact, Schildergasse was one

139. The shopping precinct in Strøget.

of the most historic parts of the city, having been the Roman decumanus maximus. Following post-war redevelopment the streets were pedestrianized against the wishes of the traders but a resulting increase in turnover of 25–30 per cent soon won them over. Schildergasse is now pedestrianized along its 500m length and is one of the busiest shopping streets in Germany. The delegation could also have visited Copenhagen where they would have seen a more linear approach to regeneration, also making use of the existing streetscape. Strøget is a now a run of individual streets that stretches for 1.1km between the two main squares of the city, the Rådhuspladsen and the Kongens Nytorv. Initially, pedestrianized for a trial period in 1962, also against fierce opposition, the experiment proved so successful that it was made permanent in 1964 and other streets and squares have since been incorporated. While the streets are pedestrianized, there are normal traffic junctions where the streets cross other roads. Vehicular access is maintained to the shops via the existing side streets. Both cities offered an example of a minimalist approach to renewal that was very successful but that required a basically healthy shopping environment to begin with. In both cases, the opposition was strong and prolonged and it was only the business' success that caused it to peter out. The value of securing the support of the business community was emphasized in delivering the project speedily and with minimum cost.

The delegation saw different methods of access for deliveries and services, from underground to separate routes and they noted that where the configuration of streets required the interaction of this kind of activity with shoppers, it could be managed successfully by limiting the times at which this could be done. In all cases, the need to provide excellent access to the centres for the users was crucial and, thus, the centre could not be developed in isolation to the transport systems in the surrounding area. Car parking was an essential component in the success of any development and they came to the view that if shoppers could not get parking in the centre, it should be available no more than five minutes away. Where there was an existing urban landscape to be renewed, all of the schemes emphasized the need to engage with the local traders. The co-operation and goodwill of existing local traders was an important factor

> in schemes for comprehensive redevelopment and it is essential, as far as possible, to effect relocation with a minimum disturbance of existing businesses. Where this is not possible, it should be the aim to provide alternative sites for those who cannot get space in the redevelopment area. Traditional traders should, as far as possible, be retained and we are convinced that such traditional retailers contribute to the success and prosperity of redeveloped shopping centres.
>
> (Report 22/1968)

The delegation was impressed. They noted that the projects had all been developed by the local authority or the local authority in partnership with a developer. This had yielded a good return.

By the end of the decade, the proposal had got to the point that the Minister for Local Government, Mr Boland, had given his approval for the compulsory purchase process to begin (*Irish Times*, 21 November 1969, p. 14). All going well, it was reasonable to expect that the centre would be well underway within about two years. This being so, the city centre would have a resource that would rival the new suburban shopping centres. Not everybody was convinced or welcomed the proposals but this was hardly unexpected and the Corporation would have taken comfort from the experience of those centres that they had visited. The Central Dublin Development Association was unconvinced by the developer's assertions about the retention of business and the protection of jobs. Opposition to the proposal from the street traders continued unabated because the street market would be displaced into a more managed and sanitized area within the development.

THREAT TO 10,000 WORKERS

We respect the memory, wishes and aspirations of the men and women who helped establish a free and independent Ireland for Irishmen, in Easter Week of 1916.

The independence and freedom of over 900 owners of property and the livelihood of 10,000 workers in this part of the centre of Dublin is presently threatened by redevelopment plans of the Dublin Corporation which intends to acquire compulsorily all property in this scheduled area and then hand it over to the foreigners we fought to get rid of 50 years ago.

These proposed redevelopment plans are repugnant to our rights as Irishmen and as citizens of Dublin.

1. It is wrong for Dublin Corporation to prepare plans for the redevelopment of this part of the city without consideration or consultation with the residents and management and workers who get their livelihood out of the area.

2. It is wrong of Dublin Corporation to prepare plans for redevelopment when these proposals are designed to get rid of approximately 80% of the people presently in the area.

3. Where are the residents, business and professional people to go?

4. How many businesses will close down when their properties are compulsorily acquired for demolition by Dublin Corporation?

5. How many workers will be thrown out of their jobs?

6. Why cannot the present owners and occupiers be permitted to redevelop their own properties in the best interests of their workers and of themselves?

7. Is it wrong to prevent Irishmen and Dubliners rebuilding their part of their own city?

8. Why should Dublin Corporation be permitted to wipe out over 900 owners and occupiers of property and why should they be permitted to become the sole landlord?

9. Socially it is desirable to have many owners of property and not just one Giant Landlord, namely Dublin Corporation.

Your jobs are threatened, your property is threatened. Your future is threatened by the sweeping compulsory purchase powers of Dublin Corporation. People, their rights and dignity, come first. Any plans of Dublin Corporation must take cognisance of people, not just property. People live and work in buildings. The people come first. We, the people who work and live in this part of Dublin, want the primitive right to continue to do so.

We will fight your cause, we will fight for your rights and for justice.

Issued by

CENTRAL DUBLIN DEVELOPMENT ASSOCIATION
7 & 8 BACHELOR'S WALK, DUBLIN 1

The CDDA is an Association formed to cater for the interests of owners, occupiers and users of property in the centre city area bounded by the Quays, Capel Street, Parnell Street and O'Connell Street

140. Central Dublin Development Association protest handbill.

Nonetheless, there was little doubt at the time that the development would occur. Those who believed this were correct but the timescale was much greater than had been envisaged. The first phase of the ILAC centre did not open until 1981 and was only a partial redevelopment of the area with much land left derelict.

The shopping experience

Up to the 1950s, the shopping experience in Dublin had been fairly consistent for decades. There were two main centres for shopping, one that focused on Grafton Street and one that focused on Henry Street. Each had its own characteristic department stores but the range of services on offer was similar, though there was debate about quality levels. Some stores maintained branches in both centres in the belief that there was a separate clientele. Grafton Street and its traders certainly believed that it was the pre-eminent street. There seems to have been broad general agreement with that view and there was a Grafton Street Development Council that aimed to keep it that way. There was also a belief that southside shoppers did not use the northern shopping district but the little data that exist suggest that the picture was more complex with flows of shoppers both ways. To varying degrees, the streets around Henry Street and Grafton Street were also shopping streets. In the case of Henry Street it was a linear system that reached down Mary Street to Capel Street while across O'Connell Street, the shopping experience reached down Earl Street into Talbot Street before gradually petering out towards Amiens Street. Grafton Street's shopping environs had more of the sense of a district about it and the parallel streets of South Great George's Street and to a much lesser degree of Dawson Street provided the framework for that. In the case of South Great George's Street, the continued presence of Pims department store ensured that there was a good footfall on the connecting street. Dawson Street was not a good shopping street but was sufficiently busy to sustain South Anne Street and Duke Street, the connecting routeways.

As has been argued above, change was afoot as the decade progressed and especially in the 1960s as the shopping centre phenomenon developed and as people's tastes came to reflect a focus on the modern. Shops and restaurants that had been a feature of the streetscape since the beginning of the century, if not longer, disappeared. They were not displaced by international chains reflecting an increasing sophistication, in fact, internationalization in that sense stalled during this time, leaving Woolworth as the most international organization on the streets, with the possible exception of the supermarkets. Rather, it just seemed that their time had come; they had run out of energy and were out of phase with the times. It seems that even Brown Thomas was not immune and that it was in some financial difficulty by 1970. These losses diminished the colour and character of the shopping experience. Nothing of the same style came in their place and the loss of tradition could not be replaced. It became difficult for Dublin to boast of the distinctiveness of its capital city experience; it became more of a regional centre, at least in shopping terms. In the first years of the 1950s, though, these changes were not yet on the horizon and the challenges faced by the retail sector generally were economic while individual streets had particular structural problems to grapple with. These will now be explored in some more detail for a range of streets, not all of them great shopping streets.

Grafton Street

A shopper on Grafton Street in the early 1950s might have experienced a variety of the responses to the shopping environment. It might have been seen as somewhat fusty and old fashioned in that it had changed very little over the previous thirty or so years. The same shops were present, doing what they had been doing successfully for years. For others, this might have represented traditional values and quality with the assurance of a professional approach to retailing underpinned by a solid reputation. The street had always been the pre-eminent shopping street in the city, a fact generally acknowledged with comparisons being variously made with Bond Street in London or Rue de la Paix in Paris. This implied the existence of expensive and fashionable stores that reflected international trends in their offerings. And so it seemed to be. There were fine shops, with royal warrants in the days of empire, and they catered to all of the needs of a well-to-do middle and upper middle class. In 1950, many of these shops were still on the street. There were furriers, jewellers, tailors, couturiers as well as many fashionable coffee shops.

Its geographical organization had not changed in decades. The lower part of the street, closer to College Green, was never as important as a retail street, although it was on the main route from north to south. The best sites were those that straddled College Green and this was a mecca for smokers with Kapp and Peterson and James Fox meeting all needs in terms of cigars and cigarettes. These were there in 1950 and they were still there in 1970. Then there was a run of premises with varied uses including travel agents, stockbrokers and the Northern Bank. There was some change in tenants over

119 Grafton Street,

Dublin

Discernment in the choice of cigars, cigarettes, pipes and pipe tobaccos make smoking one of the most satisfying pleasures on earth.

4 Burlington Gardens,

London, W.I.

JAMES J. FOX & CO. (Cigar Merchants) LTD.

141. Advertisement for James Fox cigars in 1968.

DIXON & HEMPENSTALL

OPHTHALMIC OPTICIANS

"The House of Axpel Spectacles"

View of Lower Grafton St., including Dublin University, T.C.D.

THE LARGEST STOCKISTS OF

CAMERAS and BINOCULARS

IN THE REPUBLIC OF IRELAND

111 Grafton St.   Dublin

TELEPHONE 71333

142. Advertisement for Dixon and Hempenstall on Grafton Street in 1954.

143. Grafton Street looking northwards from Harry Street. Slyne is on the immediate left.

the twenty years to 1970 but travel agent tended to replace travel agent, stockbroker replaced stockbroker, so the look of the street did not change.

Closer to Suffolk Street was Dixon and Hempenstall and Hamilton Long. Both were chemists but the former had a strong interest in optics. Proving the point that exclusive stores do not require prime locations, the firm of Barnardo had no difficulty in getting customers for its furs to cross over to Suffolk Street from the main shopping area of Grafton Street.

Grafton Street was always somewhat unusual in that the main attractions on the street were located together. The two big department stores of Brown Thomas and Switzers faced each other across the street while the quality furnishing store of Millar and Beatty was beside Brown Thomas. The mid-street location meant that shoppers were drawn from both ends of the street and this provided very good footfall on the remainder of the street.

All of the major stores had organized fashion shows or fashion weeks prior to the war as a way of enticing customers into the shops. This practice changed somewhat in the post-war period. While they continued, they now tended to be in a major hotel and for the benefit of a particular charity. This raised the question as to how to maintain the necessary air of exclusivity. This was done in Brown Thomas by adding exclusive elements. Thus, in 1950, it opened its Dior Boutique. There is an excellent history of Brown Thomas (and

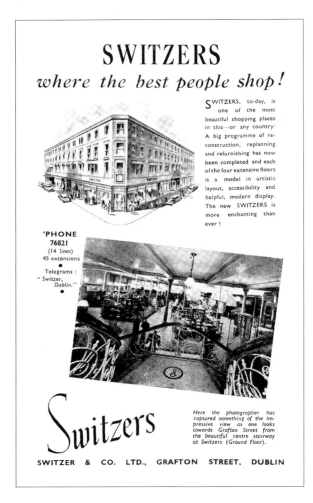

144. Advertisement for
Switzers in 1950.

incidentally Switzers) by Anne Haverty (1995) and she describes how an elegant Dior dress was displayed every day in the tea-room. They introduced big names in cosmetics, such as Estée Lauder, Guerlain and Laszlo, and they insisted that staff wear a traditional uniform.

Switzers made a significant effort to meet the needs of American tourists who visited Dublin in the 1950s and who were wooed by Waterford glass. This was not unique to Switzers, other stores capitalized upon the idea, but it was part of maintaining the image of quality. Another element was the shopping experience. While the days of carriages waiting outside were gone, both stores continued to employ commissionaires to escort customers. Favoured customers could expect individual attention and to be escorted from

"One Waspie, and take that look off your face!"

145. The demands of fashion. (*Dublin Opinion,* 1953, p. 341.)

When in Dublin, shop at

Brown Thomas

of Grafton Street, Ireland's loveliest store. Here you will find all the Irish specialities . . . Irish linen, Waterford cut glass crystal, fashions by Clodagh of Dublin, laces, souvenirs, bawneen sweaters, pottery, handwoven skirts, blouses, stoles. There's also an excellent Information Bureau where you can book theatre tickets.

Brown Thomas & Co. Ltd.,
Grafton Street, Dublin
Telephone 76861

146. Advertisement for Brown Thomas in 1968.

department to department. Undesirables were discouraged and customers were expected to be well dressed and suitably intimidated.

Switzers went through a refurbishment at the end of the 1950s. Modern plate glass replaced the old displays. Record booths were installed and the concept of selling to teenagers developed strongly with the 'young and gay' department. Gone was the soda fountain that was so much a feature of the Switzers of old. Gone too by the end of the decade was the grand staircase which had conducted shoppers to all floors. A sense of what it looked like can be obtained from looking at that which survives in today's M&S.

One of the other important draws on the street was Slyne at the corner of Harry Street. It had rather a small footprint but it used all the floors to such effect that it was a major force in quality retailing and it came into its own particularly with weddings. Next door was Scully's, who still described themselves as 'mantle makers'. Richard Allen was an important costumier and there were two other furriers on the street – Swears and Wells beside Slyne and Vard near Brown Thomas. A new arrival on the street in 1950 was Mrs Anna Black who took over the shop vacated by the fashion house of Leon who retired in the late 1940s. She was described at the time as someone who had twenty-five years of experience in New York and who was lured back into the business out of her Dublin retirement (*Irish Press*, 28 February 1949, p. 3). Not surprisingly, this did not turn out to be a long-term project. These were by no means the only clothing opportunities for women on the street and there were many tailors and dressmakers on the upper floors. With clothing came shoes and there was a fine range of offerings on the street: Dolcis, Tyler, Saxone and Boylans. Furnishing was provided by Millar and Beatty, Cavendish and Ellis, the house furnishers who had transformed into Drages, house furnishers, by the middle 1950s.

Men were always less sought after as customers but they tended to be better served in Grafton Street then elsewhere. The 1950s selection of stores was unsurprising. Tradition was maintained by Tyson for shirts, who would have been familiar to shoppers in the 1880s. Burtons had arrived some twenty years previously as the main herald of mass-produced tailoring and the 50/- tailors had brought their value-based approach from their original base in Henry Street. There were still a number of bespoke tailors with shop fronts and it remained possible for the well-to-do man to dress in style by a visit perhaps to Lynn (directly beside Tyson) or to W.J. Kelly, beside Switzers. In the late 1960s, W.J. Kelly was still advertising that more handshaping (at least 40 per cent more) went into their suits than other brands. It was not quite handmade,

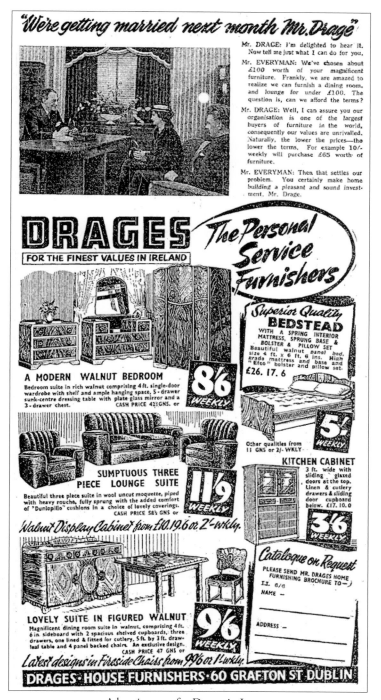

147. Advertisement for Drages in June 1955.

148. Advertisement for
Tyson from 1881.

149. Grafton Street at the St Stephen's Green end in the middle 1960s.

as it would have been in previous generations, but this was all that the market could bear.

Grafton Street had always been a place of resort in a way that other streets were not. From the beginning of the century, there was emphasis on promenading as people of leisure used the street and its many coffee houses (no pubs) to meet with their friends and acquaintances. It was a very Continental practice but one with a long tradition in Dublin despite the vagaries of the weather. After all, Sackville Mall had been designed with this in mind in the middle of the eighteenth century and the Rotunda had been built as a wet day alternative. Promenading had declined somewhat by the 1950s, though a saunter might be possible, but there was still a wide range of restaurants and cafés. Mitchell's had tradition while the Monument Café had excellent cakes. Bewleys had developed a reputation for its coffee while the Cameo Café or Robert Roberts Café were two of a number of alternatives on the street.

If a person having visited in 1950 was to have returned at the end of the 1960s, would the street be recognizable? In broad terms, the answer is 'yes'. There had been relatively little change in the mix of uses on the street and most of the shops and units still occupied the same locations as before. It was still the place to visit to go to Switzers or Brown Thomas and there had been no influx of international brands. Some brands had been replaced by others but the function was the same. Thus, Fitzpatrick Shoes now traded where Dolcis had been. The Cameo Café had become the El Habano Café and then, at the beginning of the 1960s, the Kum Tong Chinese Restaurant, part of Dublin's introduction to Chinese cuisine. Yet the street had changed fundamentally because many of the older tenants were gone; tenants that people would have come to associate with the street. Mitchell's was gone, as was Millar and Beatty, Slyne, Noblett's and the Monument Café and Creamery. Businesses come and go and so it is not entirely surprising that losses would occur. What is noteworthy is that these were businesses that were long established; some had survived two world wars, a rising and a civil war. The reasons for their departure were complex and a single explanation will not do. It is certain that the business environment of the 1950s was difficult and there was not the money around for high-end stores such as Millar and Beatty or Slyne. It may also be the case that their style of business no longer suited a city which was embracing the new and the plastic in their homes and places of entertainment. The owners may simply have run out of steam and decided to do other things. The fact that liquidations were voluntary would bear this out. Mitchell's made it only to 1956 and it closed in May of that year, having been on the street since 1805. It had long been regarded as one of the best restaurants on the street, if not in the city, and was also viewed as being somewhat expensive. Its reputation for quality was well established when Dublin Corporation's guide to the city for 1914/15 (*Dublin – Ireland's Capital*) noted that 'it is the most popular rendezvous in the capital, and in its fine rooms one will recognize many of the leaders of the Irish social world' (p. 143). There was a major sale of fixtures and fittings and many a household or bed and breakfast obtained their silver dinner services as a result. The *Irish Times* reported that Newbridge dinner knives went for £5 per dozen while teaspoons were 35s. The decision to sell seems to have been made quickly and there was no general sense that the place was about to disappear. As late as 1953, Mitchell's had been referring to their longevity on the street and their quality. As they said in one advertisement: 'As the *Chicago Tribune* said: "particularly is Mitchell's of Grafton Street, Dublin, Ireland, noted for its excellent cuisine and dainty teas with luscious cakes". Our customers of today enjoy the benefits of long experience in the comfortable and modern rooms of our premises in Grafton Street, the original site of no. 10' (*Irish Times*, 31 December 1953, p. 8). Certainly it came as a surprise to the 100 staff who were simply given a week's notice. No similar establishment came to replace Mitchell's, which is instructive in itself. Instead, the premises became the sales office for the Irish Hospital's Sweepstakes until a later transformation brought the joys of a Big Mac to the hungry populace. Millar and Beatty, almost neighbours of Mitchell's, went equally quickly. The store had been on the street since 1887 but the business dated back to 1851. It had enjoyed numerous royal warrants and was regarded as the finest furniture store in the country with a range of services to match. Back in the early years of the century, it was noted for its own range of furniture which it manufactured in both Dublin and Derry. Not only did it offer new and antique furniture but it did contract work for hotels, companies and even boasted that it fitted out Dublin Castle and the Viceregal Lodge. It was particularly noted for carpets and not only supplied and fitted carpets but offered a carpet cleaning service. For most of the century it was seen as a high-end store but ownership passed into the hands of a larger business group and it was decided in 1959 to close. This was a large store with a frontage of 48ft (15m) and an area of 30,000 sq. ft (2,800 sq. m) which reached back to Dawson Street. This resulted in a plot depth of 166ft (51m) and it was this that pointed to its future use because no store emerged able or interested in occupying the four-storey building.

150. Advertisement for the Monument Café in 1963.

When you visit

DUBLIN

enjoy a delightful and varied
menu at a most reasonable
price at our two lovely cafes —
both in the busiest shopping
thoroughfares.

BREAKFAST, LUNCHEON, TEAS, SUPPER

MONUMENT CAFÉS

55/56 UPR. O'CONNELL ST. Tel. 44661

39 GRAFTON ST. Tel. 74587

The company that had owned the Millar and Beatty brand continued in business and in 1977, they decided to revive the brand in the Dún Laoghaire shopping centre. It was reckoned that Dún Laoghaire was the place to sustain the price level but the tone had been changed to better reflect the times:

> A spokesman for Millar and Beatty said that they have assembled there what is claimed to be possibly the most comprehensive collection of antique reproduction and modern furniture ever seen in Ireland. The difference with the past is the recognition in the pricing structure that this is the day of the salary earner, and not the sinecure-holder. The equivalent today of the cachet that once went with the appointment as supplier to the Great Houses lies in the challenge involved in becoming fashionable in the new housing estates.
>
> (*Irish Times*, 23 December 1977, p. 14)

Unfortunately, the challenge proved too much and the revival of Millar and Beatty was shortlived and the space was on the market again by October 1979.

Slyne, who had been on Grafton Street for over half a century, had attempted to change with the times and at the end of the 1950s was noted for its low-priced goods.

Low priced cotton dresses are selling fast and being as speedily replaced. For 2 guineas there are fine cotton ones with wide horizontal stripes in two shades of tan, white and grey, or two shades of yellow, white tan and grey, and they have scoop neck·lines, set-in, short sleeves, and gathered skirts with big patch pockets set at hemline level. Much the same style, only with frontal buttoning from neck to hem, comes in plain cotton with a ribbed surface in such colours as scarlet, butcher blue, yellow, natural and pure white, and they are also 2 guineas.

(*Irish Times*, 13 July 1960, p. 4)

They left their Grafton Street premises in 1967, where they had five floors and moved around the corner to 13 Wicklow Street, which had recently been the Nobbitt Grill. Though it was explained that the Grafton Street premises were no longer suited to their method of doing business, the reality of moving from a premier business street to a side street was much more telling (*Irish Times*, 5 October 1967, p. 8). Over the previous fifty years, Knowles, the fruiterers, had gradually expanded their business so that they occupied 26 and 27, located between Duke Street and Anne Street South. They decided simply to retire from business and closed in August 1961.

As noted above, change is a natural part of the retail cycle but what makes this period different was how comprehensive the departure was of so many iconic stores over a relatively short period. The effect was not confined to Grafton Street but was experienced throughout the city centre. The losses were felt all the more because nothing particularly interesting replaced them. Slyne was replaced by Raphael footwear but a Tele Rents store replaced Sibley while the Cummiskey self-service (mentioned above) store replaced Dina Ryan, a supplier of gowns. It would be fair to say that the street was slipping somewhat in prestige but there was a tension between tradition and modernity, a point made by Mr B.J. Fitzpatrick, out-going chairman of the Grafton Street Development Council, when he said that Grafton Street was slipping backwards and was not keeping pace with modern developments (*Irish Times*, 2 July 1965, p. 6).

It was not all gloom and loss, however, and it would not be correct to suggest that the street went into a rapid decline. There was still believed to be business opportunities on the street and Arnotts decided to make the move southwards into the buildings formally occupied by West, the jewellers, near Switzers. In 1967, it was reported that the store had exceeded expectations (*Irish Times*, 15 March 1967, p. 12). The big change was the arrival of two

arcades. Arcades were nothing new in retailing. They had formed part of the
agora in Greek cities as a way of avoiding the heat of the sun and they were a
common feature of medieval cities. Indeed, Dublin Corporation decided
against allowing an arcade in the development of St Stephen's Green in the late
seventeenth century because of the potential to attract night vice. In Victorian
times, arcades perpendicular to the main line of the street were developed in
many cities as a means of extending the shopping street and they are still
found in places such as Milan, Paris or Brussels. Two arrived in quick
succession on Grafton Street. The first was the Creation Arcade which was
developed near Duke Street. The closure of Knowles provided the street
frontage while the depth was provided by the demise of one of the more
unusual uses – the Classic Roller Skating rink.

The arcade developed from the opening of Creation House in 1958, which
was not a sales location but rather a display area in which retailers, not
necessarily with a presence on Grafton Street, could display their wares. The
idea was that the better-off shoppers on Grafton Street would then be moved
to visit the store and purchase. From this was developed the idea that there
was a market for smaller, modern retail units in a managed environment. The
retailer got a new, modern unit which was not too large and where most of
the space could be devoted to selling. With careful management of the leasing,
the entire shopping offering could be very attractive. The arcade was opened
in December 1959 with units over three floors and entrances from Grafton
Street, Duke Street, Duke Lane and Lemon Street. The profile in 1961 showed
a focus on clothing with some firms choosing to have more than one unit,
suggesting that the research on unit size was not what it might have been.

1	Knitwear Boutique	2	Creation Man's Shop
3	Creation Boutique	4	Creation Man's Shop
5	Colette Modes	6	Davy Byrne's Wine Lodge
7	Colette Modes	8	Vacant
9	Donegal Shop	10	ESB
11	Donegal Shop	12	ESB
13	Martin Tailoring	14	Creation Restaurant
15	Martin Tailoring	16	Creation Restaurant
17	Charles Webb, Prints	18	Vard and Vince, Furriers
19	Chapeaux		

Davy Byrne's Wine Lodge was a logical extension of the eponymous public
house in Duke Street and it offered an exclusive range of wine and spirits. Vard
and Vince were happy to maintain their store on South Anne Street and felt

that there was business for another furriers. This was doubtless assisted by fashion advice that fur could now be worn by younger people! Caroline Mitchell, writing in the *Irish Times* in 1956, made this point, though about Barnardos. She argued that most women who wore 'valuable fur had reached years of maturity anyhow, and the magnificent skins only added to their general appearance of important prosperity. Nowadays, however, the skins are every bit as luscious as they were but the styling is all changed … [so that] an 18-year old girl can wear the most expensive full length coat (if she can pay for it), and still look 18 years old' (*Irish Times*, 7 May 1956, p. 6). Colette Modes was probably the anchor tenant and aimed at a sophisticated clientele with a special Creation Arcade range. The aim was also one-stop shopping in that it was argued that most shopping needs could be catered to and that the weary shopper could then repair to the restaurant for reviving. Public telephones were provided and there was an information desk to point people towards what they needed. It was believed that the arcade would be particularly attractive to visitors with little time (but presumably more money).

There was very little turnover in units during the 1960s, suggesting that the concept had been successful and the overall composition of the arcade was the same in the late 1960s at it had been at the beginning of the decade. The restaurant was gone by then as was Martin Tailoring and the Knitwear Boutique but Colette Modes, the Donegal Shop and the others, including Vard, were still there.

An arcade was also the solution found to the problem of what to do with Millar and Beatty. The Grafton Arcade was opened by the Lord Mayor on 30 September 1960. The initial plan was for nineteen units, all on the ground floor – unlike the Creation Arcade – with the upper floors made available for office accommodation. Brown Thomas took some additional space on the upper floors and had an entrance from the arcade.

The arcades were not a response to the development of shopping centres in the suburbs, these were still some time away, nor to the increasing interest in shopping by car, since no car parking space was available. Rather, it was an exercise in modernity, the provision of a bright, new shopping experience, a riot of glass and polished aluminium. They were also seen as an antidote to the increasing volume of traffic on the street. It seemed that the traders were not ready for pedestrianization so the arcades both increased the volume of shopping space and took people from the streets. The Grafton Arcade was initially developed by a consortium of business interests and, at a lunch to celebrate its opening, one of the directors, Mr Leslie Watson, was quoted as saying that they 'had wanted to do something that would be worthy of

151. The Creation Arcade.
(Magowan, 1961.)

152. *(below)* Advertising feature for the Creation Arcade in 1959.

Grafton street – of the old Grafton street that used to cater for what had been called "the carriage trade" ... When the buses had begun to roar down the street, everyone had been distressed ... With the bus traffic, Grafton street did, indeed, begin to go down but it had come up again' (*Irish Times*, 29 September 1960, p. 4). Naturally, he would say that the street had come up again but his remarks were indicative of the conflict between ease of access and traffic volumes, a matter discussed below. To make the arcade attractive, there was much attention to materials and design. The *Irish Times* gushed that the main impression of the arcade was one of 'restrained impressiveness with pilasters of polished Swedish emerald pearl granite and polished Honduras mahogany everywhere. The shop walls are finished externally in polished white Sicilian marble and the mahogany doors are fitted in polished bronze' (*Irish Times*, 29 September 1960, p. 4) – polished surfaces appeared to be the acme of style. For all of that, the mix of uses that they attracted was hardly indicative of high-end shopping and they also had difficulty with turnover of tenants as the 1960s moved on. The table below shows the range of tenants for three years in the 1960s, as reported by Thom's directories (and to which the usual caveats must apply).

	1961	1966	1969
1	Rentel		
3	Vacant	Iberia Airlines	
5	Vacant	Rigney Travel Agents	
7	Chez Nous, Cakes		Grafton Boutiques
9	Sir, Handcraft Tailor	Mooney, Tailor	
11	Gaytone Cleaners		
13	Boyd	Bonanza Trading Stamps	Purnell and Co., Auditors
15	Monaghan, Men's Outfitter		
17	Young Striders		Hoechst, Pharmaceuticals
19	Brown Thomas		
2	Irish Independent Branch Office		
4	La Rue Clothing (closed May 1964)	Vacant	Niagara Cycles / Massage Equipment
6	Werth, Hearing Aids		
8	Remington Shavers		Mona Lisa, Ladies' Fashion
10	Vacant	Judy, Children's	French Government Tourist Office
12	Donegal Shop	French Government Tourist Office	Warboys Ltd. Manufacturing Jeweller
14	Vision Book Shop		
16	Photax Camera Shop		Boyswear
18	Grocery Cash Prices		

This raises the question as to why this arcade did not do as well as the Creation Arcade, only a little further up the street towards St Stephen's Green. On the face of it, the Grafton Arcade was in a perfect location, directly attached to Brown Thomas and across the road from Switzers. It should have had excellent footfall and been in a good position for impulse shopping. Yet, this does not appear to have been the case and there is no obvious reason, except perhaps that there was already enough shopping provision on the street and these were not particularly interesting uses.

One of the issues raised in the development of the arcades was the question of traffic. In many ways, Grafton Street in the 1950s was the victim of its own success. There was too much traffic on the street and, despite the draconian limit on parking to twenty minutes, parking was at a premium. The footpaths were narrow and there was increasing conflict between pedestrians and traffic – all signs, it might be said, of a successful shopping street.

Dealing with traffic

There had been attempts to manage traffic on the street previously, one of which was the bizarre idea of switching the street to one way in the middle of each day (see Brady, 2014). The need to resurface major streets in the city centre, taking out the tram tracks and the last of the cobble stones, necessitated some temporary but dramatic changes to traffic patterns and one of these was to turn Grafton Street into a permanently one-way street. On the completion of the works, it was decided that the one-way system of the main portion of Grafton Street, from St Stephen's Green to Suffolk Street, was a good idea and it was retained. There was a further experiment to make the lower part of the street one-way with the flow from College Green to Nassau Street but this was quickly abandoned (*Sunday Independent*, 9 March 1952, p. 2).

Grafton Street was now one-way from south to north but traffic congestion did not really improve and parking was still possible. Indeed, while it might have been expected that the traders would have welcomed any diminution of traffic, this does not seem to have been the case. For example, parking was finally banned on the street in 1960 and at Christmas that year, they complained that the Gardaí did such an efficient job of enforcing new traffic regulations that they scared shoppers away from the street. This caused the parliamentary secretary to the Minister for Justice, C.J. Haughey, to note on the occasion of the opening of a temporary car park for 200 cars on a site in Earlsfort Terrace which was destined for the Sugar Company headquarters, that they simply could not have parking on the street (*Irish Independent*, 10 December 1960, p. 12). He felt that the four-minute walk to the street from the new car park should go some way to addressing the issue. Note the precision of 'four minutes'! The traders also had mixed views on one-way streets and when the one-way system was significantly extended in 1966, they claimed that Grafton Street suffered greatly as people were now being dropped off by buses in places as far flung as Pearse Street and O'Connell Street. A delegation from the Grafton Street traders to the General Purposes Committee of Dublin Corporation was quoted as saying that shoppers 'cannot be expected to make their way on foot across the city' (*Irish Times*, 25 February 1966, p. 8).

There were also ambitious plans to make the shopping experience on the street more attractive and one of the more interesting was the suggestion that the street be roofed over. This was not as major an undertaking as it might seem for the street is quite narrow. A company, Marketing Centres Estates, was established in 1959 with the aim of developing such a project and they reckoned that it could be delivered for about £250,000 and could be completed within a year. It would be placed about 10 ft (3m) above the buildings, leaving space for air circulation and would be supported on about twenty narrow supports from ground level on each side of the street. These would be placed so as not to obstruct shop windows. An outline drawing was provided in the *Irish Times* (10 June 1959, p. 9). The main advantage was the obvious one of keeping the rain out which, it was claimed, fell on six days out of every ten. Alas, there was not the necessary support for the idea and it went away. With the later pedestrianization of the street, it might have proved to be a very useful asset.

By the end of the 1960s, it was coming to be realized that Grafton Street had to change if it was to maintain its eminent position. In a Christmas feature for 1969, there was the usual piece which extolled the virtues of the street with an emphasis on its style. With the slogan 'Grafton Street is Quality Street', the following description was offered.

> And luxury, in the objective sense, is the essence of Grafton Street. In this one short street there is a higher concentration of the best that the world can offer than can be found anywhere else in Ireland.
>
> It's an unimposing street architecturally, but it has character. It's stamped in the mind of every Dubliner as the street of quality, and much of our social history has been played out on its pavements.
>
> (*Irish Times*, 19 December 1969, p. 12)

But on the same page, juxtaposed with this piece extolling the virtues of the street, was one that put forward a more sober reality. It was noted that a shopper could find anything that was desired on Grafton Street but you needed a lot of time on your hands or luck because of the crowds and the congestion. 'The window-shoppers often block solidly the sidewalks; pedestrians with an immediate destination to reach – and in a hurry – are forced on to the roadway and then have to battle their way back through the crowds when the shop of their choice is sighted'. Pedestrians were only one problem, the traffic on the street was so heavy that it was constantly thronged at Christmas with the result that it was difficult to do business. 'Frustration, exasperation, monstrous time-wastage and the useless burning-up of nervous energy' was the consequence; hardly the ideal image for the primary shopping street.

So while the *Dublin – Guide and History* edition for 1970 declared that Grafton Street was 'still the most popular and probably best-known shopping street and the ideal place to stroll to savour the shopping and the atmosphere of the newer Dublin' (p. 34), it seemed that matters could not continue as they were. The shopper might still have found many old favourites on the street. Switzers and Brown Thomas still offered the wide range of high quality products to be complemented by the nearby jewellers of Wests and Weirs and there were many other fine shops but the shopping centre in the suburbs was the coming 'thing'. Pedestrianization was seen as an inevitable response to the need to improve the shopping experience.

George's Street

George's Street put up a significant struggle in the 1950s and 1960s to retain its position as a prominent shopping street. Its traffic problems were different in that it was a wide thoroughfare and traffic movement had been improved by the widening of the eastern side as it approached Dame Street. It was well served by buses and shoppers found themselves deposited right in the middle of the shopping district. There is no doubt but that the key to George's Street's attraction was the presence of Pims. This was a huge store that occupied most of the lower west side of the street from 75–88. Because they had been there for over a century they were synonymous with the street and everyone knew what Pims had on offer. There were other important draws as well. There was Kelletts' large drapery store on the corner with Exchequer Street. They had been there since 1881 and the store had been gradually extended and rebuilt. In 1915, they advertised that 'in every branch of the drapery and millinery trade they will be found to offer great attractions and advantages to their patrons, and a visit to their showrooms is at all times a pleasant and interesting experience'. Winstons, ladies' outfitters, was further up the street towards

Stephen Street and by the middle 1950s, expansion of their store made it one of the biggest in the locality. On the other side of the road was Cassidy's, also a ladies' outfitters, which occupied nos 53–7, while a little further down the street and directly beside Pims was Macey, yet another ladies' outfitters. Macey now occupied the premises of what had been Holmes Ltd, who always made a big play of their tracking of Parisian fashions. These were all big stores and, though they might not have had the cachet of some of the stores on Grafton Street, they were a formidable business draw. In a somewhat different sphere but also important was Dockrell, which specialized in hardware of all kinds and was also a household name. It too had a long history, having been founded in the 1840s. It had a small street frontage but the extent of the store is clear in the extract from the Goad plan shown below and it also had extensive stores and warehouses nearby. There was a lot more besides on the street. Naturally, there were shoe shops: Fitzpatricks, Tyler, Saxone, Denson, Connolly. Edwards had a cake and coffee shop and so did Bewley's, Kilmore (later Kylemore) and the Monument Creamery. There was more potential for day-to-day shopping on the street compared to Grafton Street with Eastmans and Hafners butchers, Becker Bros for teas (in business since 1867), Home and Colonial, the Maypole Dairy and, of course, a branch of Findlater. There was a stray furrier, several tailors, chemists, a wallpaper store. If the shopper strayed into the South City Markets, s/he would have found two florists and fruiterers (Daly and Kenny) and two good fishmongers, Daly and McCabe. Though McCabe's premises were to be taken over by Daly during the early 1950s, this had been such a fashionable store that in the early 1900s it did not bother to advertise its products, it simply mentioned its clients. The rest of the markets though were not in good shape and were either vacant or given to storage or manufacturing.

It cannot be denied that the quality of shopping was good on George's Street. Many of the shops, such as Becker Bros (teas), Whyte's (glass and china) and Bewley's, had well-established reputations and had been on the street for fifty years or more. Indeed, as Grafton Street began to lose some of its oldest and more characteristic shops during the 1950s, there was a degree of convergence in the overall quality of the experience, for a time at least.

The battle for the hearts and minds of shoppers was co-ordinated by the George's Street and Exchequer Street Traders' Association. Originally the South Great George's Street Traders' Association, it had been founded in 1927 to promote the street. The Association was given great coherence by the fact that many of the major stores on the street were family businesses: the Cassidy,

153. South Great George's Street in 1957. Note the extent of stores such as Pims, Macey and Kelletts (outlined). (Goad Fire Insurance plan, 1957.)

Keep in touch...

A walk round Pims will convince you that here is the store that greets you with a thousand-and-one newer and more interesting ways to approach modern living.

Forty or more stimulating departments present you will an unrivalled panorama of things fashionable to wear . . . useful in the home and most desirable to own . . . in fact Pims is an ever changing, continuous programme of delightful suggestions and surprises.

Come to Pims . . .
Come Often . . .
Keep in Touch . . .

Pims

Departmental Store
SOUTH GREAT GEORGE'S ST.
DUBLIN   Phone 53061

154. Advertisement for Pims on South Great George's Street.

By Royal Warrant   to H.M. the King.

McCABE'S,

Fish, Poultry, Game, and Ice Merchants.

Patronised by His Majesty the King ; the late Queen Victoria ; Duke of Connaught ; His Excellency the Lord Lieutenant ; Chief and Under Secretaries ; the Nobility, Gentry, principal Clubs, Military Messes, and Hotels.

COUNTRY CUSTOMERS SPECIALLY CATERED FOR.   Every Attention Guaranteed.

LARGE DAILY ARRIVALS of . . . . .
FISH, POULTRY and GAME, as in Season.

South City Markets, DUBLIN.

ALSO,

11, Rathgar Road, Dublin ; 10, Ranelagh, Dublin ;
85, Main St,, Bray; Curragh Camp, Co. Kildare.

155. Advertisement for McCabe's from 1908.

156. Advertisement for Whyte's from 1906.

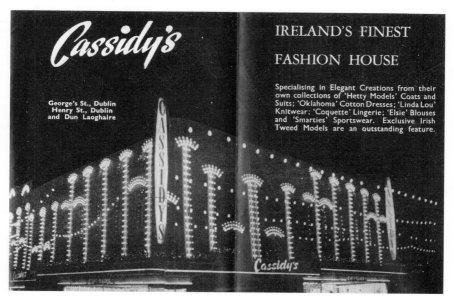

157. Advertisement for Cassidy's fashions from 1961.

158. Advertisement for Winstons. Note the concern for the 'fuller figure'.

159. Fuller Figure!
(*Dublin Opinion*,
1955, p. 185.)

" *I have one myself, madam, and I'm sure, like myself, you will
find it will create a sensation amongst your friends.*"

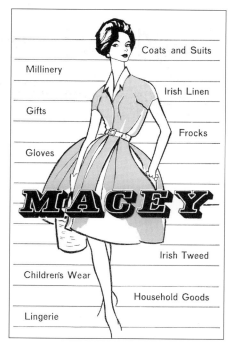

160. Advertisement for
Macey in 1961.

Dockrell and Kellett families were all important members. It was very good during the 1950s and 1960s at keeping the street in the public gaze and there were more Christmas shopping features for the street than for Grafton Street or, indeed, any other street. Nor was it just at Christmas that the street was featured. They obtained excellent coverage during An Tóstal, as being particularly attractive to American guests.

Typically, the suggestion was that it was a one-stop shopping destination (probably to a greater degree than Grafton Street) as demonstrated in this 1956 feature:

> The housewife, of course, is concerned first and foremost with provisions and delicacies for the festive boards. These she finds in abundance and variety at prices calculated to suit even the most modestly filled pocketbook.
>
> Her groceries and provisions purchased, she passes on to the problems on her gift list and here she is joined by her husband and family who also flock to George's Street to do their Christmas shopping.
>
> With chemists, sweets, jewellery, china, furnishing and radio stores at their command the problems are easily solved and all that remains is that piece of personal finery to which most of us treat ourselves at this time of year.
>
> (*Irish Independent*, 30 November 1956, p. 7)

An example of the style of advertising can be seen in the advertisement for Winstons (on p. 290) for 1956. In addition, they provided a postal service for country shoppers and they also maintained their service for the fuller figure, though they were now referring to 'outsizes'!

Another key element at Christmas was the variety and novelty of the street illuminations. Most of the main shopping streets were illuminated but the Association in George's Street sought to have theirs stand out. They also ensured that the Pims Santa was there to serve the entire street. By the 1960s, it was the same theme:

> To go shopping anywhere at Christmas in a world of illusion of snow-capped peaks, reindeers, sleighs, silvery fir trees and, magic is for the young adventure, the old a tonic and the rest a pleasure – especially if one has enough money to buy the attractively displayed goods that seem so much better than any other time of the year.

One of Dublin's more dazzling shopping areas these days is South Great George's Street. And there, under an awning of coloured lights, you'll find a number of windows devoted to haute couture to shoes and knitwear from Italy, to goods ranging from glamorous rainwear and snowboots to cocktail and evening wear, coats and suits, children's wear and toys and the tempting accessories that tempt any woman's heart.

(*Irish Press*, 18 December 1962, p. 4)

The traders were not going to surrender the high fashion stakes to Grafton Street easily and Colette Modes, which had another store on Grafton Street, aimed to provide top-end brands and to emulate Paris fashions.

The traders' association had embraced **Exchequer Street** as part of their group and that made sense because of its role as a conduit between the two major shopping streets. There was not a huge variety of retailing on the street – it had a hotel and the strangely located P&T telephone exchange, but it did

BRING THE CHILDREN TO MEET SANTA CLAUS in his *Venetian Fairyland*

Yes Children, come and ride in my magic Gondola, and then visit my Toyland packed with lovely toys for boys or girls. Gift Parcels. 2/-. Afterwards have a Teddy Bear Tea in our Restaurant.

All toys are available on our Budget Account; write for our Toy list.

BUMPER XMAS PARCELS

Pims

SOUTH GEORGE'S STREET, DUBLIN

161. Advertisement for Santa at Pims.

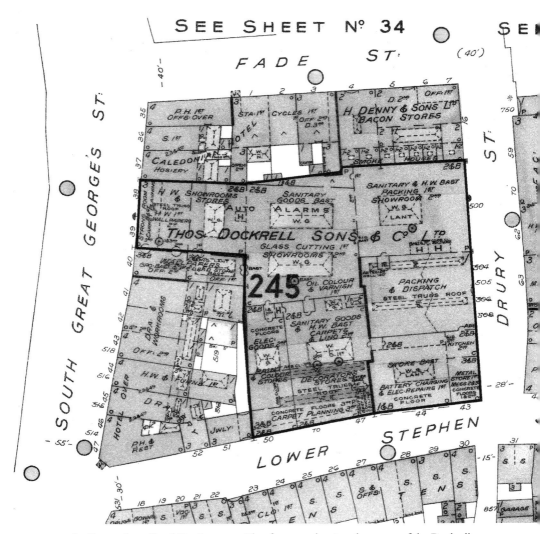

162. Extract from Goad Fire Insurance Plan for 1957 showing the extent of the Dockrell store.

have Nicholls and the Belfast, Damask and Linen Co. These were drapers and outfitters who sold a vast array of goods and were an inevitable destination for any shopping trip. This made it worth the walk into Exchequer Street and the walk might then be continued in one direction or another to George's Street or Grafton Street. Another important draw on the street, near Drury Street, was Dimond and Co., ladies' outfitters, and the expanding Roxy hairdressing operation.

The shopper then moved into **Wicklow Street**, which also had good shopping mixed in with different uses such as hotels and business premises. There were dressmakers and tailors, such as Femina Gowns at no. 9 and Geldof, dressmakers, at no. 11, who later changed into Budget Fashions. There were mantle makers, shoe shops, more drapers – Allshire occupied nos 33–5 – and there was even a furrier. There were some refugees from Grafton Street, the best known of which would have been Horton's, the gent's outfitters, who earlier in the century had occupied the key location at the junction of Grafton Street and Suffolk Street. They would soon be joined by Slyne. As would be expected on a street with lower rents, there were restaurants and cafés, dry cleaners (Bells and Burtols, the latter becoming Prescotts) and a number of good public houses, notably the International Bar.

Shops on Exchequer Street survived the 1950s and 1960s very well and there was relatively little change with the exception that Nicholls became even more dominant by taking over the Belfast, Damask and Linen Co. premises by the middle 1960s. There was much more turnover on Wicklow Street but no particular trend. One outfitter was replaced by another, and restaurants came and went in the same locations. For example, the Flamingo Restaurant had taken over from Bobby, gent's outfitter, in the middle 1950s and then it became the Pagoda Restaurant in the early 1960s (Chinese restaurants were 'in'), which in turn morphed into the Glass and Household Linen store at the end of the decade. Allshire, the drapers, were gone by the end of the decade to be replaced by four different stores, including a shoe repairers, a delicatessen and a fabric shop. There was, of course, a Tele Rents shop there by the early 1960s.

It has been mentioned above that George's Street began to rival Grafton Street's eminence but this promise was not fulfilled. The street experienced a number of very significant changes during the 1950s and 1960s and these contributed to a change in its character, despite the advertising. It started to lose its key shops. Kelletts, which had occupied the key location at the junction of George's Street and Exchequer Street, ceased trading in 1959. The business was bought by Dunnes Stores and the new store opened in May 1960, while Whyte and Co. were replaced by Power Supermarkets by 1963. The street might have absorbed these losses but the biggest issue lay with Pims, which had been in decline for some time. It had long since passed from the Pim family and was owned by the British company, Great Universal Stores. At the end of the 1950s, it had been decided to split the operation into Pims, concentrating on drapery, and Smarts, concentrating on house furnishing. Despite further reorganization, which involved selling a site to Woolworth, a

163. Horton's shop front on the corner of Suffolk Street in 1924.

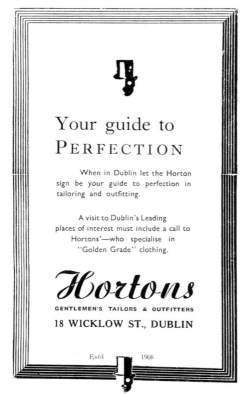

Your guide to
PERFECTION

When in Dublin let the Horton
sign be your guide to perfection in
tailoring and outfitting.

A visit to Dublin's Leading
places of interest must include a call to
Hortons'—who specialise in
"Golden Grade" clothing.

Hortons

GENTLEMEN'S TAILORS & OUTFITTERS
18 WICKLOW ST., DUBLIN

Estd   1908

164. Advertisement for Horton's on Wicklow Street in 1953.

deal that fell through, the holding company was not satisfied with the return they were getting and decided to close the drapery division on 30 September 1967. With this decision went one of the most distinctive stores in Dublin and the decision to redevelop the site as offices with relatively little retail had very serious implications for the street.

At the end of the 1960s, a piece in the *Irish Independent* suggested that the street was in trouble and losing businesses because of the lack of parking space and the failure of Dublin Corporation to facilitate multi-storey units. Galen Weston of Power Supermarkets was quoted as saying that when he first opened his supermarket, he had hoped for a bigger site. He was now glad that he did not get it. Ben Dunne of Dunnes Stores said that he would not be renewing his lease (*Irish Independent*, 30 August 1969, p. 22). It was further suggested in the piece that the departure of stores such as Kingstons and Nicholls men's outfitters (both across the road from Pims) was indicative of this decline. This produced a furious response the following week led by Keane, Mahony and Smith – advisers to MEPC property developers – who said that there was no shortage of demand for property (*Irish Independent*, 5 September 1969, p. 22). There had been new arrivals in the form of the Nathesco store and Colette Modes had doubled their property. He further stated that Denson's, Cassidy's and Winstons had reported an increase in business. His argument was that the lack of car parking was not the problem it was in Grafton Street because of the bus service. Their data suggested that 89 per cent of shoppers came by bus and there was no traffic to speak of on Saturdays when 40 per cent of business was done. He also argued that the nearby presence of so much local authority housing secured the future of the street. Michael O'Neill, chair of the traders' association, was more measured. He agreed that the trading environment had been difficult in recent times and that the Pims end of the street appeared dead. He felt that Wicklow Street, Exchequer Street and George's Street were coming back and that trading was better. However, there was not much he could say about Pims; it was not coming back. He seemed to put some hope in the building of multi-storey car parks. Interestingly, when the decision to close Pims was announced, the holding company had suggested that the lower part of George's Street was not good retail territory with flows going northwards from Exchequer Street. If that was true, though, it would be hard to explain why the company survived for so long (*Irish Times*, 7 August 1967, p. 10). Laurence Cassidy of Cassidy's was definitely upbeat. The street was on the up and up, he said, and this was fact, not propaganda (*Irish Independent*, 26 September 1969, p. 23). Now, despite that denial, none of the views expressed were value free and each was playing to his own interests. It is interesting to note, though, how parking had become an issue since this was the driving force behind the suburban shopping centres. There could not be continued reliance on people coming to shop by bus and the notion that the street could be supported by local authority housing was odd. In any event, the street did decline though multi-storey car parks were built and Dunnes did not move from its location. However, many other shops disappeared over the next decade and the street declined into the secondary street that it remains today.

As has been mentioned before, the streets around Grafton Street benefitted from the footfall generated by the main shopping attractions. The development of the Creation Arcade was an attempt to capitalize on this and to draw customers from the street directly into a shopping centre type concept. Both **Duke Street** and **Anne Street** had, in previous generations, provided space for services that needed the customers flowing down Grafton Street but which could not afford the rents of a major shopping street. There had been personal services of all kinds – dancing masters, hairdressers, language schools and, while they still existed, servants' registries. By now, most of these more exotic uses had gone but these streets remained home to a mixture of uses that included pubs, restaurants, outfitters, opticians and even a grocery and a dairy. These were combined with ground floor commercial offices for electrical engineers, wholesalers, decorators and quantity surveyors. Anne Street was a good location for antique shops and specialist print shops. Both Anne Street and Duke Street catered to the betting needs of Dubliners and there was a Kilmartins bookmaker on both streets combined with a branch of Mirrelson on Anne Street and these were constants during the two decades. Not much changed in terms of the character of the streets during the 1950s and 1960s though there was some turnover in individual businesses. However, there was no particular pattern to these changes; for example, a ladies' outfitter became a boutique and then a restaurant. There was a little bit of movement so that Fitzgibbon, sports outfitters, moved from 12 Anne Street to 8 Anne Street.

Dawson Street was always a surprising contrast to George's Street. As a parallel street to Grafton Street, it could easily have been a retail street, especially as the cross streets leading to it are short and direct. It never did take on that character and instead became the commercial core of the city, a process that intensified during the 1960s. No overwhelming explanation presents itself. It was a busy traffic artery but so was George's Street and the most reasonable explanation must lie in the fact that the main draws on the street did not have the attraction of a store such as Pims. While it had Hodges Figgis,

165. The streetscape on Dawson Street, 1960s.

128 years a-growing . . .

A TRUE KNOWLEDGE OF WINE is the fruit of long and patient experience. In 1825 Mr. John Morgan, already a noted authority on wines, founded the retail business which still bears his name and has continued in unbroken succession in the family from that day to this. For 128 years discriminating citizens have graced their tables with wines from the House of Morgan cellars, and have benefitted from a tradition of personal service and expert knowledge that has remained unchanged since Mr. Morgan first took down his shutters. To those whose steps have not yet strayed in the direction of Dawson Street we can but suggest a perusal of our latest Wine List as a preliminary to closer acquaintance with the myriad treasures of the finest cellars in Dublin.

THE HOUSE OF

MORGAN

36 DAWSON STREET

DUBLIN

Wine and Cigar Merchants

166. Advertisement for Morgan on Dawson Street. An example of a specialist use on a secondary street.

one of the specialist bookshops in the city, the main retail draw was the large store of Maguire and Gatchell. They sold all sorts of hardware, ironmongery, china, fittings, baths, electrical goods, as well as offering an installation and repair service for items such as boilers and water tanks. They had been on the street since the 1890s and had built impressive new premises during the 1930s (see Brady, 2014). They also sold seeds for flowers and vegetables and there was a little concentration of seedsmen on the street with the businesses of Drummond and Dixon at 57–8 and 61 respectively, near Duke Street. Given the range of their goods and the fact that parking was less frenetic nearby, it is rather surprising to find that they were in trouble by the late 1950s. There was no sign of the impending threat when the opening of their television department was reported in 1959.

> In accordance with their policy of keeping up with every new business development, Messrs. Maguire and Gatchell have now opened their new television and radio department, which is located on the ground floor of No. 13 and 14 Dawson Street, Dublin, adjoining their electrical appliances department in one of the finest showrooms in this country with an area of more than 4,000 square feet. The new department has a full stock of radio and television sets produced by the leading manufacturers, including Pye, Bush, Philips, Ekco, Pilot and G.E.C. In the new department can be seen a wide variety of sets ranging from the smallest transistor portables – so popular for summer days – to de-luxe radiograms and television sets from 17" to 21" screens in great variety. If desired, customers can avail of hire purchase facilities at most attractive terms.
>
> (*Irish Times*, 8 July 1959, p. 8)

They probably reckoned on selling more radios than televisions, which were expensive. A 17-inch Philips set cost £76 while a Pye set was available for £80. At those prices, it is not surprising that hire purchase was popular but even more so were the rental companies that were popping up on all the main streets. Nonetheless, Maguire and Gatchell must have had confidence in their new departure as part of the development involved the installation of a 180ft (55m) aerial on the roof of their business. That forward-looking business development was in July 1959. Within three years the company had gone into liquidation, having first retrenched its premises into Dawson House, its purpose-built store. There was no indication as to what happened in particular

THE JEWELLERS SINCE 1875

J O H N   M O R T O N   L T D.,
48/49 NASSAU STREET   -   DUBLIN
(Corner of Grafton Street, opposite Trinity College)
Jewellers, Silversmiths, Watchmakers.   Specialists in Antique Silver and Souvenirs.

167. Morton on Nassau Street. Capitalizing on the footfall towards Grafton Street.

to cause the collapse. The slowdown in the building trade was probably a major factor, even though they had a nationwide reach and were prepared to do work in any part of the country. The closure was announced on 30 June 1962 and the business was wound up almost immediately with a closing down sale in July that continued well into the autumn. Although the buildings moved into the commercial sector, they did not find permanent tenants and they were set for redevelopment by the end of the 1960s. The departure of this store ended any significant retail business on the street, though Elvery's continued at the junction with Nassau Street. The developing office sector prompted demolitions and redevelopments and by 1970, Dawson Street was commercial.

If the main streets were finding it hard to retain their long-established businesses, then little better might be expected in the secondary streets. This section on the streets around Grafton Street concludes with a look at **South King Street**, the street that terminated the main shopping district. It was never an important shopping street and was always a mixture of pubs, manufacturers

168. New insurance development on Dawson Street, 1967.

and their agents, combined with local provision for the housing schemes in the locality.

In the early 1950s, a visitor turning into South King Street would immediately have met three pubs, perhaps reflecting the fact that there were no pubs on Grafton Street itself, though the need was met in the side streets. Further down there were two newsagents and the offices of the American Window Cleaning Company, which had been around since the latter years of

169. St Stephen's Green awaiting redevelopment in 1983.

the nineteenth century. A little further on and the premises of Booth Bros, who produced mechanical tools, was reached and then on past shopfitters, plumbers, automotive engineers and the goods of Peter Kennedy, the baker. The other side of the road was a similar eclectic mix with the Gaiety Theatre providing the focal point. This was an area in transition in the 1950s and 1960s as one manufacturing outlet replaced another for a time. Thus, Alan Gay Ltd, dress manufacturer, replaced Booth Bros in the early 1960s, Tillie and Henderson, shirt manufactures, replaced Peter Kennedy. A large section of the northern side of the road beside the Gaiety Theatre was vacant in the late 1960s, having once been the location of Sunbeam Wolsey, hosiery manufacturing. Industry was either closing or moving to the suburbs and the area was changing. This was not just on South King Street but in the block immediately to the south where the St Stephen's Green shopping centre would eventually replace the current buildings – but not before they had performed the important function of being Dublin's flea market during the 1970s, the Dandelion Market.

One use, though, that was ahead of its time and which was found on North King Street and Anne Street in the early 1950s was cycle parks. These were locations where bicycles could be parked in safety, or at least in relative safety; there was a court case in 1951 that would have raised concerns. One Christopher Russell, cycle park attendant and master criminal, was sentenced to two months' imprisonment for having in his possession four bicycles, five mud splashers, four pumps, five battery lamps, four bicycle pump connections and one bell. The articles were found in his home. Unfortunately, the cycle parks did not survive into the 1950s, perhaps because of activities such as the above.

Westmoreland and D'Olier streets

D'Olier Street and Westmoreland Street were designed by the Wide Streets Commissioners as shopping streets and their outline plans for the buildings show shops on the ground floor. Presumably, it was believed that the flows of people along the monumental axis from Sackville Street and on into College Green would be sufficient to generate good business for the traders there. The streets did, indeed, develop as shopping streets but only to a degree and with a significant difference between Westmoreland Street and D'Olier Street. The latter suffered from not being on the direct route to College Green until the modern one-way traffic system was put in place.

Like many other streets in the early 1950s, the shops would have been familiar to people from an earlier generation. The most notable buildings on the west side of Westmoreland Street were Rowan Seeds which had large premises beside the Bank of Ireland, and the impressive Bewley's Café with its fine coffee and excellent cakes. Others might have been drawn to this part of the street to make use of the travel offices of the shipping companies.

Crossing to the triangular island that divides Westmoreland Street from D'Olier Street was not always the easiest of occupations because of the volume of traffic that used the street. The trams, and later the buses, made the crossing almost as exciting as getting across O'Connell Bridge. On the Westmoreland Street side of the island was an interesting mix of uses. John Purcell had the greatest vantage point from his position on the apex. Otherwise, there was a run of outfitters, Kennedy and McSharry, Best, Menswear Ltd and Woodrow Hats. It was a little enclave of outfitters for men, without any sign of ladies' stores. Watson, the fish merchant, closed in the later 1960s by which time both Woodrow Hats and Menswear Ltd were also gone. The newcomers included the offices of Pan Am and expanded offices for the Educational Building Society and the Provincial Bank.

D'Olier Street did not have much retailing, with the exception of Kennedy and McSharry which also opened on to Westmoreland Street. Its most distinctive characteristic was that it was here that Dubliners came to buy their coal from the large number of coal suppliers on the street. In the early 1950s,

170. Aerial photograph from late 1940s, showing the island between Westmoreland and D'Olier streets.

there was the Diamond Coal Co., Wallace, Tedcastle McCormack, Murphy and Co., with Donnell Coal on Westmoreland Street. Over time, there was some change to the company line up but the general concentration was maintained. Otherwise, it was a mix of commercial businesses with auctioneers, shipping companies, publishers and some singular uses such as the Dublin Bible Depot and the Irish Family Burial Society. The most impressive of these operations was the Dublin Gas Company's fine art deco façade with its symmetry and finely etched glass panels. There was one major change, though. D'Olier Street was home to the Red Bank Restaurant, which was famous for its seafood and which had developed an air of danger during the Second World War because of its regular use by the staff of the German and British embassies. In the 1950s, it was doing good business and it supplied oysters and seafood until 1968. Its closure sent ripples across the city and there

Shopping is easy and pleasant at McBirneys, the famous departmental store at O'Connell Bridge, Dublin. Easy because so many items for you, every member of your family and your home can be selected under one roof. Pleasant because a grand variety of merchandise—with prices clearly marked—can be seen at a glance as you leisurely stroll around . . . and, of course, the excellent value offered in all departments is more than pleasant—it's sensational !

By the way, you should visit our café before or after your shopping. It opens at 9 a.m.—the food is delicious, the service excellent.

171. McBirney's advertisement from 1955. Note the emphasis that it is at O'Connell Bridge.

was a feeling that another essential part of the city had been lost. The fact that it was bought by the Blessed Sacrament Fathers as a church and shrine suppliers left Dubliners, who usually can deliver a quip at a moment's notice, speechless.

A left turn from Westmoreland Street would have brought the shopper onto Aston Quay. This was where McBirney's continued their long-term strategy of trying to persuade shoppers that they were only forty paces from O'Connell Bridge, because, otherwise, there was little to attract the casual shopper down the quays. McBirney's was a national household name and it offered a postal service to all parts of the country. At one time it had the added advantage that the country buses stopped almost outside the door. This ended with the building of Busáras but McBirney's soldiered on and was still there at the end of the 1960s, even though many of the other properties around it were either vacant or demolished.

172. Worth jewellers with the Nelson Pillar still in place.

O'Connell Street

The appearance of O'Connell Street was dramatically changed by the destruction of the Nelson Pillar in 1966. The Pillar had been the 'city centre' and with its loss and non-replacement, that concept became much more ambiguous. The closure of Laird, the chemist, in the early 1950s, had already removed a very distinctive element from the street. Laird had always advertised themselves in large letters on the façade of their building and they featured in many photographs and postcards of the Pillar. Worth, the jewellers who replaced them, carried on this tradition, though in a somewhat more muted way.

O'Connell Street was always a mixture of land uses with more retail on the lower part of the street and more business and commerce on the upper part. While there was not much change in the kind of business undertaken on the street, or its distribution, some iconic elements were lost. During the 1950s, there were many banks, a smattering of ice cream parlours, the various cinemas, the Gresham Hotel and a mixture of retailing that encompassed nationally known brands and much smaller operations.

The shops that everybody knew included Clerys, Findlater, Eason, the Monument Creamery and Café and Lemon's sweet shop. Clerys was an institution and central to the business life of O'Connell Street. It was multifunctional in that it offered a restaurant, café and a ballroom as well as a

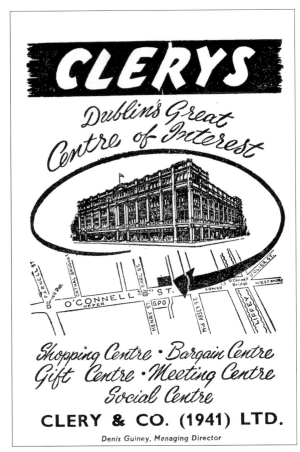

173. Clerys advertisement from 1959.

convenient clock under which couples could meet. It vied with Switzers and Brown Thomas in terms of the range of goods that it offered and it by no means surrendered the high-fashion arena to them – take for example, the fur week in 1952. They offered across the range of retailing from clothing to furniture, cookware, crockery and sporting goods. They even had a men's department hidden away in a corner. Up to the middle 1960s, they used to offer a postal service but, as another reflection of changed times, this was discontinued. Because Clerys was owned by Dennis Guiney who also ran Guiney's shop on Talbot Street, the marketing of the two stores could be dovetailed to allow Guiney's to focus on those for whom value was a more pressing concern while allowing Clerys to take the middle ground. Despite the economic circumstances of the 1950s, Clerys did well financially (see Costello and Farmer, 1992) and maintained an air of formality by maintaining long

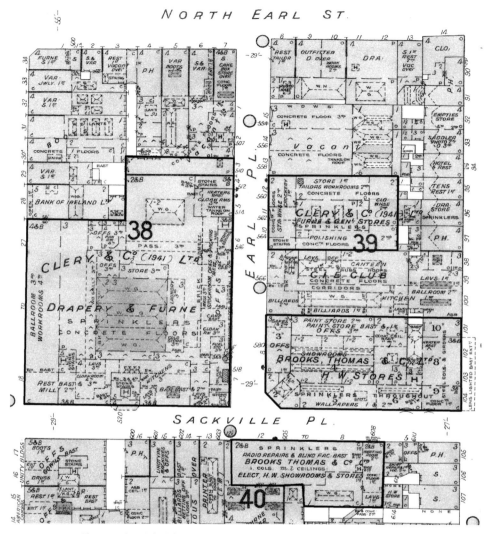

174. Clerys and Brooks Thomas. (Extract from Goad Fire Insurance Plan, 1961.)

wooden counters and requiring the staff to be dressed formally. This model had
to change in the 1960s and it seems that this posed challenges for the store.

Clerys occupied most of the block, as can be seen on the extract from the
Goad Fire Insurance Plan, and also had a warehouse across Earl Place.
Sackville Place was also a retail street in its own right because of the presence
of Brooks Thomas, the hardware store. It occupied most of the block on the
northside. Indeed, because of its extensive stores and yards on Lower Abbey

Street (now the Irish Life Centre), it may well have been the largest business in the area. At the end of the decade, having such a land-intensive use in a city centre was an anachronism and it would have disappeared long before had that part of the city been a zone of assimilation. Even so, it eventually gave way to the Irish Life development of the early 1970s, the first phase of which was completed in 1977.

Fortunately for the street, Clerys continued unchanged during the 1960s but the iconic Findlater store was lost and replaced by an anonymous office block. Moving up the block from North Earl Street, there were three well known outfitters – Burton on the corner, Madame Nora for higher class dresses and Kingstons for menswear. In addition was the 'Happy Ring House', which still carries the logo. Kingstons had been on O'Connell Street since the rebuilding of the Hammam block in 1927 and they had gradually expanded to occupy 9–13 O'Connell Street and the important corner site onto Cathedral Street. Following a major refurbishment in 1965, they were said to have the largest window area of any man's outfitters in Ireland and they also had a branch on George's Street and Grafton Street. The location also emphasizes the point made earlier about men's clothing. They tended not to occupy prime sites, either on streets or in department stores. Thus, there was a little run of them on the island between Westmoreland Street and D'Olier Street. Here the store was a big one but it was on the edge of the shopping district. This simply reflected the fact that men were not the best comparison shoppers and that, generally, men regarded shopping as merely a task to be completed as quickly as possible. All that mattered was that the store was reasonably convenient. Kingstons' particular claim to fame was their range of shirts and they were known for their slogan 'A Kingston shirt makes all the difference'. They also sold suits, hats and shoes and they were not afraid to cater to the more adventurous man! As their general manager put it in 1965: 'today men want light jacket colours – fawns and biscuit colours or different shades of grey. It is all part of the average man's increasing fashion-consciousness, a trend which, Mr Anderson hopes, will naturally evolve to include hats. For no man, he insists, is well dressed without one' (*Irish Independent*, 4 June 1965, p. 18).

Findlater was so synonymous with the upper part of O'Connell Street that the corner on which it stood was called Findlater's corner. The reasons for its demise have been dealt with earlier and reflected its inability to adjust to the changed terms of grocery retailing. Its loss was also a loss for the street because no use was found for its extensive premises and they were vacant at the end of

175. Advertisement for Kingstons.

the 1960s and soon to be demolished. This left that upper part of the street mainly to entertainment services. The Savoy Cinema also maintained a high quality restaurant and the Gresham Hotel occupied most of the remainder of the block. This also had an effect on the stores between Cathal Brugha Street and Parnell Street and they went through a range of changes, though the newsagent at the strategic corner of Parnell Street gave itself a distinctive identity as Heraldic House. The Monument Creamery was also a casualty of the 1960s and their premises beside the Carlton Cinema passed to the Revenue Commissioners.

It has already been noted that Laird, the chemist, had been replaced by Worth, the jewellers. The Metropole had been a quality hotel before it was destroyed in 1916 and it was redeveloped as a cinema and restaurant complex. Not obvious to the casual visitor because it was hidden from sight, the Capitol

176. Upper O'Connell Street at the beginning of the 1950s.

Cinema was another popular place for Dubliners in Princes Street. The queues outside the Metropole, Capitol, Carlton, Savoy and Ambassador testified to the popularity of cinema. But it was not enough to sustain the Metropole in the long term and, while it was part of the life of the city during the 1950s and 1960s, it was demolished and redeveloped by British Home Stores (BHS) in 1972. Eason was the other well-known store on the block while Mansfield Shoes occupied the strategic corner of lower O'Connell Street and Middle

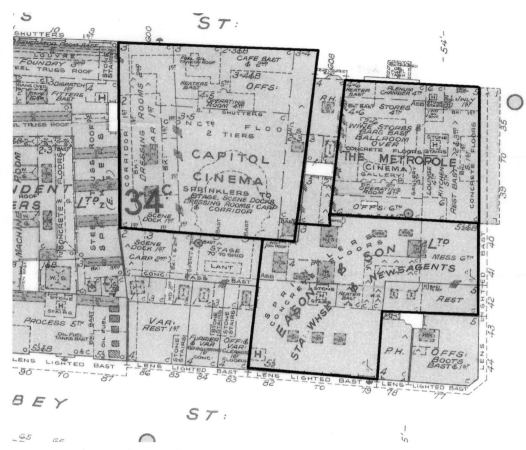

177. The Capitol, Metropole and Eason. (Extract from Goad Fire Insurance Plan, 1961.)

Abbey Street. While the brand disappeared in the early 1950s as did the True Form Boot Company, the stores continued their role as Tylers. Dubliners' love of ice cream was facilitated by Cafollas near O'Connell Bridge on the east side and 'the Ice Cream Parlor' on the opposite side.

Lemon's pure sweets was another iconic store. It was a relatively small unit on the block between Bachelor's Walk and Middle Abbey Street but the business dated back to 1852 and their tooth defying boiled sweets were part of every Christmas, if not other times of the year. They also had a distinctive façade, identifying The Confectioner's Hall and it was brightly lit in the evening; remnants of the name still survive. Unfortunately, it was gone by the late 1960s and replaced by the Kentucky Chicken Restaurant, though manufacture of the sweets continued in Drumcondra until the 1980s.

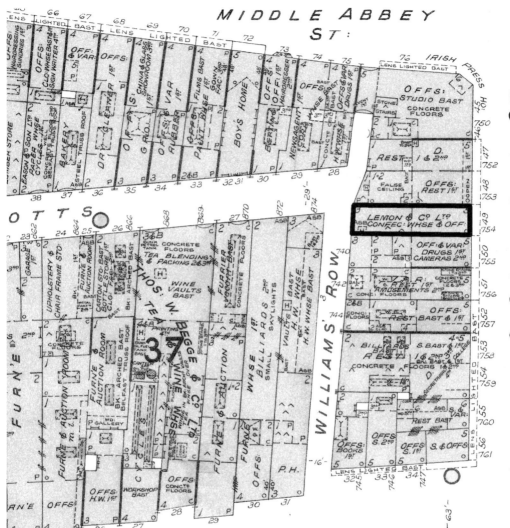

178. The layout of the west side of Lower O'Connell Street. Note the small size of the individual units. (Extract from Goad Fire Insurance Plan, 1961.)

Though most of the land uses present in 1950 were still there in the late 1960s, the character of the street was different because of the significance of what had been lost. This was probably felt more during the working day when the street functioned as a business centre and had far less significance at night when the street became the entertainment hub of the city with its cinemas, clubs and restaurants.

179. A view of the west side of Lower O'Connell Street. Lemon's is highlighted.

180. Advertisement for Lemon's sweets in 1954.

Henry Street

This street was always the competition to Grafton Street on the northside and it had some heavyweight draws in the form of Arnotts department store and Roches department store across the road from it. Further down the street at the junction of Mary Street and Jervis Street was the equally impressive Todd Burns department store. Add to the mix a Woolworth and a Monument Creamery and it is clear why it was an important shopping destination in the early 1950s. The focus on Henry Street, like Grafton Street, was mainly on clothing with perhaps a few more food stores than Grafton Street. It was dominated both in commercial and spatial terms by the two big stores of Arnotts and Roches and there was space for relatively few other uses. While Todd Burns ultimately struggled, see p. 323, Arnotts did very well during this period. The picture painted by Nesbitt (1993) is of steady growth in retail (though not as good in wholesale) during the 1950s and 1960s which resulted in the confidence to go ahead with a long term major refurbishment of the store. In 1958, a contract for the rebuilding of nos 7–10 was signed and provided the store with wider spaces, an extended balcony, ground and basement level. To this was added additional workshop and wholesale space. The length of window display on Henry Street increased by more than half and there were forty retail departments where there had been thirty-five. Profits had been steady at £50,000 per year during the late 1950s but broke through the £100,000 barrier in 1961 and reached £200,000 in 1964. In all, as Nesbitt put it, the Consumer Price Index rose by 60 per cent during the 1960s and while the wholesale department managed to beat it slightly by increasing by 66 per cent, the retail managed 189. Clearly, things had gone well for Arnotts.

In the 1950s, Woolworth had a large and popular store and Slowey's, ladies' outfitters and drapers, would also have been a well-known shop. The 50/- tailors had spread from here to Grafton Street with their offer of good suits for low prices but there were quite a number of other tailors on the street, including three branches of Premier Tailors as well as Galligans. Food was supplied by the Home and Colonial stores (later to be merged with Liptons), the simply named Bacon Shops (who also had a branch on Grafton Street), Hafners as well as Liptons in its own right and the Monument Creamery. H. Williams had large premises between nos 45–7. They were not yet organized as a supermarket but their scale was an indication of what was to come. Very little changed between 1950 and 1970. Cassidy's fashions arrived to replace Dolcis shoes and Morris tailoring and the Monument Creamery closed but, otherwise, the same stores were trading in the same places.

181. Advertisement for
Arnotts, 1965.

200
steps
in the
right
direction . . .

From Nelson Pillar
in O'Connell Street, focal point of the
city's activity, take 200 steps down Henry
Street—no more, no less. On your left is
Arnotts, one of Dublin's leading department
stores. Arnotts stock all that's best in
Irish quality goods—tweeds, linens, lace
and Waterford glass—and the choicest
merchandise from overseas. Smart
restaurants, too.

Arnotts

HENRY STREET, DUBLIN   TELEPHONE 46801

182. The Moore Street redevelopment site.

As the 1960s passed, there was anticipation along the street about Dublin Corporation's plans for redevelopment of a large area of the north inner city. Feelings were mixed about the potential impact on the street but it was agreed that there was a need to do something about the decay that was close by Henry Street. Take, for example, Denmark Street where Roches stores occupied the corner side. A short walk along the street in the early years of the 1950s and the walker would have met tenements, Hendron Brothers machinery, a run of demolished or ruinous buildings from nos 10–15, more tenements, the occasional grocer, furniture dealer and manufacturer and then, returning on the other side of the road would have seen yet further tenements until Denmark House was reached, still a fine building amid the ruination around it. Five years or so later and much of Denmark House was vacant, there was more demolition and the transformation of the sites into surface car parks. It remained ripe for redevelopment at the end of the 1960s.

Despite the nearby decay, such was its popularity at Christmas that the street would be so crowded that any attempt at rapid movement was impossible. Its impact on the traffic flows on O'Connell Street at Christmas was mentioned earlier. A feature of the street at that time was the street traders who, then as now, were allowed to sell on the street on payment of a licence fee, which in 1969 was 5s. They operated on the basis of a small profit and quick return based on little or no overheads but they too were finding that the supermarkets were able to outprice them (*Irish Times*, 20 December 1966, p. 6).

If Grafton Street was the best shopping street in Dublin, then Henry Street might be taken to be the busiest one. That, at least, is how it was presented in an uncommon puff piece in the *Irish Times* in 1969, though there was concern that business had reached its peak. The writer seemed to think that depopulation in the locality would pose a threat but that would assume that the street depended on local shopping to a far greater extent than was the case.

> One need only have eyes in one's head and a moderate degree of perception to realize that Dublin's Henry Street is a very successful shopping street. The high level of shoppers at all times, the milling crowds at week-ends, the evidence of thousands, perhaps hundreds of thousands of pounds, poured into expansion and modernization of premises and the attraction of new shops to the street, some of them branches of businesses established in other parts of the city, are evidence that a success story has been building up in Henry street and now perhaps has reached its peak.

CRIES OF DUBLIN

" The last o' the long decoraychains ! "

183. Tradition on Henry Street. The Christmas crowds in 1954 and the Tower Bar not allowing standards to slip in 1957.

While the response of Mr Doody of the Henry Street Association was positive and he asserted the quality of business on the street, his logic was not entirely convincing in explaining the particular success of Henry Street:

> The reasons for success Mr Doody ascribed first to the physical factor of location. 'Proximity to the G.P.O. is important,' he said. 'The Post Office is a stable institution, and areas associated with general post offices are usually stable also. Then, it is a known fact that the best shopping streets are those which run off main arteries. O'Connell Street is a terminal for many bus services, and we believe that many of our customers even those who are car owners, travel by bus, particularly women. Any street thus located which has a variety of shops must succeed'.

The description of the street in this piece was not greatly different to that offered in the 1940s and so perhaps little had changed. The street had been called 'democratic' on a previous occasion (*Irish Press*, 19 January 1934, p. 13) and it is an interesting description for a street. Its repetition so many years later must say something about the way that other streets were perceived. The idea of dressing up to go shopping now seems bizarre but it appears that certain stores, Switzers for example, had certain expectations of shoppers, even in the 1950s.

> I have always thought of Henry Street and its colourful, perpetually noisy, rather smelly little sister-street round the corner as essentially places for family shopping – the bread and butter type throughout the year, the cake and pudding type at Christmas, with occasional forays, for fashion or the special gift, into one of the department stores. But times are changing and the street with it. Nothing has been lost but much has been added. More glamour, more fashion, more tempting displays with prices going higher but starting even lower. It's still a family street, with fathers, mothers and children still dominant, but more and more of the other age groups to be seen – young teenagers, late teenagers, courting couples and the newly married. It's certainly the most democratic street in Dublin, with every income group from poorest to richest, the child with 5/- out of his money-box, the woman in pursuit of a new fur coat, rubbing shoulders in the packed square yards of the pavement and roadway.
>
> (*Irish Times*, 18 December 1969, p. 18)

184. Henry Street following pedestrianization. (A.J. Parker.)

Mary and Talbot streets

The reason for grouping **Mary** and **Talbot** streets together in this discussion is because of the function they performed. Whereas the southside shopping district was to be found on either side of Grafton Street, though to a far greater extent on its western side, the northside equivalent was essentially linear with Henry Street in the middle. Talbot Street was the main route to Henry Street from Amiens Street Railway Station and many of the northside buses made their way to their terminus via Talbot Street. Mary Street led ultimately into Capel Street but it was not a major transportation artery.

Both streets offered a range of local services as well as hosting some well-known stores. Mary Street was probably the better shopping street, mainly because Todd Burns, the department store, drew shoppers all the way down as far as the junction with Jervis Street. It had a mixture of outfitters, shoe shops, chemists, grocers, tobacconists and some less common uses such as Jackson's Loan Office (i.e., a pawnbroker) at no. 29. There was also the Mary Street Cinema at nos 12 and 13 but this was gone by the early 1950s and replaced by another store which became very well known – the O'Dea Upholstery and Furniture store. This already had a large manufacturing establishment on Wolfe Tone Street, so it was a logical expansion to take over the cinema. In an example of the phenomenon that specialist stores need not

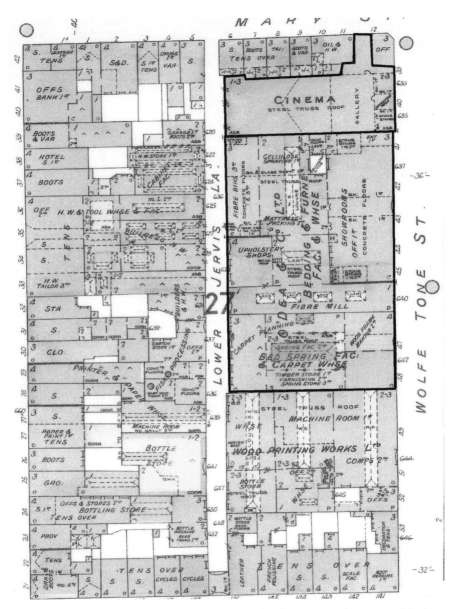

185. Lower Mary Street showing the cinema. Notice also the presence of tenements (Tens) on a shopping street. (Extract from Goad Fire Insurance Plan, 1953.)

follow the normal rules on location, the fashion store of Sydenham was located very near Capel Street. This was a high-fashion store and it survived into the 1950s.

186. Advertisement for Todd Burns in 1953.

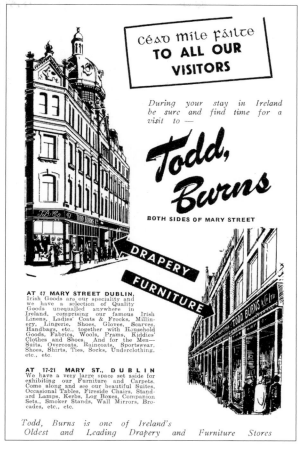

céad míle fáilte
TO ALL OUR VISITORS

During your stay in Ireland be sure and find time for a visit to —

Todd, Burns

BOTH SIDES OF MARY STREET

DRAPERY
FURNITURE

AT 47 MARY STREET DUBLIN, Irish Goods are our speciality and we have a selection of Quality Goods unequalled anywhere in Ireland, comprising our famous Irish Linens, Ladies' Coats & Frocks, Millinery, Lingerie, Shoes, Gloves, Scarves, Handbags, etc., together with Household Goods, Fabrics, Wools, Prams, Kiddies' Clothes and Shoes. And for the Men— Suits, Overcoats, Raincoats, Sportswear, Shoes, Shirts, Ties, Socks, Underclothing, etc., etc.

AT 17-21 MARY ST., DUBLIN We have a very large space set aside for exhibiting our Furniture and Carpets. Come along and see our beautiful Suites, Occasional Tables, Fireside Chairs, Standard Lamps, Kerbs, Log Boxes, Companion Sets, Smoker Stands, Wall Mirrors, Brocades, etc., etc.

Todd, Burns is one of Ireland's Oldest and Leading Drapery and Furniture Stores

Todd Burns was the anchor store on the street and it had been there since the middle of the nineteenth century. While it focused on fashion, as they all did, there was a particular emphasis on making goods available on credit and they marketed themselves heavily to engaged couples as to how they could finance the furnishing of their home. However, that model did not sustain itself into the 1950s and it was in trouble by the end of that decade. This led the directors to consider an entirely new model which involved a fundamental change. The new operation, named Todco, opened in 1962 and had a brief flirtation with a branch on Grafton Street. It brought the supermarket concept to the selling of clothing as well as food. Dresses, suits and clothes were displayed on racks with size and price indicated. There were dressing rooms where the clothes could be tried on and there was a returns system for those that did not fit when tried at home. This is now the standard method of

The opening of Todco's new Self-Service Superstore signals a revolution in Irish Shopping values. Todco is not just a new shop, but a new concept of shopping. Come and see for yourself. Select from a wonderful range of popular top-quality goods — at bargain prices. For the first time glamorous fashions come to you at prices everyone can afford. At TODCO you shop at your leisure — its self-service all the way from selection to check-out. TODCO — the modern self-service superstore — there's nothing like it!

Don't miss the Grand Opening Ceremony at 10.30 a.m. on Friday Family Christmas Hampers to be won by early shoppers.

TODCO LTD., MARY ST., DUBLIN 1

187. Opening day feature for Todco. (*Irish Independent*, 28 November 1962, p. 6). The caption reads: 'The opening of Todco's new Self-Service Superstore signals a revolution in Irish Shopping values. Todco is not just a new shop, but a new concept of shopping. Come and see for yourself. Select from a wonderful range of popular top-quality goods – at bargain prices. For the first time glamorous fashions come to you at prices everyone can afford. At TODCO you shop at your leisure – it's self-service all the way from selection to check-out'.

188. Car parking opportunities while awaiting development around Moore Street.

clothes shopping but it was very new at the time and generated quite a lot of interest. The principle was that the shopper, having chosen the goods, then went to one of the checkouts where they were paid for and wrapped. Downstairs was a food supermarket with an area of 4,500 sq. ft (420 sq. m). There was also a change in emphasis in that the goods were now aimed at the price conscious and they aimed to project a 'cut price' image. In all they had 30,000 sq. ft (2,800 sq. m) of shopping space on the ground floor. The store opened on 30 November 1962 and another innovation was that they capitalized on the dereliction around them to provide supervised car parking for shoppers, the cost of which could be set against purchases.

Talbot Street had Guiney's, a more price-conscious version of Clerys that was very popular with country shoppers during the Christmas season. Being located at the junction with Gardiner Street, it was important in encouraging flows along the street. In 1963, they advertised that the goods in their sale were at cost price or less. 'Buy now … the simple truth is that this time the savings offered you at Guiney's are the greatest you have seen in years. This applies to all departments. Many prices as you will see below are literally slashed. In several departments, there are items that are almost "for nothing"' (*Irish Independent*, 2 May 1963, p. 3). This was no different to the message in 1959 when it was: 'Reductions in a big way bring truly tremendous savings' (*Irish Independent*, 25 June 1959, p. 1) or in 1966 when it was 'Guiney's small profit

189. Advertisement for Blacks on Talbot Street in 1953.

policy as successful as ever' (*Irish Independent*, 28 April 1966, p. 3). However, like Clerys they had abandoned their postal service by 1966, explaining that the postage costs had often been inadequate or had been entirely omitted.

Otherwise, Talbot Street was a mixture of local shopping and specialist stores. In the latter case was the Varian Brush at nos 91 and 92 or Richardson's Wet Weather clothing company at no 5. As with Mary Street, there were tobacconists, chemists, butchers, drapers and a good supply of pubs. Because of the lower rents on this secondary shopping street, it was possible for uses that required more space to locate there. The most notable of these was the furniture stores and there was the Talbot Street Furnisher who later became Guiney's Furniture Stores, Sheeran's lino and carpets, Black and Co. (regarded as high quality furnishers) as well as quite a number of wallpaper and paint shops.

190. Another location awaiting redevelopment. Ormond Quay in the middle 1980s.

There was a flirtation with the supermarket concept during the early 1960s when Kelly's Restaurant and the National Home Stores became Cummiskey Supermarkets (they had been pioneers of self-service on Grafton Street), then Stewarts Supermarket before becoming Newbarrys Furniture Store. Perhaps the most interesting uses were at the Amiens Street end where McHugh Himself was a legendary supplier of bicycles and radios. Almost next door was the New Electric Theatre, which was transformed into Cinerama and specialized in showing very wide-screen versions of movies. It was a street where there was a lot of change during the 1950s and 1960s but with the exception of the Monument Creamery, these were individual stores rather than chains and local rather than iconic.

While there were shopping opportunities in many streets other than the ones described above, there was also an increasing amount of under-utilization and even decay in many of these secondary and tertiary streets. Liffey Street Upper and Lower was an important pedestrian routeway from north to south city across the Ha'penny bridge. It had figured strongly in Abercrombie's plans for a new route linking South Great George's Street to Dominick Street. It led directly onto the junction of Henry Street and Mary Street but an examination of its land use shows that it was largely given over to large scale, space intensive uses such as furniture sales. These were not necessarily high-end furniture stores and there was quite an amount of second-hand sale rooms among them.

There was even a car sales operation at the junction with Middle Abbey Street. The lower part of the street was even more diffuse, though the most coherent use was that of McGrath Tea and Sugar warehouse that occupied much of the eastern side. The remainder included tenements in the upper storeys of buildings that sold curios, paint and yet more furniture. There was no great demand for these properties and it can be easily understood why Dublin Corporation was so anxious to develop the area. Indeed, the low demand for properties along the quays generally resulted in the landscape shown in figure 190.

A polycentric city

By 1970, the shift towards a polycentric city was well underway. Though the road and bus network would continue to focus on the city centre for decades to come, there would soon be an increasing number of competitive nodes for the city centre. Shopping centres would now become part of the normal provision of suburban areas and, as many household names opened stores in these centres, the dominance of the city centre was seriously challenged. It was no longer necessary to make an increasingly fraught journey to a city centre where parking was difficult to obtain and could be at quite a distance from the shops. As time went on, higher-order convenience goods could increasingly be obtained in suburban centres. This, eventually, would lead to the current circumstance where a journey to a suburban centre is now necessary to purchase particular items such as building materials, white goods or electrical items, there being few such outlets in the city centre anymore. Industrial production had gradually been drifting out of the centre since the 1930s but in the later decades of the century, light manufacturing and businesses of all kinds would move to suburban locations to what were first called 'industrial estates' but which later became the more sophisticated sounding 'business parks'. The drift from the centre was faster than the capacity of the city centre to respond either by building alternative in-centre locations or by finding new uses to occupy the deserted spaces. This caused Dublin in the 1970s and 1980s to be characterized by vacant lots in prime locations that had been cleared and left unused. For many years, these provided very useful parking opportunities for Dubliners and the 'bomb site' car parks were a lucrative if unattractive land use for a variety of companies. It would not be until the economic boom of the 1990s that these sites were taken up and streetscapes restored to normality, though there still remain pockets of derelict land that serve as reminders to what was once the case far more generally.

Today, as with many European cities, Dublin is a polycentric entity with a well-developed edge characteristic. Edge cities have large volumes of retail and commercial development at the edge of the city, usually along the major transportation routes. These serve a population drawn from the outer suburbs as well as from the older city and the level of services in these edge developments can easily rival or exceed those of the city centre. The range of large regional scale centres along or close to the M50, including IKEA at Ballymun, is typical of what is found around many European cities today. They attract large volumes of shoppers from considerable distances and the size of the car parking provision is a simple indicator of what makes this kind of development possible. Such is the draw of these centres that consumer flows in the older city are reversed and flow out of the city towards the edge. Essentially, the city has been turned inside out.

Another casualty of increasing suburbanization is local provision. As shopping increasingly became car based and as the frequency of shopping changed, so the local grocery store, butcher and chemist found it increasingly difficult to compete. They could not compete on price and the services they offered were not sufficient to keep them in business. They closed in large numbers and it was not until the 1990s that opportunities opened up again for local stores in some areas selling to a cash-rich, time-poor population who wished to shop at odd hours and for whom price was not a defining characteristic.

Dublin for visitors

Dublin at the beginning of the 1950s

If a visitor was contemplating a visit to Dublin in the 1950s, s/he might have taken a look at *Ireland, An Introduction*, produced by the Department of External Affairs in that year. It aimed to provide an introduction to history, institutions, resources and culture and this it did in the course of forty-six pages. The book pulled no punches on the 'national question' by stating that the territory of the State was a work in progress and that in order to make her full contribution to the world 'she must first obtain full freedom' (p. 11). The Ireland it described was an agricultural nation with 644,000 people directly employed in agriculture compared to 212,000 people in industry. It was expected that most visitors to the country would be attracted by its natural beauty. 'An overnight journey by rail and sea from London, or by air from America, takes you from crowded streets and workshops to the finest ocean coast in Europe with glorious sandy beaches, narrow green fjords running for miles between mountains and outside, when the wind rises, a panther sea that can leap hundreds of feet upon the cliffs' (p. 44). Dublin was not seen as part of that tourist menu, though the author was positive about the city. Writing about the eighteenth century, he noted that 'its chief monument is Dublin which, with its great public buildings, its spacious planning, its many squares and streets of tall dignified houses, has few rivals as a Georgian capital. Large districts of the city – for example the Merrion Square-Fitzwilliam Square area – are intact survivals from this epoch' (p. 40). But the visitor should not expect too much for 'it is true that unlike some other countries Ireland has not great and long traditions of catering for foreign visitors as a highly specialized industry, as a science – indeed, almost as an art. She does not boast palatial hotels, fashionable spas and casinos or elaborately equipped resorts' (p. 44). Despite having to rough it, one million visitors came each year.

John Ryan's picture of Dublin at the beginning of the 1950s is of a rather dull physical city with a bohemian atmosphere. While the extent to which that bohemian nature was enjoyed by the citizenry at large has been challenged, there are others who can attest to the veracity of the experience for some at least. While Ryan's memoir was published in 1975, with all that is implied by that, he saw the city at this time as being in many respects the city that Joyce had left. Granted the city had expanded into places such as Howth, Clontarf,

Cabra, Drumcondra, Kilmainham, Clondalkin and Dundrum but, as he put it, 'the concrete had not yet seeped through every nook and cranny of what was metropolitan Dublin and her four companion boroughs' (Ryan, 1975, p. 5). He makes the point that Dublin was already a 'faded eighteenth century beauty' when Joyce was around and she was in greatly reduced circumstances (though even in poverty, gracious)'. Writing about the 1940s, he argued that this was 'substantially the same city that continued to stand or, with occasional lapses, fall around us; in other words, Joyce's physical city but with motor cars and neon lighting' (p. 6). Yet, this was a city which accommodated the literary and where 'most of the Dubliners I knew then had an alcohol problem – they couldn't get enough of it' (p. 20). Notwithstanding the comment on alcohol, the comment on faded grandeur will chime with those made below on how Dublin was presented to visitors in the 1950s. Ryan saw Dublin as a Georgian city with artistic coherence to which even the Victorian speculators had managed to accommodate themselves. In his view, it was only recent times (i.e., the 1960s and 1970s) that 'developments wholly alien to the eighteenth century idea were pile driven and implanted on the original Georgian matrix'. Whether he would have been as concerned in the 1950s is a moot point. Seeing the city as a valuable organic whole from Georgian times was a relatively new concept and one not recognized in previous periods when people focused on individual buildings and not streetscapes. Ryan offered the reader a window into the world of the literati who inhabited Dublin's pubs; very much a view from the inside. A view from an entirely different perspective was offered by Chiang Yee.

He was a Chinese poet, painter, author and calligrapher who made quite a reputation, especially after the war, for a series of books entitled *'The Silent Traveller in …'* where he offered an outsider's view of places such as London, Edinburgh, New York, San Francisco and Boston. The New York book, first published in 1950, was a particular success but the Dublin volume, published in 1953, failed to sell well because, it was suggested, it was too expensive. It was not a guide to the city but rather a series of experiences from which it is possible to glean a sense of what Chiang Yee felt about Dublin. As with all his books, it is charming, polite and positive but he saw nothing remarkable and we get no sense of Ryan's bohemia from his encounters. Perhaps the most geographical chapter is chapter II, 'How I was going down O'Connell Street', a reference to Gogarty's book, whom he wished he had met. While O'Connell Street was described as being busy with heavy traffic, he found the pace of the city to be much slower than might be expected. As he put it: 'the curious fact

Branches at:
120 Terenure Road, North.
Tel.: 95024.
92 Terenure Road, East.
Tel.: 95112.
6 Summerville Park.

Branches at:
16 Upper Rathmines Road..
Tel.: 92392.
10 Church Gardens.
Bankers—ROYAL BANK.

DEVENEY'S

WHOLESALE & RETAIL PROVISION MERCHANTS

Head Office:

92 Terenure Road East, Dublin

EXPORTERS OF ALL CLASSES OF DRIED AND CANNED FRUIT.   . SUPPLIERS TO THE TRADE..

All Orders to Head Office.   Telephone 95112.

XMAS GIFT PARCELS OF FRUIT MAKE IDEAL PRESENTS FOR YOUR FRIENDS.

Dear Sir/Madam,   November/December, 1949.

Arrangements have been made for sending parcels of undermentioned goods to Great Britain by post. It has been officially announced that these facilities will extend till further notice.

SPECIAL XMAS LOT.

4-lb. Tin Xmas Pudding, Choicest Grade (including postage and packing), 18/-.
Xmas Cake (3-lb. approx.) Almond Paste with Royal Icing. Guaranteed to contain only Purest Irish Butter and Eggs and Richest Fruit (including postage and packing) 25/-.

SPECIAL LOT.

We have been appointed Sole Agents for the largest Canners in Éire.
4 1-lb. Tins Choice Irish Stewed Steak 12/- (plus 2/- Posting and Packing).

XMAS HAMPER.

4-lb. Xmas Pudding
1 Large Xmas Cake, Almond Paste with Royal Icing
6 Packets Chivers Jellies
1 Tin Rich Biscuits   £5
1 Box Sweets   (including Packing
4 Tins Choice Canned Fruit   and Postage).

A

XMAS ORDER.

All Goods Guaranteed No. 1 Quality and Well-known Brands.
1-lb. Whole Almonds
1-lb. Ground Almonds
1-lb. Currants
1-lb. Raisins   s. d.
1-lb. Sultanas   28 0
1-lb. Desic. Coconut   Postage &
½-lb. Glacé Cherries   packing,
1-lb. Sweet Mince   2/-.
Meat
½-lb. Candied Peel

B

	s.	d.
3-lb. Butter	13	0
Postage	2	0
	15	0

Packed in Tin Box.

C

	s.	d.
2-lb. Tin Fruit Salad	4	6
2-lb. Tin Choice Apricots	4	6
2-lb. Tin Pineapple	4	6
Postage	2	0
	15	6

D

	s.	d.
1-lb. Ground Almonds	6	0
1-lb. Whole Almonds	4	0
2-lb. Desiccated Coconut	8	0
Postage and Wrapping	2	0

Special 4-lb. or 8-lb. Boxes Assorted or all one kind of above.
8-lb. Cocoanut at 3/9 per lb.

E

	s.	d.
2-lb. Tin Choice Apricots	4	6
2-lb. Tin Cling Peaches	4	6
2-lb. Tin Pineapple	4	6
2-lb. Tin Bartlett Pears	4	6
Postage and Box	2	0
	20	0

F

	s.	d.
2-lb. Minced Meat	16	0
1-lb. Almond Paste	including	
1-lb. Desic. Cocoanut	Postage.	

G

1-lb. Currants   1-lb. Raisins
1-lb. Sultanas   2-pkt. Jellies
1-lb. Cocoanut
1 Tin Sardines
Small Tin Grape Fruit
15/-. Postage 2/-.

H

4-lb. Sweet Mince Meat. Guaranteed by one of Ireland's leading manufacturers. (Including postage & packing) 12/6.

I

	s.	d.
12 Tins Sardines	18	0
Postage and Packing	2	0
	20	0

J

	s.	d.
12 Jellies, Lamb's or Chivers	12	0
Postage and Packing	2	0
	14	0

K

	s.	d.
2-lb. Rich Fruit Cake, Almond Iced	11	6
3-lb. Rich Fruit Iced Brack	5	0

L

	s.	d.
2-lb. Tin Guavas	3	1
2-lb. Tin Fruit Salad	3	1
Tin, My Lady Pineapple	3	1
Incl. post & packing	11	3

M

Ladies' Fully Fashioned Nylon Stockings, 16/6 & 19/6.

N

3 Large Tins Choice Fruit Salad 15/6.
including Packing and Postage.

O

4-lb. Desiccated Cocoanut, including postage and packing, 18/-.
8-lb. at 3/9 per lb.

P

1-lb. Currants, 1-lb. Raisins, 1-lb. Sultanas, 1 Tin Sardines, 1-lb. Butter, 2 Jellies—15/6.
(Including postage).

Q

1-lb. Tin Fruit Salad, 1-lb. Tin Pineapple, 1-lb. Tin Pears, 1-lb. Tin Apricots—12/- incl. postage.

S

8-lb. Dried Fruit:—Assorted Raisins, Currants and Sultanas for 18/-. incl. postage.

T

BISCUITS.

	s.	d.
4-lb. Choc. Marshmallows	20	0
4-lb. Cocoanut Creams	20	0
4-lb. Butter Creams	20	0

including postage and packing.

U

4 Tins Fruit from the following selection: Peach, Pear, Pineapple, Apricots or Fruit Salad 14/- including Postage.

Irish Dairy Butter, Chilled Before Packing, and Packed in Special Waxed Containers. Guaranteed to Arrive in Good Condition.

TO PREVENT PILFERING ALL PARCELS SECURELY PACKED AND BOUND WITH WIRE BAND BY SPECIAL MACHINE.

CONTINUED OVERLEAF.

191. Order form for Deveney's of Terenure.

is that no one appears to walk fast on O'Connell Street. Dublin seems to retain all its eighteenth-century calm and to get along very happily without any of the fuss and bustle characteristic of modern capitals' (p. 16). The image of O'Connell Street was one of drapers and eating places. At the time of his visit, there were a lot of British tourists in the city and they still seemed to be interested in the dining attractions which Dublin offered (see *Dublin, 1930–1950*). In the years immediately following the end of the Second World War, Dublin emerged as a tourist destination for those anxious to enjoy the ready availability of foods, especially steaks, which remained rationed in Britain. He mused that 'most of the visitors to Dublin seemed to be combining their pleasure-seeking with their eagerness for better food and coupon-free clothes' (p. 21).

This had been good business while it lasted and for those who could not travel there was also a mail order service. The image here from Deveney's (p. 332) in Terenure shows how developed the business was and what was on offer. Not only was there a full range of Christmas fare, and it might be expected that business would be particularly good at that time of year, there was a wide range of other goods including butter, tinned fruit, dried fruit, biscuits, sweets, sardines as well as ladies' fully formed nylon stockings. These goods could be imported free of duty to the UK and there was no limit to the number of parcels. What makes it all the more remarkable was that much of the produce had to come from the colonies and there was a particularly strong representation from Australia. Thus, there was the phenomenon of goods being imported from Australia and then sent to the motherland.

Chiang Yee noticed that not all visitors were British; he heard many different accents and languages, especially when he did the 'tourist things' such as climbing the Nelson Pillar. His hosts were the Earl and Countess of Longford and they brought him to see the environs of Merrion Square where he felt that he had found the Dublin 'of old fame'. He admired the tall, fine houses, the size of the square pleased him and he felt that one could easily appreciate the grandeur of the square in its time of greatness. And therein lies an important observation, there is no reference to modernity in his text. Dublin was a pleasant, peaceful and rather sleepy town.

> On my way out of the square, I met nobody on Upper Mount Street, which is very wide and exceptionally neat, with clear-cut buildings of the same style on both sides. St Stephen's Church, at the far, end, was lit up brightly in the midday sun, and the whole district wore a still and peaceful air.
>
> (p. 58)

Chapter 12 of a *View of Ireland*, produced by the British Association for the Advancement of Science in 1957, offered an excellent essay on the development of the city and it chimes rather well with Chiang Yee's view. R.B. McDowell's essay was probably as close to an objective view of the city as it was possible to get. It correctly identified the then-contemporary forces of change in the city: the solidification of the middle-class areas of the city, the impact of Dublin Corporation's housing programme on the city's geography and the role of renovation and renewal in the city. However, the focus here is on the more impressionistic view that ended the essay and it is a good point of comparison (and corroboration) with the books and guides discussed in this chapter. The author was speaking of the city of Joyce's era.

> It left also a larger and more elusive legacy, the latest layer of tradition of which the historically conscious Dubliner is aware. If Georgian Dublin still provides a framework of frozen dignity for the central nucleus which remains the focus of the city's life, what can be fairly termed Joycean Dublin provides the intellectual with memories from which he can extract standards, style and anecdotage. To this is due the widely held conception of Dublin as a place where seedy splendour rubs shoulders with noisy squalor, where the decline and fall of a ruling caste are clearly perceptible, where creation is often sacrificed to conversation and where conversation is characterized by agile pugnacity and exuberant verbal flamboyance, a reckless mixture of bold and sustained speculation, paradox and romanticised anecdote. This Dublin is fast vanishing in the new age of the film, television and spreading suburbia; but the myth still exercises a potent influence, and Dubliners are kind enough to see to it that the visitor who seeks for traces of the era of *Ulysses* is never wholly disappointed.
>
> (p. 237)

The culinary experience

If one was a visitor and wished to dine out in the early 1950s, then one might have been directed to one of the restaurants associated with the cinemas such as the Metropole or Savoy as a reasonable compromise between the fine dining of the Shelbourne and the day-to-day offerings of a café. In 1952 or 1953, the fare was in solid trencherman style and was not unduly influenced by Continental traditions. The Savoy was open from 10 a.m. to midnight during the week but only from 1 p.m. to 8 p.m. on Sundays. The Savoy trio entertained from 1 p.m. to 2.30 p.m. and from 8.30 p.m. to 11 p.m. A diner could enjoy tomato or kidney soup for 1s. or the consommé royale for 1s. 3d. Entrées comprised minute steak (4s.), curried chicken (5s.) or bacon and 2 eggs at 3s. 6d. There were joints of beef and lamb at 3s. 3d. but chicken was the really expensive item at 5s. 6d. for boiled chicken and ham or roast wing of chicken and bacon. This was before the era of battery chickens, which did so much to turn chicken into the cheap meat that it is today. The specials in March 1952 comprised a grilled pork chop and straw chips for 4s. 6d. or boiled gammon and cabbage for the same price. Fish was also available and ranged from kippers at 2s., to turbot at 5s. 3d. with sole available at 4s. 3d. Among the better value fish was whiting at 3s. and haddock at 2s. 6d. The vegetables were sure to excite and the Savoy followed the modern habit of charging extra for them. Peas were 11d. and baked beans were an impressive 1s. 3d. but potatoes could be had for 7d. and cabbage for 6d.

Ice cream in various forms and flavours formed the dessert opportunity and the diner could expect to pay between 8d. and 2s. 9d. Indeed, there were lots of opportunities for ice cream on O'Connell Street from the various ice cream parlours.

Drinks were more interesting. In a previous volume (Brady, 2014), it was noted that good wine was available at very reasonable prices in Dublin but not differentiated from very ordinary bottles in menus. So it remained in the 1950s. Tastes had not changed. White wine was either Chablis or Liebfraumilch and surprisingly the sweeter wine commanded 20s. per bottle compared to 16s. per bottle for Chablis. Red wine was either Burgundy or Bordeaux but with little differentiation between classed wines and ordinary. Thus, Chambertin, Pommard and Volnay were available for 15s. 6d., less than the Liebfraumilch. As a point of comparison today, a commune-level Chambertin will cost €50 in an off-licence, the sky is the limit in a restaurant, but a decent Liebfraumilch will not cost much more than €10; it can be bought for under €5. From Bordeaux, one could enjoy St Émilion, St Julien and Médoc for between 12s. and 13s. per bottle. Vintages and vineyards were not specified and seemed unimportant, except for the two classed growths available for much the same money. Chateau Palmer was available for 14s. while Chateau Mouton Rothschild was at 16s. 6d. It is to be hoped that those who could afford it enjoyed their Chateau Palmer and maybe put some under the stairs; the 1948 vintage is still alive and sells for about €500. Mouton Rothschild is now stratospheric since it got itself promoted to a first growth in 1973 and a 1947 bottle will cost over €5,500 today. A more recent vintage

Please Remove this Card for Wine List

3/6 LUNCHEON 3/6 TABLE d'HOTE	SPECIAL HIGH TEAS

**3/6 LUNCHEON 3/6
TABLE d'HOTE**

Tomato Juice
or
Consomme Julienne
or
Kidney Soup

———

Fillets of Plaice A L'Orly
or
Braised Steak Menagere
or
Curried Lamb, Rice
or
Minced Chicken and Ham
or
Roast Sirloin Beef, Yorkshire Pudding
or
Assorted Cold Meats, Salad

———

Cabbage, Peas, Grilled Tomatoes
Boiled, Mashed or Chipped Potatoes

———

Coffee

Sweets Extra:

Tapioca Pudding	...	6d.
Apple Tart, Custard	...	6d.
Orange Chantilly	...	6d.
Stewed Prunes, Custard	...	6d.
Strawberry Ice	...	6d.

DINNER ROLLS, 2d. EACH

IN THE CINEMA:
Joseph Cotten : Marilyn Monroe
"N I A G A R A"
Showing at: 3.25; 6.15; 9.05

15/6/53

SPECIAL HIGH TEAS

Including Pot of Tea, Bread and Butter,
Served from 3 p.m. each day.

—⋆—

Steak Garni Savoy	... ...	6/6
Grilled Sirloin Steak & Chips	... ...	5/-
Ham Salad	... ...	4/6
Fried Plaice & Chips	... ...	4/6
Rasher, Sausage, Egg & Chips	... ...	3/9
Dressed Lamb Cutlet & Chips	... ...	3/6
Mushrooms on Toast & Chips	... ...	3/6
Double Egg Omelette & Chips	... ...	3/6
Scrambed Egg on Toast	... ...	3/-
Fried Eggs & Chips	... ...	3/-
Hamburg Steak, Onions & Chips	... ...	3/-
Double Poached Egg on Toast	... ...	2/9
Grilled Kippers	... ...	2/9
Mixed Salad	... ...	2/6

IN THE CINEMA:
Joseph Cotten : Marilyn Monroe
"N I A G A R A"
Showing at: 3.25; 6.15; 9.05

15/6/53

192. Lunch and High Tea menu for Savoy Restaurant, June 1953.

such as the 2007 (regarded as average and therefore more accessible in price terms) will cost at least €500 per bottle for Rothschild while Palmer will cost at least €200 and these are not restaurant prices. So the strange imbalance continued. Sherry or port at 1s. 3d. per glass was also a good bet as long as the brown sweet sherry was avoided and the Cockburn's tawny port was chosen. The food might not have been interesting but there was certainly the opportunity to enjoy good wine. For those of teetotal tastes, tea at 8d. was dearer than coffee at 7d. A year later and the menu had become even less exciting but the same basic range was available as the menu shown above demonstrates.

There was one entertainment available in Dublin in the first half of the decade that was a novelty: speedway racing.

Speedway

Motorcycle races had taken place in Dublin before the Second World War and the Phoenix Park had been a popular venue since 1927. Speedway had been popular in the UK since the late 1920s as both an individual and team sport. It comprised motorcycle races, usually with four but sometimes six competitors, racing around an oval track. What made it different was that the cycles were standardized and had no gears and no brakes. It really was rider against rider. The newspapers of the day reported considerable interest in racing on the Continent and in the road races that occurred but the idea of a dedicated track in Dublin had to wait until the post-war period. Northern Ireland was more advanced in this regard and in 1946, the *Irish Times* reported that the track at Bangor would soon reopen. It noted that speedway was billed as the great sport of the future with all its thrills and spills and that the Bangor track was adjudged one of the best in the British Isles. It reported that speeds of 80mph (130km) had been recorded (*Irish Times*, 9 February 1946, p. 4). By December of that year, the *Irish Times* was reporting that nineteen speedway tracks had been approved in the UK and they were set to inject £250,000 (7 December 1946) into the business. The attraction of daredevil riders on gearless, brakeless bikes was huge and by 1948, a promoter was offering to open a 'dirt track' in Santry (29 May) and by mid-1948, the Santry Saints was competing there against British teams. The popularity of the sport grew and was such that it both attracted international stars to Dublin and facilitated the opening of another speedway track at Shelbourne Road in the greyhound stadium. The new track opened on 9 May 1950 before a crowd of 10,000 and this became the primary venue for the sport. It proved popular to begin with and good crowds attended. The matches were reported in the major newspapers and there was a dedicated slot on the radio. The Shelbourne Tigers enjoyed success against visiting English league teams and this helped boost popularity. All throughout 1950, the newspapers reported victories by the Shelbourne Tigers against UK opposition in front of capacity crowds.

Racing was an afternoon event with races on Sunday afternoon in Shelbourne Road, usually at 3.30 p.m. By 1951, the greyhound racing track at Chapelizod had been refitted for speedway with a capacity of 20,000 and the possibility of racing under lights. The opening meeting took place on 28 March and the *Irish Times* reported that 'in spite of the rain which slowed the track, the racing was of the highest class, the riders providing a thrilling spectacle in the artificial lighting glittered on the machines as the riders hurtled around' (p. 8). The Dublin Eagles enjoyed success against British teams, just as the Shelbourne Tigers did.

A typical meeting might have fourteen heats between the teams with four riders in each heat. Points were awarded for first, second and third and the

Charles Arthur

Good Afternoon Everybody,

Well ! After a long trip in Britain the "Tigers" are back here to-day and looking forward to a fine match with Harringay. Welcome again to Jeff Lloyd, and of course to the new Match Race Champion "Split" Waterman, who won the title from Jack Parker last week. Jack Biggs was a star of the Fourth Test Match at Birmingham, scoring 16 out of 18 points, an exceptionally fine achievement, which together with Jack Young's performance gave the victory to Australia.

To-day, if the "Tigers" can defeat this leading London Team, they will really feel they have achieved something.

Bristol last Sunday really fought hard in every heat and I'm pleased to-day to record that the "Tigers" kept up their winning sequence.

What have the "Tigers" been doing this last week ? Well—they travelled away to Aldershot right after last Sunday's meeting—then down came the rain so the team, wet and bedraggled, made their way back from Aldershot to London—arrived at midnight and then were on the train next morning for a 230 mile ride to St. Austell in Cornwall. We managed to draw this match by some very fine riding in the last heat by Jimmy Gibb and Royal Carrol. Four points down before the last heat—and the local riders were already thinking they had won the match, but Jimmy and Royal shot away to a flying start to make it a 5 points to one heat victory and a drawn match.

On Wednesday we went to Aldershot where the postponed Monday night's Meeting was held. Jimmy Gibb was out of action with his motor blown up, so took no part in the match. All the "Tigers" rode exceptionally well but we had to accept defeat by Trevor Redmond and his team, who have not yet been defeated at Aldershot. However, the "Tigers" want to go back there again as soon as possible since they know that being now used to the tricky track that they could defeat Aldershot. We'll see !

Johnny Roccio took a bad spill at Aldershot, the mechanics are taking his bike to pieces trying to straighten the frame and forks which were bent a little, so here's hoping they fix it in time.

Johnny Gibson did some good riding and twice laid down his bike to save running into fallen riders. Good work Johnny.

Yours Sincerely,
CHARLES ARTHUR.

193. Pages from a Speedway programme for 1951.

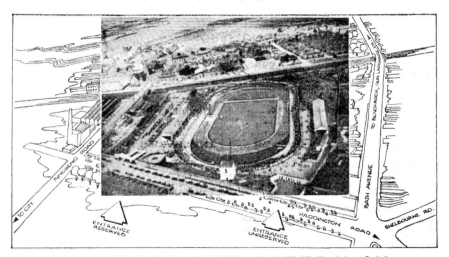

SHELBOURNE SPEEDWAY

EVERY SUNDAY - - 3.30 p.m.   BOOKING AT MESSRS. CLERY'S, O'CONNELL ST.,
Promoter—RONNIE GREENE, M.B.E.   EACH THURSDAY, FRIDAY & SATURDAY.

ADMISSION: RESERVED STAND, 4/6 & 3/6. CHILDREN HALF-PRICE. UNRESERVED
COVERED STAND, 2/-. CHILDREN, 1/-.

HOME TEAM — Ronnie Moore (Capt.), Norman   VISITING TEAMS—ALL ENGLISH 1st DIVISION
Parker, Ernie Roccio, Cyril Brine, Denis Grey,   TEAMS.
Geoff. Marden, Reg. Trott, Des. Monson, Don Terry.

194. Speedway advertisement for 1952.

cumulated score determined the winner. As an additional incentive, there was the Irish National Championship trophy, which was presented by Independent Newspapers. In addition, there were novelty events such as that for Sunday 12 August 1951 in Shelbourne Park when event 15 was a 'mass cycle race' open to boys only aged '7–12 years and 65–85 years'.

It was truly an international sport with stars moving between teams as opportunities arose, but it was short lived in Dublin. By 1952, Speedway was in trouble and was having difficulty attracting the crowds and in spring of that year, several evenings in Shelbourne were cancelled and there was no money to support the Tigers. Nonetheless, a speedway event was part of the official programme for the opening season of An Tóstal in 1953 on 19 April and there was an international meeting between England and New Zealand in Shelbourne Road on 26 July, at 3.30 p.m. Its success was seen as important in deciding the continuing fate of the sport. It was expensive to run and the management were not making enough money to sustain the teams; public interest was waning as the novelty wore off. The sport continued to splutter and the *Irish Times* reported in March 1954 that the owners of the Chapelizod track were trying to get a match between a team of Irish riders and a UK side and, if successful, 'Dublin would once again hear the roar of the machines of the crash-helmeted steel-booted dare-devils that had been silent in the metropolis for the past two years' (p. 19). They were successful for a time in 1954 as the all-Dublin team – the Chapelizod Falcons – competed, as before, against UK stars. The Shelbourne Tigers also revived and enjoyed success. But this was to be a short-lived revival and by January 1955, the *Irish Press* was told by the managing director of Shelbourne Park, Mr Paddy O'Donoghue, that there were no plans for speedway for 1955. As he put it, there was no real spirit of competition and the Irish public had lost interest (*Irish Press*, 21 January 1955, p. 8). Stock car racing had replaced it in the minds of some of the public but, though it had a following, it never managed the sheer enthusiasm of the early days in Dublin. It had been only a five-year phenomenon but it had seen the establishment of an international sport in the city which added a little more colour to a wet Sunday afternoon. There was an attempt to revive speedway racing in 1970 at Shelbourne Park with a new generation of Shelbourne Tigers. The programme for Sunday 5 July stated that 'it's great to be back in Shelbourne Park after so many years and hear to roar of the bikes and see the red shale flying again'. It was not to be; the attractions of dog racing won out over motorbikes.

To recap, in the early 1950s, Dublin was a pleasant place to visit with a genteel, if faded, streetscape but with an ability to enjoy itself, if you knew the right places. Visitors had returned after the Second World War and they were now more diverse than ever. English tourists initially came to eat well but even towards the end of the 1940s, visitors from further afield were being seen in the city. The chapter will explore this in more detail and see how Dublin was presented to its visitors and what might have been on the agenda for an interested tourist.

Dublin and tourism

Dublin had been an important tourist destination since Queen Victoria popularized the idea of tourism in Ireland by her appreciation of Killarney and an industry developed around the production of guides to the city. Even in the dark days of the Second World War, these guides continued to be printed and new editions were produced to assist with the surge in visitors that occurred at the end of the war. The big change for Dublin was the improvement in connectivity that took place as a result of the development of transatlantic and Continental air routes. It is important to recall that Dublin was not easy to reach as a tourist destination before the days of air travel. The sea journey was long and uncomfortable and involved less than glamorous rail travel. Motoring holidays were becoming more common despite the complex customs rules and ships that were not set up for transporting cars. They had to be carried in the hold and winched aboard. It was not speedy and must have been somewhat heart-stopping for the car owners to watch. Granted there had been a drive-on, drive-off service between Larne and Stranraer since the 1930s but there was still the issue of customs to be dealt with in crossing the border.

The Second World War changed the global horizons of many US citizens and Europe became an important tourist destination. This also prompted an increased effort to market Ireland abroad, though the advertisement reproduced here seemed to have forgotten about Dublin. The Irish diaspora was an obvious target for visits to Ireland and An Tóstal, held for a number of years from 1953, was an organized attempt to encourage such travel especially in the spring season. It gradually fizzled out after 1958 because it could not be shown that it had achieved any significant increase in tourist numbers.

Connectivity

The era of air travel only became a reality for Dubliners in the 1930s with the opening of Aer Lingus routes to Bristol and then to London. The building of a fine airport at Collinstown provided the infrastructure for a rapid expansion and it offered facilities that were as good as anywhere in Europe. Not that

195. Extending the season. Advertisement for tourism in Ireland in 1954.

196. An Tóstal and its targets. (*Dublin Opinion*, 1953, p. 22.)

197. Aer Lingus advertisement in 1953.

everyone believed that the future lay in land based aircraft; there was a strong body of opinion at first which believed that seaplanes were the future.

The post-war period proved busy for Dublin Airport and data for 1949 indicated that passenger numbers had reached over 200,000 with marginally more arrivals than departures. Aer Lingus accounted for the greater part of these, over 193,000, because it had a virtual monopoly on the airport. The remainder was due to charters and a shared arrangement between KLM and Aer Lingus on the Amsterdam route. Aer Lingus itself did not hugely alter its pattern of routes in the early 1950s but it was central to making Dublin much more accessible. It did this by developing a series of relationships with other European airlines and 'through ticketing'. Of course, such travel involved a change of aeroplane but this was not seen as the annoyance it is today. This worked both ways, of course, so that it facilitated the Irish going further afield

AER LINGUS

PASSENGER FARES

ALL FARES AND RATES ARE SUBJECT TO ALTERATION WITHOUT NOTICE

Route	One-Way £ s. d.	17-Day Excursion £ s. d.	Round-Trip £ s. d.
Between DUBLIN			
and Birmingham ...	5 16 0	8 10 0	10 9 0
Bristol ...	6 2 0	8 19 0	11 0 0
Cardiff ...	5 11 0	8 3 0	10 0 0
Edinburgh ...	5 16 0	8 2 0	10 2 0
Glasgow ...	5 5 0	7 4 0	9 2 0
Isle of Man ...	2 10 0	3 10 0	4 10 0
Liverpool ...	4 8 0	6 11 0	7 15 0
London ...	8 2 0	12 10 0	14 5 0
Manchester ...	4 15 0	6 16 0	8 6 0
Shannon ...	3 3 0	4 10 0	5 8 9
Jersey ...	10 10 0	—	18 18 0
From DUBLIN		Valid for 23 days only	
To Paris ...	13 0 0	—	23 8 0
Lourdes ...	20 0 0	30 9 0	36 0 0
Rennes ...	12 15 0	—	22 19 0
Barcelona ...	26 12 0	42 7 0	47 18 0
Biarritz ...	20 0 0	30 9 0	36 0 0

198. Aer Lingus passenger fares for September 1955. (*Red Guide*, p. 55.)

as well as the locals of these distant lands finding out about this exotic place called 'Ireland' and its capital, Dublin. By 1953, Aer Lingus could advertise: 'Fly Aer Lingus to Paris – Europe's gayest city – thence by Air France to Nice, Geneva, Barcelona and other famous continental cities. Only 3½ hours flying time to Paris – you'll have no queues or luggage worries'. The prices quoted were significant – over £44, for example, for a 'low cost tourist fare to Milan'.

In the same year, by using Paris or London and Swissair, a traveller could travel from Zurich, Basle, Berne or Geneva, the latter for £36 4s. return. For those who preferred London as a gateway, there were opportunities to fly BEA from Nice or Rome (£49 16s.) with one booking, one ticket. This was all very well but it meant that Aer Lingus obtained only part of the booking fee.

The September 1955 *Red Guide* showed that Dublin had direct connections with Lourdes, London, Liverpool, Shannon, Paris, Barcelona, Bristol, Cardiff, Manchester, Amsterdam, Birmingham, Isle of Man, Glasgow and Jersey. The best connection was with London where there were four flights daily. In most other cases, there were only one or two flights per day. Flights from Paris, for example, were at 11.40 on Sunday, Monday and Friday, at 19.25 on Wednesday and at 20.35 on Tuesday and Thursday. Biarritz and Rennes opened up travel from the South of France, from which there was a flight every Tuesday and Thursday.

This was still a somewhat limited selection of direct routes but this began to change when the Aer Lingus monopoly ended and BEA started flying directly into Dublin Airport in 1957. Initially, this was on the Dublin-London route but other routes quickly opened up. By the end of the 1950s, there was excellent connectivity to the UK and improving connectivity elsewhere. In an attempt to woo a wider range of customers, Aer Lingus offered its dawnflights and starflights to London in 1960 for £11 return. In 1962, it addressed the other end of the market and introduced first-class fares on the London route, having successfully developed them on the transatlantic routes. This was impressive service for the £19 9s. return because you could enjoy prawn cocktail, grilled salmon steak, peaches and cream, salmon mousse in aspic followed by veal cordon bleu. Naturally, the drinks and cigarettes were free. All of this meant that by 1960 it was possible for visitors to access Dublin quite easily from the UK as the table here for March 1960 shows.

Table 10. Aer Lingus timetable from Britain, effective 14 March 1960.

City	Departure time for Dublin	Frequency
Birmingham	1500	Daily
Bristol	1435	Weekdays
Cardiff	1510	Weekdays
Glasgow	1915	Daily
London	1305	Monday, Tuesday, Thursday, Friday and Saturday
	1725	Monday, Wednesday and Saturday
	1805	Monday, Tuesday, Thursday, Friday and Saturday
Liverpool	1030	Weekdays
	1935	Daily
Manchester	2225	Daily except Saturday

Ireland was now open to the United States as transatlantic aircraft became a regular feature in the skies. As early as 1952, Aer Lingus had an arrangement with BOAC which provided it with connections, via London, to fifty-one countries. There was an overnight service that connected London with

199. Advertisement for KLM
hub in 1953.

Comfort above all to and from Ireland . . .

Because you can fly comfortably, fast in luxurious KLM airliners to and from the Americas from SHANNON or to and from the Continent, the Near, Middle and Far East and Africa, it will pay you all ways to take a KLM round-trip ticket whenever and wherever you travel.

Reservations arranged through any Travel Agent or your nearest KLM Office. In Ireland, call the Aer Lingus Booking Office, 40 Upper O'Connell Street. Tel: DUBLIN 42921

KLM
ROYAL DUTCH
AIRLINES

Montreal or New York. For strategic reasons, no Irish government would allow any airline other than Aer Lingus to fly into Dublin airport from the Americas. They had to use Shannon instead and travel onwards to Dublin by Aer Lingus or use Shannon as the gateway to Ireland. Despite many attempts by the US authorities to change things, the status quo with Shannon was maintained. By 1966, Aer Lingus had developed a feeder system whereby travellers using TWA or Pan Am could use a morning turnaround service from Shannon to Dublin. Aer Lingus had to respond directly to the increased competition by developing its own routes to a far greater extent. This they did by securing government approval for the purchase of BAC One-Eleven jets, which they introduced in 1965 on their Continental European routes. By the end of the decade, the first 737s had arrived and the days of turbo prop on the UK routes came swiftly to an end. Not only was travel now more direct, it was also much quicker.

Brussels	2 hours 20 minutes
Copenhagen	3 hours
Frankfurt	2 hours 45 minutes
Dusseldorf	2 hours 35 minutes
Zurich	2 hours 10 minutes
Rome	4 hours 5 minutes
Paris	1 hour 35 minutes
Lourdes	2 hours 5 minutes
Barcelona	2 hours 25 minutes

Air travel was still a minority experience in the 1950s, though proportionately more visitors used it to visit Dublin and Ireland than locals used it to leave. For most, though, getting to Dublin involved using one of the sea routes. In addition to the main Dún Laoghaire-Holyhead and Liverpool-Dublin port routes, people could travel via Larne-Stranraer, Fishguard-Rosslare and Glasgow-Dublin Port. The Dún Laoghaire-Holyhead route was the mail route and the oldest and best known. In the early 1950s, there were two sailings per day each way in the summer season, except on Sundays, and one per day in winter when only the night boat sailed. The principle was that the traveller could reach Dublin or London by the early morning, the boat journey taking three hours. The Ward Lock guide claimed that 'British Railways have several twin-screw steamers which, in the luxury of their appointments and in their precautions for the safety of passengers, rival the great ocean liners' (p. 10). This might have been true in first class but it was certainly not true in second/third class where crowded conditions were the order of the day and the journey was often far from comfortable. An insight into the travelling conditions was provided in Seanad Éireann on the occasion on the second reading of the Bill to acquire the B&I line (see below). Mr E. Maguire, described as a company director, recalled his experiences as a traveller.

> For instance at Dún Laoghaire, we know that year after year travellers were treated more like refugees fleeing from a country, and sometimes like cattle, rather than like human beings and tourists. It took a long time to get efficiency ... Since 1946 or 1947 I have had to go across on business practically every ten days, and only on two occasions were we in time coming into Euston Station. We varied from being half an hour late, to three or four hours late. Even now after all those years, I think it is fair to say that there are little or no facilities at Dún Laoghaire for meeting or seeing off friends or relatives, or even children. In this country we are looking to our tourist trade, and also we have relatives

and friends who go backwards and forwards across the Channel. There are also the Irish people who are living in England and who cross the Channel.

Things were so bad that it was even suggested that there was a positive desire to prevent people coming to Ireland, or at least to make it unpleasant and difficult for them to do so. Quite frankly, I do not think that is the case. I do not want to be too anti-anyone, or to say anything out of turn, but it is true that part of the fault has been the inefficiency of British Railways. Dr Beeching has made some attempt to put things in order. It was thought at one time that the inefficiency was directed at the Irish Mail. I have had experience of travelling in England outside of London, and British Railways are equally inefficient in areas which have nothing to do with Ireland. However, the fact was that so far as Ireland was concerned, they provided an inefficient and bad service, which was uncomfortable for travellers between Ireland and England.

(Seanad Éireann Debates, 58(14), col.1223)

Travel was a segregated business with the distinction between classes maintained on the ship as it had been on the railway element of the journey. Fares had a complex structure and involved deals for mid-week and special excursions. They also varied with the seasons and for that reason there is no meaningful 'average' fare. However, a sense of the changes in fares over the decade and the difference in the experience available can be seen in the tariff charged for berth accommodation on the mail boats, shown in the table here. There was a very significant difference between the cost of an open berth and a cabin de luxe or even an ordinary single berth cabin in first class. The table also shows that fares increased steadily during the 1950s, as prices did generally. This was all for a journey of less than 3¼ hours, though those with berths were allowed to sleep on a little later. It was also usual to get a cup of tea and a biscuit, invariably Jacob's Marietta, in the cabins.

A berth made more sense on the B&I line because of the nine hours which the passage took from Liverpool to Dublin. They had a simpler fare structure and in 1953 a berth in first class cost 9s. 4d., one in a cabin cost 3s. while one could sleep in a dormitory for 2s. 4d. This was a night service with a sailing each way on each evening during the Summer (except Sunday) and on Monday, Tuesday, Thursday and Friday from Dublin and Monday, Wednesday, Thursday and Saturday from Liverpool in the winter.

Table 11. Cost of mailboat accommodation, 1953–60.

First Class (Saloon)	1953	1958	1960
Cabin de luxe (One passenger)	35s.	42s. 6d.	50s.
Cabin de luxe (Two passengers)	45s.	50s.	60s.
Single berth cabin with toilet	18s.	22s. 6d.	25s.
Berth in two berth cabin with toilet	13s.	17s. 6d.	17s. 6d.
Ordinary single berth cabin	12s.	16s.	20s.
Berth in ordinary two berth cabin	6s.	8s.	10s.
Open berth – made up bed	4s. 6d.		8s.
Third Class			
Berth in two, four or six berth cabin	4s. 6d.	6s.	8s.
Open berth – made up bed	3s. 6d.	5s.	7s.
Open berth	3s.	4s. 6d.	6s.

Despite whatever inconveniences there were, it seems that visitors were prepared to travel to Dublin, even for very short stays. Excursions to Dublin were regularly on offer from all parts of Britain. It might be expected that these would appeal to Irish people living there but the shortness of the stay in Dublin meant that the focus had to be on visitors. An Tóstal provided an opportunity to encourage this traffic and this was featured in the advertising for such trips in the earlier part of the 1950s. Typical of this was an An Tóstal day excursion to Dublin on Monday, Wednesday and Friday between 19 April and 7 May 1954. This left Doncaster at 6.25 p.m., picking up others at Rotherham and Sheffield, and got back there some forty hours later at 10.37 a.m. And all this for 50s. in third class! An Tóstal might have faded but the availability of excursions did not and two handbills are reproduced here. One from 1955 was for a single-day excursion from London to Dublin which had the traveller on the go for thirty-four hours. It involved an evening departure from Euston at 9.45 p.m. on Friday with a return to Euston 6.30 a.m. on Sunday morning. This ran during the winter only (and not at Christmas) and it cost 70s. 6d. for third class throughout though it was possible to upgrade to first class on the ship for an extra 20s. Such trips were also available from other locations. Another example, this time from the winter/spring of 1958–9, was aimed at people living in Manchester, Oldham, Rochdale and Stockport. This involved leaving at around 9 p.m. on Friday to catch the night boat to Dublin and arriving in Westland Row on Saturday morning. The return took place over Saturday night for a charge of about 70s. in first class and around 47s. 6d. in second class. A less arduous trip was offered in 1966 when there was a day excursion from the Isle of Man to Dublin, departing Douglas at 8.30 a.m.

200. Handbill advertising a day trip to Dublin from London in 1955.

with a return from Dublin at 5 p.m. The fare was 27s. in first class and 23s. in second class. This gave only a very short stay in Dublin but a bus tour of the city lasting 2½ hours could be taken for an additional 8s. 6d. It must have been a popular offering given the frequency with which it was offered and it was still on offer in 1969 but the fare had risen to an egalitarian 30s. with the optional bus tour available for 10s. It seems that travellers were made of stern stuff.

The car ferry was the other element in Dublin's changing connectivity and the changing profile of visitors. As car ownership grew in Britain, and in Europe generally, there was a natural desire on the part of car owners to use their cars for touring and car ferry connections with the continental mainland were quickly developed. By 1961, agencies such as Bord Fáilte saw the tourism potential and the need for improved services. In the first nine months of 1957, for example, it was found that 6,227 cars were brought into the country by sea. In 1959 that figure was 9,434 and by 1961 it had further increased to

THE ISLE OF MAN STEAM PACKET COMPANY LTD.
(Incorporated in the Isle of Man)

1966 DAY EXCURSIONS
TO
DUBLIN

The Company may alter, withdraw, or curtail any service or suspend or cancel any sailing as the Company may think necessary.

MAY—
    THURSDAY, 26th
JUNE—
    WEDNESDAYS, 22nd and 29th
    THURSDAYS, 2nd, 9th and 16th
    FRIDAY, 24th
JULY—
    TUESDAY, 12th
    WEDNESDAYS, 6th, 20th and 27th
    THURSDAY, 14th
    FRIDAYS, 1st. 8th, 22nd and 29th
AUGUST—
    EVERY WEDNESDAY AND FRIDAY
SEPTEMBER—
    FRIDAY, 2nd
    WEDNESDAY, 7th
    TUESDAY, 13th

DOUGLAS depart 08 30 hours   DUBLIN depart 17 00 hours
    FARES : 1st Class 27/- ; 2nd Class 23/-
Children under 3 years of age FREE ; 3 years and under 14 Half-fare.
Infants must be accompanied by an adult.
All fares are current at time of publication and are liable to alteration without notice.

TICKETS, which may be purchased before the actual sailing day, can be obtained at :
DOUGLAS—Company's Booking and Enquiry Office, Sea Terminal Buildings, Victoria Pier, or Imperial Buildings, The Quay.
    Isle of Man Railway Enquiry Office, Villa Marina. The Promenade.
    W. H. Chapman Ltd., Travel House, Victoria Street.
    Paul Gelling and Partners, Duke Street.
RAMSEY—Company's Office, The Quay.
DAY EXCURSION PASSENGERS ARE NOT PERMITTED TO CARRY LUGGAGE
    CUSTOMS REGULATIONS—RE PURCHASE OF GOODS
1—The Customs concessions normally given to ordinary travellers arriving from Foreign Ports do not apply to day excursion passengers and for these there are no concessions.
2—All goods obtained in the Republic of Ireland (Eire) whether marked "Made in England or Great Britain, etc." or not may be liable in the Isle of Man to Customs Duty, or Purchase Tax, or both. See Special Notices exhibited in the booking offices and on board the vessels.
    H.M. Customs Officers will be in attendance.

DURING JUNE, JULY and AUGUST ONLY
Motor Coach Tour In and Around Dublin
including a stop in the Main Shopping Centre.   FARE 8/6d.
Bookable in advance at the Company's Offices at Douglas and Ramsey ONLY
SEE BACK FOR DETAILS

Passengers and their accompanied luggage will only be carried subject to the Company's Standard Conditions of Carriage of Passengers and Passengers' Accompanied Property as exhibited in the Company's Offices and on board its vessels. Acceptance of a ticket issued by the Company binds the passenger to these Conditions.
Breakfast, Luncheons, Teas and Refreshments can be obtained on board.
Imperial Buildings,   A. J. FICK,
    Douglas.   General Manager.

January, 1966.   ISLAND DEVELOPMENT CO. LTD.

MOTOR COACH TOUR OF DUBLIN
(2½ hours duration)

In connection with the above special coaches accompanied by Guide-Lecturer, will leave Sir John Rogerson's Quay for Tour of Dublin City as follows :—

Depart Sir John Rogerson's Quay 1-30 p.m. via Moss Street, Pearce Street, Dame Street (City Hall and Dublin Castle), Lord Edward Street. Christ Church Place (Christ Church Cathedral), Winetavern Street, Winetavern Street Bridge, Northern Quays (Four Courts and Guinness's Brewery), Main Road to Phœnix Park, Phœnix Monument, North Circular Road, Phibsboro', Glasnevin Cemetery, Botanic Gardens (half-hour visit), North Frederick Street, O'Connell Street, Nelson Pillar, Abbey Street, Bursaras arrive 3-40 p.m. (approximately 30 minutes allowed to visit shopping centre). Depart Bursaras at 4-10 p.m., Memorial Road, Butt Bridge, George's Quay to arrive at Sir John Rogerson's Quay by 4-30 p.m.

FARE 8/6d.

Children 3 years and under 14 — Half-fare.

Conditions

Coras Iompair Eireann organised Tours and/or The Isle of Man Steam Packet Co. Ltd.. as Agents only give notice that all Tickets are issued upon special express conditions that they shall not be in any way liable for any injury, damage, loss, accident, delay, or irregularity which may be occasioned either by reason of any defect in any vehicle, or through the acts or defaults of any Company or person engaged in conveying the passenger or carrying out the purpose for which the ticket is issued, or otherwise in connection therewith. Such conveying, etc., is subject to the laws of the Country where the conveyance, etc.. is provided. Baggage is at "Owner's Risk" throughout the tour unless insured. Small articles, coats, wraps, umbrellas, and other hard baggage are entirely under the care of the passenger, who is cautioned against the risk attached to these being left in conveyance when sight-seeing.

201. Handbill advertising a day trip from the Isle of Man to Dublin in 1966.

14,253. This was despite all of the difficulties in doing this and it was reckoned that, with proper facilities, something of the order of 40,000 cars could be brought from Britain per year. This would have a national benefit since it was estimated that each car resulted in a spend of £115 and that people covered upwards of 2,000 miles (3,200km).

For a while, it seemed that there was even potential in combining the improved air connectivity with the provision of a car ferry service. It was reported in the *Irish Times* in 1960 that British Rail was contemplating

202. Aer Lingus Carvair in the middle 1960s.

replacing its boat services with an air-based one (*Irish Times*, 7 January 1960, p. 1). Given that the spirit of the age was in favour of axing railway systems and Beeching was about to begin his analysis of the British system, the enthusiasm for air travel is understandable. The model being considered was that people would make a short hop by air and then continue their journey by coach. In that context, it seemed sensible to move cars by air too and Aer Lingus began to offer such a service from Liverpool to Dublin in May 1963. The first flight took place on 8 May of that year when their Carvair (a converted DC4 Skymaster) landed at Dublin Airport with five cars and sixteen passengers. The plane had a capacity of five cars and twenty five passengers and the service operated seven times per week but increased to thirteen times during the summer period. It was said at the time that such was the demand that Aer Lingus expected to ferry 4,000 cars in 1963 (*Irish Times*, 9 May 1963, p. 11). Aer Lingus were not alone in offering this service, most airlines did so and it was very popular with British tourists travelling to France. By 1966, the service linked Dublin-Liverpool, Dublin-Bristol and Dublin-Cherbourg. The cost varied with the size of the car so that, for example, the fare for a 14.5 ft (4.4m) car from Cherbourg to Dublin was £78 return plus a passenger fare of £15 16s. A more modest car of 12.5 ft (3.5m) in length cost £50 return. This was a significant premium to pay for the savings in time; the flights were no more than two hours long but perhaps the excitement of flying in the plane itself was an important element. However, 1966 was as good as it got and by 1968 Aer Lingus had divested itself of three of its Carvairs as competition from the sea ferries began to bite.

Despite the optimism over the future of air transport, the sea ferries were always going to be the way forward and there were two potential services for Dublin, each building on the existing services. British Rail (as Sealink) operated from Holyhead to Dún Laoghaire and B&I from Liverpool to Dublin Port. There were other services to Dublin Port, such as from the Isle of Man or from Scotland, but these two services dominated the market. It came as no surprise when it was announced that each would operate a car ferry service to Dublin. British Rail decided to continue its association with Dún Laoghaire though this was not to everyone's delight locally as there were fears that the town would be swamped by tourists. There was also annoyance when it was announced that the east pier would be used as a temporary berth for the ferry while the permanent one at St Michael's wharf was completed. The Dún Laoghaire Protection Society did not like that proposal either and they agitated to have the terminal moved to Trader's Wharf, which was closer to the west pier and therefore nearer to Dublin and away from the town. As was always the case, the project took longer than anticipated, it being announced in 1963 that there would be two new ferries on the service by 1965. The intention was to build a one-class car ferry with accommodation for 155 cars, 1,000 passengers and 80 sleeping berths. There would be two large lounges, a smoking room, a tea bar and a cafeteria on board. The new ships would complement the existing ships, the Hibernia and the Cambria, but the third ship on the route, the Princess Maud, would be retired. The Princess Maud was a relief ship that was used if the demand for either of the two ships was such that passengers were left behind. Her retirement would have come as a relief to anyone who had to endure travel on that particular vessel. It was truly a dreadful experience in rough weather as the ship had no stabilizers and was even rumoured to have a flat bottom. Class distinctions would, of course, be maintained on the Hibernia and Cambria. Holyhead Ferry I (no better name could be found it seems) was launched by Mrs Lemass on 18 February 1965, with a projected start date for the service of 9 July 1965. It was announced on the day that 8,000 advance bookings had been made and the future seemed bright (*Irish Times*, 18 February 1965, p. 1). In the event, the first sailing was on 19 July and the new ferry seemed to have caught the public imagination. On 7 October 1965, some 4,000 people took the opportunity of a tour of the ferry at an admission cost of 1*s*. each in aid of the Royal National Lifeboat Institution. On that day, British Rail announced that since coming into service

203. The Holyhead Ferry I.

that 23,000 cars and 70,000 passengers had been carried. It was only a summer service to begin with, operating only between 20 May and 15 October, but it was an important element in changing the nature of tourism in the city and in Ireland generally. To promote ferry usage, a rail sleeper service for car users was announced, to run three times a week, but it was quickly found to have little demand. While the ferry concept was successful, the ferry itself had only a short tenure on the Irish Sea. Its lack of a front loading capacity and only a single car deck resulted in its replacement in 1973.

It was a popular service and there was some suggestion that there was price gouging going on because of this. A table published by the *Irish Times* in 1965 showed that, while exact comparison was not possible, it seemed that the traveller to and from Ireland was being charged more per unit of distance. Regardless, the ferry was much cheaper than the air ferry as the comparative figures given above show.

Table 12. Comparative costs for ferry travel (car not exceeding 12.5 ft) in 1965.

Route	Hours	Car	Passenger
Larne-Stranraer	2½	£6 5s.	16s. 6d.
Holyhead-Dún Laoghaire	3¼	£8 15s.	£1 12s.
Dover-Dunkirk	3¼	£4 5s.	£2 1s.
Liverpool-Isle of Man	3¼	£6	£1 11s.
Southampton-Le Havre	6¼	£5 10s.	£2 18s.
Hull-Rotterdam	16	£8	£8 10s.
Tilbury-Antwerp	16	£8 15s.	£5 10s.

(*Irish Times*, 23 February 1965, p. 8)

The B&I company was in transition during this period and so it can be forgiven for not being as fast. It had been an element of government policy to increase Irish participation in the Irish sea trade. The most cost effective way, it seemed to the government, involved the acquisition of an established company rather than attempt to set up a new one. During the early 1960s, discussions took place with Coast Lines, the owners of the company, with a view to acquiring it. This led to the British & Irish Steam Packet Company Limited (Acquisition) Act in 1965 and a subsequent reorganization of the company. It decided that a car ferry was a necessary feature for the city and it set about developing a new terminal in Dublin Port for such a drive-on, drive-off facility. This led to a contract being signed in March 1967 for a ship capable of handling 220 cars and 1,000 passengers with a second ship being ordered in September. The M.V. Munster began service in May 1968 and transported 3,000 cars in each direction per week, together with 14,000 passengers. It was quickly decided that the company would run a car ferry service all-year round, in contrast to British Rail. Ready to try out any new idea, B&I announced in September 1968 that it would study the possibility of a hovercraft on the Irish Sea (*Irish Times*, 14 September 1968, p. 12). Common sense soon prevailed!

There were, of course, those who saw the cloud around the silver lining. By the end of the 1960s, it was confidently believed that about 250,000 cars would visit the country each year with about 150,000 coming directly into Irish ports, the remainder via Northern Ireland. The income associated with this was about £10 million in 1968. During the summer, it was estimated that about 3,000 cars per week came into Dublin, rising to 7,000 during the peak weeks in July and August. To these would be added another 8,000 making their way from other locations. The complaint was these were adding to the traffic chaos in the city and that not enough was being done to keep the flows moving. The *Irish Times* was particularly concerned about pedestrians trying to cross at O'Connell Bridge and it noted that there were long delays before the crossing could be negotiated safely (*Irish Times*, 19 July 1968). However, unless there had been a sea change in the behaviour of Dublin pedestrians, very few were likely to be waiting around for the opportunity to cross in safety.

By the end of the decade connectivity was better than it had been before. In addition to the standard two sailings per day to Dún Laoghaire in the summer time, two extra sailings were needed during August. The car ferry sailed twice daily also. A similar level of service was available to Dublin port from Liverpool via the B&I line. Air travel was now facilitated not only by Aer

204. An early invitation to visit Dublin
Airport, no longer feasible by 1953.

Visit

DUBLIN AIRPORT

When in Dublin pay a visit to Dublin Airport—the
home base of Aer Lingus—which operates regular
services to the principal cities of Britain, Paris and
Amsterdam. The sunlit restaurant overlooking the
Airfield and with its view of the distant Dublin
mountains is only 20 minutes drive from the centre
of the city.

AER LINGUS

205. The new terminal building in the 1970s.

Lingus operating jet aircraft from most major European centres but also by other airlines providing services into Dublin. By 1970, most major airlines had offices in Dublin and the airport was regarded as being one of Europe's finest. Dublin was also linked directly and indirectly via Shannon to the Americas. In fact, from the early 1950s, it was felt that the airport was not going to be big enough to cope with the numbers that would use it. As early as 1953 it was announced that the ground floor of the terminal building would be closed to sightseers (*Irish Times*, 23 January 1953, p. 3). There was speculation that another airport might be needed when it emerged that Dublin Airport was the fourteenth busiest in Europe during 1960. That speculation was quickly dispelled and it was instead decided that the airport would be expanded by the building of new terminal buildings and the provision of a multi-storey car park (which was quickly closed for security reasons) to facilitate the growing number of car users. Soon the clean lines of the original terminal building were to be swamped by the massive constructions of the 1960s to the point that it is very hard to see the original today.

Selling Dublin

To be a successful tourist destination, Dublin had to be clever in projecting its image. It was not a spectacularly beautiful city in the mould of Prague, Venice or Rome. Little survived from the medieval period and the Georgian landscape, which came closest to defining an image for the city, was not particularly valued in itself at this time. It had some fine buildings but they were not in attractive settings and most of its finest architecture dated from the eighteenth century. It was a cultural centre with a good reputation for the arts, especially literature. In addition, it was generally believed that it was a hospitable city.

The question of how to define the city can be demonstrated by looking at a slim volume produced in 1951 with the rather odd focus of Ulster and Dublin (Farrer and Turnbull, 1951). Faced with the problem of how to describe Dublin, they found it best to describe it in terms of its past and not its present. As they put it: 'Dublin – like Florence or Edinburgh – lives leisurely now, proud of its stone heritage, hiding its business and prosperity under the mantle of eighteenth-century grace, an easy going, above all pleasant city, with a deep strength' (p. 17). They were being positive but they could find nothing more enthusiastic to say of modern Dublin – 'Dublin became capital of a free and independent Ireland, and Dáil Éireann took office in Leinster House' (p. 19).

In fact, they went on to say that:

> the best – though expensive – shopping area lies in the region of O'Connell Street. Grafton Street has been compared to Bond Street. An open air market in Moore Street attracts many visitors. The tourist, however, should remember from the start that this heart of the city is not Ireland, is not even Dublin. Let him go a little way further into the city and he will come on grimmer streets and lanes where something closer to the old pagan heart of Ireland beats its slow rhythm.
>
> (p. 20)

Whatever message they were trying to convey about Dublin, there was no such confusion about Belfast.

> If Dublin stands for the past of Ireland, for historic stone and the arts of the Gael, Belfast is the present, the child of modern invention, industrialism and capitalism. Belfast has not much history to speak of, for it is too busy creating its own history. A century ago its population was fifty thousand; to-day it is nearly half a million. Belfast has the largest linen mills, the largest rope-works, the largest tobacco factory and the largest shipyards in the world. The city speaks in superlatives.
>
> (p. 28)

So, Dublin was about the past, Belfast was about a superlative present.

'With the authority of Dublin Corporation'

There was a long tradition of officially endorsed guides to Dublin, which went back to the beginning of the century. They provided a useful means for Dublin Corporation to make political statements such as in the 1914 guide to the city when it was stated that 'for many centuries the control of the Dublin Corporation was in the hands of people who had little in sympathy with the great body of the citizens, and it was not till 1841 that a really representative assembly was elected with the great Irish leader, Daniel O'Connell, as the first Lord Mayor' (p. 4). Moreover, while there was the 'hope that in a few years [Dublin] will be again the centre of Irish Government' (p. 2), it should be remembered that Dublin 'is at present a prosperous and an attractive place, and one which may be justly termed the second city in the Empire' (p. 3). In the 1930s, with independence achieved, these guides provided a vehicle to discuss the plans for the development of the city and the ending of poverty.

Corporation endorsement passed to the Irish Tourist Association guides in the 1940s, though for two years in the early 1940s there was the *Lord Mayor's Handbook* – as much an economic prospectus for the city as a guide to it.

The production schedule for these guides was somewhat erratic, often a flurry in consecutive years and then a long gap until the next one. This publishing schedule was probably unsurprising during the 1950s, not because there was a diminution in visitors, but because all sources of expenditure were under pressure and these guides were a fairly obvious area in which to save. They were also different to commercial guides in that they had no difficulty in dating them because of the practice which developed of including a greeting from the Lord Mayor. A very substantial guide with high production values was produced in 1953 and again in 1954. It was doubtless encouraged by An Tóstal, which was hoped to result in large numbers of visitors to the city. As in previous versions, it could not quite make up its mind as to whether it was a practical guide or an academic tome. With almost 300 pages on good quality paper it would have been quite heavy to carry around but a greater problem with its use while out walking was the thematic rather than locational manner in which the information was organized. It also lacked practical information, the kind of thing for which guides are generally purchased. Instead, the greater part of the book was devoted to learned articles on various aspects of the city. There were chapters on the history of the city, on arboreal Dublin, on humorous Dublin, on the port of Dublin, on commercial Dublin and so on. These were penned by various experts on the topic and written in formal academic style.

The guide was somewhat lacking in practical information on matters such as how to get about or where to eat or any of the myriad things that visitors need to know. These official guides were never great at providing this information but there had been the beginnings of a recognition in those produced during the 1940s that such information might be welcomed and that the guide should focus on 'tourism' as an activity. While there were plenty of advertisements for various services, there was no attempt to sell the city as a shopping destination. It did not seem to cross the minds of the Corporation that people might have money to spend. There was a lot of very good writing on aspects of the city that people might actually want to go and see but the reader had to work to find it. The chapter on 'architectural Dublin' by Maurice Craig introduced the reader to many of the principal buildings of the city. It is a scholarly paper and a sense of the style can be gleaned from the following extract. Writing about the finest streets such as Dominick Street, North Great

206. Dublin Corporation's official guide to Dublin, 1950s.

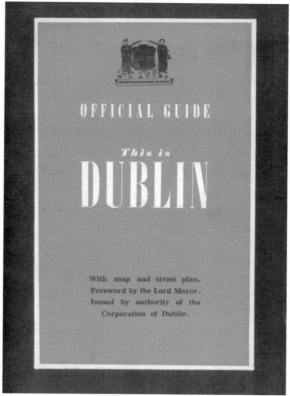

George's Street, Eccles Street and Gardiner Street on the northside he noted: 'The houses are almost all of red-brick, the elevations simple to the point of severity, making their effect by pure proportion and ornamented only as to the doorways and the ironwork' (p. 163). There was no sense in his descriptions though about the general decay of these streets and the developing threat to their future. 'Arboreal Dublin' was, in fact, a good essay on the parks and open spaces. The chapter entitled 'touristic Dublin' contained details of four interesting walks through the city. These will be discussed a little later because they were staple fare for these guides. None of these sections were organized in a manner which would have made it easy for the visitor to find them or, indeed, to use them. The books also contained two fine maps, produced not by the Ordnance Survey but by Bartholomew, which would also have appeared in the Ward Lock guides. These were good quality maps with excellent detail, though the Dublin one at a scale of 1:20,000 approximately would have been awkward to use if out and about. They were strange guides in many ways. They provided a high-quality introduction to the city but not in a particularly visitor-friendly manner. This stands in contrast to some of the guides produced in the 1960s, discussed below, which went to the other extreme by not discussing enough about the city and its heritage.

A new 'official' guide was produced in the early 1960s as part of the *Green Guide* series and they were available for 2s. 6d. This presumably was a reaction to the Ward Lock guides, which were now being marketed as *Red Guides*. These *Green Guides* were later transformed into *Dublin – Official Guide* but their general format remained unchanged. As before, the official nature of the endorsement was emphasized by the picture of the current Lord Mayor and the reproduction of his letter of endorsement. In fact, so assiduous was the Corporation in ensuring this that there are two editions for 1964, with exactly the same information except for the change in Lord Mayor. The 1969 version was hardly different, apart from some slight alterations in presentation.

The books were still written in a formal style but they had been reorganized into guides for visitors. There was much more by way of practical information and a lot of space was devoted to shopping, both in descriptions of products that were available and in advertisements for the shops that could provide them. There was some experimentation with the order of the features but it was finally settled on that, following an introduction to the city, the visitor would be guided towards four routes that would meet their needs. They would also be told of some additional places of interest, mainly information on major public buildings, and there, also, the practical information was provided.

This major improvement on previous versions included such details as to where parking for nine hours, two hours or one hour could be obtained. Details were given on CIE's bus tours and rail tours. For example, a tour to the Boyne Valley was available in 1969 as follows:

> CD.12. Tour of the Boyne Valley (7 hours), visiting Tara, ancient seat of the High Kings, Slane with its castle, the burial chambers of Brugh na Boinne and the scene of the Battle of the Boyne. 11 a.m. on Mondays, Wednesdays and Fridays from May 11 to June 12, daily (except Saturdays) from June 14 to September 27, and Mondays and Fridays from September 28 to October 30. Fare 20s.

This was the same tour as described in 1964 but the price had risen from 15s. The books also shed light on such mysteries as the arcane procedures for parking a car, as well as the mysteries of the licensing laws; this would have been of interest to visitor and local alike. The needs of visitors had once been

207. The 1960s' *Green Guides* to Dublin.

given particular consideration under the bona fide provision in the legislation. This was intended to allow thirsty travellers to get a drink outside the normal licensing hours but the reality was that it provided this service to more locals than travellers. The key element was that the person seeking the drink had to be a traveller and that meant that he/she had to have travelled at least 5 miles (8km) if s/he had been lodging in a county borough on the previous evening or 3 miles (5km) if anywhere else. The strange governance structure of Dublin with its county borough that did not encompass the entire city facilitated thirsty revellers in travelling relatively short distances and making a nonsense of the law. Attempts to end the practice had failed in 1943 but the opposition to it soon regained their wind and once again grew. As is often the case with these matters, nothing happened overnight or, in this case, for a decade. Following the establishment of a commission in 1956 to investigate the matter, legislation was introduced into the Dáil in 1959. As the Minister for Justice, Mr Oscar Traynor, put it during the introduction to the second stage debate in the Dáil on 11 November 1959: 'The primary provisions are contained in a couple of sections dealing with (1) the abolition of the so-called bona fide trade, (2) the fixing of more suitable hours of trading on weekdays and (3) the general opening of licensed premises throughout the country on Sundays and on St Patrick's Day'. This was the careful balance that was to be struck. To compensate for the loss of bona fide drinking, there would be more liberal opening hours during the week and especially on Sunday. It had to change because:

> By the end of 1955, however, demands for liberalization of the licensing laws had become increasingly persistent; there had been a substantial increase in the number of area exemption orders granted by the Courts; the abuses associated with the bona fide traffic on Sundays and late on weekdays were the cause of constant complaints by law-abiding persons; and, finally, there was a considerable amount of illegal drinking.
>
> It must be apparent to all—publicans and public alike—that scarcely any of those persons who patronise the bona fide houses are genuine travellers: they are, almost entirely, persons travelling to get drink and availing themselves of the bona fide provisions to get it in the knowledge that the motive for these journeys is not something that could be satisfactorily proved in proceedings against them in court.
>
> (Dáil Debates, 177(7), col. 939)

So it ended, leaving drinkers with the following system, though of course the sprinkling of early houses, which could open at 7 a.m. across the city centre, did provide some solace.

> Drinking Licensing hours in Dublin are:
> Summer (April to October): Weekdays, 10.30 a.m. to 2.30 p.m., 3.30 p.m. to 11.30 p.m. Sundays, 12.30 p.m. to 2 p.m., 4 p.m. to 10 p.m. Winter (November to March): Weekdays, 10.30 a.m. to 2.30 p.m., 3.30 p.m. to 11 p.m. Sundays, 12.30 p.m. to 2 p.m., 4 p.m. to 10 p.m. Closed all day on Good Fridays and on Christmas Day. Hours for St Patrick's Day as on Sundays.
>
> Hotel residents can get alcoholic drink any time except on Good Friday when it is only supplied with meals. Non-residents who are having meals in licensed hotels or restaurants may get drink, outside the normal hours, as follows: on weekdays during the closed hour (2.30 to 3.30 p.m.), and from the general closing hour until 12.30 a.m.; on Sundays from 2 p.m. to 3 p.m., and from the general closing hour until

11 p.m.; on Christmas Day from 1 p.m. to 3 p.m. and from 7 p.m. to 10 p.m.

Extensions are given occasionally, generally in connection with dances.

(*Green Guide*, 1969, p. 83)

The guides also contained a substantial feature on shopping, a major innovation but perhaps not as effective as it might have been. It was arranged thematically rather than locationally, unlike the commercial guides described below.

The guides offered four tours through the city. These did not change greatly over the years though there was some reorganization and variation in the order in which places were visited. They were well-considered tours and would have given the visitor a comprehensive view of the city. The tone was generally positive and while there was mention of some of the decay that was evident in the city, it was passed off in a matter of fact way, unlike the guides of the 1930s and early 1940s that felt the need to explain it. The 1964 guide was provided with a good map of Dublin at a scale of 1:14,080 (4.5 inches to the mile) but the earlier and more elegant Ward Lock map had now been replaced by a map drawn by a member of the Town Planning Institute. It was functional but lacking in style, perhaps because of its green and yellow colour scheme. The 1969 edition replaced this map with one at the larger (but odd) scale of 1:9,400 (6.75 inches to the mile). This made it more unwieldy but it was of more conventional design with clearer print and better colours.

The tours in 1969 were not quite an exact copy of those on offer in 1964 but they were close. There was some editing of material to note that the statue to Thomas Davis had been erected in College Green and that Nelson had been blown up but there was no change to the general style or tone of the prose. The first tour involved the south-east city and this was the opportunity to explore Grafton Street and to see the Georgian city. What was encouraging was that it included a short recognition that the city was more than individual buildings, though that was primarily the focus, and that the streetscape was of interest. It was noted at Fitzwilliam Street that:

This is one of the most splendid architectural sights in Dublin, a spacious series of late Georgian boulevards, running down almost three quarters of a mile to Holles Street Maternity Hospital, the whole crowned (alas) by Dublin's oldest skyscraper, the gasometer, some of the houses on the right hand side were demolished to make way for the new Electricity Supply Board headquarters.

(p. 23)

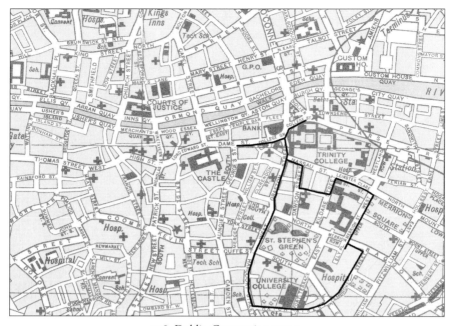

208. Dublin Corporation tour 1.

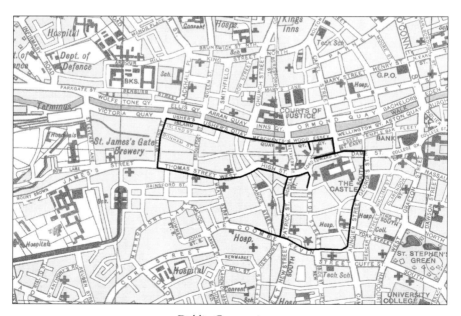

209. Dublin Corporation tour 2.

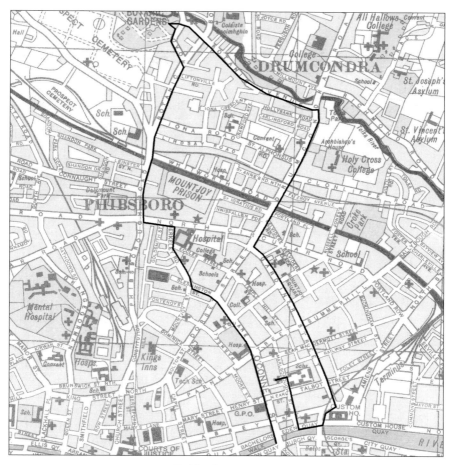

210. Dublin Corporation tour 3.

The next tour was also well considered in that it focused on the old city, taking in the cathedrals and castle as would be expected. As in previous generations, it did not shy from taking the visitors into the less glamourous parts of the city. Indeed, the guide claimed that the area around Kevin Street provided one of the most interesting walks in Dublin and included the ruins of St Sepulchre, Marsh's Library, St Patrick's Cathedral and into the Coombe where it was said that it was, at the time, 'the home of a lusty, vital cross-section of Dublin's population, and most of the people in the environs have roots of many generations in the area' (p. 32). Moving up towards Christ Church Cathedral and into High Street, the guide made reference to the obvious: the houses were in the process of demolition. However, the explanation that this was because the foundations on this part of the ridge were poor because of the poor soil was not quite the reason for their disappearance which, the reader will realize, had everything to do with road widening. The trip then wandered along James' Street as far as Guinness, which was still offering tours of the brewery on demand in the summer, before cutting down to the quays and heading back towards Capel Street. This was hardly the most salubrious part of the city but it was the most historic and it was good to read that the Corporation was happy that people would see these parts of the city, despite the obvious dereliction that would have been on view.

It had been recognized that the third tour was previously too short and the fourth too long. In order to balance this out, the third tour was modified to bring the visitor on a trip to the Botanic Gardens. On foot, this was a substantial walk, though it did offer a very good transect across the landscapes of the north inner city. It began with a visit to the northside Georgian city, along O'Connell Street, up Parnell Square and onto Dorset Street via a look at Hardwicke Street. The visitor then crossed into Berkeley Street and up to Phibsborough and, eventually, crossed the Royal Canal at Cross Guns. From there it was a relatively short walk to the Botanic Gardens. Having enjoyed the Botanic Gardens, the visitor then headed to Drumcondra and back into town via Gardiner Street. The guide was accurate in its description:

> Beyond the North Circular a turn left brings us down Gardiner Street and once again into the territory of that famous family of town planners. Gardiner Street, with its adjacent Mountjoy Square, was, perhaps, their greatest achievement. Time has dealt harshly with it, but today, standing at the south-west corner of Mountjoy Square, and looking down the long slope of Middle and Lower Gardiner Street, one can envisage the magnificent sight this must have made in the days of its glory, running right down to the Custom House.
>
> There is little of interest in present day Gardiner Street, except the Jesuit Church of St Francis Xavier in the upper street.

(p. 41)

The fourth and final tour appealed to the more adventurous in spirit and was more historically interesting than visually appealing, though some good architecture was to be seen. With a starting point of Grattan Bridge, the visitor went up Capel Street and took some short detours to look at the remains of St Mary's Abbey and to explore Wolfe Tone Street. While the bustle of the markets might have been interesting, then, as now, access to the Chapter

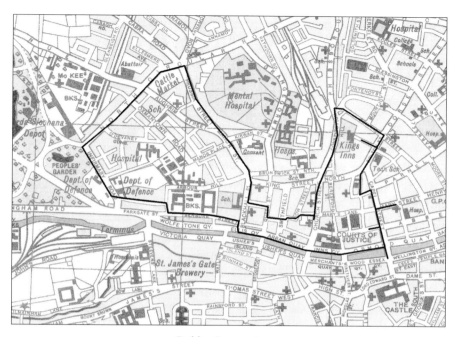

211. Dublin Corporation tour 4.

House of the abbey would have been a hit and miss affair. The walk then proceeded up Capel Street with a detour into Green Street to view the court house, another location not generally on the tourist trail, before joining Bolton Street and walking to Henrietta Street. While Henrietta Street was once the primary street in the city, attracting the tag of Primate's Hill, it had fallen far from grace by 1960 and would have presented a ruinous aspect to the visitor and it would have been hard to work out why it was supposed to, as the guide suggested, 'give delight to the eye' (p. 96). At the junction with Dominick Street, the visitor paused. There was the opportunity to explore a little of Dorset Street and to chance Granby Row where Matt Talbot lived but the main route involved heading up the hill to Broadstone where a good view of the city could be had and the King's Inns admired before heading down Church Street, correctly described as 'dilapidated but picturesque', to the inevitable encounter with St Michan's and thence into Smithfield via the Jameson distillery and across to view the buildings of the Law Society (the Bluecoat school). From there it was uphill through Stoneybatter and Prussia Street to view the cattle market, still on the North Circular Road. Thence it was along the North Circular Road to the Phoenix Park, though it was recognized that this could only be a reconnaissance as the park held enough

attractions to make it a destination in its own right. Once at the bottom of
Infirmary Road, the visitor was heading for home but first note had to be
taken of Collins Barracks and Croppy's Acre. Then it was back towards town
but via Benburb Street rather than the quays. This was a rather strange choice.
The guide described it in bohemian terms as being once one of the liveliest
streets in the city with many musical taverns. It retained its lively nature in
1960 – but probably more in the evening than during the day – as one of the
main centres of prostitution, not to mention being dilapidated. The Four
Courts were visited on the route back and finally Grattan Bridge was once
again reached. It was an interesting route for a visitor and would have brought
him/her to some of the more out of the way locations in the city, if not the
downright insalubrious. It was all the more fascinating for that and certainly
carried on the Corporation's tradition of presenting an honest view of the city.

Bord Fáilte

Fógra Fáilte (later Bord Fáilte) produced a parallel series of guides in the 1950s,
also designated as 'official guides'. These were pocket sized and were a simpler
production with a two-colour cover depicting a famous building in Dublin
such as the GPO for 1950 and again for 1953, the campanile in Trinity
College for the 1955 edition or the Custom House for the 1959 edition.
Unlike the Corporation guide, the reader had to work out the printing date
but it did not really matter because there was little change in the guide over
the decade, nor, indeed, did the content vary greatly from what had been on
offer in the 1940s. Thus, in the 1943 version, the following comment was
offered on the twentieth century.

> With the birth of the Irish Free State, Dublin became once more an
> independent capital, the metropolis of a country old in history, fresh in
> promise and achievement. Progress under the new dispensation has
> been remarkable. Better cleansing of thoroughfares, improved methods
> of public lighting, great new housing schemes are but a few results of
> enlightened municipal administration.
>
> (p. 43)

This was reproduced exactly in the 1959 edition. Perhaps nothing much had
changed and the editors did not feel it necessary to revise their text. The only
change of significance was in the order of the sections. There were short essays
on matters such as learned institutions, notable public buildings, art galleries,

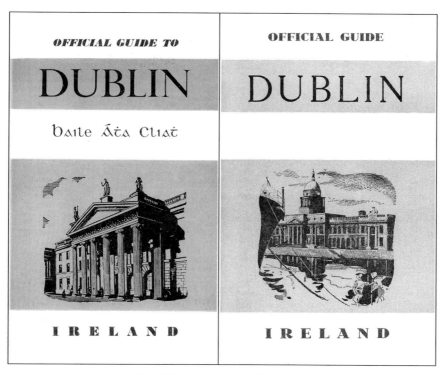

212. Bord Fáilte guides to Dublin in the 1950s.

the national museum, parks and gardens as well as a concise but useful history of the city. The visitor was also encouraged to venture a little out of town and enjoy what county Dublin had to offer. The general practical information was far better than in the Corporation guide and provided details on banks, places of worship, taxi companies, location and contact details for embassies and consulates, as well as postal and transport information. Particularly useful was a small section on what buses to take to various locations and where the terminus for them was to be found. It seemed particularly important to inform visitors about opportunities for bathing. Detailed information was provided for locations such as Tara Street baths. The information below is from the 1959 edition and it should be noted that prices had risen over the decade by at least one third. Note the existence of a first- and second-class swimming pond. Naturally, mixed bathing was not allowed; indeed, females seemed barely tolerated. However, in the more liberal Dún Laoghaire mixed bathing was permitted in the public outdoor sea baths.

Tara Street Baths, Dublin City.
Open (at the times stated below) all the year round, except for a period
of two or three weeks after Christmas.

First Class Swimming Pond (Male only). Week-days 10 a.m. to
7 p.m. Summer Season. – Men, 8*d.*; boys, 4*d.*; club members (on
production of Members' Cards), 6*d.* Winter Season (water heated) –
Men, 10*d.*; boys, 4*d.*;. club members (on production of Members'
Cards), 6*d.*

Second Class Swimming Pond (Male only). Weekdays, 10 a.m. to
7 p.m. Summer. – Men, 4*d.*; boys, 2*d.* Winter (water heated) –
Secondary School boys (accompanied by teacher), by arrangement, 2*d.*

Ladies' Day, Monday, 3 p.m. to 7 p.m. Charges as foregoing.

This guide also offered four tours of the city and these were basically
unchanged in 1959 from those on offer in the 1940s; nothing modern in the
city was deemed worthy of note and, as was usual, there was no recognition
of the interest or value of the Georgian streetscapes. The Nelson Pillar had
gradually crept into the guides following a long period of omission. There was
a reference to a splendid view being available from the top in another section
of the guide on historic streets and houses but it got short shrift in the actual
tours and its mention in the walking tour was only as a location marker for
the GPO. It may have stood for 157 years by the time it was finally toppled
but it was certainly not on every visitor's 'must do/see' list.

> Near the Nelson Pillar is the General Post Office, which in Easter
> Week, 1916, was made the headquarters of the Provisional Government
> set up by the Irish Volunteers. Military hostilities at that period and in
> subsequent years resulted in the almost complete destruction of
> O'Connell Street. But it has risen in splendour from the ashes and as
> an appropriate symbol of Dublin's irrepressible spirit. This fine
> thoroughfare has seen history in the making for it has witnessed every
> great national demonstration of triumph or sorrow.
>
>   (p. 29)

While this was a better *tourist* guide than that of Dublin Corporation, it must
say something about Bord Fáilte's view of the business that it too ignored the
potential for shopping in Dublin. Were it not for the few advertisements, the
reader might have formed the view that there were no shops in Dublin.

Tour 1 brought the visitor around College Green, up Grafton Street and into St Stephen's Green. From there the visitor visited Earlsfort Terrace to see UCD and then down Dawson Street, pausing to look up Molesworth Street at Leinster House before turning right at the bottom and heading into Merrion Square. With a tour of Merrion Square, the visitor retraced his or her steps back towards College Green. There was not a word about the architecture or the streetscape. Instead, attention was drawn to the fact that St Andrew's Church was near the site of the Thingmote: 'This is an historic spot ... The Thingmote was a huge mound, and it afterwards supplied material for the construction of Nassau Street' (p. 83). It is fascinating that attention should be drawn to a feature, not a trace of which remains, but nothing said about the existing urban landscape.

The second tour was of old Dublin and included Dublin Castle and the two cathedrals. This was to be expected on any visit but what was good about it was that, just as with the Corporation guides, there was no directing the visitor away from the dilapidation of the Coombe.

Tour 3 was described as being along the quays but it was really a tight loop that took the visitor from Pearse Street across O'Connell Bridge, up O'Connell Street and Parnell Square before heading east along Great Denmark Street and back down to the quays via Marlborough Street. It gave the visitor a chance to see some of the busier streets as well as admire the building of Belvedere College and to see the Pro-Cathedral. As in previous editions, all that was said about North Great George's Street was that many of the fine houses had fallen into disrepair but they still had good interiors.

The final tour was more complicated, it involved getting on and off buses, and had elements in common with the fourth Dublin Corporation tour. The main object was the Phoenix Park but this was also the only way to see the Four Courts and to have the obligatory visit to St Michan's and a view of Collins Barracks. Attention was drawn to the Arbour Hill Detention Barracks where the graves of the executed leaders of the 1916 Rising were to be found. But since this could not be seen from the quays, there was little point in mentioning it unless it was intended to get the visitor to slog uphill to see it. This part could have been done on foot but once the Phoenix Park and the Zoo had been enjoyed it was necessary to take a bus to get to Phibsborough via the North Circular Road to connect with the no. 19 bus, which would leave them at Finglas Road from where they could walk to Glasnevin Cemetery. Here, the purpose was to see the republican plot and other graves of note, especially O'Connell's. On completion, they were to return to Finglas

Road to get the no. 19 again and journey to the Botanic Gardens. This bus journey was totally unnecessary since the walk would have taken less time than the wait for the bus. However, perhaps the bus would have been necessary after all, since this was an exhausting day and would have left any visitor footsore.

All in all, there was little fundamental difference in the locations included in these guides compared to the Corporation guides. The packaging was a bit different with the main contrast between the short third walk and the much longer fourth tour. The other difference is that the Corporation had toned down the political aspect and did not see the need for the visitor to visit the honoured dead in Glasnevin. The coverage of the city centre was good. Most of the important historic sites were visited and the visitor would have got a sense of the geography of the city if s/he was minded to visit some of the other locations mentioned in the book. It was also good in that it took in the north side of the city, rather than concentrate on the more fashionable south.

What was disappointing about all of these guides was that, according to their contents, the twentieth century did not appear to have happened for Dublin. It was a criticism of the city in early decades of the century that it was living on the memory of its past. Cosgrave and Strangways (1907) argued in their guide that this view was somewhat harsh but the same criticism could be levied some fifty years later. The guides reflected the historical discourse of the time and so the history of the city stopped at 1921 and there was a failure to find much of the twentieth century that was worth seeing. For example, the 1964 edition simply says: 'at the General Election of 1918, there was an overwhelming majority for Sinn Féin, the separatist party. There was fighting again between Irish and English forces before the Truce of 1921; and again the following year when a Civil War broke out. Now Dublin, after a long and chequered career, is the Irish capital of an Irish nation. No longer the bulwark against Ireland, but the nerve centre of an independent nation' (p. 15). It is hard to find a more succinct summary of the twentieth century that raises so many questions and answers none.

There were some alternative guides available in the 1950s that were more practical. The *Visitor's Guide to Dublin* was printed by the Parkside Press and it was full of practical information, including an adequate map of the central city. There had been a previous but not as comprehensive version some years previously, produced by the City Directory Company and available for 1s. 6d. The map in the *Visitor's Guide to Dublin* was no work of cartographic skill but it did show the main features of the city and there was a substantial street

213. The admission charge to the Nelson Pillar in the early 1960s.

index to help visitors find their way around. Although the essay on Dublin was short in the extreme, it was very good as a topographical snapshot and at least it recognized the importance of the Georgian squares:

> The topography of the city may be quickly grasped by the visitor if he stands on O'Connell Bridge (which, incidentally, is wider than it is long). Immediately in front is O'Connell Street and the monument to Daniel O'Connell, Lord Mayor in 1841 and champion of Irish Freedom; in the centre is the Nelson Pillar, next to the General Post Office, and at the far end a monument to Parnell. On the right of the bridge can be seen the Custom House, completed in 1791. Ireland's most impressive public building and one of the noblest in Europe; beyond stretches the city's large dockland area and the North Wall where passengers embark for Liverpool.
>
> Looking from O'Connell Bridge in the opposite direction, College Green and Trinity College, founded in 1591, can be discerned at the end of Westmoreland Street. Facing the College is the old Parliament House (now the Bank of Ireland) begun in 1729; here the Act of Union with England was passed in 1800. Just beyond is Grafton Street, Dublin's fashionable shopping centre, which leads to St Stephen's Green, 22 acres in extent, the largest and prettiest park within the city. It is surrounded by fine 18th century houses, and the beautiful Georgian Fitzwilliam and Merrion Squares are near here.

This was as succinct as it was brief and, with a few more paragraphs in this vein, the city was summarized. The tourist for whom this guide was written would enjoy the history of the city but only as part of a wide-ranging schedule that would include shopping, going to the races or other sporting events and enjoying the night life. S/he would want to have a good meal and enjoy a pleasant drink and know where to hire a car or find a place to dance (p. 7).

'Seven Days in Dublin'

In the 1960s a new series of guides was printed by the Mount Salus Press. Initially entitled *Seven Days in Dublin* by 'Endymion', they developed into *Dublin – Guide and History*. They were roughly A5 in size, printed in landscape format and while the earlier editions came with a small black and white map, the later ones offered a four-colour map. At A2 size, it showed the streets very clearly but it was unwieldy and not particularly robust. However, the series was well received and it was chosen by the Irish National Teachers Organization as a guide to delegates to the Assembly of World Confederation of Organizations of the Teaching Profession which took place in Dublin in 1968 as part of the INTO's centenary year celebrations.

This series was another step in a gradual loosening up of the style of guides. They had been rather worthy and wordy in the 1930s and a great deal was expected of the average visitor. Tourism was meant to be a serious business, learning about the culture and mores of the society being visited. This guide was noted for the fact that it took a more light-hearted view. One of the endorsements printed at the beginning of the guide was from Quidnunc in the *Irish Times* who found the guide 'most readable and informative' with 'very succinct and racy information on all sorts of things'. From today's perspective it is rather difficult to appreciate the racy nature of the information but the style is certainly chatty, friendly and engaging. The information is interspersed with commentary and opinion but not in any heavy-handed way. There is a confidence in these texts and it is no longer felt necessary to explain Dublin. Rather, she is 'presented'.

In 1963 Dublin was presented as a growing city with improving infrastructure and an increasing standard of living, though this was supported to some degree by emigration to the United Kingdom. The final paragraphs of the description are reproduced below. By the late 1960s and the 1968 edition, the reference to the United Kingdom had been removed and the implication given was that work had been created at home for a growing labour force. Now attention was drawn to the skyline of Dublin with its many new and striking landmarks reflecting 'the dynamic spirit of progress which is characteristic of Ireland in the 1960s', though he added that 'unhappily few of these great blocks add anything to the grace and charm of the city. Progress is not altogether an unmixed blessing' (p. 12).

> The development of Dublin goes on to this day. Much credit is due to the municipal authorities for the way in which they have tackled our

slum clearance problems. New artisan estates have been built where many Dubliners have found comfortable homes undreamed of by their fathers. Like other countries in modern times, Ireland has been experiencing a movement from the land to urban areas. Dublin has attracted many country-born people and the population is now over 600,000. In addition to providing housing to keep pace with rapid expansion, work has been found for the bulk of this additional labour force. The port facilities have been extended, new electric power stations built and new industries established, particularly in the sphere of light engineering. The chaotic number of cars everywhere in evidence and the generally well-fed appearance of our citizens are indicative of our rising standards of living. We are indebted to the United Kingdom which absorbs our surplus labour, with the result that unemployment is seldom a serious problem in Ireland.

(*Seven Days in Dublin*, 1963, p. 12)

It was a positive view of the city, one that became even more so by the end of the decade. The sense of fun that is evident in the guide can be seen from this final paragraph on the city which offers a 'word of warning' to visitors. Nothing was to be taken too seriously.

There is much more we could say about Dublin and its history; but we think that we have given a sufficient sketch of our background to help you understand Dubliners and to enjoy our city. A word of warning: many foreigners, who have never been to this country before, harbour all manner of strange and often quaint illusions about Ireland and the Irish. Perhaps in the interest of your peace of mind we should shatter one such impression; nowadays, our battles seldom transcend the verbal plane and are usually conducted among ourselves on issues which you may well find incomprehensible. Dubliners are naturally friendly and hospitable. It is true that some of us are inclined to live in the past and to regard change with a certain suspicion, but we like to surround ourselves with the advantages of the present, and we look to the future with a quiet confidence which we know is not misplaced. Wherever you come from you will feel at home in Dublin and will be assured of a welcome.

As the title indicated, the guide offered a range of activities to be completed on each of seven days. Despite the modern style and approach of the guide, the Dublin on offer was very traditional and deviated little from the menu that had been around since the beginning of the century. The cathedrals and other important buildings, mostly from the eighteenth century, were to be visited on the first day but the streetscape was not of any great interest. Neither was much of interest in the twentieth-century city. The city centre was returned to only on Friday, when the visitor was invited to view Georgian Dublin, mostly in the south-eastern sector, and to enjoy St Stephen's Green. There was one interesting segue which would have taken the visitor way out of this zone and this was to the bottle museum that was 'appropriately located in cellars beneath Kingsbridge Station'. The only modern building worthy of note was Busáras. It was described as an 'exceptional example of progressive modern design' but it was visited only because the tourist would have ended up there while taking one of the bus tours out of the city. Strangely, there was no mention of the Nelson Pillar, even in the pre-destruction editions of the guide, nor any focus on O'Connell Street and its monuments. While the descriptions of the individual buildings were good, the visitor would have had a rather perfunctory experience of the city. Certainly, there was little chance that s/he might get lost north of the Liffey.

Most of the attractions were in the outskirts and the visitors were sent to places such as Howth or Dún Laoghaire. One day was devoted to what they called 'the far off hills' and this meant heading into Wicklow and day trips to Glendalough and the Vale of Avoca.

If these guides were to be followed, tourism was now intimately associated with entertainment and a great effort was put into linking this with the cultural experience. Pit stops were suggested during the cultural activities and the night life was extolled. Pubs were an important element in this but there was also an emphasis on good eating and fine dining. In 1963, the visitor was directed to Jammet's as the place par excellence on Nassau Street where the *faisan en voliere* was 'out of this world'. Guests were warned, however, that this did not come cheap and that they could expect to pay 42s. Another favourite was Bernardo's off Lincoln Place. This was a relatively new arrival and was described as being quite small, unpretentious with none of 'Jammet's mature opulence'. It offered superb Italian cooking but this time for about 28s. There seemed to be a new interest in Italian cuisine and also recommended was the Unicorn and Quo Vadis on St Andrew Street. Somewhat of a novelty, and therefore mentioned, were the Chinese restaurants. It seems that there had been several attempts at these but also many casualties. The visitor was directed to the best of the survivors – Wong's on Chatham Street – but this

214. Advertisement for the Metropole.

215. A Wimpy burger, the new taste sensation.

CONTINENTAL LOUNGE BAR
32   L O W E R   S T E P H E N   S T R E E T,   D U B L I N   2
(TWO DOORS FROM MERCER'S HOSPITAL)
YOU ARE INVITED TO VISIT US—Unusual in character, continental in atmosphere
A breath of Paris, reminiscent of les Bistros. Cosmopolitan clientele. Left bank mood.
Rendezvous of intelligentsia, Bohemian, literati, theatre personalities, socialities, beatniks,
artists, aristocrats and gay fashionable young ladies; businessmen and professionals —
from followers of Hippocrates to ambitious young advocates.
ALL WITH A ZEST FOR LIFE — YOU ARE INVITED TO JOIN OUR COTERIE
VISITORS — MEET YOUR FRIENDS IN . . .
THE HOUSE WITH THE CONTINENTAL ATMOSPHERE — Telephone 53137

216. Advertisement for Bartley Dunne's with its 'unusual character'.

would cost £1. There were other attractions and the hotels were still to be recommended. The Shelbourne had both reputation and price to match. À la carte could cost about 35s., table d'hôte was 15s. The Grill Bar apparently offered exceptional value for a quick bite. The Russell Hotel, a little off centre on the Harcourt Street side of the Green, was described as having both high standards and high prices and a bill of 42s. and more could be expected. The Gresham got praise for its five-course table d'hôte for what seems to have been a standard 15s. while the Metropole Georgian rooms in O'Connell Street was quite plush and inclined towards sophistication. The table d'hôte was also 15s. while à la carte would probably put you back about 26s. The Dolphin was offered as a 'home from home'. The suggested ritual was to have a martini in the lounge before retiring to dine where excellent steaks were prepared before your eyes and where the sole bonne femme was superb. The menu was described as extensive and without frills but at the same time it would cost 25s. There were also opportunities to dine well in Dún Laoghaire and Goatstown. Less expensive options were the Ship Grill in Westmoreland Street and, of course, the Green Rooster on Lower O'Connell Street. This had long been the haunt of ordinary Dubliners on a late-night outing. It was open until 2 a.m. and the hungry could get its famous chicken dinner for 9s. 6d., though wine was extra. Mind you, the fact that a Wimpy burger was being advertised as a new taste sensation must raise doubts about Dublin's palate.

However, it was the pubs that received special mention. They were described as an acquired taste – more rugged and down-to-earth than their UK counterparts 'with the emphasis on characters rather than character'. The 'singing taverns' were recommended, especially Lalor's of Wood Quay where there were few concessions towards creature comforts and it was usually full of characters of the O'Casey-Behan tradition. Whether O'Casey would have seen himself as a Behan, especially in relation to pubs, must be a matter of dispute but the chance to experience such real Dubliners was encouraged. Other pubs recommended were the Brazen Head, the Pearl and Groome's while Bartley Dunne's in Stephen Street was recommended for its 'odd mixture of bohemians and down-to-earth Dubliners' in an atmosphere that would have delighted James Joyce. Whether the author was aware that this was one of the few gay friendly bars in Dublin at the time must remain a moot point. The author clearly liked Davy Byrne's:

> But first an aperitif in Davy Byrne's, one of our most fashionable hostelries, in Duke Street off Grafton Street. Between six and seven most evenings, particularly in autumn and winter, you will find a fair cross-section of our social elite, others climbing in that direction, angry young men, gay young things, businessmen and professionals ranging from lawyers to punters. At its best, Davy's is the most congenial drinking haunt in town. Iced draught lager is a specialty. Cocktails are served in the rarefied atmosphere of the inner bar – but we always drink with the rabble outside.

Once upon a time, guides simply ignored the concept of shopping as a suitable tourist activity, now an entire day was to be devoted to it. There was confidence in the quality of Irish products as suitable purchases and even the souvenirs were said to have improved in quality – a good quality blackthorn shillelagh could be had from 13s. to £3. There was a focus on Waterford Glass, Donegal carpets (how would they get them home?), china, pottery and tweed. There was also recognition of a growing couture industry in Ireland and visitors were directed to Sybil Connolly and Irene Gilbert. Mind you, it was assumed that shopping was generally an activity for women because 'most men look on it as a penitential exercise, especially accompanying their wives'.

The image of Dublin presented had not changed much by the end of the decade. The visitor was still invited to visit the same list of historic buildings and there was nothing of the modern era found interesting enough to be included. In fact, the description of Busáras was watered down to read that it was 'one of Dublin's largest and most modern public buildings'. The Georgian era was given the same short shrift as it had been in 1963, despite the growing controversy about the replacement or retention of buildings. There was more enthusiasm for it in an advertisement for the Irish Hospitals' Sweepstake,

Joyce's Dublin

In reading Joyce you will come across Mountjoy Square, Georgian, tall and commanding. Architectural reliquary of departed taste. Dignified consort of brick and tree and noise of playing children. Rejoice in a city's prospect of the past. Rejoice in a thought for the future. The thought of a ticket. The prospect of a win.

4 Sweeps Annually

IRISH SWEEPS LINCOLN
(March)

IRISH SWEEPS DERBY
(June)

CAMBRIDGESHIRE
(October)

SWEEPS HURDLE
(December)

NUMEROUS FIRST PRIZES OF

£50,000

IRISH HOSPITALS' SWEEPSTAKES, BALLSBRIDGE, DUBLIN 4.
Branch Sweep Offices at Cork, Sligo, Galway and at 9-11 Grafton St., Dublin 2.

TICKETS £1 EACH

217. Advertisement for Irish Hospitals' Sweepstake. (*Dublin – Guide and History*, 1970, p. 17.)

which suggested that 'in reading Joyce, you will come across Mountjoy Square, Georgian, tall and commanding. Architectural reliquary of departed taste. Dignified consort of brick and tree and noise of playing children' (p. 17).

Neither had there been any revolution in dining. In fact, the author seemed to suggest that matters were not as good as they were. It seemed that people were now time poor, if a little better off financially, and their attitude to fine dining had suffered. We, the author suggested, had 'reduced it to a colourless, almost mechanical process' (p. 49). Jammet's and the Dolphin Hotel were gone but the visitor was once again pointed in the direction of Italian cuisine, in the form of Bernardos, the Unicorn or Quo Vadis. The Trocadero also offered possibilities on St Andrew Street. The Chinese arrivals seem to have settled and there was now the Chop Stick in Dame Street and Wong's on the Naas Road. The hotels remained places with good restaurants and the Shelbourne, Gresham and the Russell still maintained high standards. The Mirabeau in Sandycove was now being recommended as this 'small and at first sight unpretentious restaurant is a welcome newcomer which has attracted praise from satisfied and discerning patrons. The quality of cuisine is superlative and is matched by the loving care with which it is prepared and served' (p. 53).

Prices had risen over the decade. A table d'hôte in the Gresham had now moved to 21s. (plus 10 per cent). The Metropole offered a five-course dinner

Styled in Tweed

Stylish coat in pure new wool Donegal Hand-woven Tweed. Ideal for the more mature figure. With slight drape at back, and, for the Autumn, the new ' just below the knee ' fashion length.

In delightful Coffee/Cream, Black/White, rich Reds or Violet and Blue tones.

Sizes 10 thru 16   Price £15. $36.50
Size 18   £15.10. $37.50

Just one from our New Season Collection.

66 Sth. Great George's St. • 24 Grafton St., Dublin 2

218. Couture at Colette Modes.

(with dancing on Wednesdays) for 18*s.* 6*d.* Dipping into the à la carte menu in the Shelbourne would cost 50*s.* (including drinks) while the Russell would cost somewhere of the order of 55*s.* However, more reasonable fare was available. The Saddle Room in the Shelbourne offered beef plus trimmings, rolls, butter and coffee for 30*s.* while this would also get you the à la carte menu in Bernardo's.

According to the guide, Dubliners devoted Saturday mornings to coffee drinking with the obligatory stroll down Grafton Street, which was 'entertaining and enlightening. Indeed, you will travel far to find a more fascinating concentration of pretty girls' (p. 51). The pub scene was still to be recommended but this was changing. The 'singing pub' was now firmly established and it was said that traditional customers had been swept away by ballads and their followers, who are mostly cheerful boys and girls in for the company, the singing and pints of Guinness, Cokes and the odd glasses of gin or port. There were still good pubs, which in the author's view were those that had retained their traditional fixtures and fittings (including the customers). Decried was the arrival of the modern pub with its chrome and plastic, venues that were tasteless, shoddy places with nothing to recommend them. As he wrote about Toner's and Doheny and Nesbitt's: 'long may they flourish, and may they never change'.

By the later 1960s, shopping was firmly on the tourist agenda. The reputation of Dublin for haute couture continued to be praised but now readers were also directed to 'off the peg' fashions in Colette Modes and

Richard Alan of Grafton Street and Donald Davies of Enniskerry. There was a change in this guide compared to the previous edition in that it now focused on the shopping district of Dublin, rather than on the goods which were available. As would be expected, the main shopping district was in the environs of Grafton Street because it does 'contain in a very convenient area, most of the shops in which the average visitor may be interested', though it was agreed that there was more to Dublin shopping and that the visitor should take the opportunity to prowl around the rest of the city.

The end of an era of Ward Lock guides

It is as well that these other guides had appeared because an old friend was on the cusp of departure. Ward Lock had produced detailed and comprehensive guides to the city since the 1880s on a frequent but irregular schedule. The guides dealt not only with Dublin but also with the Boyne Valley and Wicklow. There were not many advertisements but photographs were provided as well as three very good maps. The map of the city, at a scale of 3.25 inches to 1 mile (about 1:19,500), was high quality and was produced by Bartholomew for the company while the other two dealt with the environs of the city and of the region. By the 1950s, they were claiming to be in their twenty-fifth edition. The edition under consideration here was undated but can be placed in the early years of the 1950s.

The guides were positive about Dublin, as expected, but it was the physical environment that was the first selling point, noted in the very first paragraph that the reader met. They shared the same problem with the other guides; it was not clear what it was about Dublin, *per se*, that was really attractive. They put it thus:

> Few cities are more fortunate than Dublin in charm of situation and beauty of environs. The city proper stands at the head of the beautiful bay which bears its name, and centres on the estuary of the Liffey by which (and by the smaller rivers Tolka and Dodder) it is watered. To the east the noble bay stretches away to the circling shore where the waves lap the coastline and spill upon the silvery sands; to the northeast the rocky promontory, familiarly called the Hill of Howth, constitutes the most remarkable feature of what is otherwise a flat, extensive plain; westward stretches the spacious, Phoenix Park, and the lovely vale through which the Liffey flows; and to the south, the villa-studded shore of the bay extends along the nine miles from the city to the granite hills of Dalkey and Killiney. Behind all, the mountains of

Dublin and Wicklow spread their undulating length to where Bray Head is lashed by the oft-times turbulent Irish Sea. The whole presents a scene which for grandeur is almost without a parallel in Europe.

(p. 9)

Decoding the florid prose tells the visitor that Dublin is set in a nice bay with a number of rivers where the only feature of interest is Howth Head and a large park. Nothing about the city itself features in this description and it is a while before that entity is introduced to the visitor.

That issue aside, what was particularly useful about the Ward Lock guides was that they combined a great deal of practical information with very detailed descriptions of locations and buildings. In this, they were probably the best guides to the city, though they were not as assiduous as they might have been at ensuring that *all* of the information was up to date. However, this edition had noted the transition to a republic though they incorrectly noted that the name of the country had changed from Éire to Republic of Ireland (p. 19) – an error for which they might easily be forgiven. The format was well established by the 1950s, from page size, to the typeface used and the writing style. They did not provide much by way of any historical overview for the reader and carefully avoided stepping into the contested history around the events of 1916 or 1921. Their comments on that time period were factual and to the point but, to their credit, they did at least note that the centre of Dublin had been destroyed by both rebellion and civil war, though the latter was described as an 'outbreak'. In common with the other guides, their view of Dublin had not changed much by the early 1950s in comparison to earlier editions. Dublin was an industrial capital with a fine port and excellent educational facilities:

> The street architecture of Dublin is, in comparison with other European cities is not strikingly beautiful but there are many stately buildings of the Georgian period worthy of notice. What is wanting in architectural splendour is, however, supplied by the spaciousness of some of its business avenues; of O'Connell Street in particular, which, having been for the most part destroyed during the Rebellion of 1916, and during the subsequent outbreak in 1922, has been entirely rebuilt. Many of the public buildings and churches of Dublin are noteworthy in character and design and other features of the city, notably the two and a half miles of walled quays and parallel avenues through which the Liffey flows; the spacious parks, gardens, and open places; the splendid

monuments; the charm of its environs; the courtesy of its citizens – all
combine to make the city a pleasant place to visit, and to sustain its
deserved designation of Dear, Delightful Dublin.

(p. 22)

Apart from the fact that the soubriquet was just as likely to be 'dear, dirty
Dublin', this text (and much else in the guide) was unchanged from the 1930s.
It is a small thing but the reader will note that there was positive comment on
the 'business avenues' and that many public buildings (and some of them were
new) were worthy of note. In this, they went further than other guides.

Once the reader had worked his or her way through the practical
information with details on buses and taxi fares and golf and religious services
as well as some information on shopping, it was time for the visit to the city.
While they did recognize that shopping might be an activity to be indulged
in, unlike the 1960s guide described above, they just pointed to the main
streets and let the visitor get on with it. There were three comprehensive routes
offered and these were unchanged from those offered in previous volumes and
which were discussed in *Dublin, 1930–1950*. They were designed as loops and
covered about 3 miles (5km) but with opportunities to retreat by bus if the
going became too tough. Three miles seemed to be taken by most guides as
the limit of tolerance for even an avid walker. Route One was an extended
loop that encompassed O'Connell Street, Bank of Ireland, Trinity College and
then moved up Dame Street towards Christ Church. Some time was spent in
the Liberties before moving down the hill to St Patrick's Cathedral and then
back towards the centre of town via Aungier Street and South Great George's
Street. It was a good comprehensive route through most of medieval Dublin
with full commentary provided. This was the only guide that really featured
the Nelson Pillar. It was described as:

> standing at the junction of North Earl Street on the left or east side
> (leading to Amiens Street Station), and Henry Street, on the right, with
> O'Connell Street, is a lofty fluted column in the Doric style, about 120
> feet high, surmounted by a colossal statue of Nelson by Kirk, a native
> of Dublin. The monument was erected in 1806. Spiral stairs lead to a
> railed platform at the top (admission 6*d.*), whence may be obtained a
> splendid panoramic view of the city, bounded by the Bay on the east,
> by the Carlingford and Mourne Mountains on the north, and by the
> Dublin Hills and the Wicklow Mountains on the south-west and south.
> Many buildings, hotels, and business houses in O'Connell Street and

the adjacent streets were destroyed during the 1916 Rebellion and subsequent troubles; the reconstruction has produced a number of notable buildings.

(p. 49)

A flavour of the style of the guide and the level of detail supplied can be seen from the following extract for Aungier Street, as well as the helpful insertion as to how to salvage weary feet by translating them to a bus:

> In Aungier Street, which we reach after passing along the south side of the Convent, is the Birthplace of the Poet Moore. The house, No. 12, is still standing, and, as in the poet's time, is occupied by a shopkeeper … The 'little gable window by which I penned my earliest verses, the Melodies, etc.,' is gone, and the shop front is altered, but otherwise very few interior or exterior changes have been made.
>
> Buses run down Aungier Street to College Green and Nelson's Pillar, or the return can be made down York Street into Stephen's Green and Grafton Street.
>
> The continuation of Aungier Street forms the busy thoroughfare of South Great George Street, where once stood the stately church of St George of Windsor and the houses of many of the Irish earls. On the right is the commodious South City Market, in the Scottish Baronial style, with a long street frontage.

(p. 68)

Route two was also a loop of about three miles (5km) and began in Grafton Street, moving to St Stephen's Green, thence to UCD and back towards the National Museum and Library with a segue to the National Gallery. Then the visitor was taken on a long salient to visit the Custom House and Pro-Cathedral. It would have taken quite a long time to complete all of the visits involved but the visitor would have had a good cultural education from both museum and gallery. Ward Lock was never particularly interested in the Georgian landscape of the city so the best that could be said of Merrion Square was that it had many fine Georgian houses and that 'this was once the fashionable centre of Dublin; and, though many of its fine residences continue to be occupied by Dublin's leading citizens, as many have been converted into offices of the government and important societies or institutions' (p. 79).

It was always a feature of the Ward Lock guides that the third tour took the visitor into the northside and this was no exception. It was a similar tour

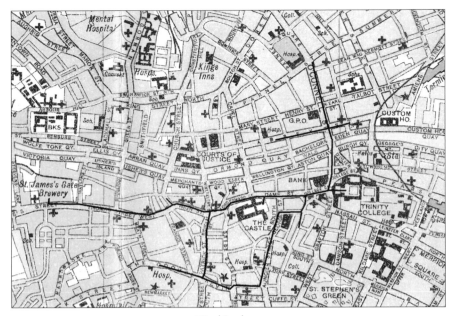

219. Ward Lock route 1.

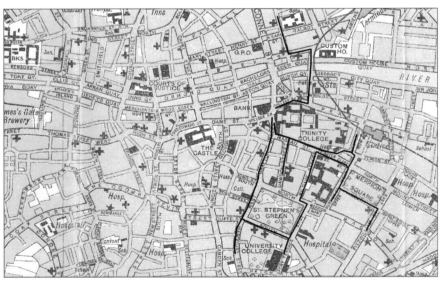

220. Ward Lock route 2.

to Route 4 of Dublin Corporation's tours, described above, and it took the visitor more off the beaten track into little side streets. The route took them down towards Capel Street from O'Connell Street, pausing on the way to look

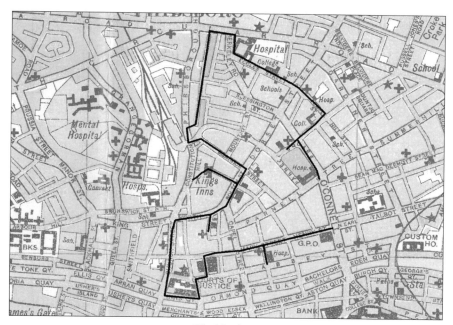

221. Ward Lock route 3.

at Jervis Street Hospital. They crossed Capel Street into the markets and the area around St Mary's Abbey. This would have been a noisy and bustling part of the city, especially early in the day, and in its first guides, earlier in the century, Dublin Corporation preferred not to bring the visitor down that way to the Four Courts, the first main destination. Ward Lock also noted that a bus could assist in getting to the Four Courts but that was only for those for whom the walk was too much. From there, a detour along the quays was possible but the main route was along Church Street and the obligatory visit to St Michan's. As they walked along North King Street, they could take a short diversion into Green Street to view the courthouse and then a little later on, they could leave Bolton Street and view Henrietta Street and the King's Inns and even venture through the park to view the various nearby institutions, the Hardwicke, the Richmond and Whitworth hospitals, the Richmond Lunatic Asylum and the Richmond Penitentiary. One way or another, the tourist eventually would end up at the Broadstone Station, from where a good view of the city could be obtained. Then it was northwards along Phibsborough Road or, alternatively, an inner route along what had been a spur of the Royal Canal. It was still a canal at this time but would have been filled in by 1956. From the heights of Phibsborough another view of the city was obtained and the unusual sight of Mountjoy Prison came into view. Thence it was back into the centre via the streets of the Gardiner estate and the municipal gallery. The guide noted, as they had noted in previous editions, that 'the north side of Dublin, part of which we have just traversed, was long the most fashionable residential quarter, and the interiors of the houses, especially those in North Great George Street, which runs parallel to the east side of Parnell Square, are very fine' (p. 92). Alas, though, they also noted that 'no longer a fashionable quarter, many of the houses on the north side are now let out as tenements, and have fallen into sad neglect and disrepair.'

The environs of Dublin, involving a trip to the Phoenix Park, the Irish National War Memorial and onwards to Lucan, Leixlip, Celbridge and Maynooth comprised the fourth route. This is perhaps the most interesting of the tours from a socio-political perspective. Both series of official guides had sections on the Royal Hospital and Kilmainham Gaol, though neither felt that they were important enough to include in a tour. The Ward Lock Guide took these in and also directed the visitor to the Irish National War Memorial.

> THE IRISH NATIONAL WAR MEMORIAL occupies an area of about 20 acres on the southern slopes of the Liffey valley, directly opposite Magazine Hill, Phoenix Park. It lies in the centre of the 150 acre parkway which stretches from Islandbridge to Chapelizod. The Memorial, the design of Sir Edwin Lutyens, R.A., is a Garden of Remembrance and includes a spacious level lawn with a sunk garden at either end. In the centre of the lawn stands the War Stone with a fountain on either side of it. Southwards of the War Stone, at the head of an imposing semi-circular flight of steps stands the Great Cross. Paved pergolas, of granite columns and teak beams, divide the lawn from the sunk gardens. At the ends of the pergolas stand the Book-rooms or Shrines, four in number, which house the beautifully illuminated volumes in which are written the names of the 49,400 Irishmen who gave their lives in the Great War. Granite piers and niches are set in the rustic whinstone walls around the lawn.
>
> (p. 95)

This reference first appeared in the Ward Lock guide that was published at the end of the Second World War. It is not found in any other guide to the city and a useful comparison may be made with another, smaller, commercial guide to the city that visited the same locale. *A Short Guide to Dublin and District* was produced by Browne and Nolan Limited for 1s. 6d. This was pocket sized, less than A6, and while it concentrated on the history of the city, rather than practicalities, these were not totally ignored. A lot was covered in its 48 pages and the tours within Dublin were arranged by the cardinal points while visits to the environs of Dublin such as the Boyne Valley, Maynooth and Wicklow were also suggested. This guide too is undated but appeared sometime during the 1950s and before 1958. While it has no difficulty in pointing out the attractions of a trip up the Nelson Pillar, it ignores the war memorial, despite, and this in itself was unusual, bringing the visitor to its environs and having them take a trip around the Royal Hospital and Kilmainham. It seems that the war memorial was contested not only in popular or political discourse but also as a tourism destination.

> Continuing up James's Street, Guinness's Brewery (map ref. B.5) is reached. This is well worth a visit. (For details see page 7.) Just beyond the brewery the street widens, and in the centre is James's Street Fountain. To the right of this a long avenue leads to St Patrick's Hospital (map ref. A.6) – a mental institute founded by Dean Swift but a short time before his own mind gave way. To quote Swift himself: 'He left such little wealth he had To build a house for fools and mad Showing, by one ironic touch, No nation needed it so much.' Proceeding in the direction of Inchicore a turn to the right leads to Kilmainham Gaol of sinister memory. The old prison – now closed – has figured largely in Irish history. Here Parnell was imprisoned during the Land agitation, and here was signed the 'Kilmainham Treaty'. From here, also, some of the leaders of the 1916 Insurrection went to face a firing squad (map ref. A.5). Just opposite the prison is the entrance to the Royal Hospital for maimed soldiers, founded by Charles II as a companion institute to Chelsea. Originally the site of a hospice of the Knights of Malta, the present building was erected from a design of Sir William Robinson. The apartments are magnificently proportioned, and contain many splendid works of art. The Royal Hospital was, for generations, the headquarters of the Commander-in-Chief of the British troops in Ireland, and is rich in memories of great soldiers, notably the 'Iron Duke'. A turn to the right past the Royal Hospital leads down a long hill to Kingsbridge Railway Station, headquarters of Córas Iompair Éireann (Irish Transport Organization) and terminus for all trains for the south and south-west.

(p. 14)

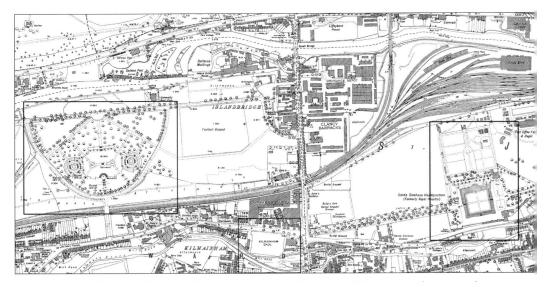

222. The Royal Hospital, Kilmainham Gaol and the National War Memorial juxtaposed.
(Ordnance Survey plan, 1:2,500, Sheet 18(X), 1939.)

223. An aerial view of the National War Memorial gardens.

This was to be the swansong for the Ward Lock guides, at least for the Dublin and Wicklow edition. By the 1960s, they had been transformed into the *Red Guides*, focusing on the fact that they had had a distinctive red cover since the 1890s, and the decision was made to focus almost entirely on the

United Kingdom. Dublin was now rolled into an Ireland volume with the result that the coverage given to the city was greatly diminished. There was still a good map of the city centre, produced in the same manner as previously, and the routes described above were retained but in a summarized form. This was a loss and nothing around in the 1960s was quite as good.

The practicalities

Visitors to Dublin had many hotels from which to choose at all grades. The supply of rooms available seemed to be in line with demand except during the Spring Show in May and the Horse Show in August when rooms were at a premium both in availability and in price. The Ward Lock guide listed the following hotels in its 1950s guide but there were many others.

Anchor	2 Parnell Square
Belvedere	North Great George's Street
Buswells	25–6 Molesworth Street
Caledonian	South Great George's Street
Central	Exchequer Street
Clarence	6–8 Wellington Quay
Dolphin	49 Essex Street
Four Courts	Inns Quay
Gresham	Upper O'Connell Street
Ivanhoe (Temperance)	7–8 Harcourt Street
Jury's	College Green
Moira	15 Trinity Street
Mont Clare	14 Clare Street
Parkside	North Circular Road
Regent	D'Olier Street
Royal Exchange	5–7 Parliament Street
Royal Hibernian	Dawson Street
Russell	St Stephen's Green
Shelbourne	St Stephen's Green
Standard	82 Harcourt Street
Wicklow	Wicklow Street
Wynn's	35–9 Lower Abbey Street

The best of these would have been the Gresham, Shelbourne, Russell, Jury's and the Royal Hibernian and, with the exception of the Gresham, all were located south of the river in the south-eastern sector. One of the results of the 1916 Rebellion was to shift the focus of quality hotels away from O'Connell Street. There had been the Metropole, Hammam and Imperial and these were of the highest quality. Of course, visitors were not confined to the city centre. Thom's directory for 1956 listed just under 100 establishments within the

224. Advertisement for the International Hotel and Royal Hibernian Hotel, 1950.

environs of Dublin. Most were within the canals and many were associated with the various transportation termini. Thus, the visitor could expect to find accommodation in and around Harcourt Street, around Amiens Street and Talbot Street and Westland Row; there were fourteen hotels on Harcourt Street alone. Visitors using Broadstone or Kingsbridge were not particularly catered to but Parnell Square was the site of another cluster. Suburban hotels were still relatively few and far between and tended to be concentrated in attractive and well-off coastal locations such as Howth, Sutton, Dún Laoghaire, Killiney and Bray. The International Hotel in Bray, for example, wooed guests on the basis that it was only 12 miles (19km) from Dublin, though it was unclear what else they offered to make it worthwhile travelling the distance. The practice of hotels providing a detailed guide to visitors did not resume after the Second World War and so the researcher is denied a useful source of information. Not only did the guides provide a sense of what elements of Dublin were being 'sold', they provided great detail on the range of services provided and the charges for those services.

Some idea of continuity and changing prices may be obtained from an advertisement for the St Andrew's Temperance Hotel on Exchequer Street in 1960. The concept of temperance hotels was long established in Dublin and the Ivanhoe on Harcourt Street, mentioned above, was another long-term survivor. Miss Johnson was still presiding over her hotel in 1960, as she had been in the 1940s when the hotel's guide to visitors stated that it was the city's most conservative temperance hotel. It still offered sixty rooms with hot and cold water. The tariff from the 1940s may be compared with that of 1960. The consumer price index prepared by the CSO with a base of 1947, suggested that prices generally had risen by 46.2 per cent by 1960. These prices suggested that Miss Johnson had applied increases generally in line with the overall experience of the decade but that she had rounded up or down to the nearest shilling or six pence.

	1940s	1960
Bedroom with full breakfast	10s. 6d.	16s. 6d.
Luncheon	2s. 6d.	4s.
High tea	3s. 6d.	5s.
Weekly rate (inclusive)	£5 5s.	£9 9s.

Unfortunately, in the 1960s Thom's directories ceased providing lists of hotels and instead moved to an alphabetical index only of services, which is not nearly as useful to the researcher. At the same time, the major hotels returned to producing information guides for the visitor, this time with the Shelbourne and Hibernian using the same template. Unfortunately, they decided that these would be advertising guides only and they provided none of the information of previous decades. Something was learned, though, of what pastimes Dublin had to offer and these will be looked at below.

One version of the Shelbourne guide offered a little more information than other editions and it seems that radio in each bedroom was seen as a plus in that it was advertised as being free of charge from 6 a.m. to midnight. They presumably did not want guests messing with long wave after Radio Éireann had gone to bed or before the strains of O'Donnell Abú in the morning. The hotel still maintained a gift shop and a gentleman's hairdresser, as they had always done, and women continued to need to look elsewhere. Other services included chauffeur-driven vehicles and full valet service was available on each floor. The Gresham's booklet was a little more informative and pointed out that 185 of the 220 rooms had private bathrooms and showers together with guest-controlled heating and radio. There was 'a gay ballroom' and excellent

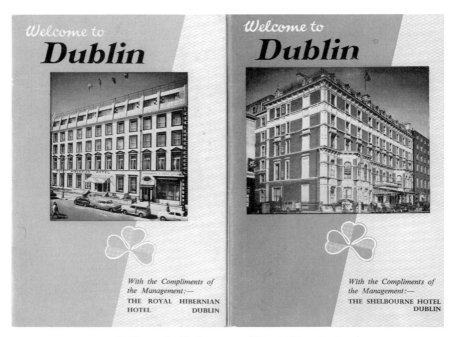

225. Guides to the Shelbourne and Royal Hibernian hotels.

dining. For those prepared to pay, there were the terrace suites, each with a large sitting room with a cocktail bar, a kitchenette and a twin-bedded room with private bathroom. They were furnished with hand-painted furniture, Irish-made carpets and linens and rare Connemara marble fireplaces in the sitting rooms. Since they opened onto a 50 ft (15m) terrace, they gave excellent views of the city and the sea (or so they claimed). Unfortunately, no indication was given as to the cost of this luxury. The hours of service were what would now be seen as standard. Breakfast began at 7 a.m. and ended at 10.30 a.m. while dinner was served from 6.30 p.m. to 9.00 p.m with the grill room available until 11 p.m.

Dublin Tourism produced a booklet of practical information for the city for 1970. It was a series of typed sheets, foolscap size and colour coded by topic. It might not have been the best produced document but it did contain a great deal of information. By this time, Bord Fáilte had begun its practice of grading hotels using a system of letter codes. In Dublin, they recognized 7 A* hotels and a further 17 A grade hotels. There were 14 hotels that merited B* and a further 13 at B and 16 at C. Bringing up the rear were two hotels on Parnell Square – Blossoms and Parkway – which were graded D. At this time, there were also a number of new unclassified hotels such as the Royal Dublin on O'Connell Street and the Tara Towers on the Merrion Road.

The list of hotels with a grade of better than B* is given below together with the minimum and maximum approved high-season prices for bed and breakfast. These are useful only at a broad level of comparison since all sorts of deals were available to alter these prices.

Table 13. Top-class hotels in Dublin in 1970 by price and location.

Grade	Name	Minimum	Maximum	Location
A*	Gresham	115s.	115s.	O'Connell Street
A*	Intercontinental	139s.	149s.	Ballsbridge
A*	Jury's	75s.	85s.	College Green
A*	Royal Hibernian	95s.	95s.	Dawson Street (room only)
A*	Russell	125s.	125s.	St Stephens Green (room only)
A*	Shelbourne	92s.	112s. 6d.	St Stephen's Green
A	Anchor	45s.	45s.	2 Parnell Street
A	Central	52s. 6d.	62s. 6d.	Exchequer Street
A	Claremont	42s.	42s.	Howth
A	Clarence	47s. 6d.	55s.	Wellington Quay
A	Crofton Airport	65s.	65s.	Whitehall
A	Four Courts	47s. 6d.	57s. 6d.	Inns Quay
A	Green Isle	47s. 6d.	55s.	Naas Road (room only)
A	Ivanhoe	47s. 6d.	55s.	Harcourt Street
A	Marine	55s.	55s.	Sutton
A	Moira	65s.	75s.	Trinity Street
A	Montrose	41s. 6d.	55s.	Stillorgan Road (room only)
A	Powers Royal	55s.	65s.	Kildare Street
A	Skylon	47s. 6d.	55s.	Drumcondra Road (room only)
A	South County	70s.	80s.	Stillorgan Road (room only)
A	Sutton House	40s.	30s.	Sutton (room only)
A	Wicklow	65s.	65s.	Wicklow Street
A	Wynn's	47s. 6d.	55s.	Lr Abbey Street
B*	Ashling	45s.	45s.	Parkgate Street
B*	Belvedere	40s.	40s.	Great Denmark Street
B*	Buswell's	45s.	45s.	Molesworth Street
B*	Caledonian	35s.	35s.	South Great George's Street
B*	Grosvenor	38s. 6d.	38s. 6d.	Westland Row
B*	Hollybrook	35s.	35s.	Howth Road
B*	Lansdowne	50s.	50s.	Pembroke Road
B*	Lenehan	35s.	35s.	Harcourt Street
B*	Mont Clare	40s.	42s. 6d.	14 Clare Street
B*	North Star	45s.	45s.	Amiens Street
B*	Ormond	52s. 6d.	52s. 6d.	Ormond Quay
B*	Ormsby	40s.	40s.	Eccles Street
B*	Rosslare	30s.	30s.	Harcourt Street
B*	West County	40s.	40s.	Chapelizod

226. The South County Hotel in south county Dublin.

There are no surprises in the top hotels and no change since the 1950s. The main difference was the development of suburban hotels, which was a consequence of the increased suburbanization of population and facilities coupled with the advent of the car ferry. More people were now motorized, whether on organized tours, hiring cars or bringing their own and suburban locations offered greater capacity for parking and ease of travel. The South County Hotel was an example of these new facilities and the prices show that suburban location did not result in lower tariffs.

Entertainment
Dublin did not offer any particularly local forms of entertainment unless the singing pubs which had become more commonplace at the end of the 1960s fall into that category. Looking at the hotel guides, it was assumed that people would be interested in the pubs, the theatre and would wish to play golf, go fishing or go racing or even hunting. By the end of the 1960s, the Abbey had returned to its original location in Abbey Street and there was still the Gaiety, Olympia and Gate as well as a number of smaller theatres. However, the theatre scene was much diminished by the loss of the Theatre Royal in 1962 and the Queen's Theatre was heading for closure by the end of the decade.

There was much variety on offer in the various theatres as the table below shows. This is a random selection of the offerings and it showed that

GAIETY THEATRE

Proprietors: THE GAIETY THEATRE (DUBLIN) LTD.
Resident Manager: PHIL O'KELLY

IRISH PREMIERE

FOR TWO WEEKS ONLY
COMMENCING MONDAY, 27th APRIL, 1959
Nightly at 8 p.m.   Matinee Saturday at 2.30 p.m.

EITHNE DUNNE

IN

HILTON EDWARDS' PRODUCTION

OF

BRECHT'S

MOTHER COURAGE

AND HER CHILDREN

(English Version by Eric Bentley)

WITH

CHRISTOPHER CASSON	JOHN COWLEY
MILO O'SHEA	PATRICK BEDFORD
LAURIE MORTON	LELIA DOOLAN
PAUL FARRELL	DERMOT TUOHY
FAY SARGENT	JAMES NEYLIN
CHARLES MITCHELL	BRIAN PHELAN

Costumes designed by MICHEÁL MAC LIAMMÓIR
Settings : ROBERT HEADE
Musical Director : PETER HELD
MALE VOICE CHOIR FROM DUBLIN MUNICIPAL SCHOOL

Stage Director		JOSIE MacAVIN
Stage Manager	For	CHARLES ROBERTS
Assistant Stage Manager	P. J. O'Connor	WILLIAM STYLES
Press and Public Relations Officer	Productions	
		FRANKIE BYRNE
Stage Manager	For Gaiety	TOM JONES
Chief Electrician	Theatre	HARRY MORRISON

The public may leave at the end of the performance by all exit doors. Persons shall not be permitted to stand or sit in any of the gangways intersecting the seating, or to sit in any of the other gangways.—Copy Bye-Law.

227. *Mother Courage* in the Gaiety, 1959.

OLYMPIA THEATRE, DUBLIN

Dame Street, Dublin
Managing Directors : Stanley Illsley and Leo McCabe

COMMENCING MONDAY, JULY 18th, 1960
NIGHTLY AT 8. p.m.   SATURDAY, TWO PERFORMANCES, 5.30 and 8.15 p.m.
STANLEY ILLSLEY and LEO McCABE by Arrangement with
LINNIT and DUNFEE Ltd. and JACK HYLTON
present The BRISTOL OLD VIC PRODUCTION of

SALAD DAYS

by DOROTHY REYNOLDS & JULIAN SLADE
Music by JULIAN SLADE. Directed by DENIS CAREY.
SAME PRICES AS LAST VISIT: Stalls: 10/- & 7/6. Circle: 8/6, 6/-, 4/-.
Boxes: 40/- and 35/-. Gallery: (unreserved) 2/6.

NEXT ATTRACTION

NOEL COWARD GIVES STANLEY ILLSLEY AND
LEO McCABE YET ANOTHER WORLD PREMIERE
PRODUCTION AUGUST 8th — AT OLYMPIA (FOR
TWO WEEKS)

In association with MICHAEL REDGRAVE Productions Ltd. F.E.S. PLAYS LTD. presents

SYBIL THORNDIKE

MARIE LOHR   LEWIS CASSON

in

"WAITING IN THE WINGS"

A Play by **NOEL COWARD**

with

NORA NICHOLSON	MAUREEN DELANY	UNA VENNING
JESSICA DUNNING	WILLIAM HUTT	MARY CLARE
MAIDIE ANDREWS	MOLLY LUMLEY	BETTY HARE
EDITH DAY	NORAH BLANEY	MARGOT BOYD
JEAN CONROY	ERIC HILLYARD	

and **GRAHAM PAYN**

Directed by MARGARET WEBSTER. Scenery and Costumes by MOTLEY

PRICES FOR THIS OUTSTANDING ATTRACTION SAME AS " NUDE WITH
VIOLIN "—MR. COWARD'S LAST WORLD PREMIERE AT THIS THEATRE.

GALA DRESS OPENING AT WHICH MR. COWARD WILL BE PRESENT.
PRICES: (OPENING NIGHT ONLY) Stalls: £1. 1. Circle: 15/-, 10/6, 7/6.
Prices following performances: Stalls: 12/6, 8/6. Circle: 10/6, 7/6, 5/-.
Postal Bookings (with stamped addressed envelope) are now being accepted for the 1st week

228. *Waiting in the Wings*, world premiere in the
Olympia, 1960.

ABBEY THEATRE
Dublin

Playing at
THE QUEEN'S THEATRE

Pending Rebuilding and Enlargement
of the Abbey

Monday, 21st March, 1966 and following nights at 8

The Call

A Play in Three Acts by Tom Coffey

Characters:

PETER BURNS	Liam O Foghlú
MAY BURNS	Aingeal Ní Nuamain
JIM BURNS	Roibeárd Carladhal
FRANK BURNS	Domhnall MacCanna
NANCY KELLY	Máire Ní Néill
DOCTOR MORAN	Pádraig MacLéid
FR. JOHN, O.F.M.	Eamon Guailli
KATHLEEN COLLINS	Eadaoin Ní Ceallaigh

The scene is the living-room of the Burns' house in a small
town in the south-west of Ireland.

ACT I: Scene 1:   Afternoon early June.
          Scene 2:   Late evening, a week later.
          Scene 3:   Same, a few hours later.

In the interests of public health this Theatre is disinfected with
JEYES' FLUID and sprayed with JEYES' FLORAL SPRAY

ACT II: Scene 1:   Mid afternoon on the following day.
          Scene 2:   A week later.

ACT III: Scene 1:   Three weeks later.
          Scene 2:   Same day, a few hours later.

There will be Intervals of Ten Minutes between the Acts

Play produced by PROINSIAS MacDIARMADA
Setting designed by LIAM MILLER and
painted by BRIAN COLLINS
Stage Manager: JOE ELLIS

THE CALL

THE CALL is the fourth play by Tom Coffey to be produced in the Abbey.
It comes after an interval of practically five years during which he has had
work produced elsewhere.
His first play in this theatre was entitled STRANGER BEWARE. It was
staged on 17th September, 1959. His second play ANYONE COULD ROB A
BANK was first put on in August 1960 and was revived in November of the
same year. Both the above were full-length plays in three acts. His third play
in the Abbey was THE LONG SORROW, a one-act play the scene of which
was situated in a graveyard near the border. It was first performed on 19th
September, 1961.
All three plays mentioned above dealt in one way or another with crime
and had casts which included policemen on duty. In the long plays the police
were members of the Civic Guards. In the short play, however, there was a
member of the Royal Ulster Constabulary.
Mr. Coffey's new play has no police in it and no connection with crime. It is a
comedy of family life in a small south-western country town.

COFFEE COUNTER NOW OPEN IN STALLS BAR

SMOKING WILL NOT BE PERMITTED IN THE AUDITORIUM

229. *The Call* in the Abbey, 1966. The programme layout and design had not changed since the 1940s.

Dubliners could enjoy a range of European and Irish offerings from the classics to the modern and from the serious to farce. International companies visited Dublin on a regular basis and there was clearly an audience, as evidenced by the high prices charged, as well as the presence of such distinguished visitors as the Bristol Old Vic or the Bolshoi Ballet. It may well have been that visitors would have been disappointed by the lack of regular offerings of classic Irish drama, though the Abbey could generally be relied upon in that regard. In an atmosphere of censorship, the theatre was quite outgoing but it was badly shaken by the furore over the production of *The Rose Tattoo* in 1958 (see the excellent account by Whelan and Swift, 2002). After that, the industry took a careful path during the 1960s. Thus, for example, in 1960, the Abbey's offering for the Theatre Festival in September was *Song of the Anvil* by Brian McMahon and *The Quare Fellow* by Brendan Behan. The Olympia offered *Macbeth* by the Old Vic Company while the Gaiety presented Siobhán McKenna in *The Playboy of the Western World* and *Voices of Doolin* by Walter Macken. By 1968, there was more of an international flavour with the Black Theatre of Prague appearing in the Olympia and Arthur Millar's *After the Fall*

Table 14. Random selection of events in Dublin theatres, 1950–69.

Theatre	Opening	Artist / Play	Author
Abbey	12 February 1951	*Juno and the Paycock*	Seán O'Casey
Abbey	24 March 1951	*The Shewing-Up of Blanco Posnet*	G.B. Shaw
Theatre Royal	6 May 1952	Katherine Dunham	
Theatre Royal	17 November 1952	Betty Hutton	
Theatre Royal	3 December 1952	Gracie Fields	
Abbey	13 May 1954	*Crabbed Youth and Age*	Lennox Robinson
Abbey	13 May 1954	*Twenty Years a Wooing*	John McCann
Olympia	4 October 1954	*Blythe Spirit*	Noel Coward
Gaiety	12 July 1954	Gilbert and Sullivan Operas (D'Oyly Carte)	
Abbey	13 February 1956	*The Shadow of a Gunman*	Seán O'Casey
Gaiety	25 February 1957	*Julius Caesar (AD 1957)*	Version by Hilton Edwards, Michael MacLiammoir
Gaiety	25 March 1957	*Anastasia*	Marcelle Maurette
Abbey	15 February 1958	*Give Me a Bed of Roses*	John McCann
Gaiety	27 October 1958	Ballet Rambert	
Gaiety	27 April 1959	*Mother Courage and her Children*	Bertolt Brecht
Gaiety	7 July 1959	*Festival of Fun*	Jimmy O'Dea
Gaiety	6 October 1959	*The Boy Friend*	Sandy Wilson
Olympia	22 February 1960	*Lily of Killarney*	Glasnevin Musical Society
Gaiety	16 May 1960	Royal Ballet	
Abbey	15 July 1960	*The Country Boy*	John Murphy
Olympia	18 July 1960	*Salad Days* (Bristol Old Vic)	Dorothy Reynold and Julian Slade
Olympia (World Premiere)	8 August 1960	*Waiting in the wings* (Mr Coward present for first night)	Noel Coward
Olympia (TF)	12 September 1960	*Hassan*	James Elroy Flecker
Gaiety	4 July 1961	*The Golden Years*	Donal Giltinan
Abbey	26 April 1963	*The Devil's Disciple*	G.B. Shaw
Gaiety	29 July 1963	Bolshoi Ballet	
Gaiety (TF)	23 September 1963	*A Little Winter Love*	Alun Owen
Gaiety (TF)	30 September 1963	*The last P.M.*	Conor Farrington
Olympia (TF)	30 September 1963	*Carrie*	Michael Coffey, Wesley Burroughs
Abbey	11 February 1964	*Juno and the Paycock*	Seán O'Casey

Table 14. Random selection of events in Dublin theatres, 1950–69. *(continued)*

Theatre	Opening	Artist / Play	Author
Gaiety	15 June 1964	Savoy Operas	
Gaiety	23 August 1965	Bolshoi Ballet	
Gaiety	6 September 1965	Gaels of Laughter	Maureen Potter
Abbey	22 November 1966	*Tarry Flynn*	Patrick Kavanagh
Abbey	21 March 1966	*The Call*	Tom Coffey
Gaiety	6 March 1967	*Bitter Sweet*	Noel Coward
Abbey	18 March 1968	*The Saint and Mary Kate*	Frank O'Connor
Gaiety	9 June 1969	*Alfie* (Eamon Andrews Studios)	Bill Naughton
Gaiety (TF)	7 October 1969	*On the Rocks*	G.B. Shaw
Abbey	17 August 1970	*A Crucial Week in the Life of a Grocer's Assistant*	Tom Murphy

Note: (TF): Theatre Festival production.

Table 15. Prices for a selection of performances in Gaiety and Olympia theatres.

Gaiety	Dress Circle	Parterre	Grand Circle	Special event
1954	10s.	7s. 6d.	5s.	D'Oyly Carte
1957	10s.	7s. 6d.	6s., 4s.	
1960	12s. 6d.	10s.	7s. 6d., 5s.	Royal Ballet
1960	10s.	7s. 6d.	6s., 4s.	
1963	55s.	45s., 20s.	30s., 10s. 6d.	Bolshoi Ballet
1964	13s. 6d.	10s. 6d.	8s., 5s. 6d.	D'Oyly Carte Savoy Operas
1967	12s. 6d.	10s.	7s. 6d., 5s.	
1969	14s., 12s. 6d.	12s. 6d., 10s.	7s. 6d., 5s.	Alfie Saturday was 1s. dearer

Olympia	Stalls	Circle	Gallery	Special event
1960	12s. 6d., 8s. 6d.	10s. 6d., 6s. 4s.	2s. 6d.	Theatre Festival
1960	10s., 7s. 6d.	8s. 6d., 6s. 4s.	2s. 6d.	Old Vic Theatre
1960	£1 1s.	15s., 10s. 6d., 7s. 6d.		Opening night for Noel Coward
1960	12s. 6d., 8s. 6d.	10s. 6d., 7s. 6d., 5s.		
1963	15s., 12s. 6d., 8s. 6d.	10s. 6d., 6s., 4s.	2s. 6d.	Carrie

230. The Metropole and crowds at night.

on at the Gaiety while Deirdre O'Connell's tiny Focus Theatre offered Lillian Hellman's play *Toys in the Attic*. The Gate offered *The Au-pair Man* by Hugh Leonard while the Peacock presented *The Taylor and Anstey*, which was an edgy enough choice but the Abbey was playing safe with *The Playboy of the Western World* followed by *The Cherry Orchard*. That there was an audience can be seen from the fact that prices could be raised to suit the event. For example, a special event such as a visit by Gracie Fields to the Theatre Royal in 1952 cost between 3s. 6d. and 15s.

Whatever was being offered, until the middle 1960s theatregoers would have recognized the distinctive odour of Jeyes Fluid as part of their experience. For reasons of public health, the theatres were regularly washed with Jeyes Fluid and this fact was advertised on the programmes. Attempts were made to disguise the effect by the addition of Jeyes floral spray but that just made it worse.

The cinema was also identified as a popular pastime, as testified by the queues that formed outside cinemas for the various showings. The location of cinemas had not changed over the years, though the smaller houses in the city centre had closed. There was a concentration on O'Connell Street and environs and patrons would go to the Ambassador, Carlton, Metropole, Savoy and Capitol and the nearby Adelphi on Abbey Street, the Astor and Corinthian on Aston Quay and the Cinerama on Talbot Street and its equivalent, the Plaza, on Parnell Square, both of which specialized in large-format movies. Only the Grafton newsreel cinema on Grafton Street or the Academy in Pearse Street would have brought people south of the river.

The revival of interest in Irish folk music led to the development of Irish cabarets and Jury's Hotel was seen as the mecca for this in the city centre. The Gresham Hotel was pleased to draw the attention of its guests to the following towards the end of the 1960s. The pricing in US dollars was recognition of the increasing importance of this market.

> Irish Cabaret
> A gay evening of Irish song and dance, humour and wit, choice food and drink. 8.30–11 nightly (incl. Sundays). Adm. Spectators £1 ($2.50) (incl. two drinks). Diners at Cabaret 10/– ($1.25) (à la carte menu). May–mid-October.

> Molly Malone Night
> All the fun, gaiety and excitement of an evening in 19th century Dublin. Marvellous food and drinks. Nightly (Mon.–Sat.) 8.30–11 p.m. Adm. 45/– ($5.60), includes dinner, wine, entertainment. June–mid-September.

> Intrepid Fox
> Dancing in a pleasantly sophisticated atmosphere from 8 to 12, Wednesday to Saturday with a break for our special entertainment. Delicious meals, popular drinks available, from 8 p.m. Adm. 10/– ($1.25) à la carte menu. October–May.

Coffee table views

Another way in which to present Dublin to the visitor was by means of coffee table books and this chapter ends with a look at three such publications which date from the 1960s. *Dublin and Cork* by R.S. Magowan is largely a picture book. There is very little text but it is provided in three languages – French and German in addition to English. The introduction was by Kate O'Brien and it may be wondered just how well it resonated with those who were anxious to promote the newly industrializing city and country. Ms O'Brien saw charm in our old-fashioned look, for 'we always seem to keep a good few years behind the rest of the world in the things that show outward results – in the sciences, in mechanical and industrial progress; and in architecture, literature and the fine arts'. This happy accident had prevented the city from making some of the mistakes that other, more eager cities had done but it gave the city an old-fashioned look. So it is not surprising perhaps that there is a picture of sheep in the streets, horse-drawn carts as well as the inevitable series on horses and horse-racing. The overall assessment was that Dublin was a county-town-capital.

> I showed these photographs to an English friend, a painter who knows Ireland well, who has often worked here and loves its whole ambience, as painter-material. She smiled affectionately at times, murmuring, 'How old-fashioned they look!'
>
> I knew what she meant. These children, sitting in glorious eighteenth-century doorways, or hanging over Liffey walls, or awaiting their turn at the Horse Show, do look old-fashioned in that they look truly shy, but also friendly, and a bit puzzled by the picture-taker's interest in them. Also, their clothes – though mostly quite good, for in Ireland too, thank God, we are eliminating the great savageries of poverty – they too look old-fashioned.
>
> (p. 5)

Closer to the end of the decade, Desmond Guinness produced *A Portrait of Dublin*. The aim of the book was to develop an appreciation of the Georgian heritage of the city as that landscape was increasingly threatened. It was an exercise in education for a population that was not particularly architecturally literate. While the author claimed that the architecture of Dublin was among the most distinguished in the British Isles, he made no such claim for life in the city. Despite the 'business world computing and the medical world commuting' Dublin was still 'very much a county town, the capital of a nation with its roots in the soil, almost untainted by industrialization. It is not uncommon to find a herd of cattle being driven through the street; horse traffic can still be seen, and the jangle of harness mingles in O'Connell Street with the liturgical cries of the newsvendors' (p. 9).

In Guinness' view, the 'city is at its best by night, when marvellous plaster ceilings will come to life in the most surprising places and when the giant grey stone buildings are asleep. Then you can breathe the spirit of the eighteenth century, as faithfully as in a Malton print' (p. 11).

Small wonder it was then, that there was no meeting of minds between those who sought to preserve this heritage and those who saw Dublin on the cusp of the 1970s as a modern city, ready for modern architecture and ways of doing business as it prepared for membership of the European Economic Community.

Dublin – A Portrait by V.S. Pritchett is a different sort of coffee table book. Published in 1967, it contains many wonderful photographs of the city and its people but the text is an intensely personal reflection of the city from a political perspective and the author leaves us in no doubt about his views. From an urban point of view, he saw that 'Dublin is a capital city and it looks like one' (p. 28). He then went on to contradict himself some pages further on when he declared that Dublin was a village where 'everyone knows everyone else; certainly a rural ethos prevails' (p. 31). What he meant by Dublin being a capital city was that it now had the apparatus of a city, what he termed the red and white housing estates, the tall television masts and the fact that the 'Londonish' appearance began to appear as one nears the centre. While the northside was dilapidated, he noted the change taking place. The new office blocks have appeared: 'two appalling skyscrapers stand near O'Connell Bridge and vandals have sliced down one corner of a fine Georgian Street at the corner of Merrion Square' (p. 28). Yet for all that, the city retained its Georgian and early Victorian character, though Dubliners did not like their city. They were realists in a short-sighted way. They saw the opportunities presented by demolition and they embraced them.

Despite this, he describes a city that was spacious and airy, not in a Napoleonic sense but rather something that was easier and lighter. In this he reflected the earlier memoir of Chiang Yee – there was a sense of idleness in the city still. But this was the work of an earlier generation, even the reconstruction of O'Connell Street in the 1920s struck him as modern (and not in a positive way) and he wrote of 'harsh and gloomy inconvenience in its interiors'. It is this tension that permeates the text. Time and again, the author praises some aspect of the city that he finds pleasing and charming but then immediately is brought back to a reality in which this is under threat. Thus, he likes the colours of the residential areas of the city with their speckled brick in different shades. He likes the proportions of the Georgian environment, the doors, the fanlights. Above all he likes the scale of the city. 'For although Dublin is a low city, its chief effect upon the eye is one of verticality and height, which is due to the carefully diminished proportions of the tall narrow windows. The illusion of height is preserved also in the Victorian terraces, where the basements have been raised to ground level and the front doors are usually approached by a broad flight of twelve or fifteen steps' (p. 37). But quickly, the tone of the text changes and on the next page we read:

> Many parts of the north side of Dublin and around St Patrick's are ragged and dilapidated, but there has been a really powerful drive at re-housing in these neighbourhoods. Neither the planning nor the building is attractive; there is little civic imagination; but a lot has been done to the worst slums in Europe. The familiar sight is of the shafts of timber propping up walls rising out of ruined lots. Despair and the bizarre go together, and here one feels Dublin has gone beyond caring either because money is short or the foreign sense of planning has been lost. A large part of the noble Mountjoy Square is overcrowded slum, left behind because Dublin's commerce, money and fashion have moved to the south side. The admirable Georgian Society is doing what it can to save Mountjoy Square, but the chances are not great and the speculators are busy.

And this perhaps sums up best the tensions between the old and new in the city at the end of the 1960s. The city was seeing the benefits of economic growth, people had more money in their pockets than before. More and more were becoming home owners, the motor car was becoming more common. But modern economic growth required a modern city and what had been taken for granted in previous generations was now under threat. The eighteenth- and nineteenth-century streetscape had never really been noticed by Dubliners, even when it fell down, because there was no pressure to replace it with something else. Now there was a tension. Should Dublin become modern or should Dublin retain its heritage? The tension was made all the more manifest because the pressure for change was greatest in the areas where the old streetscape had been best preserved. Pritchett demonstrates this juxtaposition very well as he presents the classic coffee table pictures of the city with the dilapidation of those parts of the city where there was no pressure for economic development. A generation previously, there would have been no real need for texts such as that by Guinness to build an appreciation of these older, fine streetscapes. By the end of the 1960s, the battle had clearly been joined.

Sources and bibliography

Sources

This volume builds on the topics developed in the six previous volumes of the series and especially on the two previous thematic volumes that deal with Dublin in the twentieth century. The reader is encouraged to explore these volumes in building up a comprehensive view of the city.

- *Dublin through space and time, c.900–1900*
- *Dublin, 1910–1940: shaping the city and the suburbs*
- *Dublin, 1745–1922: hospitals, spectacle and vice*
- *Dublin docklands reinvented: the post-industrial regeneration of a European city quarter*
- *Dublin, 1930–1950: the emergence of the modern city*
- *Dublin, 1950–1970: houses, flats and high-rise*

As usual, the bibliography below aims to provide the reader both with details of the sources used in this volume but also to act as a guide to wider reading in the area. The bibliography is very similar to that of the previous volume *Dublin, 1950–1970: houses, flats and high-rise* since both volumes deal with the same time period and there is considerable overlap in the topics.

This volume was as reliant as ever on maps to illustrate the ideas being discussed. Unfortunately, the 1950s and 1960s have rather sparse offerings. The revision of the 25 inch (1:2,500) series of Ordnance Survey plans was complete by the middle 1940s and they were not revised again. Local revisions were produced by organizations such as Dublin Corporation but they were not for public release and the quality of the output, though sufficient for their purpose, was variable. These OS maps remain the most useful scale for the purposes of this book but they become somewhat dated by the time discussion moves to the 1960s. They were replaced by the 1:1,000 series towards the end of the 1960s and this meant that there was now a highly detailed map resource available. The issue was that they were too detailed and too many sheets were needed to look at even a small urban area. This is perhaps to look a gift horse in the mouth but it remains the case that the 1:2,500 was a more useful scale for urban analysis.

In the 1930s the Ordnance Survey began to produce its Popular Edition maps of the city of Dublin at a convenient scale. There is a provisional edition (265b) dated 1933 and then an edition at 1:25,000 which has an imprint of 1948. Publication of these maps became a more regular feature during the 1950s and 1960s and provide a very useful overview of suburban development. The degree of revision varied from edition to edition and it is important not to assume that the printing date means that the map is current as of that date. The scale of maps also varied from 1:25,000 to 1:20,000 and 1:18,000. This is not a major issue but it means that temporal comparisons sometimes require some digital manipulation. As the city began to grow so the 1:63,360 sheet of the Dublin District became more useful. A number of editions of this map were produced from the 1950s into the 1970s and they provide a really useful overview of the growth and expansion of the city.

To these must be added the extremely useful Geographia plans which provide a view of the city for approximately 1935, 1948, 1958 and 1968 at a scale of 4 inches to the mile (about 1:15,800).

A considerable number of guides to Dublin were produced during the 1950s and 1960s. Dublin Corporation resumed production of its guides and these were additional to those published by Fógra Fáilte, later Bord Fáilte. Both had the imprimatur of being 'Official Guides'. To these were added a number of useful guides by commercial publishers, especially in the 1960s. Ward Lock had been one of the staple guides to the city since the 1890s but this period saw the end of that engagement. While a standard guide was produced in the early 1950s, the 25th edition, the 1960s saw Dublin subsumed into a guide to Ireland and most of the detail was lost. It was quite a loss because none of the other commercial guides came close to the detail or the quality. Though the kernel of the information provided in these guides did not change all that much over time, they changed at the margins and they add to our understanding of a developing city.

Unfortunately the golden age of the postcard was long over by the 1950s. These had proved particularly useful in the earlier volumes of this series but their geographical scope became steadily more and more limited. The views now concentrated on the main streets with relatively few images of lesser locations. This volume, like the others in the series, relies on ephemeral material quite a lot because it is trying to build a picture of what it was like to live and use the city during the 1950s and 1960s. The advertisements that are contained in the various guides and often on the margins of maps are central to understand how people spent their time and on what they spent their money. To these may be added the information on the margins of theatre programmes and other events. The availability of this material is very much hit and miss and a matter of luck. While the tradition of the better hotels producing guides for visitors resumed after the war, they were but a poor reflection of what had been provided previously.

A census was undertaken in 1951, 1956, 1961, 1966 and 1971 and though only the printed volumes are available, they remain a valuable source. The amount of detail in the 1951 census is limited and even more so in the 1956 version. Much of the information was presented at the level of the city but there was some data available at a smaller spatial scale. The big change came in 1971 when it was decided to publish census results for small spatial units – almost 200 in the case of Dublin. These permitted a much finer look at the city and the author was one of the first to get the opportunity to work with these data.

As noted in the previous volume, the debates in the Oireachtas should never be overlooked. There was much discussion there about matters relating to the development of the city and information was provided in debates and answers to parliamentary questions which is not easily available elsewhere. However, the great joy of recent times and a huge improvement for the researcher is the availability of newspapers online. The archives of the *Irish Times*, *Irish Press* and *Irish Independent* and a host of local newspapers are now available electronically. For a time, only the search engine for the *Irish Times* was of any value but there was been a huge recent improvement in the ease with which all the publications can accessed.

This archive allows for a significant increase in productivity and enables us to follow up stories in a way that would have been hit and miss otherwise. Another repository of great use is that of Dublin Corporation, referred to as Report x/19xx, and held in the City Archive. While surprisingly little of the record of the work of committees of the Corporation has survived, it is fortunate that these committees reported regularly to the entire Corporation and that these reports were printed and bound for the members.

Bibliography

Aalen, F.H.A. and K. Whelan (eds) (1992) *Dublin city and county: from prehistory to present*. Dublin: Geography Publications.

Abercrombie, P. (1944) *Great London plan*. London: Stationery Office.

Abercrombie, P. and J.H. Forshaw (1943) *The county of London plan*. UK: Macmillan and Company Ltd.

Abercrombie, P., G. Duffy and L.F. Giron (1942) The Dublin Town Plan [with Comments], *Studies: An Irish Quarterly Review*, 31(122), pp 155–70.

Abercrombie, P., S. Kelly and A. Kelly (1922) *Dublin of the future: the new town plan*. Liverpool: University Press of Liverpool.

Abercrombie, P., S. Kelly and M. Robertson (1941) *Dublin sketch development plan*. Dublin: Dublin Corporation.

Abrams, C. (1961) Urban renewal project in Ireland (Dublin), prepared for the Government of Ireland by Charles Abrams, appointed under the United Nations Programme of Technical Assistance. NY: United Nations.

Allan, C.M. (1965) The genesis of British urban redevelopment with special reference to Glasgow, *Economic History Review*, 18 (2) series, pp 598–613.

Alonso, W. (1964) *Location and land use*. Cambridge: Harvard University Press.

Baillie Scott, M.H. et al. (1910) *Garden suburbs, town planning and modern architecture*. London: Fisher Unwin.

Ballymun Amenity Group (1974) *Ballymun: the experiment that failed*. Dublin: Ballymun Amenity Group.

Bannon, M.J. (1973) *Office Location in Ireland and the role of central Dublin*. Dublin: An Foras Forbartha.

Bannon, M.J. (1978) Patrick Geddes and the emergence of modern town planning in Ireland, *Irish Geography*, 11(2), pp 141–8.

Bannon, M.J. (ed.) (1985a) *The emergence of Irish planning, 1880–1920*. Dublin: Turoe Press.

Bannon, M.J. (1985b) The genesis of modern Irish planning. *In*: Bannon, M.J. (ed.) *The emergence of Irish planning, 1880–1920*. Dublin: Turoe Press, pp 189–260.

Bannon, M.J. (1988) The capital of the new State. *In*: Cosgrave, A. (ed.) *Dublin through the ages*. Dublin: College Press.

Bannon, M.J. (ed.) (1989a) *Planning: the Irish experience, 1920–1988*. Dublin: Wolfhound Press.

Bannon, M.J. (1989b) Irish planning from 1921 to 1945. *In*: Bannon, M.J. (ed.) *Planning: the Irish experience*. Dublin: Wolfhound Press, pp 13–70.

Bannon, M.J., J. Eustace and M. O'Neill (1981) *Urbanisation: problems of growth and decay in Dublin*. Report 55. Dublin: National Economic and Social Council.

Barlow (1940) *Royal Commission on the distribution of the industrial population. Chairman: Sir Montague Barlow*. UK: HMSO.

Barnett, J. (1986) *The elusive city: five centuries of design, ambition and miscalculation*. New York: Harper and Row.

Barr, A.W. (1958) *Public authority housing*. UK: Batsford.

Barrett, H. and J. Phillips (1987) *Suburban style: the British home, 1840–1960*. London: Macdonald & Co. Ltd.

Bater, J. (1980) *The soviet city*. UK: Edward Arnold.

Behan, B. (1963) *Hold your hour and have another*. London: Hutchinson.

Behan, D. (1961) *Teems of times and happy returns*. London: Heinemann.

Behan, D. (1965) *My brother Brendan*. London: Leslie Frewin.

Bolger, D. (ed.) (1988) *Invisible cities, the new Dubliners: a journey through unofficial Dublin*. Dublin: Raven Arts Press.

Bowley, M. (1945) *Housing and the State, 1919–1944*. London: Allen & Unwin.

Brady, J. (1986) The impact of clean air legislation on Dublin households, *Irish Geography*, 19, pp 41–4.

Brady, J. (2001a) Dublin in the nineteenth century – an introduction. *In*: Brady, J. and A. Simms (eds), *Dublin through space and time*. Dublin: Four Courts Press, pp 159–65.

Brady, J. (2001b) Dublin at the turn of the century. *In*: Brady, J. and A. Simms (eds), *Dublin through space and time*. Dublin: Four Courts Press, pp 221–81.

Brady, J. (2001c) The heart of the city – commercial Dublin, *c*.1890–1915. *In*: Brady, J. and A. Simms (eds), *Dublin through space and time*. Dublin: Four Courts Press, pp 282–340.

Brady, J. (2004) Reconstructing Dublin city centre in the 1920s. *In*: Clarke, H., J. Prunty, and M. Hennessy (eds) *Surveying Ireland's past, multidisciplinary essays in honour of Anngret Simms*. Dublin: Geography Publications, pp 639–64.

Brady, J. (2005) Geography as she used to be, *Geographical Viewpoint*, 31, pp 29–39.

Brady, J. (2006) Dublin – growth and economic prosperity, 1995–2005. Archived paper for XIV International Economic History Congress. Helsinki. http://www.helsinki.fi/iehc2006/papers3/Brady.pdf.

Brady, J. (2014) The Liffey and a bridge too far: bridge-building and governance in Dublin, 1870–1960, *Irish Geography*, 47(2), pp 75–103.

Brady, J. (2014) *Dublin, 1930–1950 – the emergence of the modern city*. Dublin: Four Courts Press.

Brady, J. (2015) Dublin – a city of contrasts. *In*: Fogarty, A. and F. O'Rourke (eds) *Voices on Joyce*. Dublin: UCD Press, pp 77–95.

Brady, J. and A. Simms (eds) (2001) *Dublin through space and time, c.900–1900*. Dublin: Four Courts Press.

Brady, J. and A. Simms (eds) (2006) *Dublin 1745–1922 Hospitals, spectacle and vice*. Dublin: Four Courts Press.

Brady, J. and A. Simms (2008) *Dublin Docklands Reinvented – the post-industrial regeneration of an industrial quarter*. Dublin: Four Courts Press.

Brady, J. and A.J. Parker (1975) The factorial ecology of Dublin – A preliminary investigation, *Economic and Social Review*, 7(4), pp 35–54.

Brady, J. and A.J. Parker (1986) The socio-demographic structure of Dublin 1981, *Economic and Social Review*, 17(4), pp 229–52.

Brady J. and P. Lynch (2009) The Irish sailors' and soldiers' land trust and its Killester Nemesis, *Irish Geography*, 42(3), 261–92.

Brooke, H. (1952) *Living in flats: report of the flats subcommittee of the central housing advisory committee*. London: H.M.S.O.

Buchanan, C. (1963a) *Traffic in towns* – A study of the long term problems of traffic in urban areas – Reports of the steering group and working group appointed by the Minister of Transport. London: HMSO.

Buchanan, C. (1963b) *Traffic in towns*. The specially shortened edition of the Buchanan report. UK: Penguin.

Burnett, J. (1978) *A social history of housing, 1815–1970*. London: David & Charles.

Burnham, D. and E. Bennett (1909) *Plan of Chicago*. Chicago: The Commercial Club.

Cahill and Co. (1939) *Dublin by day and by night. A new guide to the city*. Dublin: Cahill.

Callanan, M. and J.F. Keogan (2004) *Local government in Ireland: inside out*. Dublin: Institute of Public Administration.

Chiang Yee (1953) *The silent traveller in Dublin*. London: Methuen.

Cherry, G.E. (1974) *The evolution of British town planning*. Leighton Buzzard: Hill.

Cherry, G.E. (1988) *Cities and plans*. London: Edward Arnold.

Colman, H. (ed.) (1947) *Eire to-day*. Dublin and London: Metropolitan Publishing Company.

Cooke, P. (ed.) (1989) *Localities: the changing face of urban Britain*. London: Unwin Hyman.

Corden, C. (1977) *Planned cities: new towns in Britain and America*. London: Sage Publications.

Corpus Christi Parish (1991) *Golden Jubilee, 1941–1991* [private publication, no details].

Cosgrave, E. and L.E. Strangways (1907) *Visitor's guide to Dublin and neighbourhood*. Dublin: Sealy, Bryers & Walker.

Costello, P. and T. Farmar (1992) *The very heart of the city*. The story of Denis Guiney and Clerys. Dublin: A&A Farmar.

Cowan, P.C. (1918) *Report on Dublin housing*. Dublin: Cahill & Co. Ltd.

Craft, M. (1971) The development of Dublin: the southern suburbs, *Studies: An Irish Quarterly Review*, 60, pp 68–81.

Creese, W.L. (1967) *The legacy of Raymond Unwin: a human pattern for planning*. London: MIT Press.

CSO (1958) *Censuses of population 1946 and 1951*. General Report. Dublin: Stationery Office.

CSO (2000) *That was then, this is now. Change in Ireland, 1949–1999*. Dublin: Stationery Office.

CSO (2012) *Older and younger*. profile 2. Dublin: Stationery Office.

Curriculum Development Unit (1978) *Divided city, portrait of Dublin 1913*. Dublin: O'Brien Educational.

D'Arcy, F. (2007) *Remembering the war dead: British Commonwealth and international war graves in Ireland since 1914*. Dublin: Stationery Office.

Dalton, G. (1994) *My own backyard – Dublin in the fifties*. Dublin: Wolfhound Press.

Daly, M.E. (1984) *Dublin: the deposed capital, a social and economic history, 1860–1914*. Cork: Cork University Press.

Daly, M.E. (1985) Housing conditions and the genesis of housing reform in Dublin, 1880–1920. *In*: Bannon, M.J. (ed.) *The emergence of Irish planning, 1880–1920*. Dublin: Turoe Press, pp 77–130.

Dawson, J.A. (1983) *Shopping centre development*. Topics in applied geography. UK: Longman.

Dawson, J.A. (ed.) (1980) *Retail geography*. UK: Croom Helm.

Department of Local Government (1948) *Housing – a review of past operations and immediate requirements*. Dublin: Stationery Office.

Department of Local Government and Public Health [various] Annual Reports, Dublin, Stationery Office.

Dickinson, P.L. (1929) *The Dublin of yesterday*. London: Methuen & Co.

Dillon, T.W.T. (1945) Slum clearance: past and future, *Studies: An Irish Quarterly Review*, 34, pp 13–20.

Dix, G. (1978) Little plans and noble diagrams, *Town Planning Review*, 49(3), pp 329–52.

Dix, G. (1979) Patrick Abercrombie: pioneer of planning, *Architectural Review*, 990, pp 130–2.

Dixon, D. (2014) *Dublin – the making of a capital city*. UK: Profile Books.

Douglas, R.M. (2009) *Architects of the resurrection: ailtirí na haiséirghe and the fascist 'new order' in Ireland*. UK: Manchester University Press.

Doyle, L. (1935) *The spirit of Ireland*. London: B.T. Batsford Ltd.

Dublin and District House Builders' Association (1939) *The contribution of private enterprise to Greater Dublin's needs* [pamphlet]. Dublin: Sackville Press.

Dublin Corporation (1942) *Lord Mayor's handbook*. Dublin: Dublin Corporation.

Dublin Corporation (1944) *Lord Mayor's handbook*. Dublin: Dublin Corporation.

Dudley, Earl of (1944) Design of dwellings. The Dudley Report. *Report of the design of dwellings sub-committee of the central housing advisory committee and study group of the ministry of town and country planning*. UK: HMSO.

Egan, M.J. (1961) *The parish of St Columba, Iona Road, Glasnevin* [private publication].

Evans, H. (ed.) (1972) *New towns: the British experience*. UK: Charles Knight.

Farrer, R. and A. Turnbull (1951). *Ulster and Dublin*. London: W&R Chambers.

Ferriter, D. (2006) *What if? Alternative views of twentieth-century Ireland*. Ireland: Gill and Macmillan.

Ferriter, D. (2007) *Judging Dev: a reassessment of the life and legacy of Eamon de Valera*. Dublin: Royal Irish Academy.

Ferriter, D. (2010) *The transformation of Ireland, 1900–2000*. UK: Profile Books.

Fishman, R.L. (1984) The origins of the suburban idea in England, *Chicago History*, 13(2), pp 26–35.

Fleming, M.C. (1965) Economic aspects of new methods of building with particular reference to the British Isles, the Continent and America, *JSSSI*, 21(3), pp 120–42.

Galligan, M., M. Glynn and C. Ward (1968) *New homes: a pilot social survey*. Dublin: An Foras Forbartha.

Garrett, A. (1970) *From age to age, history of the parish of Drumcondra, North Strand, St Barnabas*. Dublin: Blackrock Printers.

Garvin, T. (1996) *The birth of Irish democracy*. Dublin: Gill and Macmillan.

Gaskell, S.M. (1987) *Model housing*. London: Mansell.

Gaskell, S.M. (ed.) (1990) *Slums*. Leicester: Leicester University Press.

Gaughan, J.A. (ed.) (1981) *Mount Merrion, the old and the new*. Naas, [no publisher].

Genders, R. (1947) *Holiday in Dublin*. Worcester: Littlebury and Company.

Gibberd, F. (1972) The master design: landscape; housing; the town centres. *In*: Evans H. (ed.) *New towns: the British experience*. UK: Charles Knight, pp 88–101.

Greater Dublin Commission (1926) *Report of the greater Dublin commission of inquiry*. Dublin: Stationery Office.

Guild, R. (1989) *The Victorian house book*. New York: Rizzoli.

Guinness, D. (1967) *A portrait of Dublin*. New York: Viking Press.

Gumley, F.W. (1982) Remembering ... *Dublin Historical Record*, 35(3), pp 95–8.

Hall, P. (1985) The rise and fall of the planning movement: a view from Great Britain, *Royal Geographical Society of Australia, South Australian Branch, Proceedings*, 85, pp 45–53.

Hall, P. (2002) *Cities of tomorrow*. Oxford: Blackwell Publishing.

Hanna, E. (2013) *Modern Dublin: urban change and the Irish past, 1957–1973*. UK: Oxford University Press.

Harkness, D. and M. O'Dowd (1981) *The town in Ireland*. Belfast: Appletree Press.

Harris, R. and P.J. Larkham (eds) (1999) *Changing suburbs: foundation, form and function*. London: E. & F.N. Spon.

Harrison, B. (1966) Philanthropy and the Victorians, *Victorian Studies: An Irish Quarterly Review*, 9, pp 353–74.

Harvey, J. (1949) *Dublin – A study in environment*. London: Batsford.

Haverty, A. (1995) *Elegant times – A Dublin Story*. Dublin: Sonas.

Hayward, R. (1949) *This is Ireland – Leinster and the city of Dublin*. London: Arthur Barker.

Hobson, B. (ed.) (1929) *A book of Dublin*. Dublin: Corporation of Dublin (1st edition).

Hobson, B. (ed.) (1930) *A book of Dublin*. Dublin: Kevin J. Kenny (2nd edition).

Horner, A.A. (1985) The Dublin region 1880–1980. *In*: Bannon, M.J. (ed.) *The emergence of Irish planning, 1880–1920*. Dublin: Turoe Press, pp 21–76.

Horner, A.A. (1992) From city to city-region – Dublin from the 1930s to the 1990s. *In*: Aalen, F.H.A. and K. Whelan (eds), *Dublin city and county*. Dublin: Geography Publications, pp 327–58.

Horsey, M. (1990) *Tenements and towers – Glasgow working-class housing, 1890–1990*. UK: HMSO.

Houghton, J.P. (1949) The social geography of Dublin, *Geographical Review*, 39, pp 237–77.

Housing and Public Health Committee (1937) *London housing*. London: King and Staples Ltd.

Housing Inquiry (1885) *Report of the Royal commission appointed to inquire into the housing of the working classes*. Minutes of evidence etc., Ireland, British Parliamentary Papers, cd. 4547, London.

Housing Inquiry (1914) *Report of the departmental committee appointed by the Local Government Board for Ireland to inquire into the housing conditions of the working classes in the city of Dublin*. British Parliamentary Papers, 19, 1914, cd.7272/7317-xix, London.

Housing Inquiry (1944) *Report of inquiry into the housing of the working classes of the city of Dublin, 1939–43*. Dublin: Stationery Office.

Housing Manual (1944) *Housing Manual 1944*. Ministry of Health, Ministry of Works. UK: HMSO.

Housing Manual (1949) *Housing Manual 1949*. Ministry of Health. UK: HMSO.

Housing Manual (1952) *Houses 1952*. Second supplement to the Housing Manual 1949. Ministry of Housing and Local Government. UK: HMSO.

Housing Manual (1953) *Houses 1953*. Third supplement to the Housing Manual 1949. Ministry of Housing and Local Government. UK: HMSO.

Howard, E. (1898) *Tomorrow: a peaceful path to real reform*. London: Swan Sonnenschein.

Hoyt, H. (1939) *The structure and growth of residential areas in American cities.* Washington DC: Federal Housing Administration.

Hubbard, E. and M. Shippobottom (1988) *A guide to Port Sunlight Village.* Liverpool: Liverpool University Press.

Hughes, J.B. (1914) Poverty in Dublin, *Irish Messenger Social Action Series*, 13. Dublin: Irish Messenger Office.

Hunter, M. (1981) *The Victorian villas of Hackney.* London: Hackney Society.

Hyland, J.S. (Ltd) (1898) *Ireland in pictures.* Chicago: J.S. Hyland and Co.

Igoe, V. (1990) *James Joyce's Dublin houses.* London: Mandarin Paperbacks.

Ikonnikov, A. (1988) *Russian architecture of the soviet period.* USSR: Raduga Press.

Johnston, J.H. and C.G. Pooley (eds) (1982) *The structure of nineteenth century cities.* London: Croom Helm.

Jordan, D.P. (1995) *Transforming Paris: the life and labors of Baron Haussmann.* USA: Free Press.

Kelly, P. (1990) Drumcondra, Clonliffe and Glasnevin township, 1878–1900. *In*: Kelly, J. and U. MacGearailt (eds), *Dublin and Dubliners.* Dublin: Educational Company of Ireland, pp 36–51.

Kennedy, T. (ed.) (1980) *Victorian Dublin.* Dublin: Albertine Kennedy Publishing.

Khan-Magomedov, S.O. (1987) *Pioneers of Soviet architecture.* London: Thames and Hudson.

Killen, J. (1992) Transport in Dublin: past, present and future. *In*: Aalen, F.H.A. and K. Whelan (eds) *Dublin city and county.* Dublin: Geography Publications, pp 305–25.

Knox, P.L. (1982) *Urban social geography, an introduction.* London: Longman.

Kopp, A. (1970) *Town and revolution. soviet architecture and city planning, 1917–35.* NY: Braziller.

Kostof, S. (1991) *The city assembled: elements of urban form through history.* London: Thames and Hudson.

Kostof, S. (1992) *The city shaped: urban patterns and meanings through history.* London: Thames and Hudson.

Lawless, P. and F. Brown (1986) *Urban growth and change in Britain: an introduction.* London: Harper & Row.

Le Corbusier (1929: 1987) *The city of tomorrow.* Translated by Frederick Etchells. USA: Dover Books.

Lichfield and Associates (1966) *Preliminary appraisal of shopping centre redevelopment in Dublin Centre.* Report No. 1. London: Nathaniel Lichfield and Associates.

Lincoln, C. (1992) *Dublin as a work of art.* Dublin: O'Brien Press.

Local Government (1938) *Report of the Local Government (Dublin) Tribunal.* Dublin: Stationery Office.

Long, H.C. (1993) *The Edwardian house.* Manchester: Manchester University Press.

Lynch, K. (1990) *City sense and city design.* Cambridge, Massachusetts: MIT Press.

MacLaren, A. (1993) *Dublin, the shaping of a capital.* London: Belhaven Press.

Magowan, R.S. (1961) *Dublin and Cork.* London: Spring Books.

Malone, P. (1990) *Office development in Dublin, 1960–1990.* UK: Manchester University Press.

Marley Committee (1935) *Departmental committee on garden cities and satellite towns.* Ministry of Health. UK: HMSO.

McCartney, D. (1999) *UCD: a national idea: the history of University College Dublin.* Dublin: Gill and Macmillan.

McCullough, N. (1989) *Dublin: an urban history.* Dublin: Anne Street Press.

McDonald, F. (1985) *The destruction of Dublin.* Dublin: Gill and Macmillan.

McDowell, R.B. (1957) The growth of Dublin. *In*: Meenan, J. and D. Webb (eds), *A view of Ireland.* Dublin: British Association for the Advancement of Science.

McGrath, F. (1931) The sweep and the slums, *Studies: An Irish Quarterly Review,* 20, pp 529–54.

McGrath, R. (1941) Dublin panorama: an architectural review, *The Bell,* 2(5), pp 35–48.

McManus, R. (1996) Public Utility Societies, Dublin Corporation and the development of Dublin, 1920–1940, *Irish Geography,* 29(1), pp 27–37.

McManus, R. (1998) The Dundalk Premier public utility society, *Irish Geography,* 31(2), pp 75–87.

McManus, R. (1999) The 'Building Parson' – the role of Reverend David Hall in the solution of Ireland's early twentieth-century housing problems, *Irish Geography,* 32(2), pp 87–98.

McManus, R. (2002) *Dublin, 1910–1940: shaping the city and the suburbs.* Dublin: Four Courts Press.

McManus, R. (2004) The role of public utility societies in Ireland, 1919–40. *In*: Clarke, H., J. Prunty and M. Hennessy (eds) *Surveying Ireland's past: multidisciplinary essays in honour of Anngret Simms.* Dublin: Geography Publications, pp 613–38.

McManus, R. (2005) *'Such Happy Harmony', early twentieth-century co-operation to solve Dublin's housing problems.* Dublin: Dublin City Public Libraries.

McManus, R. (2006) The growth of Drumcondra, 1875–1940. *In*: Kelly, J. (ed.), *St Patrick's College, Drumcondra, 1875–2000: a history.* Dublin: Four Courts Press, pp 41–66.

McManus, R. (2008) *Crampton built.* Dublin: G.&T. Crampton.

McManus, R. (2011) Suburban and urban housing in the twentieth century, *Proceedings of the Royal Irish Academy,* 111C, pp 253–86.

McManus, R. (2012) 'Decent and artistic homes' – housing Dublin's middle classes in the 20th century, *Dublin Historical Record,* 65(1 & 2), pp 96–109.

McManus, R. (2012) Upper Buckingham Street: a microcosm of Dublin, 1788–2012 (with Sinead O'Shea), *Studia Hibernica,* pp 141–79.

McManus, R. (2013) An introduction to Dublin's first citizens (with Lisa-Marie Griffith). *In*: R. McManus and L. Griffith (eds) *Leaders of the City: Dublin's first citizens, 1500–1950.* Dublin: Four Courts Press, pp 15–34.

McManus, R. (2013) Lord Mayor Laurence O'Neill, Alderman Tom Kelly and Dublin's housing crisis. In: McManus, R. and L. Griffith (eds) *Leaders of the City: Dublin's first citizens, 1500–1950.* Dublin: Four Courts Press, pp 141–51.

Meenan, J. (1957) Dublin in the Irish economy. *In*: Meenan, J. and D. Webb (eds), *A view of Ireland.* Dublin: British Association for the Advancement of Science.

Meghen, P.J. (1963) *Housing in Ireland.* Dublin: Institute of Public Administration.

Meller, H. (1990) *Patrick Geddes, social evolutionist and city planner.* London: Routledge.

Mikhail, E.H. (ed.) (1982) *Brendan Behan*. London: Macmillan.

Miliutin, N.A. (1974) *Sotsgorod – The problem of building socialist cities*. Cambridge Massachusetts: MIT Press. This is a translation by Arthur Sprague of the original 1930 text in Russian.

Miller, M. (1989) Raymond Unwin and the planning of Dublin. *In:* Bannon, M.J. (ed.) *The emergence of Irish planning, 1880–1920*. Dublin: Turoe Press, pp 189–260.

Miller, M. (1992) *Raymond Unwin, Garden Cities and town planning*. Leicester: Leicester University Press.

Milne, K. (ed.) (2010) *Christ Church cathedral Dublin: a history*. Dublin: Four Courts Press.

Mingay, G.E. (1986) *The transformation of Britain, 1830–1939*. London: Routledge.

Ministry of Local Government (1925) *House designs. Prescribed by the Minister of Local Government under the Housing Act, 1924*. Dublin: Stationery Office (5 vols).

Moody, T.W. and F.X. Martin (eds) (1967) *The course of Irish history*. Cork: Mercier Press.

Mumford, L. (1961) *The city in history*. London: Penguin.

Municipal Boundaries (1881) *Report of the Municipal Boundaries Commission (Ireland)*. British Parliamentary Papers, Vol. 50, c.2827, Dublin.

Murphy, F. (1984) Dublin slums in the 1930s, *Dublin Historical Record*, 37 (3/4), pp 104–11.

Murphy, R.E. (1972) *The central business district*. London: Longman.

Murphy, R.E. and J.E. Vance (1954a) Delimiting the CBD, *Economic Geography*, 30, pp 189–222.

Murphy, R.E. and J.E. Vance (1954b) A comparative study of nine central business districts, *Economic Geography*, 30, pp 301–36.

Murphy, R.E., J.E. Vance and B.J. Epstein (1955) Internal structure of the CBD, *Economic Geography*, 31, pp 21–46.

Muthesius, S. (1982) *The English terraced house*. New Haven: Yale University Press.

Nesbitt, R. (1993) *At Arnotts of Dublin, 1843–1993*. Dublin: A&A Farmar.

Nowlan, K.I. (1989) The evolution of Irish planning, 1934–1964. *In:* Bannon, M.J. (ed.) *Planning: the Irish experience*. Dublin: Wolfhound Press, pp 71–85.

O'Brien, J.V. (1982) *Dear dirty Dublin, a city in distress, 1899–1916*. Berkeley: University of California Press.

O'Brien, M. (1950) The planning of Dublin, *Journal of Town Planning Institute*, 36(6), pp 199–212.

O'Dwyer, F. (1981) *Lost Dublin*. Dublin: Gill and Macmillan.

O'Rourke, H.T. (1925) *The Dublin civic survey*. Liverpool: Liverpool University Press.

Oliver, P., I. Davis and I. Bentley (1994) *Dunroamin: the suburban semi and its enemies*. London: Pimlico (Random House).

Osborough, N. (1996) *Law and the emergence of modern Dublin*. Dublin: Irish Academic Press.

Owen, D. (1965) *English philanthropy, 1660–1960*. Cambridge, Massachusetts: Harvard University Press.

Park, R.E. and E.W. Burgess (1925) *The city*. Chicago: University of Chicago Press.

Parker, A.J. (1973) Intra-urban variations in retail grocery prices, *Economic and Social Review*, 5(3), pp 393–403.

Parker, A.J. (1973) The structure and distribution of grocery stores in Dublin, *Irish Geography*, 6(5), pp 625–30.

Parker, A.J. (1974) An analysis of retail grocery price variations, *Area*, 6(2), pp. 117–20.

Parker, A.J. (1974) Changing retail grocery prices in Dublin, *Irish Geography*, 7(1), pp 107–11.

Parker, A.J. (1975) Hypermarkets: the changing pattern of retailing, *Geography*, 60(2), pp 120–4.

Perle, E.D. (1979) Scale changes and impacts on factorial ecology structures, *Environment and Planning*, A9, pp 549–58.

Power, A. (1993) *Hovels to high rise: state housing in Europe since 1850*. London: Routledge.

Pritchett, V.S. (1967) *Dublin – A portrait*. London: Bodley Head.

Prunty, J. (1998) *Dublin slums, 1800–1925: a study in urban geography*. Dublin: Irish Academic Press.

Prunty, J. (2001) Improving the urban environment. *In*: Brady, J. and A. Simms (eds), *Dublin through space and time*. Dublin: Four Courts Press, pp 166–220.

R. Travers Morgan and Partners (1973) *Central Dublin Traffic Plan*. London: R. Travers Morgan.

Ratcliffe, J. (1974) *An introduction to town and country planning*. London: Hutchinson.

Ravetz, A. (1974) From working class tenement to modern flat. *In*: Sutcliffe, A. (ed.), *Multi-storey living: the British working-class experience*. London: Croom Helm, pp 122–50.

Reith (1946) *Reports of the new towns committee. Ministry of town and country planning and Department of health for Scotland*. Chairman: Rt Hon. Lord Reith of Stonehaven. Interim Report cmd 6759, second report cmd 6794, final report cmd 6786. UK: HMSO.

RIBA (1931) *Dublin*. Handbook for delegates. Conference of the Royal Institute of British Architects.

Robertson, M. (1933, 1934) *A cautionary guide to Dublin*. Dublin: Royal Institute of the Architects of Ireland (RIAI).

Rockey, J. (1983) From vision to reality: Victorian ideal cities and model towns in the genesis of E. Howard's Garden City, *Town Planning Review*, 54(1), pp 83–105.

Rogers, H.B. (1962) The suburban growth of Victorian Manchester, *Journal of the Manchester Geographical Society*, 58, pp 1–12.

Rosenau, H. (1983) *The ideal city, its architectural evolution in Europe*. London: Methuen, 3rd edition.

Rothery, S. (1991) *Ireland and the new architecture, 1900–1940*. Dublin: Lilliput Press.

Ryan, J. (1975) *Remembering how we stood – Bohemian Dublin at the mid century*. New York: Taplinger Publishing.

Schaechterle, K. (1965) *Dublin traffic plan. Part 1*. Germany: Ulm/Donau.

Schaechterle, K. (1968) *Dublin traffic plan. Part 2*. Germany: Ulm/Donau.

Schaffer, F. (1970) *The new town story*. UK: MacGibbon & Key.

Scott, W.A. (1916) The reconstruction of O'Connell Street, Dublin: a note (including sketch), *Studies: An Irish Quarterly Review*, 5, p. 165.

Shaffrey, M. (1988) Sackville Street/O'Connell Street, *GPA Irish Arts Yearbook*, Dublin, pp 144–56.

Sheehan, R. and B. Walsh (1988) *The heart of the city.* Dingle: Brandon.

Sies, M.C. (1987) The city transformed: nature, technology and the suburban ideal, 1877–1917, *Journal of Urban History,* 14(1), pp 81–111.

Simms, A. and P. Fagan (1992) Villages in County Dublin: their origins and inheritance. *In*: Aalen, F.H.A. and K. Whelan (eds), *Dublin city and county.* Dublin: Geography Publications, pp 79–119.

Simpson, M. and T. Lloyd (eds) (1977) *Studies in the history of middle-class housing in Britain.* Newton Abbot: David & Charles.

Skilleter, K.J. (1993) The role of PUSs in early British planning and housing reform 1901–1936, *Planning Perspectives,* pp 125–65.

Slater, T.R. (ed.) (1990) *The built form of western cities.* Leicester: Leicester University Press.

Smith Morris, E. (1997) *British town planning and urban design.* UK: Longman.

Spence, N. (1982) *British cities: an analysis of urban change.* Oxford: Pergamon Press.

Stationery Office (1948) *National nutrition survey. Part 1. Methods of dietary survey and results from Dublin investigation.* Dublin: Stationery Office.

Stationery Office (1955) *National commission on emigration and other population problems, 1948–1954.* Dublin: Stationery Office.

Stedman-Jones, G. (1971) *Outcast London: a study in the relationship between classes in Victorian society.* Oxford: Clarendon Press.

Stenhouse, D. (1977) *Understanding towns.* Hove: Wayland Publishers.

Stevenson, G. (2006) *The 1930s home.* Shire Books

Stevenson, J. (1984) *British society, 1914–45.* London: Penguin.

Stuart, M. (1972) *The City: Problems of Planning.* UK: Penguin.

Sutcliffe, A. (ed.) (1980) *The rise of modern urban planning, 1800–1914.* London: Mansell.

Sutcliffe, A. (ed.) (1981) *British town planning: the formative years.* New York: St Martin's Press.

Swenarton, M. (1981) *Homes fit for heroes.* London: Heinemann.

Tarn, J.N. (1968) Some pioneer suburban housing estates, *Architectural Review,* 143, pp 367–70.

Tarn, J.N. (1973) *Five per cent philanthropy.* Cambridge: Cambridge University Press.

Telesis Consultancy (1982) *A review of industrial policy.* Report 56. Dublin: National Economic and Social Council.

Tetlow, J. and A. Goss (1965) *Homes, towns and traffic.* UK: Faber and Faber.

Thomas, R. and P. Cresswell (1973) *The new town idea.* Unit 26 of urban development course. The Open University. UK: O.U. Press.

Thompson, F.M.L. (1988) *The rise of respectable society: a social history of Victorian Britain 1830–1900.* London: Fontana Press.

Thompson, F.M.L. (ed.) (1982) *The rise of suburbia.* Leicester: Leicester University Press.

Thrift, N. and P. Williams (eds) (1987) *Class and space: the making of urban society.* London: Routledge.

Tudor Walters Report (1918) *Report of the committee appointed by the President of the Local Government Board and the Secretary for Scotland to consider questions of building construction in connection with the provision of dwellings for the working classes in England, Wales and Scotland.* London: HMSO.

Tutty, M.J. (1958) Drumcondra, *Dublin Historical Record*, 15 (3), pp 86–96.

Unwin, R. (1912) *Nothing gained by overcrowding*. London: Garden Cities and Town Planning Association.

Unwin, R. and B. Parker (1909) *Town planning in practice* (1994, reprint). Princeton: Princeton Architectural Press.

Ward, C. (1969) *New homes for old. Human sciences in industry, study number 3*. Dublin: Irish national productivity committee.

Ward, S. (2002) *Planning the twentieth-century city*. UK: Wiley.

Whelan, G. (2002) *Spiked: Church-State intrigue and The Rose Tattoo*. With Carolyn Swift. Ireland: New Island.

Whelan, W. (2003) *Reinventing modern Dublin*. Dublin: University College Dublin Press.

Whelan, Y. (2001) Scripting national memory: the Garden of Remembrance, Parnell Square, *Irish Geography*, 34(1), pp 11–33.

Whelan, Y. (2001) Symbolising the state: the iconography of O'Connell Street , Dublin after Independence (1922), *Irish Geography*, 34(2), pp 145–50.

Whelpton, E. (1948) *The book of Dublin*. UK: Rockcliff.

Wilson, W.H. (1994) *The city beautiful movement*. USA: Johns Hopkins University Press.

Wright, L. and K. Browne (1974) A future for Dublin. Special Issue, *Architectural Review*, November, pp 268–330.

Wright, M. (1967) *The Dublin region. Advisory regional plan and final report*. Dublin: Stationery Office.

List of illustrations

1.   Extract from the north city housing survey of 1918 showing contemplated developments.   14
2.   Dereliction in Liffey Street, late 1970s.   23
3.   Outline of road system for Finglas West.   24
4.   Portion of the new tangent route showing road widening in the High Street area.   25
5.   The new route across the Liffey at the Ha'penny Bridge with the two new bridges.   26
6.   Suggested Liffey bridge and associated roads.   28
7.   An example of the extensive land reservations for housing on the northern edge of the city.   30
8.   Demolition and renewal from Patrick Street and the Coombe into Clanbrassil Street.   32
9.   Demolition and renewal along Clanbrassil Street.   33
10. Example of protected structures in Dublin planning scheme, 1957.   35
11. St George's Church in its heyday.   36
12. Harcourt Terrace as it was in 2009.   36
13. Howard's concept of a city system – a central urban area with satellite towns.   50
14. Wright's new towns in their regional context.   51
15. Miliutin's plan for Stalingrad.   52
16. Residential areas in the new towns.   53
17. Industrial and residential areas in new towns.   53
18. Outline plan for Cumbernauld.   57
19. Aerial view of town centre of Cumbernauld.   57
20. Outline plan for Runcorn.   58
21. The outline plan for Harlow.   61
22. Temporary local shopping provision in Tallaght as houses were completed in 1970s.   62
23. The first 'town centre' in Tallaght in the middle 1970s.   63
24. The '3 Guys' shopping centre at Tymon, Firhouse, just prior to opening in 1977.   63
25. The city centre in Burnham's plan for Chicago.   66
26. View of Ballyowen Sanatorium.   67
27. View of the Belfield campus.   68
28. Landing in the pool.   71
29. The Liffey returns the flames.   73
30. The bowl of light without the flames.   73
31. O'Connell's ice cream soda fountain.   75
32. The monument as a flower bed, 1959.   77

33.	Support for a garda signalman.	77
34.	The Councillors preserve 'the Thing'.	78
35.	Adding to the weight of the structure.	79
36.	The end of 'the Thing'.	81
37.	The site for the Civic Offices at the time of Abercrombie's sketch development plan.	83
38.	The St Anne's demesne before redevelopment.	84
39.	Rates and Dublin.	87
40.	Portion of late-nineteenth century handbill for the Irish House.	88
41.	The Irish House and Wood Quay prior to clearance.	88
42.	*Dublin Opinion*'s plan for the new offices.	92
43.	'You must reduce'.	94
44.	The Wood Quay site in 1977 showing portions of the city wall.	100
45.	An aerial view of Merrion Square in the early 1950s.	102
46.	Nelson concerned.	107
47.	The monument to Lord Gough in the Phoenix Park.	110
48.	Statue of Lord George Carlisle in the Phoenix Park.	111
49.	'Misneach' in the grounds of Ballymun Comprehensive School.	112
50.	The Nelson Pillar post-explosion on 8 March 1966.	113
51.	O'Connell Street after Nelson.	114
52.	The Irish National War Memorial at completion.	116
53.	The Rotunda Gardens.	121
54.	An aerial view of the Rotunda Gardens, looking south in 1949.	121
55.	Garden of Remembrance as opened without the signature sculpture.	123
56.	The 'Children of Lir' installed in the Garden of Remembrance.	123
57.	William III in context in Dame Street.	124
58.	Thomas Davis statue in Dame Street.	124
59.	Opera in the Gaiety in May 1941.	127
60.	The concert hall.	128
61.	The Haddington Road / Beggar's Bush site.	129
62.	The Dancing House in Prague.	132
63.	The Flatiron building in New York.	133
64.	An aerial view of the Liberty Hall site in the early 1950s at the junction of Burgh Quay and Beresford Place.	134
65.	The Liberty Hall site cleared.	134
66.	Liberty Hall under construction.	135
67.	Liberty Hall completed.	135
68.	Liberty Hall as an addition to the urban landscape.	137
69.	The site for Busáras being cleared in the late 1940s.	137
70.	A design for the new Port and Docks HQ.	138
71.	View from Carlisle Bridge, later O'Connell Bridge.	140
72.	View from O'Connell Bridge in the 1930s.	140
73.	O'Connell Bridge House in place.	141
74.	Hawkins House, the replacement for the Theatre Royal, from Liberty Hall.	142

75. Office building and showrooms for Heiton McFerran Ltd, Tara Street, 1967. 142
76. Hume House, Ballsbridge, 1967. 143
77. Lansdowne House, Ballsbridge, 1967. 143
78. Fitzwilton House, Grand Canal, 1969. 144
79. ESB offices on Fitzwilliam Street, perhaps the best example of the conflict between the old and the new. 147
80. The cause célèbre of Stein, the opticians, who stood against the demolition of their shop in 1983. 147
81. Advertising hoarding from the 1980s inviting development projects in the north city centre. 148
82. The houses on Upper Mount Street following demolition in February 1989. 151
83. The restoration process almost complete in 1990. 151
84. The Hume Street/St Stephen's Green site. 154
85. Oblique aerial image of the east side of St Stephen's Green in the early 1950s. 154
86. Court appearance. 163
87. Regulations. 163
88. Multi-storey car park in Marlborough Street. 167
89. Parking on O'Connell Street near Parnell monument. 169
90. Parking on O'Connell Street Lower. 169
91. Prospects. 171
92. The ever-present attendant. 171
93. Twenty minutes only. 173
94. Parking meters and nose-to-kerb parking on Eden Quay. 176
95. An example of the up-line service between Greystones and Dublin in 1955. 183
96. Bumper to bumper traffic on Grafton Street in the 1960s. 187
97. Church Street demolitions. 190
98. 'Save our strand'. 193
99. Buchanan system of roadways servicing a complete redevelopment of an existing centre. 201
100. A schematic for a multi-level centre. 202
101. The Royal Canal and associated railway lines near Spencer Dock. 206
102. Transportation Study outline network. 210
103. Dublin Corporation's plan for an inner tangent square. 211
104. The recommended plan by Travers Morgan for the central city area. 212
105. Recommended route for the northern part of the tangent. 213
106. Recommended route for the western part of the tangent. 214
107. The Kevin Street/Patrick Street interchange as imagined by the *Architectural Review*, 1974. 215
108. The Liffey bridge as suggested by Travers Morgan. 216
109. The Liffey bridge as imagined by the *Architectural Review*, 1974. 216
110. A view of the M8, Glasgow's inner ring road. 218
111. The basic Alonso bid-rent model. 221
112. Self-service comes to Grafton Street. 227
113. H. William's 'hypermarket' in Dundrum in the early 1970s. 229

114. Five Star supermarket in Rathmines in 1968. 229
115. Superquinn in Finglas. 231
116. Finglas shopping centre in the 1970s. 231
117. The Findlater store in O'Connell Street, Dublin. 233
118. Findlater site post-redevelopment. 233
119. Kansas City Country Club Plaza in the 1940s. 236
120. The Highland Park shopping centre in Dallas. 236
121. The Bull Ring shopping centre in Birmingham. 237
122. Elephant and Castle in London. 237
123. An aerial view of the Trafford Centre. 239
124. Ground floor of the Trafford Centre. 239
125. An example of uninspired shopping centre design. 241
126. The Lijnbaan in Rotterdam in the 1950s. 241
127. Stillorgan shopping centre and environs upon opening. 242
128. The Stillorgan shopping centre upon opening. 243
129. The site for the Phibsborough centre. 245
130. The Phibsborough centre with a Power supermarket in 1969. 245
131. Advertisement for Ford Prefect in 1952. 251
132. Advertisement for Ford Zephyr in 1952. 251
133. Advertisement for Vauxhall cars in 1955. 252
134. The central business districts as seen by the Central Statistics Office, 1971. 255
135. The area to be redeveloped in Dublin city centre. 257
136. Detail of the redevelopment area, showing extensive dereliction in 1957. 258
137. The town centre of Stevenage. 261
138. The town centre of Amstelveen. 261
139. The shopping precinct in Strøget. 263
140. Central Dublin Development Association protest handbill. 265
141. Advertisement for James Fox cigars in 1968. 268
142. Advertisement for Dixon and Hempenstall on Grafton Street in 1954. 268
143. Grafton Street looking northwards from Harry Street. 269
144. Advertisement for Switzers in 1950. 270
145. The demands of fashion. 271
146. Advertisement for Brown Thomas in 1968. 271
147. Advertisement for Drages in June 1955. 273
148. Advertisement for Tyson from 1881. 274
149. Grafton Street at the St Stephen's Green end in the middle 1960s. 274
150. Advertisement for the Monument Café in 1963. 277
151. The Creation Arcade. 281
152. Advertising feature for the Creation Arcade in 1959. 281
153. South Great George's Street in 1957. 287
154. Advertisement for Pims on South Great George's Street. 288
155. Advertisement for McCabe's from 1908. 288
156. Advertisement for Whyte's from 1906. 289
157. Advertisement for Cassidy's fashions from 1961. 289

158. Advertisement for Winstons.   290
159. Fuller Figure!   291
160. Advertisement for Macey in 1961.   291
161. Advertisement for Santa at Pims.   293
162. Extract from Goad Fire Insurance Plan for 1957 showing the extent of the
     Dockrell store.   294
163. Horton's shop front on the corner of Suffolk Street in 1924.   296
164. Advertisement for Horton's on Wicklow Street in 1953.   296
165. The streetscape on Dawson Street, 1960s.   299
166. Advertisement for Morgan on Dawson Street.   299
167. Morton on Nassau Street.   301
168. New insurance development on Dawson Street, 1967.   302
169. St Stephen's Green awaiting redevelopment in 1983.   303
170. Aerial photograph from late 1940s, showing the island between
     Westmoreland and D'Olier streets.   305
171. McBirney's advertisement from 1955.   306
172. Worth jewellers with the Nelson Pillar still in place.   307
173. Clerys advertisement from 1959.   308
174. Clerys and Brooks Thomas.   309
175. Advertisement for Kingstons.   311
176. Upper O'Connell Street at the beginning of the 1950s.   312
177. The Capitol, Metropole and Eason.   313
178. The layout of the west side of Lower O'Connell Street.   314
179. A view of the west side of Lower O'Connell Street.   315
180. Advertisement for Lemon's sweets in 1954.   315
181. Advertisement for Arnotts, 1965.   317
182. The Moore Street redevelopment site.   317
183. Tradition on Henry Street.   319
184. Henry Street following pedestrianization.   321
185. Lower Mary Street showing the cinema.   322
186. Advertisement for Todd Burns in 1953.   323
187. Opening day feature for Todco.   324
188. Car parking opportunities while awaiting development around
     Moore Street.   325
189. Advertisement for Blacks on Talbot Street in 1953.   326
190. Another location awaiting redevelopment: Ormond Quay in the mid-1980s 327
191. Order form for Deveney's of Terenure.   332
192. Lunch and High Tea menu for Savoy Restaurant, June 1953.   336
193. Pages from a Speedway programme for 1951.   338
194. Speedway advertisement for 1952.   338
195. Extending the season. Advertisement for tourism in Ireland in 1954. 341
196. An Tóstal and its targets.   341
197. Aer Lingus advertisement in 1953.   342
198. Aer Lingus passenger fares for September 1955.   343

199. Advertisement for KLM hub in 1953. 345
200. Handbill advertising a day trip to Dublin from London in 1955. 349
201. Handbill advertising a day trip from the Isle of Man to Dublin in 1966. 350
202. Aer Lingus Carvair in the middle 1960s. 351
203. The Holyhead Ferry I. 353
204. An early invitation to visit Dublin Airport, no longer feasible by 1953. 355
205. The new terminal building in the 1970s. 355
206. Dublin Corporation's official guide to Dublin, 1950s. 359
207. The 1960s' *Green Guides* to Dublin. 361
208. Dublin Corporation tour 1. 364
209. Dublin Corporation tour 2. 364
210. Dublin Corporation tour 3. 365
211. Dublin Corporation tour 4. 367
212. Bord Fáilte guides to Dublin in the 1950s. 369
213. The admission charge to the Nelson Pillar in the early 1960s. 373
214. Advertisement for the Metropole. 377
215. A Wimpy burger, the new taste sensation. 377
216. Advertisement for Bartley Dunne's with its 'unusual character'. 378
217. Advertisement for Irish Hospitals' Sweepstake. 380
218. Couture at Colette Modes. 381
219. Ward Lock route 1. 386
220. Ward Lock route 2. 386
221. Ward Lock route 3. 387
222. The Royal Hospital, Kilmainham Gaol and the National War Memorial
juxtaposed. 390
223. An aerial view of the National War Memorial gardens. 390
224. Advertisement for the International Hotel and Royal Hibernian Hotel, 1950. 392
225. Guides to the Shelbourne and Royal Hibernian hotels. 394
226. The South County Hotel in south county Dublin. 396
227. *Mother Courage* in the Gaiety, 1959. 397
228. *Waiting in the Wings*, world premiere in the Olympia, 1960. 397
229. *The Call* in the Abbey, 1966. 398
230. The Metropole and crowds at night. 401

List of tables

1. Dublin planning scheme 1957, maximum density expressed as average acreage
required by dwelling. 29
2. Dublin planning scheme 1957, minimum back garden dimensions. 29
3. Population projections for the Dublin region, 1966–71. 47
4. Population projections for the Dublin region, 1971–85. 47
5. Office development in Dublin, 1960–70. 145
6. Third-class fares from Harcourt Street Station in 1955. 185

7.   Shop numbers in Dublin, 1951–71.   222

8.   Shops classified according to employment numbers, 1956–71.   224

9.   Central area shopping profile, 1966–71.   254

10. Aer Lingus timetable from Britain, effective 14 March 1960.   344

11. Cost of mailboat accommodation, 1953–60.   348

12. Comparative costs for ferry travel (car not exceeding 12½ ft) in 1965.   353

13. Top-class hotels in Dublin in 1970 by price and location.   395

14. Random selection of events in Dublin theatres, 1950–69.   399

15. Prices for a selection of performances in Gaiety and Olympia theatres.   400

Index

Page numbers *in italics* contain images

Abbey Street, 27, 177, 313, 396, 402
Abbey theatre, 396, 398, 399–401
Abercrombie, Patrick, 27, 44–5, 49, 55, 66, 82–3, 85, 89–91, 161–2, 182, 186, 192, 208, 327
access roads, 200, 208, 211
Aer Lingus, 340, *342–5*, 351–2
  Carvair, *351–2*
aerial, 57, 102, 121, 134, 239, 300, 334, 390
air, 13, 69, 305, 308, 330, 340, 346, 351, 354
Air France, 343
airport, 19, 49, 130, 213, 340, 342, 356
Amiens Street, 139, 167–8, 177, 182–4, 189, 193, 253, 266, 321, 327, 384, 392, 395
Amstelveen, *260–2*
Amsterdam, 260, 262, 342–3
anchor tenant, 238, 240, 243–4, 246–7, 280, 323, 391, 395
Anglesea Road, 35
Annamoe Drive, 179
Anne Street, South, 278, 298, 303
arcades, 238, 279–80, 282–3
Archbishop, 101–4
archdiocese, 27, 104
architects, 16, 39, 69–70, 85, 87, 89–90, 93, 95, 97–8, 103, 117, 129, 141, 144, 152, 159
Architectural Association of Ireland, 69, 130
Architectural Associations, 91
architecture, 65, 69–70, 99, 139, 158, 366, 371, 403
  colonial, 158
  finest, 356
  modern, 70, 97, 404

Ardee Street, 195
Ardoyne House, 18
areas, central, 18, 195, 202, 209, 253–5, 260, 262, 383
Arnotts, 278, *316–17*
Arran Quay, 213
Arts Council, 125, 128
assimilation, 146, 148, 310
Aston Quay, 74, 306, 402
atmosphere, 285, 379, 398, 402
  bohemian, 330
  rarefied, 379
attractions, 133, 269, 285, 298, 318, 333, 337, 339, 368, 376, 378, 389
Aungier Street, 178, 384–5
Authorities, 17, 20, 41–3, 96, 111, 114, 174–5, 187, 357
  see also City Council; Dublin Corporation
  civic, 108
  hospital, 120, 122

Baggot Street, 230, 232
Balbriggan, 175
Baldonnel, 106
Baldoyle, 208
Balfe Street, 174
Ballast Office, 138–9
Ballsbridge, 127, 143–4, 160, 179, 395
Ballybough, 34
Ballybough Road, 213
Ballyfermot, 105, 167, 179, 204, 230, 232, 234
Ballymun, 15, 48, 110, 192, 208, 234, 247–8, 256, 260, 329
  Comprehensive School, 112
  shopping centre development, 247
Bank of Ireland, 118, 304, 373, 384

bathing, mixed, 369
beauty, 65, 80, 382
   dignified, 76
   faded eighteenth-century, 331
   manmade, 159
   natural, 330
Beggar's Bush, 129–30, 136
Belfast, 74, 294–5, 357
Belvedere, 391, 395
Belvedere College, 371
Benburb Street, 368
Bennett, Edward, 66
Beresford Place, 134, 139, 177, 189
Berkeley Street, 366
Berlin, 129
berth accommodation, 347–8, 352
B&I line/company, 346–7, 352, 354
bicycles, 192, 220, 250, 303–4, 327,
   337, 339
Birmingham, 236, *237*, 260, 343–4
Black Church, 35
Blackhall Place, 205
Blackhorse Bridge, 204
Blackpitts, 213
Blackrock, 232, 234
Blanchardstown, 45, 49–51, 60, 62, 64,
   67, 106, 207–8
blocks
   central, 89, 139
   flat, 18
Boland, Kevin, 118, 156, 158–9, 218,
   264
Bolshoi Ballet, 398–400
Bolton Street, 367, 387
bona fide drinking, 361–2
Bond Street, 267, 357
Bord Fáilte, 349, 368–70, 394
borough boundary, 105, 191–2
boroughs, 20, 40, 192
Botanic Gardens, 366, 372
bottleneck, 109, 186
Bowl of Light, 70, *71*, *73*, 72–4, *77*, 82,
   150
   copper, 72

flames, 72–4
long woman's grave, 74
semi-submerged submarine, 74–5
'the Thing', 74, *78–9*, *81*
tomb of the unknown gurrier, 74
Boyne Valley, 360, 389
brands, 229, 243, 248, 272, 275, 277,
   307, 313
Bray, 183–5, 234, 250, 392
Bray Head, 383
Bray Urban Council, 185
Brazen Head, 379
Bride Street, 164
bridge, 27, 39, 72, 74–6, 78, 80–1, 89,
   162, 170, 173, 187, 192, 194, 203,
   206, 215, 217, 373
   new, 26, 162, 192, 203, 205, 208
Bridge Street, 25, 195
Bridgefoot Street, 195
Britain, 54, 56, 59, 235, 262, 333, 344,
   348–50
British Legion, 117–19
British Rail, 350, 352, 354
Broadstone, Station, 27, 367, 387, 392
Brooks Thomas, 134, 309
Brown Thomas, 267, 269, 271–2, 275,
   280, 282–3, 285, 308
Buchanan report, 59, 196, 199–200,
   201–2, 217
buildings, new, 93, 96, 150, 198
Burgh Quay, 136
Burnham, Daniel, 66, 132
bus/buses, 59, 168, 180–2, 185–6, 191–
   2, 209, 282, 284–5, 297–8, 304,
   320, 369, 371–2, 384–5, 387
   fares, 181, 185–6
   lanes, 193
   services, 52, 179, 181–2, 186–7, 297,
   320, 328
   speeds, 182
Busáras, 137, 306, 376, 379
business, 16, 23, 29, 62, 70–1, 131, 145–
   6, 192, 198, 200, 220–1, 224, 234,
   238, 248, 256, 258, 263–4, 272,

275–8, 280, 285–6, 295, 297–8,
300–1, 307, 313, 318, 320, 328–9,
333, 337, 346, 356, 370, 374, 404
business avenues, 383–4
Buswells, 391, 395
butchers, 240, 249, 253–4, 278, 326,
329
Hafners, 286
Butt Bridge, 27, 39, 162, 170, 178,
186–7, 192, 195, 203, 205
butter, 249, 333, 381
imported, 250
supplies, 250
bye-laws, 146, 178
Byrne, Davy, 379

cabin, 347–8
Cabra, 13, 106, 230, 246, 331
Cabra Road, 194
cafés, 275, 295, 307, 334
Bewley's, 304
Cameo, 275
El Habano, 275
Caledonian, 391, 395
Cambria, 352
Camden/George's Street, 211
canal, 31, 144, 170, 196, 203–5, 207,
216, 387, 392
route, 194
Capel Street, 178, 253, 255, 266, 321–
2, 366–7, 386–7
car ferry, 349, 351–4, *353*, 396, 426
Cardiff, 343–4
Cardiffsbridge Road, 179
Carlingford, 384
Carlisle Bridge, *139–40*
Carlisle Building, 139, 141
Carlisle monument, 110
Carlisle statue, *111*
Carysfort Avenue, 232
cash, 226, 232, 250
Cassidy, 286, 297
Castleknock, 45, 106
Cathal Brugha Street, 177, 311

cathedral, 27, 83, 85, 89–91, 95–8,
102–4, 161, 365, 371, 376
civic-sponsored, 101
cathedral plan, 27, 98, 101
Cathedral Street, 177, 310
Cavendish Row, 109
Celbridge, 388
census, 17, 166, 191, 221–3
comprehensive traffic, 191
census of distribution, 221–2, 224–5,
253
Central Business District (CBD), 146,
196–7, 253, 255
Central Dublin Development
Association, 264
Central Statistics Office, 255
centre, 64, 74–5, 109, 156, 162, 167–8,
172, 192, 195–8, 202, 207–9, 220–
1, 224, 232, 234–6, 238, 240, 242–
4, 246–8, 256, 259–60, 262, 264,
266, 328–9, 357, 373, 378, 382,
388–9, 404
large, *see* shopping centre
regional, *see* shopping centre
Charlemont Street, 196
Richmond Street, 34
Charles Street, 34
charm, 80, 374, 382, 384, 402
Chatham Lane, 174
Chatham Street, 174, 376
checkouts, 228, 234, 325
chemists, 240, 244, 254, 269, 286, 292,
307, 311, 321, 326, 329
Chicago, *66*
Childers, Erskine, 75, 149
Christ Church Cathedral, 82, 87, 90,
93, 95, 98, 161, 365, 384
Christmas, 186, 188, 283, 285, 292,
313, 318, 320, 333, 348, 370
church, 35, 54, 60, 69, 95, 102, 167,
306, 383
Church of Ireland, 90, 117
Church Street, 25, 34, 40, 189–90, 195,
213, 367, 387

Church Street (continued)
    demolitions, 190
    Lisburn Street, 40
CIE, bus tours, see Córas Iompair
    Éireann (CIE)
cigarettes, 267, 344
cinemas, 74, 126, 141, 259, 307, 311–
    12, 314, 321–2, 334, 401
    Adelphi, 402
    Ambassador, 312, 401
    Astor, 402
    Capitol, 126, 311–13, 402
    Carlton, 311
    Casino, 230
    Cinerama, 327, 402
circulation system, 59
citizens, 72, 101, 112, 218, 357, 375,
    384–5
city, 13, 15–20, 23, 28–31, 35, 37, 39,
    41, 43–5, 48–52, 58, 60, 64–5, 67,
    69–71, 74, 76, 96, 98–9, 101, 103,
    105–6, 120, 122, 126, 132–3,
    144–6, 148–50, 152, 155–6, 158,
    160–221, 224–5, 248–9, 253, 263,
    275–6, 306, 329–31, 333–4,
    339–40, 353–4, 356–61, 363,
    365–70, 372–6, 382–5, 387–9,
    393–4, 403–5
    boundary, 44, 106
    capital, 46, 65, 102, 116, 199, 260,
        404
    central, 372
    congestion, 41, 192, 260
    developing, 141
    development, 13
    early, 34, 101
    Irish, 70, 158, 238
    large, 131, 178
    old, 41, 161, 365
    south, 106, 192, 327
    tallest building, 138
City Architect, 37, 83–5, 87, 90, 260
city authorities, 94, 109, 161
City Beautiful, 65, 356

city centre, 15, 18, 31, 35, 45, 48, 66,
    70, 139, 145–6, 160, 162–4, 166–
    8, 175, 177, 179, 182, 184, 186,
    188–9, 192–5, 197–8, 202–3, 207,
    209–12, 220–1, 224–5, 228, 230,
    232, 234–5, 238, 240, 242, 244,
    250, 253–4, 256–7, 260, 264, 278,
    283, 307, 310, 328–9, 362, 372,
    376, 391, 401
    congested, 166
    north, 146, 148, 224, 255–7
    south, 224, 256
city centre locations, 228
City Council, 13, 15–23, 27, 37–41,
    43–5, 47, 55, 60, 70, 74–6, 78–83,
    85–6, 90–1, 93, 95–6, 98–101,
    105, 107–9, 112–13, 115–16, 126–
    7, 130–1, 136, 139, 149, 152–3,
    155, 161, 165–6, 176–8, 189, 191,
    198, 204–5, 223, 248, 257–60,
    262, 264, 279, 297, 328, 334, 357–
    9, 364–5, 367, 370, 386–7
    boundary, 31
    cathedral, 103
    civic offices, 82, 84–6, 89, 92, 98
    conservation, 34, 39, 41, 149, 155,
        206, 215
    Grand Canal, 204–5
    monuments, 108, 117
    Moore Street, 257–9
    new towns, 45, 48
    planning, 37, 40, 42
    regional, 44
    renewal, 31, 150, 152, 189, 203, 255
    roads, 39, 41, 165, 167, 177, 189,
        191, 210, 284
    An Tóstal, 71, 76
    tourism, 357, 360, 366, 372
    Wood Quay, 95, 101
City Directory Company, 372
City Engineer, 37, 81–2, 170, 204
city functions, 58, 201
City Hall, 37, 96
    Dublin Castle area, 178

City Manager, 76, 79–81, 85–7, 90–1, 93–4, 100, 182, 257, 310
'city of tomorrow', 200
city planning, formal, 182
city services, better, 166
city system, 50
city wall, 35, 100, 161
civic centre, 82–5, 89–90, 96
Civic Offices, 25, 82–3, 85–6, 95–6, 99, 161
Civic Offices Committee, 83–4, 87
Clanbrassil Street, 25, 32–4, *33*, 213
Clare Street, 180, 391, 395
Claremont, 395
Clarendon Street, 174
class, social, 56, 58, 64, 252, 267, 337, 346
clearances, 65, 88, 190, 196, 203
Clerys, *307–10*, 325–6
Clondalkin, 19, 45, 50, 64, 106, 207, 331
Clondalkin/Lucan, 60
Clonskeagh Road, 192
Clontarf, 184, 189, 330
closing hours, 249, 362
clothes, coupon-free, 333
clothing, 224, 254, 272, 279, 282, 308, 310, 316, 323
Coast Lines, 354
coastal locations, 35, 182, 392
   rejected, 49
Cole's Lane, 164, 177, 196
College Green, 125, 186, 371, 373, 385, 391, 395
College Street, 174
Collins Avenue, 27
Collins Barracks, 368, 371
Collinstown, 340
colonial, 16, 158, 230, 286
commemoration, 70, 107, 115–18, 122, 125
   annual, 117, 119
   national, 125

commercial development, 43, 144–5, 160, 329
commercial sector, 96, 139, 148, 160, 220, 301
communities, balanced, 55–6
commuter, 180, 182–6, 193, 195, 198, 209, 219
   displaced, 185
   reducing, 219
commuters, 179
compensation, 42–3, 115, 155, 184
concert hall, 126, *128*, 130, 136
conflict, 146–7, 152, 282
congestion, 54, 162, 164, 180–1, 198, 200, 207, 209, 219, 285
connectivity, 145, 340, 354
conservation, 156–7
   movement, 100, 157, 159
consultants, 44–6, 48–9, 54, 166, 195, 198–9, 205, 207, 211, 215–17
Consumer Price Index, 316, 393
control, 22, 37, 39–40, 42–3, 45, 65, 96, 158, 195, 205, 218, 248–9, 357
Cook Street, 35
Coolock, 19, 194
Coolock-Raheny area, 31
Coombe, 32, 34, 67, 195, 205, 213, 365, 371
Copenhagen, 263, 346
Córas Iompair Éireann (CIE), 180–2, 185, 204, 360, 389
Cork Street, 34, 195, 213
Cornelscourt, 232, 244
   see also shopping centre
corner, 159, 272, 278, 285, 296, 308, 310, 320, 404
   Findlater's, 310
   strategic, 311–12
Cornmarket, 164, 215
Corporation employees, 93
Corporation officials, 90, 108
councillors, 31, 38, 74, 76, 78–81, 165, 178
Country Club Plaza, Kansas City, *236*

country shoppers, 292, 325
countryside, 43–4, 51, 158
county, south, 44, 395
county area, 19, 105–6
county borough, 19, 31, 44, 105, 191, 225, 361
County Dublin, 369
    south, 396
County Manager, 60
courts, 21–2, 72, 90, 96, 164, 362, 368, 371, 387, 391, 395
Crampton G. & T., 97, 99, 144
Crawley, 56
Creation Arcade, *279–81*, 283, 298
    see also Grafton Street
credit, 225, 232, 323, 374, 383
cross-city movements, 208
crowds, 152, 285, 337, 339, 401
Crumlin, 13
Cuffe Street, 164, 213
Cumbernauld, *57*, 59
Cummiskey's self-service, 226
    see also supermarkets
Custom House, 136, 178, 206, 208, 366, 368, 373, 385
Custom House Quay, 35
customers, 181, 224, 228, 232, 235, 253, 262, 269, 272, 276, 298, 300, 320, 344, 381
cycle parks, 109, 303–4
cyclists, 164–5, 168

Dáil, 114, 118, 120, 122, 128, 218, 361
Dáil Debates, 42, 114, 119–20, 122, 156–7, 159, 205, 219, 362
Dalkey, 183, 230, 232, 382
Dallas, Highland Park, *235–6*
damages, 111, 119, 172
Dame Street, 27, 124, 195, 285, 380, 384
Dandelion Market, 303
Davis, Thomas, 124–5, 363
Davitt Road, 194
Dawson House, 300

Dawson Street, 172, 235, 266, 276, *298–302*, 395
Dean's Grange, 241
decay, 22, 116–17, 145, 148, 204, 253, 318, 327, 359, 363
    genteel, 37
delegation, 89, 260, 262–4, 284
demolition, 22, 25, 27, 31–4, 82, 111–12, 114–15, 147, 149–53, 155–6, 196, 203, 246, 318, 365, 404
    demolition and renewal, 32–4
Denmark House, 318
Denmark Street, 27, 196, 259, 318
Denmark Street Little, 174, 177
Department of External Affairs, 122, 330
Department of Local Government, 38, 105, 112
department stores, 238, 247, 257, 310, 320
Deputy City Engineer, 90
Deputy City Manager, 204
derelict, 37, 148, 204
dereliction, *23*, 191, 253–4, 257–8, 266, 325, 328, 366
developers, 16, 18, 21, 43, 62, 64, 96, 145, 152–3, 155, 159–60, 238, 246–7, 259, 264
development, 13, 15–17, 19–20, 22, 31, 37–9, 41–5, 48–9, 51, 55, 59–60, 62, 64, 66, 96, 101, 105–6, 132, 141, 145–6, 153, 155, 159–60, 189, 196, 199, 202, 204, 208, 221, 223, 228, 246–7, 254–60, 264, 266, 279–80, 283, 298, 300, 329, 331, 334, 340, 357, 374, 396, 402
    awaiting, 196, 325
    companies, 96, 152, 156
    contemplated, 14
    cost, 106
    economic, 46, 107, 256, 405
    fringe, 45, 48
    lands, 31, 105–6
    low-density, 59

multi-level, 59, 202, 257, 260
private, 19, 37
process, 153, 260
projects, 148
strip, 238, 246
development control, 20–1, 149
development plan, 20–2, 27, 40–1,
    43–5, 60, 62, 64, 82–3, 153, 162,
    182, 256
    draft, 43, 155
Deverell Place, 34
Diamond coal company, 305
diocese, 101–2, 104
diplomatic missions, 117–18
display, 37, 96–7, 235, 279
distance, 28, 53, 59, 83, 106, 181–2,
    197, 217, 220, 248, 328, 353, 392
D'Olier Street, 139, 174, 206, 304–5,
    310, 391
Dominick Street, 27, 34, 196, 327, 358,
    367
Donegal Shop, 279–80, 282
Donnybrook, 241, 244
Dorset Street, 34, 196, 232, 366–7
Drages, 272–3
drapers, 294–5, 316, 326, 333
drapery, 222, 232, 285, 295
dressmakers, 272, 295
drivers, 165, 170, 175, 195
Drumcondra, 17, 221, 313, 331, 366
Dublin Brigade, 120
Dublin City
    Airport, 342, 344–5, 351, *355–6*
    bus services, 182
    Castle, 91, 94, 276
    Castle environs, 178, 371
    Gas, 305
    medieval, 99, 384
    new towns, 59, 62
    planning scheme, 29, 35
    Port, 352, 354
    region, 47–8
    Spire, 115
    visitors, 330, 363

Dublin theatres, 399–400, 426
Dublin Corporation, 13, 15–23, 27–8,
    31, 34, 37–45, 47–8, 55, 60, 70–1,
    74–6, 78–86, 89–93, 95–6, 98–
    101, 103, 105, 107–9, 112–13,
    115–17, 126–7, 130–1, 136, 139,
    149–50, 152–3, 155, 161, 165–6,
    176–8, 189, 191, 203–6, 210, 215,
    223, 248, 255, 257–60, 262, 264,
    279, 284, 328, 334, 357–60, 364–
    7, 370, 372, 386–7
    roads, *28*, 31, 38–9, 41
Dublin County Council, 20, 31
Dublin Grand Opera Society, 126
Dublin mountains, 19
Dublin Opinion, *67–8, 71, 73–5, 78–9,
    81, 87, 92, 94, 107, 128, 137–8, 163,
    171–3, 271, 291, 341*
Dublin skyline, 138
Dublin Tóstal Committee, 79
Dublin Tourism, 394
Dublin Transportation Study, 209, 211
Dublin's population, *see* population
Duke Street, 266, 278–9, 298, 300,
    379
Dún Laoghaire, 18–20, 43–5, 106, 183,
    185–6, 194, 224, 228, 232, 234,
    249, 277, 346, 352, 354, 376, 392
Dundrum, 27, 184–5, 228–30, 244,
    331
    shopping centre, *229*
Dunnes Stores, 228, 232, 234, 244, 295,
    297–8
dwellings, 15, 17–18, 29, 31, 48, 93

Earl Place, 309
Earlsfort Terrace, 67, 283, 371
East Arran Street, 174
East Essex Street, 89
Easter, 71, 115, 370
Easter Sunday, 71–2
Eblana, 99
Eccles Street, 359, 395
Eden Quay, *176, 177*

edge of the city, 18, 168, 197–8, 248,
     256, 310, 329
  developments, 64, 329
Elephant and Castle, 236–7, 262
emigration, 15–16, 46, 374
employment, 15, 46, 49, 55–6, 58, 89,
     188, 207, 209, 227, 249
  dispersal of, 207
enforcement, 164–5, 173
entertainment, 256, 275, 336, 376, 396,
     402
environment, 34, 99, 145, 159, 200,
     202
ESB, 149–50, 151, 152, 279
  Fitzwilliam Street Protest Group, 152
  offices, 147
Essex Quay, 89, 164
Essex Street, 391
estate, 16, 62
Euston, 346, 348
excavations, 99–100, 161
Exchequer Buildings, 86
Exchequer Street, 228, 285, 293–5, 297,
     391, 393, 395
excursions, 185, 347–8
experiment, 15, 179, 234, 263, 283

fabric, urban, 199, 203, 215, 260
façade, 35, 87, 89, 150, 155, 307, 313
Fairview, 168, 173, 189
families, 46, 48, 133, 170, 292, 320,
     366
fares, 179, 181, 186, 343–4, 347, 384
ferry service, 350, 352, 354
Findlater, 232–4, 243, 286, 307, 310
Finglas, 19, 24, 31, 35, 106, 167, 192,
     194, 230–2, 371
Finglas shopping centre, 231
  see also shopping centre
Fishamble Street, 86–7, 89–90
Fitzwilliam Street, 147, 149, 152, 363
flats, 15, 18–19, 29, 31, 103
flights, 344, 351, 405
flower beds, 71–2, 74–6, 78–82, 110

flows, 162, 170, 188, 191–2, 219, 266,
     283, 297, 304, 325, 329, 354
flyovers, 202, 206
footfall, 220, 238, 298, 301
footpaths, 168, 189, 283
An Foras Forbartha, 45, 209
fountain, 72, 74, 76, 124–6, 388
Foxrock, 48, 184–6, 232, 234, 241
framework, 21, 106, 207–8, 266, 334
  legal, 44
furniture, 222–3, 276, 308, 321,
     328
furriers, 267, 272, 279–80, 295

Gaiety Theatre, 126–7, 396–402,
     426
Garda, 119, 164–6, 173, 177–8
garden cities, 21, 50, 55
Gardiner Street, 34, 160, 168, 178, 195,
     205–6, 253, 325, 359, 366
General Purposes Committee, 82, 86–7,
     91, 94–5, 178, 205, 284
geography, 215, 224, 240, 372
George's Quay, 35
George's Street (North Great), 358, 371,
     388
George's Street (South Great), 228, 242,
     285–6, 287–5, 297–8, 310
George's Street, Pims, 288
George's Street, Traders' Association,
     286
Georgian
  houses, 34, 115, 152, 385
  landscape and streetscape, 148–9,
     356, 370, 385
Georgian Dublin, 37, 100, 148, 157,
     211, 331, 334, 363, 376, 380, 404
Goad Insurance Plans, 258, 287, 294,
     309, 313, 315, 322
government, 20, 46, 101, 112–14,
     116–18, 120, 122, 128, 130, 205,
     249, 354, 385
GPO, 125, 320, 368, 370
Grafton Arcade, 280, 283

Grafton Street, 172–3, 175, 181, *187*, 193, 226–7, 242, *266–9, 272–9*, 282–6, 292–5, 297–8, 301–2, 310, 316, 318, 321, 323, 327, 357, 363, 371, 373, 379, 382, 385, 402
   development, 266, 278
   newsreel cinema, 402
   traffic, *187*
Grand Canal, 106–7, 144, 193–5, 203–5
Grand Canal Street, 205
Grattan Bridge, 170, 366, 368
Great Denmark Street, 371, 395
Great Strand Street, 174
Green Belt, 44–5, 47, 51, 54
Green Book, 69–70
Green Property Company, 97, 99, 152
Green Rooster, 378
Green Street, 367, 387
Greystones, *183*, 186
Griffith Avenue, 194
grocery, 225
   see also supermarkets
   cash prices, 282
grocery shopping, 222–3, 226, 228, 253–4, 292, 298, 318, 321
   local, 250, 329
   non-self-service, 228
   online, 232
growth, rate, 46, 48, 182, 256–7
guide books, 149, 393
   commercial, 358, 363, 388
   Green Guide, 360, *361*, 363
   official guides, 358–60, 368, *369*, 371–2, 388
   Red Guides, 182, 343, 360, 390
   Ward Lock, 346, 359–60, 382–3, *385–8*, 390–1
guides, 45, 69, 331, 334, 340, 357–60, 363, 365–8, 370, 372–6, 379–85, 387–9, 391–2, 394
Guild Street, 194
Guiney, 308, 325
Guinness, 366, 381, 403, 405

H. Williams, 225–6, 228–30, 244, 316
Haddington Road, 129–30
hairdressers, 259, 298
hall, 126–7
   see also concert hall
Halston Street, 27, 174
Hammam, 391
handbill, 348–50
Ha'penny Bridge, *26*, 26–7, 162, 170, 189, 327
Harcourt Street, 184, 391–3, 395
Harcourt Street line, 183–4
Harcourt Street station, 185
Harcourt Terrace, *35–6*
Hardwicke Street, 35, 366
Harlow, *61*
Harry Street, 174, 269, 272
Haussmann, Baron, 65
Hawkins Street/House, *142*
headquarters, 136, 139, 160, 370, 389
height, 15, 28, 37, 91, 99, 131–3, 138–9, 146, 170, 215, 387, 404
Henrietta Street, 37, 41, 367, 387
Henry Street, 177, 188, 228, 230, 244, 257, 266, 272, 316, *318–21*, 327, 384
   Association, 320
heritage, 149, 152, 157, 160, 360, 404–5
   colonial power, 158
hierarchy, 59, 200, 220
High Court, 21–2, 42, 113
High Street, 25–6, 34, 99–100, 127, 161, 195–6, 215, 365
Highland Park Centre, 235
history, 69, 161, 330, 357–8, 368–70, 372–5, 380, 389
Hogan Place, 196
Holyhead Ferry, 352–3
hotel guides, 393, 396
   Andrews, 69
   Gresham Hotel, 149, 393
   Russell Hotel, 378
   Shelbourne, 393

hotels, 259, 276, 293, 295, 378, 380,
    384, 391–5
  Ashling, 395
  Clarence, 391, 395
  conservative temperance, 393
  grade, 394
  Gresham Hotel, 307, 311, 378, 380,
    391, 395, 402
  International, 392
  Jury's Hotel, 402
  major, 269, 393
  Metropole, 311–13, 334, *377*, 380,
    391, *401*
  North Star, 395
  Royal Hibernian, 391, *392*, 394–5
  Russell, 380–1, 391, 395
  Shelbourne, 334, 339, 378, 380–1,
    391, 393, 395
  St Andrew's Temperance Hotel, 393
  suburban, 392, 396
houses, 15–18, 41, 45, 54, 56, 58, 62,
    86–7, 95–6, 130, 132, 138, 141,
    149–53, 159, 164, 246, 248, 250,
    260, 295, 359, 363, 365, 367, 370,
    385, 388–9, 401
  early, 362
  nineteenth-century, 34
  ruined, 130
  semi-detached, 15, 69
  standard, 225
  tenement, 87
housing
  local authority, 13, 15–18, 37, 64,
    105, 220, 297–8
  middle-class, 19
  private, 15–16, 19, 105
  programme, 23, 31
  provision, 48, 55–6
Housing Committee, 40
housing inquiry, 15
housing projects, 31, 34, 96, 244, 253
housing renewal, 32–4
housing schemes, 15, 24, 105, 244,
    247–8, 277, 302, 368
  Ballymun, 247

housing stock, 17–18, 34, 146
Howth, 16, 20, 44, 105–6, 179, 184,
    208, 232, 330, 376, 382, 392, 395
Howth Head, 29, 35, 106, 383
Howth Junction, 184
Howth Road, 194, 395
Hume House, *143*
Hume Street, 152–3, *154*, 155, 159
hypermarket, *229*, 234

ice cream (parlour), 74, 307, 313, 335
Inchicore, 180, 204, 389
income, 16, 64, 101–2, 108, 115, 176,
    182, 241, 354
industry, 29, 46, 55, 207, 303, 330,
    340, 398
Infirmary Road, 368
infrastructure, 67, 340
inner city, 13, 18, 31, 144, 191–3, 195–
    9, 203, 318, 366
Inns Quay, 391, 395
Irish Hospitals' Sweepstake, 276, 379
Irish House, 87, *88*
Irish Independent, 104–5, 155, 227,
    248–9, 282–3, 292, 297, 310,
    324–6
Irish Life centre, 310
Irish National War Memorial, *see*
    Islandbridge
Irish Press, 104, 152, 272, 293, 320,
    339
Irish Sea, 353–4
Irish Times, 71–2, 74–5, 89, 91, 93, 96–
    9, 104, 112, 114–20, 122, 125–30,
    136, 139–41, 146, 149–50, 156,
    164–5, 168, 172, 175–81, 185–8,
    191, 198, 203–5, 217–18, 225–6,
    230, 232, 234, 240, 242–4, 246,
    248, 255, 260, 264, 276–8, 280,
    282, 284, 297, 300, 318, 320, 337,
    339, 350–4, 356, 374
Irish Tourist Association, 358
Irish Transport and General Workers'
    Union (ITGWU), 70, 131, 136

Islandbridge, 111, 116–18, 125, *388–90*
islands, 70, 172, 304–5, 310

James' Street, 366, 389
Jervis Street, 174, 316, 321, 387
Jeyes Fluid, 401
    floral spray, 401
John Dillon Street, 35
journeys, cross-city, 187
Joyce, 330–1, 334, 380
junction, 34, 87, 126, 152, 162, 165–6,
    172, 195, 200, 203, 213, 215, 228,
    235, 247, 295, 301, 316, 321, 325,
    327–8, 367, 384

Kelletts, 285, 287, 295
Kevin Street, 34, 205, 213, 215, 365
    Patrick Street, 215
Keynes, Milton, 59
Kilbarrack, 31, 106
    area, 106
Kildare, 47
Kildare Street, 253, 395
Kildare Street Club, 118, 180
Killarney, 340, 399
Killester, 106, 184, 228, 230
Killiney, 48, 182–3, 185, 382, 392
Kilmainham, 85, 93, 230, 331, 389
    Gaol, 388–90
    Treaty, 389
Kilmore, 19, 286
Kimmage, 13
Kimmage Road Lower, 28
King's Inns, 367, 387
Kingsbridge Station, 167, 182, 195,
    389, 392
Kingstons, 297, 310–11
Knowles, 278–9
Kylemore, 286
Kylemore Road, 24, 194

Labour Party, 103, 120, 156
ladies, 159, 282, 285–6, 294, 298, 304,
    316, 333

Laird chemist, 307, 311
land reservations, *30*, 153
landscape, 41, 65, 107, 116, 148, 160,
    188–9, 194, 215–16, 254, 328,
    366, 403
    city's, 70, 108, 228
Lansdowne House, *143*
Le Corbusier, 200
Leeson Street/Earlsfort Terrace, 144,
    194
legal powers, 95, 176, 255
legislation, 23, 41–4, 103, 109, 156,
    158, 181, 185, 361
Leinster House, 107, 356, 371
Lemon Street, 279
Lemon's sweets, 313–15
Leonard's Corner, 25
Liberties, 211, 384
Liberty Hall, 70, *134–7*, 139, 142
library, 69, 129, 262, 385
Lichfield, Nathaniel, 255–7
Liffey, 26–7, 73–4, 96, 105, 139, 145,
    168, 170, 182, 192, 196, 203, 213,
    215–17, 376, 382
Liffey Bridge, 194, 203, 216
Liffey Street Upper and Lower, 23, 27,
    174, 177, 327
Lijnbaan, *241, 262*
Lincoln Place, 187, 376
Linear designs, 52
Lisburn Street, 40
Little Britain Street, 27
Liverpool, 234, 343–4, 347, 351–2,
    354, 373
Local Government, 15, 38, 40–1, 44–5,
    86, 94, 105, 112, 149–50, 153,
    155–7, 218, 247, 254, 264
    Minister, 15, 40–1, 45, 86, 94,
        149–50, 153, 155–7, 218, 247
Local Loans Fund, 96
locations
    central, 18, 117, 130, 220
    favoured, 15, 160
    good, 153, 298

locations *(continued)*
  in-centre, 328
  key, 196, 295
  mid-street, 269
  perfect, 19, 283
Lombard Street, 178
London, 55–6, 131, 176, 202, 236–7, 260,
  267, 330–1, 340, 343–4, 346–9
Long Mile Road, 24
loops, 371, 384–5
Lord Edward Street, 89, 162
Lord Gough, 109, *110*
Lord Mayor, 37, 72, 84, 93, 112, 203,
  280, 357–8, 360, 373
Lower Abbey Street, 177, 391, 395
Lower Gardiner Street, 366
Lower Mary Street, 322
Lucan, 45, 50, 60, 66, 106, 207, 388
Lucan Road, 192
luxury, 252, 284, 346, 394

Macey, 286–7, 291
machines, 337, 339
Macken Street, 194
Maguire and Gatchell, 300, 346
mains drainage, sewer, 105–6, 204
major routeways, 49, 207–8, 235
Malahide, 19, 45, 49, 106, 184, 232
  Portmarnock, 45
Manchester, 238, 343–4, 348
Manning Robertson, 21, 158
Mansion House, 130, 192
mantle makers, 272, 295
manufacturing, 282, 300–1, 303, 318
maps, base, 25–6, 30, 32–3
Marino, 13, 17, 38, 130
market, 16–17, 95, 153, 221, 230–2,
  234, 250, 252, 275, 277, 279, 286,
  344, 352, 366, 387, 402
marketing, 240, 284, 308
Marlborough Place, 177
Marlborough Street, 130, 167, 177, 371
  Beresford Place, 177
Marley Committee, 54–5

Marsh's Library, 365
Mary Street, 174, 177, 244, 259, 316,
  321–5
Mary's Abbey, 174, 253, 366
Maynooth, 388–9
Maypole Dairy, 286
McBirney, *306*
McCabe, *286, 288*
median, central, 71, 82
medieval city, 26, 41, 161, 279
memorial, 72, 107, 116–17, 119–20,
  128, 388
memorial gardens, National War, 117,
  119, 388–90
  see also Islandbridge
memory, 70, 116, 120, 128, 194, 334,
  372, 389
Mercer House, 172
Mercer Street, 164, 172
Merrion Road, 395
Merrion Row, 195, 205
Merrion Square, 35, 41, 101–4, 116,
  139, 149, 178, 180, 205, 333, 371,
  373, 385, 404
  Fitzwilliam Square area, 330
Merrion Street, 178, 195
Mespil Road, 144
Metal Bridge, 27
  see also Ha'penny Bridge
meters, 172, 177–9
Middle Abbey Street, 313–14, 328
Miliutin, N., *52*
Millar & Beatty, 269, 272, 275–7, 280
Milltown, 184–5
Milltown Road, 194
Minister, 15, 40–1, 43, 45–6, 48, 75,
  86, 95, 115, 118, 120, 122, 149–
  50, 152–3, 205, 283, 361
  Minister for External Affairs, 122
  Minister for Finance, 122, 205
  Minster for Local Government, 264
  Minister for Posts and Telegraphs, 75
  Minister for Transport and Power, 149
  Minister's approval, 42, 152

Misneach, 110, *112*
modernity, 278, 280, 333
Modes, Colette, 279–80, 293, 297, 381
Molesworth Street, 371, 391, 395
Mont Clare, 391, 395
Monument Café, 275, 277
Monument creamery, 286, 307, 311, 316, 327
monuments, 41, 72, 74, 77, 108–11, 114–15, 119–20, 125, 168, 373, 376, 384
    Parnell, 169, 181, 213
Moore, Henry, 75
Moore Street, 174, 257, 259–60, 317, 325, 357
Moore Street area, 254–5
Morehampton Road, 130
motor car, 41, 63, 70, 162–3, 165, 167, 169, 171, 173, 175, 177, 179, 181, 183, 185–7, 189, 191, 193, 195, 197, 199, 201, 203, 205, 207, 209, 211, 213, 215, 217, 219, 221–2, 224, 331, 405
motor cycles, 186, 191, 250
motorists, 71–2, 164–5, 170, 172–3, 175, 179, 187–8, 208
motorways, 209–11, 217
Mount Merrion, 238
Mountjoy Square, 34, 168, 366, 380, 405
movement, garden city, 55
multi-storey, 166, *167*, 170, 193, 197–8, 202, 247, 297–8, 356
municipal offices, 37, 85, 93–4
Myles Wright report, 19, 28, 43–5, 47, *51*, 53, 55–6, 58–60, 69, 74, 172, 180, 207–9

Nassau Street, 180, 211, 283, *301*, 371, 376
Nathesco, 297
National Museum, 108, 139, 369, 385
neighbourhoods, 59–60, 62, 64, 238, 405
    distinct, 60

Nelson Pillar, the, 70, 74, 107–9, 111–12, *113*, *114*–16, 140, 160, 192, 307, 333, 363, 370, 373, 376, 384, 389
    Bill, 115
new towns, 46, 49, 51–3, 55–6, 58, 60, 62, 64, 207–8, 247, 260
    British, 54–6, 59–60, 235, 260
New Zealand, 250, 339
newsagents, 222–3, 230, 240, 244, 254, 302, 311
newspapers, 108, 112, 179–80, 187, 252, 337
Newtownpark Avenue, 186
Nicholas Street, 25, 100, 127
North Circular Road, 25, 34, 168, 179, 194, 367, 371, 391
north city survey, 13
North Dublin Mains Drainage, 105–6
North Earl Street, 188, 310, 384
North Great George's Street, 358, 388
North King Street, 27, 34, 195, 205, 213, 303, 387
North Strand, 13, 173
northside, 105, 184, 193, 247, 316, 321, 359, 372, 385, 404

objections, 22, 37–9, 95, 141, 191
occupation, 103, 156, 159, 304
O'Connell, Daniel, 74, 357, 371, 373, 384
O'Connell Bridge, 70–1, 75, 80, 84, 140, 160, 166, 170, 186, 192, 206, 304, 306, 313, 354, 371, 373, 404
O'Connell Bridge House, 139, 141
O'Connell Street, 70–1, 108–9, 112, 114, 120, 165–6, 168–9, 177, 188–9, 206, 213, 233, 255, 266, 284, 307, 310, *312–15*, 320, 331–5, 335, 357, 366, 370–1, 373, 376, 378, 383–6, 391, 395, 401, 403–4
O'Connell Street, Traders Association, 112
office accommodation, 86, 90–1, 96, 131, 141, 145, 156, 246, 280

office development, 98, 130–1, 139, 142,
    144–6, 153, 155, 159, 246, 310
office jobs, 96, 131
Office of Public Works, see OPW
Olympia, 126, 396–400
on-street provision, traditional, 260
one-way streets, 166, 174, 178, 194–5,
    205, 213, 283–4
opening hours, 248
OPW (Office of Public Works), 120,
    122, 125, 129, 152–3, 156, 205
order
    compulsory purchase, 95, 189, 259
    maximum prices, 249
    ministerial, 101
    phone, 232
Ordnance Survey, 359
Ordnance Survey plan, 25–6, 30, 32–3,
    83–4, 116, 121, 129, 154, 190,
    206, 245, 257, 390
out-of-town centres, large, 244
outfitters, gent's, 295
outlet, 232, 240, 244, 328
owners, 17–18, 59, 141, 149, 235, 248,
    275, 320, 339–40, 349, 354
ownership, 18, 56, 59, 179, 181, 186,
    207, 217, 219, 250, 253, 276, 349

Palmerstown, 50
Palmerstown Road, 194
Paris, 65, 267, 279, 343–4, 346
parked cars, 168, 169, 197
Parkgate Street, 395
parking
    appointed street, 166
    regulations, 173, 175, 180
parking attendant, 170, 171, 172
parking bye-laws, 177
parking demand, 198, 235
parking facilities, 165, 198
parking meters, 176, 178, 197
parking provision, 43, 63, 136, 196–8,
    238–9, 246, 329
parking regulations, 174, 198, 209

parking spaces, 96, 141, 164, 167, 170,
    173, 175, 195–8, 207, 219, 232,
    234, 238, 244, 280, 297
Parliament Street, 83, 89, 178
Parnell Square, 164, 168, 193, 366, 371,
    388, 391–2, 394, 402
Parnell Street, 26–7, 166, 168, 177–8,
    195, 205, 213, 253, 255, 257, 259,
    311, 395
passengers, 168, 181, 346, 348, 351–3
Patrick Street, 25, 32, 34, 213
patrons, 285, 380, 401
pavements, 284, 320
peace, 118–19, 375
Pearse Street, 186, 195, 205, 284, 371,
    402
pedestrian refuge, 164
pedestrianization, 202, 262, 280, 284–5,
    321
pedestrians, 18, 43, 59, 164, 168, 170,
    172, 188, 260, 262, 283, 285, 354
Pembroke Road, 395
penalties, fixed, 175, 178
Phibsborough, 193, 244, 366, 371, 387
    shopping centre 245
Phibsborough Road, 25, 34, 387
Phoenix Park, 110–11, 117–18, 120,
    130, 194, 336, 367, 371, 382, 388
Pims, 228, 266, 285–7, 292–3, 295,
    297–8
planning, 20–64, 69, 86, 126, 156, 168,
    198, 217, 228, 254, 405
    permission, 42, 149, 156, 159, 246
    process, 45, 60, 160, 192
planning officer, 37, 170
planning scheme, 20–1, 39–43, 161, 191
    draft, 24–6, 30, 32–3, 38
plans, 15, 20–3, 25, 27–9, 31, 34, 37–
    40, 42–6, 48, 59–60, 62, 64, 66,
    80, 87, 89–91, 94–7, 99, 103, 106,
    114, 116, 138–9, 141, 150, 152–3,
    162, 165, 188–90, 195–6, 203,
    205–7, 209, 211, 215, 217–18,
    240, 247, 256, 259, 262, 339, 357

outline, 57–8, 60–1, 255, 304
road, 23, 31, 188, 209
Plaza, Country Club, 235
plinth, 109–10, 115, 126
policy, 13, 15, 17, 23, 42, 45, 55–6,
198, 219, 223, 300, 326
polycentric city, 253, 328
population, 13, 15, 17–18, 31, 39, 45–
8, 54, 56, 60, 63, 105–6, 149, 156,
209, 222, 225, 248, 254, 329, 357,
365, 375, 396, 403
population projections, 46–7, 60
port, 78, 138–9, 162, 189, 207–8, 336,
358, 381
Port and Docks Board, 78, *138*, 139,
162, 189
Portmarnock, 19, 45, 49, 184
Power supermarket, 228, 230–2, 245–6,
295, 297
Prague, *131–2*, 356, 398
President Kennedy, 127
President Kennedy Street, 131
prices, 62, 139, 225–6, 243, 249–50,
252–3, 292, 300, 320, 323–5,
329, 335, 343, 347, 360, 369,
378, 380, 391, 393, 395–6,
400–1, 426
bargain, 324
changing, 393
gouging, 353
high, 16, 378, 398
high-season, 395
Primate's Hill, 367
Princes Street, 312
Princess Maud, 352
priority, 23, 54, 152, 157
priority schemes, 219
private bathrooms, 393–4
private cars, 52, 250
Pro-Cathedral, 117–18, 371, 385
profit, 182, 316, 318, 325
programme, 15, 34, 60, 334, 339, 401
official, 72, 339
prospect, 18–19, 40, 93, 99, 176

prosperity, 219, 264, 356
protection, *35*, 165, 172, 247, 264
provision, 13, 18, 21, 23, 31, 37, 40,
42–3, 45, 54–6, 59, 71, 82, 85, 93,
102, 105, 122, 127, 165, 195–8,
207–9, 211, 220, 223, 238, 240,
247–8, 255, 262, 280, 292, 350,
356
local, 61, 223, 302, 329
Prussia Street, 367
public buildings, 67, 69, 71, 95, 330,
360, 368, 373, 379, 383–4
public house, 136, 222–3, 247, 254,
260, 275, 279, 301–2, 326, 376,
378–9, 396
singing, 381, 396
public inquiry, 95, 189, 259–60
public transport, 59, 179–82, 193, 197,
208, 211, 219–20, 224
role of, 182, 188, 198

quays, 27, 85, 87, 89, 96–7, 130, 139,
170, 190, 215, 217, 255, 257, 306,
328, 366, 368, 371, 387
Irish House, 88
Ormond Hotel, 327, 395
Queen Street, 195
Queen's Theatre, 396
queues, 312, 343, 401
Quinn's Supermarket, 230
Quinnsworth, 234, 243, 247

Radburn, 54
radial roads, 179, 194, 209
radio, 222, 247, 300, 327, 337, 393
Raheny, 35, 179, 184, 230
rail bed, 185, 194
railway, 166–8, 182, 185–6, 194, 208,
330
fares, 186
line, 52, 167, 194–5
Ranelagh, 185, 230
ratepayers, 86, 93
Rathfarnham, 27, 179

Rathmines, 221, 229–30, 232
Rathmines Road, upper, 40
rationing, 249–50
RDS (Royal Dublin Society), 127
rebellion, 383, 385, 391
recommendations, 20, 38, 95, 108–9,
   178, 198, 208
reconstruction, 136, 152, 385, 404
Red Bank Restaurant, 305
Reddich, 59
redevelopment, 84, 96, 146, 202, 235,
   253, 255, 257, 259, 301, 318
   comprehensive, 13, 201–2, 262, 264
   partial, 202, 266
   post-war, 260, 263
redevelopment area, 258, 264
regiments, 117–18
region, 46, 234, 238, 250, 357, 382
regulations, 37, 163–4, 172–3, 175, 249
   comprehensive, 248
   enforcing new traffic, 283
Reith Committee, 55–6
relief, 67, 74, 94, 164, 166, 196, 352
Remembrance, Garden of, 120, *123*, 388
Remembrance Day, 117, 119
removal, 34, 70, 76, 78, 80, 107–9, 112,
   209, 250
Renaissance, 65–6
renewal, 32–4, 43, 109, 196, 199, 254,
   262–3, 334
   urban, 13, 42, 246, 260
rentals, 17–18
rents, 17–18, 295, 298, 326
replacement, 48, 78, 115, 139, 142,
   150, 162, 238, 246, 353, 379
representation, 101, 108, 117
representatives, 108, 117, 244
reputation, 91, 275–6, 286, 331, 378,
   381
residential areas, *53–4*, 56, 59–60, 62,
   247, 404
residential developments, 23, 54, 59,
   256
residents, 62, 64, 103, 207, 242, 248

resolutions, 91, 166
resources, 21, 152, 203, 219, 264, 330
respondents, 224, 228
restaurants, 126, 129, 230, 244, 259–
   60, 266, 275, 280, 295, 298, 307,
   311, 314, 334–5, 362
   Chinese, 295, 376
restoration, 109, 114, 196
restrictions, 43, 119, 197, 248
resurfacing work, 186
retail, 259–60, 307, 316, 329
   floor space, 254
   street, 267, 298, 309
retailers, 173, 226–7, 235, 279
   traditional, 264
retention, 79, 150, 264, 379
RIAI, 39, 79, 90–1, 96, 98, 112
Richmond Penitentiary, 387
Richmond Place, 194
Richmond Street, 34
ring road, *24*, 27, 194, 205, 210
Ringsend, 105
Ringsend outfall, 204
rival, 256, 264, 329–30, 346
river, 25, 27, 34, 52, 74, 83, 90, 95,
   105, 116, 170, 189, 192, 195, 205,
   215–16, 244, 257, 383, 391, 402
road network, 23, 27, 34, 39, 59, 137,
   191, 198, 200, 203, *210*, 217
road systems, 24, 62, 202, 205, 207,
   211
roads, 24–6, 28, 31, 41, 46, 49, 59, 62,
   139, 165, 172–3, 175, 180, 188–9,
   193–5, 199–200, 203, 208, *210*,
   213, 215, 217, 219, 228–9, 263,
   283, 286, 297, 303, 316, 318, 328,
   366, 372
   arterial, 204
   distributor, 54, 200
   existing, 38, 210, 215
   main, 54, 59, 62, 208, 235
   Naas, 192, 208, 380, 395
   Navan, 192, 194
   new, 27, 34, 193, 208–9

roadways, 28, 32–3, 82, 185, 189, 198,
 202–3, 207, 285, 320
Rochdale, 348
Roches Stores, 230, 316, 318
Rock Road, 192
Roman Catholic, 101, 117
Roman decumanus maximus, 263
roof, 35, 86, 93, 159, 244, 300
 projecting, 262
rooms, 122, 232, 391, 393–5
Rotherham, 348
Rotterdam, 240–1, 260
Rotunda, 37, 275
Rotunda Gardens, *120–1*
routes, 24, 26–8, 34, 38, 94, 96, 179–80,
 184, 188–9, 191–5, 204–5, 208,
 211, 213, 215, 342, 344–5, 352–3,
 360, 368, 384–6, 391
 arterial, 189
 direct, 304, 344
 main, 166, 189, 194, 208, 224, 267,
  321, 367, 387
 new, 26, 34, 179, 188
 recommended, 213–14
 western, 213, 215
routeway, 27, 191, 195, 217
Rowan Seeds, 304
Royal Canal, 34, 194, 204, *206*, 208,
 210, 366, 387
 Motorway, 213
Royal Dublin Society (RDS), 127
Royal Exchange, 192, 391
Royal Hospital, 85, 91, 93–4, 130,
 389–90
 Kilmainham, 389
 Kilmainham Gaol, 388
Runcorn, *58, 59*

Sackville Street, 304
 Sackville Mall, 275
 Sackville Place, 177, 309
safety, 43, 172–3, 303, 346, 354
sailings, 346–7, 352, 354
salaries, 181, 253

sale, 139, 249–50, 325
Sallynoggin, 234
Sandycove, 380
Sandyford, 210
Sandymount, 207, 228
 Strand, 19, *193*
Santry, 194, 337
satellite towns, 45, 50
Savoy Cinema, 311–12, *334–5*, 401
 restaurant, 336
 trio, 334
Schaechterle, 191, 198–200, 203, 205,
 207, 217
scheme, 20, 42, 91, 96, 99–100, 105–6,
 178, 194, 205, 235, 247, 257, 262,
 264
Schildergasse, 262–3
school, 54, 60, 69, 87, 102, 130
scope, 105, 127, 166, 199, 217, 256
Scotland, 352
Scott, Michael, 78, 91, 97, 99
sculpture, 110, 122
 signature, 123
SDAA (Small Dwelling Acquisition
 Acts), 16
sea, 105–6, 330, 349, 394
 ferries, 352
 Sealink, 352
seasons, 76, 249, 341, 347
seats, 129, 262
Second World War, 16, 54, 226, 249,
 262, 305, 333, 336, 340, 388, 392
sector
 developing office, 160, 301
 private, 13, 15, 17
 south-eastern, 105, 144–5, 152,
  160–1, 376, 391
 south-western, 105
selection, 76, 272, 324, 400, 426
self-service, 225–7, 232, 324, 327
 experience, 226
services, 40, 42, 46, 60, 64, 70, 89, 96,
 106, 117–18, 170, 177, 179–85,
 224–5, 234–5, 238, 248, 264, 266,

services *(continued)*
    276, 292, 298, 329, 340, 347,
      351–2, 354, 356, 358, 361, 392–4
    local, 59, 321
    postal, 292, 306, 308, 326
    religious, 117, 384
settlement, 60, 95
shades, 32–3, 211, 278, 310, 404
Shanard Road, 179
Shanganagh, 106
Shankill, 184–5
Sheffield, 57, 348
Shelbourne Road, 337, 339
ship, 340, 347–8, 352, 354
shirts, 272, 310
shoes, 222, 224, 272, 293, 310
shoppers, 181, 197, 224–6, 232, 234–5,
    238, 240–2, 250, 256, 264, 266–7,
    269, 272, 284–6, 295, 297, 306,
    318, 320–1, 325, 329
shopping, 173, 196, 220, 226, 228, 232,
    240, 242–4, 247, 256, 260, 262,
    266, 279–80, 282, 285–6, 292,
    310, 320, 324, 329, 360, 363, 370,
    373, 379, 381, 384
    (re)development, 246, 255–6
    comparison, 226, 238, 240
    local, 318, 326
    one stop, 238, 242, 259, 280
    self-service, 225
shopping arcade, 244
shopping areas, 230, 253, 293, 357
shopping centre
    concept, 202, 235, 238, 244, 266,
      368
    development, 235
    new suburban, 264
    suburban, 298
shopping centres, 49, 63, 235, 238, 240,
    244–5, 247, 253–4, 256, 262, 280,
    285, 328
    redeveloped, 264
    regional, 238
    regional-scale, 238

ring, 237
Seven Towers, 247
shopping district, 192, 285, 310, 382
    central, 255
shopping experience, 256, 262, 266–7,
    270, 284–5
shopping provision, 221, 242, 244, 246,
    256, 283
shopping space, 234, 238, 246, 280, 325
shopping streets, 266, 279, 285, 304,
    322
    best, 267, 293, 298, 318, 320–1
    primary, 285
    secondary, 326
shops, 54, 87, 96, 115, 147, 200,
    222–5, 228, 230, 232, 235, 238,
    240, 244, 246–50, 254, 260,
    262–3, 266–7, 269, 272, 275, 279,
    285–6, 298, 304, 307, 316, 320,
    324, 328–9, 360, 370, 382
    food, 223, 225, 253–4
    shoe, 244, 286, 295, 321
showrooms, 142, 244, 259, 285
side streets, 166, 278, 302, 386
singing, 118, 381
site, 31, 37, 49, 69–70, 82–7, 89–91,
    93–7, 99–101, 103–4, 117, 120,
    122, 125–6, 130, 132, 136–7,
    139–40, 148, 152–3, 160, 167,
    235, 240, 245, 257, 264, 276, 283,
    295, 297, 310, 317–18, 328, 371,
    389, 392
    barracks, 130
    bomb, 148, 328
skyscrapers, 70, 131, 133, 136, 363, 404
Slyne, 269, 272, 275, 277–8, 295
Smithfield, 117–18, 213, 367
Social Welfare, 130, 136
society, 226, 374
solutions, high-density, 53–4
South Anne Street, 279
South Circular Road, 25, 189
South City Markets, 286
South County Hotel, *396*